THE
SMOOTH
LOG

ARTHUR RANDOLPH MURRAY

SEABOARD PRESS

AN IMPRINT OF J. A. ROCK & CO., PUBLISHERS

The Smooth Log by Arthur Randolph Murray

SEABOARD PRESS

is an imprint of JAMES A. ROCK & CO., PUBLISHERS

The Smooth Log copyright ©2006 by Arthur Randolph Murray

Special contents of this edition copyright ©2006
by Seaboard Press

Address comments and inquiries to:
SEABOARD PRESS
9710 Traville Gateway Drive, #305
Rockville, MD 20850

E-mail:
jrock@rockpublishing.com   lrock@rockpublishing.com
Internet URL: www.rockpublishing.com

*The United States Maritime Service Seal on the Title Page is compliments of
"American Merchant Marine at War" www.usmm.org*

Paperback ISBN: 1-59663-762-5

Library of Congress Control Number: 2006925980

Printed in the United States of America

First Edition: 2006

THE SMOOTH LOG

This work is dedicated to

Anita,

my wife

who has always been

my pilot and

inspiration

TABLE OF CONTENTS

PHOTOGRAPHS

PROLOG

The following is the story of the part of my life when I made the transition from that of a naive boy to that of a more experienced and worldly man. It spans the time from when I was a teenager to the time I reached thirty years of age. During that time monumental changes took place. The bloodiest war, World War II, was fought from September 1939 to August 1945. The effects of that war lasted for decades. New nations evolved out of what had been colonial territories. Most of them fell under the control of despotic rulers. The sun set on the British Empire. The United States emerged as the most powerful nation on the earth. Wartime allies became deadly enemies, and deadly enemies became stalwart allies. The Cold War that some refer to as World War III evolved. The world's population began to explode. Turmoil continued between and within nations. Whatever else may be said, I have to say that I had lived through interesting times during this period of the World's and my own evolution.

The title of this part of my life's story, "THE SMOOTH LOG," was derived from a procedure in common use on merchant ships. Every ship carried a log on the bridge in which the watch standing Mates made entries regarding weather, sea state, course, speed, position, and any occurrences or special circumstances affecting the ship during the period of the watch. A watch was usually four hours long when at sea, and eight hours long when in port. From time to time the Captain would make an entry in the log regarding some facet of ship's business. With four people making entries in the log it was sometimes difficult to decipher what was written. Any notation made in the log book was never erased. An erroneous notation would have a line drawn through it followed with the initials of the person striking it out. This bridge log was often referred to as the rough log. Since it was an important legal document, it was kept with the ship. During a voyage a more legible copy of the rough log was made and at the end of the voyage this copy was submitted to the owners or operators of the ship. This copy was usually prepared by the ship's Purser and did not include any of the lined out notations. Thus it was known as the smooth log. When Pursers were no longer carried on ships, the task of preparing the smooth log was given to one of the Mates. On many of my ships this task was given to me as soon as the Captain discovered that I could write and print neatly.

CHOOSING A CAREER PATH

During my youthful years I always wanted to make a career going to sea. My father had gone to sea and his father before him had gone to sea. The sea was in my blood, or more accurately the sea was in my genes. In following this ambition I had no intention of being a mere sailor. I intended to be a ship's officer and eventually captain of a ship. The Nation was in the throws of the Great Depression and my parents were struggling to make ends meet. We were not well off financially and I could not expect them to be able to provide the funds to cover any schooling beyond High School. Even getting through High School was sometimes dubious. In 1937 my father moved the family from Philadelphia to Central Islip, Long Island, New York so he could go into a business venture with his nephew. At the time of the move I was in the last six weeks of the Sixth Grade. The change of schools was a very trying experience for me. My mother gave me a great deal of attention and help with my studies and I was able to complete the Sixth Grade successfully in spite of the severe change in the curriculum. Once adjusted I did very well in the Seventh and Eighth Grades of the Junior High School and easily became the top student in my class. The problem of how to start a career at sea was still not resolved. My family's financial condition had not improved with our move to Long Island. Researching in the school library I found two possible solutions to my problem. The first was to get an appointment to the Naval Academy, and the second alternative was to get accepted at the New York State Maritime Academy. There was a book describing the Naval Academy and a brochure describing the New York State Maritime Academy. During the middle of my Eighth Grade term I began to pursue these two possibilities.

I discovered that the only way I could get into the Naval Academy would be by a Congressional appointment. At that time each United States Senator could appoint two candidates to the Naval Academy each year. I went to my school's principal, Mr. Harry W. Rude, and asked him how I might get such an appointment. My family was not involved in politics and there was no way they could influence any Senator. However Mr. Rude said that he was on very friendly terms with a Senator and that he would do all he could to get me an appointment to the Naval Academy. He told me to keep up the good work and with a good academic record I should have no difficulty getting an appointment. This sounded just a little too good to be true so I decided to pursue a back up plan. I wrote to the New York State Maritime Academy and requested that they send me their enrollment application forms. They responded with a nice letter instructing me to submit an application when I entered my Junior Year in High School, and that I would have to have a good academic record especially in mathematics and science to be considered. Furthermore if I were considered I would have to pass a competitive entrance examination and meet very high physical standards. The enrolling classes were limited to one hundred students, or Midshipmen. The tuition was free but there were the costs of subsistence, uniforms, text books, and other fees. They indicated that they would keep my request on file. Money could still be a problem for me to get into the New York State Maritime Academy. However I had four years to solve that problem and I was confident that I would be able to do so.

The four years in High School were filled with successes and achievements. The Central Islip High School was relatively small. The town of Central Islip was made up of people most of whom worked in the State Psychiatric Hospital or the small businesses that supported the community. The largest ethnic group were Irish, both immigrant and first generation. The second ethnic group were the Italians, again both immigrant and first generation. About ten percent of the population were represented by old line Americans and other European countries. The Republican Party was the predominate political force. There was very little crime, and Central Islip and the adjacent towns of Islip Terrace and East Islip were policed by one officer. This officer was Gunther Faust, a naturalized German immigrant, and he was a very strict police officer. The Irish population supported a large number of bars and taverns considering the size of the town. The intellectual level of the community was average for lower middle class. The intellectual competition I faced in High School was not significantly high.

Most of my High School years I worked evenings and weekends in a service station. I pumped gas, changed tires, lubricated automobiles, and performed related tasks for fifteen cents an hour. On some weekends the owner would take off and leave me alone to run the station. World War II started in September 1939, and in December 1941 the United States joined in. I was in my junior year of High School. The Draft had already started to affect the High School and most of our male teachers had been called up. The teachers who replaced them were generally not as competent as those we lost. The loss of the good teachers resulted in a decline in the academic standing of the school which had not been very high to begin with. Although I was still at the head of my class academically, my grade average did decline. The shortage of teachers became so bad that during the last half of my senior year the Principal assigned me to teach the mechanical drawing class when the teacher was drafted.

During the four years of High School I was involved in a variety of activities. I was manager of the basketball team. During my junior and senior years I would travel by bus to Bayshore to take Spanish language lessons. These lessons were given voluntarily by a Mrs. Hildreth in her home. Her husband was a doctor, and they had lived in the Panama Canal Zone for many years. The only language courses offered in my High School were French and Latin. Although I took Latin in High School I felt that Spanish would be more useful in my future. During the Summer vacation between my junior and senior years I worked as an attendant in the Central Islip State Hospital. Two nights a week I helped to man a lookout station for aircraft. I was also active in the local Methodist Church. I was the Salutatorian of my class at graduation. A girl had beaten me by a few points for Valedictorian.

My application for enrollment in the New York State Maritime Academy was submitted during my junior year. I also applied for the Navy's V-7 Midshipman program. At some point in my senior year I was called into New York City to interview for the V-7 program. The interviewer was a Navy Lieutenant and I was not impressed with the interview or the program described by the Lieutenant. I chose not to follow this further because I preferred to go to the New York State Maritime Academy. A short time later I was called to go to Fort Schuyler to take the competitive entrance examination. It was said that several thousand prospective candidates took that examination. Being in very high spirits I did very well on the examination. There were about three hundred candidates selected from this examination, and I was one of them. The next step was a very rigorous Navy physical examination given in a building on Pine Street in down town New York City. This weeded out a good number of the candidates. Next the remaining candidates were put through a detailed interview session conducted at Fort Schuyler to winnow the number down to the one hundred and fifty selected for the next class. I was completely unprepared for the interview. There was no one coaching me or telling me what to expect or what to say. This may have been an advantage because I could only give honest spontaneous answers to the questions the review board asked. In turn I was ushered into a large room where there were tables arranged in a "U" shape with a single chair located at the mouth of the "U." There were eight or nine senior men in officers uniforms seated behind the tables. I was invited to sit in the chair and then asked to give a brief history of myself. This I did trying not to brag or exaggerate. When I finished, the officers started shooting questions at me many of which were testing my knowledge on various subjects. Since the Maritime Academy offered only two courses, one for Deck Officers and one for Engineering Officers, I assumed that those officers represented those two departments. One of the more senior officers at the head table asked the most significant question. He asked, "Since you worked in a service station for a number of years you must know a good deal about engines and machinery. Why then have you applied for the Deck department instead of the Engine department?" My answer was simple. I replied, "Engineers do not become captains of ships." Half the reviewing officers burst out laughing and the others looked surprised to say the least when they heard my answer. That answer certainly clinched it for me for I was accepted as a Cadet Midshipman.

THE NEW YORK STATE MARITIME ACADEMY

It was June 1943 and my class at the New York State Maritime Academy was not scheduled to convene until January 1944. In the mean time I was fitted for uniforms and issued some basic instruction booklets and told to report to Fort Schuyler right after New Years day. Officially I was a Midshipman USNR. I got a job at the Grumman Aircraft Corporation in Bethpage, Long Island and worked there as a riveter until the end of December. The second or third of January I reported to Fort Schuyler with the rest of the new Midshipmen. We were scheduled for eighteen months of intensive training. The class was evenly divided between the Deck and Engine departments. The school consisted of a Battalion of Cadet Midshipmen encompassing First, Second, and Third classes. We new Cadet Midshipmen were in the Third Class. The battalion was subdivided into four companies, and each company was divided into two platoons. The whole battalion was arranged so that the taller Midshipmen were in the first company and the shorter were in the fourth company. When on parade the battalion appeared to form one straight line without any heads standing above or falling below the line. This made for a very smart looking Battalion. We had a great deal of infantry drill. It was said that when on parade, the whole battalion performed with the appearance of an expert drill team. For academic instruction each class was divided into six sections, three Deck and three Engine. We marched from class room to class room or other instructional areas by sections. Each section had a section leader who was responsible for keeping the section together and orderly. The section leader also had to account for the whereabouts of anyone who was missing from his section. When settled in a class room, the section had to snap to attention when the instructor, a uniformed officer, entered the room and remain at attention until ordered to be seated. As a rule the battalion formed up by sections five times a day, before breakfast, morning colors, then lunch, dinner, and the evening study period. At 0545 every morning the battalion formed up by divisions for forty-five minutes of calisthenics, then off to the showers to get ready for the morning formation for breakfast. It was not unusual to have to do pushups in three or four inches of newly fallen snow. After breakfast we formed up again for morning colors at 0800, and afterwards marched off to the various class rooms. There was very little time that was not closely scheduled and supervised.

Discipline was essentially enforced by the First Class. When my class was assembled on the first day, Admiral T. T. Craven gave the welcoming speech. One point he made was, "There is no hazing in this Academy." An hour later we learned what the call "One Hand" meant. When a First Class man hollered "One Hand," any Third or Second class man hearing the call had to run to him and stand at attention until directed to perform some task. Failure to respond had dire consequences. Many of the tasks were for personal service such as doing his laundry, carrying his bag, or shining his shoes. Other tasks were pure hazing or punishment for some minor infraction of the rules. First Class Battalion rates, Division Captains, Platoon Leaders, Company Commanders, and Squad Leaders had the authority to put other Midshipmen on report. A person put on report would be given some form of punishment specified at a "Captain's Mast." Demerits, loss of liberty, or some other type of restriction was the sort of punishment handed out. Whenever a Midshipman accumulated one hundred and fifty demerits, he was discharged from the Academy and turned over to the Army or the Navy as an enlisted man. The hazing by the First Class added significantly to the pressure of the academic and physical training. A few did break under the constant pressure and dropped out of the Academy. The first six weeks were the worst. The new Third Class was restricted to the Fort and contact with the outside world was discouraged.

This new Third Class, my class, was composed of men of various academic and social backgrounds. About half of them had spent some time in college. A few had more than two years of college. Many were from well off families and had gone through private schools. They were all well above average intelligence. This was the first time that I encountered real serious academic competition. I was no longer the top student. Most of my classmates were city smart or real world smart whereas I was more like a country bumpkin and very naive. My study habits and procedures were not up to the academic load and my marks quickly fell below the average. There was every possibility that I would flunk out by the mid term examination. Some of my classmates had devised less than honest ways to pass the nu-

The New York State Maritime Academy
at Fort Schuyler, Bronx, New York

Cadet Midshipman Arthur R. Murray USNR

merous tests we were given. I could not bring myself to cheat in order to pass. When I was at my lowest point Dick Kadison, a classmate, took me aside and offered to help me. He told me that my major problem was that I did not know how to study and he took it upon himself to teach me how. Dick had a year or so of college and had grown up and gone to school in New York City. He was without doubt the smartest man in my class and probably the most intelligent man in the whole school. With his help I was able to bring my marks up and was soon on an even keel with the rest of the class. There is no doubt that I would not have survived that first term without the help Dick Kadison gave me. We remain fast friends to this day.

At the end of the first six months my class advanced from Third to Second Class, and a new Third Class entered the Academy. Shortly thereafter both the Second Class and the Third Class were transferred to the U S M T S American Pilot (formerly the U S S Empire State) an old Hog

Island freighter that had been converted to a training ship and was berthed at Fort Schuyler. The tween deck spaces had been converted into class rooms and berthing compartments. The berths were troop style pipe rack bunks stacked four high. A large mess deck was located on the main deck of the mid ship house. At last my class was out from under the cruel control of the First Class, and the new Third Class was under our control. We spent six months on the training ship learning the maritime arts. Because of the submarine menace the ship was restricted to cruising in Long Island Sound. There was submarine activity at the Eastern end of the sound, but the USS American Pilot was never fired on as far as anyone knows. Long Island Sound was in the war zone and if the ship had been torpedoed with about three hundred and seventy people on board it would have been quite a loss. The routine was to cruise Long Island Sound for two weeks and then return to the pier at Fort Schuyler for a week end layover to replenish stores, and then back to cruising the Sound. Training was intense. The ship was run Navy style with very strict discipline. We were taught the skills of the seaman as well as the duties and the responsibilities of a ship's officer. At the end of six months we were advanced to First Class and transferred from the ship to quarters ashore in the Fort.

On the ship my class had dominance over the Third Class who were known as "Mugs." We were learning the techniques and responsibilities of directing and supervising the work of subordinates. At the same time the officers and instructors were teaching us how to obey orders, perform various tasks, and take on certain responsibilities. One such responsibility involved maintaining the cleanliness of the main deck mess room head. Another classmate, John Green, and I had four Mugs to supervise in cleaning the head. Every morning right after breakfast we would spend about a half hour swabbing out and cleaning this head. One morning one of the Mugs informed John and me that one of the toilet bowls was infested with crabs. We gave it a thorough examination but saw no sign of crabs. The Mug insisted that he had seen some when he was cleaning the bowl. There were no insecticides available but John being an engineering cadet said that he knew how to get rid of the crabs. He disappeared into the engine room and returned a short time later with a juice can containing about an ounce of gasoline. The gasoline was poured into the infected bowl while the cleaning crew stood just outside the doorway. Then John lit a match and tossed it into the bowl. The result was spectacular. There was a muffled explosion along with a column of bright flame that rose up

S S Empire State
Hog Island Type Ship, New York State
Maritime College Training Ship

out of the bowl and spread mushroom like across the ceiling of the head. The porcelain bowl disintegrated into hundreds of small pieces scattered across the deck along with the water the bowl had contained. The ceiling paint changed from pristine white to a charred black and burnt brown color. Blisters of various sizes covered the ceiling and the sides of the stall, and a good deal of smoke poured out of the head into the mess room. General quarters were sounded followed shortly thereafter by the fire alarm. The Executive Officer and several other officers came rushing into the mess room along with the fire fighting crew. When they assessed the damage the ship's company stood down from general quarters and the fire fighting team left the area. After John and I gave the Executive Officer our story he said, "Both of you are on report for willful destruction of government property and endangering the safety of the ship."

During the few days it took the ship to return to the dock at Fort Schuyler John and I with our Mugs scraped off the damaged paint and repainted the entire mess room head. The ship's plumbers replaced the toilet bowl John and I had destroyed, and the head was back in use before the first line went on to the dock. The morning after the ship docked the ship's company was formed up on the fore deck by sections. A formal Captain's Mast was held. The Commandant of Cadets, Commander Guy DeSimone, stood before the ship's company with everyone standing at attention. He held a clip board with a printed paper on it and ordered Cadet Midshipmen Green and Murray to step forward. John and I stepped forward smartly and stood in front of him at ridged attention. Commander DeSimone then began to recite the charges against us. He had some difficulty reciting the charges. Every few seconds he would stop and putting the clip board up in front of his face he would turn his head to the side. After a few more seconds passed he would lower the clip board and resume reciting the charges. There was some muffled laughter from the men in the ranks. He went on, "… And did willfully cause an explosion which destroyed a toilet bowl and at this point Commander DeSimone lost his composure and burst out laughing along with the whole ship's company. He quickly regained control of himself and ordered silence in the ranks. Neither John nor I were laughing. We were in deep trouble. When he finished reciting the charges he asked John and me if we had anything to say. We replied, "No sir." He then said, "You are guilty of destroying government property and each of you will receive twenty five demerits and be restricted to the ship for six weeks." The ship's company was then dismissed. John and I felt that we were very fortunate to receive such relatively light punishment.

The last six months went by quickly. The academic endeavors were still intense but the lack of hazing by an upper class made it seem much easier. When the Battalion rates were announced for my class I was given one. The rate was the equivalent of a squad leader, and it came with some additional responsibilities. The most significant was being appointed as leader of my section. However being made section leader did have its costs. As section leader I was held responsible for the actions or behavior of my section when in the classroom or standing in ranks. When they were disorderly I was put on report. Early on I picked up about fifty demerits. One clown in my section, Robert Riley, was responsible for many of them. As a Battalion rate I had the power of being able to put another Midshipman on report. I informed Robert Riley that I would make sure that he got two demerits for every one that I received. His clowning in ranks declined sharply after that warning.

During the last three months of our training and education a new course on handling and processing cargo was given. This course was taught by a civilian, Professor Harry Stocker, who was an efficiency expert and author of a text book on modern cargo operations. He had been instrumental in overhauling the cargo handling operations at the Bayonne Naval Depot making it one of the most efficient in the world. Professor Stocker was an excellent teacher and I found the subject matter extremely interesting. As a consequence I scored very high on any of the tests he gave. At the end of one of the classes he invited me to have lunch with him on the following Saturday and I accepted. As arranged, I met him at the Down Town Athletic Club in Manhattan at noon. Professor Stocker had his daughter with him and introduced us. He then led the way to an impressive dining room where an excellent lunch was served. His daughter was a very attractive brunette with a pleasant friendly personality. During lunch Professor Stocker asked me if I had any plans for a career when the war was over. I responded that I had nothing beyond following a maritime career. He then said that he was going to start a consultation firm dealing with marine cargo operations when the war ended, and he would like me to consider joining him. I told him that I appreciated his offer and would certainly like to participate. He asked me to keep in touch and to contact him as soon as my wartime commitments were completed. I was tempted to ask his daughter for a date, but was afraid that it would not be appropriate. As far as I know I was the only Midshipman he ever took such an interest in. My failure to follow up on his offer after the war was probably a mistake.

One good thing about being First Class was the weekend leave policy. On most weekends we were allowed to leave the Fort on Saturday morning and we did not have to return until Sunday evening. Sometimes we were even allowed to start our weekend leave on Friday evenings. The last two weeks at the Academy were involved in taking the final examinations, and the License examination given by the U.S. Coast Guard. Then there was the graduation banquet and ball, a very formal affair. A week later there was the formal graduation exercise. By this time the class was only about two thirds the number that had started out eighteen months earlier. A few had dropped out for medical or discipline reasons, but most had dropped out due to academic failure. There was a little over one hundred who made it through to graduation. Those who did make it were graduated as Ensigns in the United States Naval Reserve and Third Mate Oceans, or Third Assistant Engineer.

THE GRADUATION BALL

The weekend before the graduation banquet and ball I went home to Central Islip. My mother asked me who would be my date for the affair. I replied that I had no idea since I did not have a steady girl friend. However I assured her that one of my classmates would come up with a sister or cousin that would be pleased to be my date. That Sunday evening my mother and I went to the service at the Methodist Church. We sat in one of the pews at the rear of the church. Sitting in one of the pews at the front of the church was Gloria and two of her sisters. Gloria had been in my class all through junior and senior high school, and I always had a crush on her. However she had always been aloof and unresponsive any time I tried to engage her in conversation. As far as I knew she never dated anyone all through high school, and this only served to place her on a higher moral level than the other girls in my class. My mother noticed Gloria and suggested that I invite her to attend the banquet and ball as my date. I thought, "what the heck," the worst she could do was to decline my invitation. When the service was over and everyone was leaving the church, I approached Gloria and after a few minutes of small talk, I asked her if she would consider attending my graduation banquet and ball at Fort Schuyler. Much to my surprise she said yes without any hesitation. I went on to tell her that it would be a formal affair and that I would call her during the week to let her know when I would pick her up on the following Saturday.

I arranged to pick Gloria up at 1700 on Saturday. I arrived at her house fifteen minutes early wearing my white dress Midshipman's uniform. She met me at the door with her mother and two sisters. They all seemed delighted, and Gloria looked absolutely beautiful. Her sisters had spent a considerable amount of time and effort putting her together. I presented her with a corsage and amid well wishes for a good time from her family we drove off in my old car. On the two hour drive to Fort

Schuyler Gloria was effervescent in conversation, totally different from the Gloria I had known in high school. She seemed to be very much impressed when she saw Fort Schuyler. Without a doubt she was one of the best looking girls at the affair. Many of my classmates and some of the instructors made a point of saying so. The banquet was held in the mess hall and was quite impressive. After the banquet everyone proceeded over to the armory where there was a full size orchestra playing popular dance music. Tables and chairs were arranged around the sides of the dance floor, and a number of long tables were set up along one wall with nonalcoholic beverages and things to munch on. Shortly after we entered the armory I led Gloria to the dance floor. The orchestra was playing a nice slow romantic tune. Gloria gave me an embarrassed look and told me that she did not know how to dance. She was indeed a dedicated Methodist. I suggested that I could teach her now and that she should not be embarrassed. She declined my suggestion so we spent the evening sitting on the side lines and from time to time touring parts of the fort. The orchestra quit playing before midnight and everyone began to depart. On the two hour drive back to Central Islip Gloria said very little. When we arrived at her house the lights were on and her sisters were waiting up for her. I opened the car door for her and she gave me a rather curt "Good night" and went quickly into the house. I could not help but think that Gloria had reverted to her old self. Even so, I sent her a formal invitation for her and three family members to attend the graduation ceremony at Fort Schuyler the following Saturday. Typically she did not attend the graduation ceremony nor did she send regrets. There was something seriously lacking in her education regarding proper etiquette. I could not understand why she accepted my invitation knowing that she could not dance, and not even fore warning me. That she did not acknowledge the invitation to my graduation was a disappointment as well as a blow to my ego. Gloria was still an enigma, and unfortunately, I still had strong feelings for her however unwarranted they were.

The country was in desperate need of officers for the Merchant ships as well as Naval vessels, so we were given a choice of going either Merchant or Navy after graduation. The class split about fifty-fifty. Half went Navy and half went into the Merchant Marine. I chose the Merchant Marine. There were several reasons for this choice. First and foremost was the fact that this would be the fastest way of becoming captain of a ship. Some of the earlier graduates who had gone into the Navy had made brief visits to Fort Schuyler during my time as a Midshipman. They reported that their assigned duties on various types of naval vessels were of little responsibility and far below the level of their training. Most expressed disappointment with the assignments they were given by the Navy. In addition to this the political leaders in the Whitehouse and the Congress promised to give those who served in the Merchant Marine a modified G I Bill of Rights. Those who went with the Navy thought they would be given heroic assignments and would have all the benefits of the G I Bill of Rights when the war came to an end. They were right about the benefits. Those of us who went into the Merchant Marine learned how much you can rely on the promises of politicians. When the war was over those politicians broke every promise they made. Since then I have never put any faith in any statement or promise made by any politician in Washington or anywhere else. They will say or promise anything to gain their immediate objectives without any intention of fulfilling them.

SHIP ASSIGNMENT

Before the graduation exercises Dick Kadison invited me to spend our leave time with him in New York. His parents were away on vacation and we could have the apartment to ourselves for two weeks. We had two weeks leave after graduation before we had to report to the Recruiting and Manning Organization for assignment to a ship. This was too good an opportunity to turn down, so I accepted his invitation. After the graduation exercises I went home with my parents for a day and then packed a small bag for the big leave celebration in New York. I joined Dick there a day or so later and we started partying in the Village and other hot spots in the city. We wore our brand new uniforms with our gold ensign's stripes and the Maritime Administration emblem on our hats. There was no shortage of women. If anything, there were too many. Dinner, drinking, and dancing partners were always available. However in those days, women were not as promiscuous as they are these days. They were willing to hold hands, hug, and kiss, but they were reluctant to go to bed on a casual date. The liberated uninhibited female did not evolve till much later. After the second day of carousing, Dick and I were having a wake up cup of coffee in the apartment. We looked at each other and asked, "What are we doing? There is a war going on and we should be in it." We decided to report to the Recruiting and Manning Organization that morning. At nine o'clock we were in the office and by ten o'clock we had our assignments as Third Mates on different ships. Dick was assigned to a "C-1" operated by the Alcoa Line, and I was assigned to a Liberty ship, The SS Patrick C. Boyle, operated by the Boland and Cornelius Steam Ship Company. Dick and I shook hands, wished each other good luck, and proceeded to our assignments. It was almost two years before I saw Dick again.

The S S Patrick C. Boyle was berthed at the foot of 40th street in the North River. I reported aboard at about 1100 and was taken to the Chief Mate by the gangway watchman. The Chief Mate, John Ciccosanti, was a slender wiry man about my own height. He said, "Welcome aboard, I am very busy right now so I will get someone to show you to your cabin and give you a tour of the ship." He called the Navy Gunners Mate over and asked him to show me around. The Gunners Mate was friendly and showed me to my cabin which was on the starboard side in the middle of a row of cabins on the boat deck.

We next toured the bridge then on to the main deck. I looked into number two hold and was surprised to see that instead of wood battens on the side of the hull, the hold was completely sheathed with wood. The Gunners Mate saw the look on my face and said, "Yes this ship is an ammunition carrier, if we get hit no one survives." After the tour I went back to the Chief Mate to find out what he wanted me to do. He said that we were scheduled to set sea watches at midnight and that we would sail shortly after that. Then he said I could go home and get my gear and say my good-byes, but be back on board as soon as possible. The ship was taking on stores and getting some last minute repairs made. Everything seemed to be a mass of activity and confusion as I left the ship.

I took the Long Island train home and told my Mother and Father that I had been assigned to the Liberty Ship, S S Patrick C. Boyle, and that we were sailing early the next morning. They asked me what kind of ship it was and where it was going. I told them it was a cargo ship and that I did not know where it was going. It was customary during the War for ships to sail with sealed orders which were not opened until after the Pilot had been dropped off and the ship was at sea. The idea was that the enemy would not be able to take any action if they did not know a ship's destination. My father sailed in the British Merchant Marine before and during the first World War until he was drafted into the American Army by a mistake of chance. I chose not to tell my parents that the S S Patrick C. Boyle was an ammunition carrier. To do so would have caused them a good deal of extra worry. I packed the things I wanted to take with me, said my good-byes, and caught the next train back to New York City. On the train I read a letter that had come to my parents home. It was from a high school classmate, Hugh Powers, who was then a student at a college in Morgantown, West Virginia. In his letter he said that a friend of his, Harriet Weidebusch, was visiting New York City and staying at a Hotel for women on Madison Avenue. He had told her that he was writing to me and suggesting that I might be able to show her around the town. His letter gave a phone number for her hotel and a request that I look her up if I could find the time.

I got back to the ship at around 1800 and reported to the Chief Mate. He said there was not much for me to do before sea watches were set at midnight, and that I was free to go ashore for a last fling before we sailed. He did suggest that I get back on board by 2200. The ship was empty of cargo so we were fairly sure we would go to another port in the States to load cargo. I went ashore and telephoned Harriet and asked her if she would have dinner with me. She agreed without any hesitation, and I arranged to meet her in the lobby of her hotel within the hour. Harriet turned out to be a very pretty petite brunette with a pleasant personality. She was a lady down to the hat and gloves, and we had a very nice dinner at restaurant not too far from her hotel. During our dinner conversation she told me that her father was a banker and that she had at least another year of college to go. I was wearing my uniform with all the new gold braid which probably made a good impression on her. It seemed a shame that I would not have a chance to take her out again in the immediate future. She was a very nice girl and I had no commitments to any other girl. I told her my ship was sailing in a few hours and I was sorry I would not be able to ask her out again for quite a while. When we finished dinner we walked back to her hotel. I gave her a lingering farewell kiss and she responded with some eagerness, which I am sure was out of character for her. I made it back to the S S Patrick C. Boyle by 2200, and never saw Harriet again.

THE VOYAGE BEGINS

Upon return to the ship I was introduced to Captain Peter Hickey, the ship's Master, and to Roger McNeil, the Second Mate. Sea watches were set at midnight and the ship sailed at about 0200. I was assigned to the bridge to assist the Captain while the ship got underway and cleared the harbor. After the Pilot was dropped off, the Second Mate took over the bridge and I turned in for a few hours sleep. I had the eight to twelve watch so I had to relieve the Second Mate at 0800. This meant that I had to have breakfast before 0800, and be ready to take the bridge watch for four hours. Soon after dropping the Pilot the Captain opened the sealed orders and found that we were to proceed to the port of New Orleans. My first watch as a Third Mate went rather well. There was a lot of activity around the bridge. The First and Second Mates were busy in the chart room laying out our courses and taking bearings to fix our position on the chart. The Captain and the Armed Guard Officer, a Navy Lieutenant,

S S Patrick C. Boyle
War Shipping Administration, Boland and Cornelius Line

made their rounds, and the deck hands were busy squaring away the decks. There were two able seamen and one ordinary seaman assigned to my watch and they took turns on the wheel. Although the ship was equipped with a gyro compass, there was no automatic pilot or "Iron Mike." At noon the Chief Mate relieved me and his watch took over. Operating this ship was considerably different from the way the training ship, the S S American Pilot, was operated. On the training ship we had fifteen men on the bridge watch plus port and starboard boat crews on standby. The S S Patrick C. Boyle had only a Mate and three seamen on watch plus two of the armed guard on standby. The rest of the armed guard were servicing the guns or working on some training task assigned by the armed guard Officer. Still I felt this first watch went well.

The S S Patrick C. Boyle, Hull number 1786, was built in Baltimore at the Fairfield Yard of the Bethlehem Steel Company. She carried a wartime compliment of sixty men. These were the Captain, three Mates, a Chief Engineer, three Assistant Engineers, three Radiomen, one Purser, one Pharmacist Mate, one Boatswain, one Carpenter, six Able Seamen, three Ordinary Seamen, one Deck Engineer, three Oilers, three Firemen, three Wipers, one Chief Steward, two Cooks, three Messmen, one Cabin Steward, an Armed Guard Officer, and eighteen Navy men. The watch routine was four hours on watch and eight hours off. Each watch consisted of one Mate, two Able Seamen, and one Ordinary Seaman on the deck watch, and one Assistant Engineer, one oiler, one Fireman, and one Wiper on the engine room watch. Those in the merchant crew who were not on a regular watch worked an eight hour day on various tasks. All Liberty Ships had an eight by eight platform located forward and in the center of the flying bridge. On this platform there was a steering wheel, a magnetic compass, a gyro compass repeater, an engine room telegraph, and a telephone and voice tubes to the lower bridge and engine room. There was also a gyro compass repeater on the port and starboard wings of the flying bridge. A wooden pilot house had been built over this platform on the S S Patrick C. Boyle to provide shelter for the helmsman. The Mates stood most of their watches at sea on the flying bridge because the visibility was much better from there. The lower bridge had only three very small ports looking forward and these ports had drop down steel plates for protection against strafing. On the bow the ship had gun tubs containing one three inch-fifty gun and two twenty millimeter guns. Half way between the midship house and the bow there were twenty millimeter guns in tubs, one on the port side and one on the starboard side. There were four more twenty millimeter guns in gun tubs, one on each corner of the midship house on the flying bridge level. On the stern there was a five inch-thirty eight gun and two additional twenty millimeter guns, all in gun tubs. The ship was well armed with five inch and three inch cannons plus ten twenty millimeter guns.

The ship's compliment was made up of a variety of people with different backgrounds and characters. A couple of the deck hands were former prison inmates who were given an early parole in order to provide seamen to crew the ship. One ordinary seaman was a lad of thirteen. He was big for his age, right out of the hills of Kentucky, and he had lied about his age in order to be allowed to ship out. There were two college professors from some South American country who claimed to be political refugees. They were probably Communists and they did not speak English very well, especially when the Chief Mate was assigning them to some difficult task. The Third Engineer was a man in his fifties who had been a Postman and went into the Merchant Marine because the armed forces would not take him. He always longed to be back on his postal route. The captain was a graduate of the Massachusetts Maritime Academy and had made several runs to Europe carrying ammunition. The Chief Engineer was a great lover. He was paying alimony to three former wives and a fourth was suing him for divorce. The Armed Guard Officer was a ninety day wonder who had been a lawyer in civilian life. However he was an excellent officer who had his act together. The rest of the crew were the average you found going to sea in those days.

My next watch began at 2000 when I relieved the Second Mate. The sky was overcast and darkness fell rather quickly. The ship was heading south down the East Coast on our way to New Orleans. No lights were shown. The ship was completely blacked out. Even the Western horizon was dark in accordance with wartime regulations. I found myself alone on the flying bridge except for the man at the wheel in the small wooden makeshift wheel house. It was very dark and very lonely. The charted course was checked carefully before I went on watch so I was confident it was correct. With ships operating in a blacked out condition, and knowing that there was always a great deal of traffic along the coast, I was extremely anxious — hell I was scared. The lives of fifty nine people were in my hands. If I were to collide with another ship there would be a great loss of life. In those days merchant ships were not equipped with Radar. We were

Arthur Randolph Murray

lucky to have a gyro compass on board. There was no Loran. We did have a Radio Direction Finder, but the radio stations were silent because there was a war on. Navigation was crude by today's standards. Throughout the watch I strained my eyes looking ahead and to the sides. The Gyro compass was checked against the magnetic compass frequently. The helmsman's steering accuracy was checked constantly. There was a seaman on lookout on the bow, a helmsman on the bridge with me, and a seaman on standby in the mess room. The seamen rotated an hour and twenty minutes on the wheel, an hour and twenty minutes on bow lookout, and an hour and twenty minutes on standby in the mess room. To say the very least, it was a dark, lonely, and scary four hours.

The next eight to twelve morning watch went much more easily. I was beginning to get the feel of the shipboard routine. When I went on the next eight to midnight watch I felt much more comfortable, but there was still some anxiety and the fear of a collision with some other darkened ship. The remainder of the trip's night watches went better because the sky cleared and the moon and stars provided much better visibility. By the time the ship reached New Orleans I felt I was a seasoned watch officer. Still I was amazed that Captain Hickey would leave a green Third Mate alone on the bridge at night. Some months later I asked Captain Hickey why he placed the fate of his ship in the hands of a fresh out of school green third mate about whom he knew very little. He told me that I was not alone on those eight to midnight watches. He said that he had stood everyone of those watches with me. While I was on the flying bridge, Captain Hickey was on the lower bridge. When I walked to the starboard wing, he walked to the starboard wing, and when I walked to the port wing, he walked to the port wing. He knew exactly what was happening with his ship. I asked why he had not let me know that he was standing the watch with me. It would have made me feel much more at ease. Captain Hickey said that I would not have gained the confidence to be totally responsible for running the ship as quickly as I did if he had let me know that I was not alone on those first watches. Once he was satisfied that I could handle the responsibility, he no longer stood my watches with me. I was a twenty-year-old kid, but in those days one had to grow up fast. As time went by I came to realize that Captain Hickey was not only one of the best seamen I had ever known, he was also the best teacher. As Third Mate I was always on the bridge with the Captain when the ship was maneuvering in or out of a port and when docking and undocking. Captain Hickey told me to pay careful attention to everything he did while maneuvering the ship because this would be the best opportunity for me to learn. He made a point of explaining why he ordered every change of rudder angle and engine speed and how to use the mooring lines under different conditions when docking the ship. The effect that wind and current had on the ship while maneuvering was explained in great detail. Captain Hickey taught me more about ship handling in six weeks than I ever learned in six months on the training ship.

NEW ORLEANS

A week later the S S Patrick C. Boyle tied up at the Paulene Street wharf in New Orleans to load cargo. We took on a mixed cargo of munitions, machinery, PX supplies, four thousand tons of aviation gasoline in fifty-five gallon drums, vehicles, aircraft wings in crates, and some large boxed items. Many of the larger vehicles, crates, and boxes were stowed on the main deck. A wooden cat walk was built over this deck cargo so the crew could get to the guns. The ship had a full load but we had no idea where we were to take it. It took about a week to load the cargo and the crew took advantage of all the pleasures available in New Orleans. Sea watches had been broken so everyone was on day work except the mates and engineers who had to stand the night watches. Still this allowed me the opportunity of enjoying the bars, night clubs, and restaurants of New Orleans. The Court of Two Sisters was an intriguing restaurant in the French Quarter, and I left one of my personal cards with hundreds of others in Lafiette's Saloon. I soon learned to avoid the "Honey buy me a drink" girls who were present in all of the bars along Canal street. If one were foolish enough to buy them a drink, they would invariably order Champaign, and one would have to pay for a very expensive bottle. Many of the Merchant Seamen fell into this trap. This was the nasty side of an otherwise pleasant city.

Most Liberty Ships were fitted with name boards usually carried on the port and starboard rails on the flying bridge deck. They were made from wood planks and measured about two feet by twenty feet. They were painted the same gray color as the ship's hull, and the letters spelling out the ship's name were cut into the wood and usually painted white. However on the S S Patrick C. Boyle the name boards were different. Captain Hickey had the boards painted "Kelley" green with the letters painted a "Canary" yellow color. The Navy Captain of the Port for New Orleans sent word to the ship to have the name boards repainted to conform to the standards for Liberty Ship name boards. Captain Hickey ignored the Navy's request. In every port the S S Patrick C. Boyle paid a visit, the Navy would send a notice to the ship to have the color of the name boards changed to conform to the regulations. They were never changed as long as Captain Hickey was the Master. He felt that this was one way to distinguish his ship from all the other Liberty Ships, which is just what the Navy did not want.

One evening I took a four hour ride on a river excursion boat, the President. This vessel had two bands playing music on different decks, several bars, and a dining room. There were many unescorted women on board. One of them struck up a conversation with me and we spent the evening dancing and drinking. I do not remember her name, but she was very friendly. Before we parted at the dock she gave me her phone number. She said that she shared a house with several other girls and would like to throw a party. I was asked to invite some of the officers from my ship to come to her house the next evening, and to call her to let her know how many would come. About six of us went to her house and there were about ten young ladies there. They had a record player going and had set out snacks and drinks. We danced and talked and had a very tame but enjoyable party. The girls were all office workers and were hungry for some male companionship. There was no hanky-panky. These were nice decent girls. The party broke up before midnight because the girls had to be at work the next morning. The men from my ship and I were invited to come back the next evening, but that was the day we sailed. The ship sailed at mid afternoon so there was no chance for me to say a proper farewell.

We dropped the pilot at the entrance of Southwest Pass in the early afternoon and proceeded across the Gulf of Mexico to the Yucatan Straight. Our ship had been ordered to the Panama Canal port of Cristobal. During the passage to Cristobal the crew finished securing the cargo for an ocean passage and cleared away the debris left by the longshoremen and other workmen during our stay in New Orleans. The Gun Crew Officer exercised his men and some of the merchant seamen in gunnery drills and going to general quarters. By the time we reached Cristobal they were able to be at their stations with the all guns ready in under two minutes. I cannot remember this officer's name. He was a full lieutenant U. S. Navy Reserve, about thirty years old, and had red hair. The Gunners mate was in his mid twenties and the rest of the gun crew were kids like me in their late teens or early twenties. They had all volunteered for armed guard duty on merchant vessels. This duty was considered the most dangerous duty in the Navy.

THE PANAMA CANAL

The S S Patrick C. Boyle picked up the pilot and entered Cristobal Harbor on my morning watch and anchored inside the breakwater. There were several other merchant ships at anchor. They were of various sizes and some were fully loaded while others appeared to be light. Civilian and military people came aboard and informed the captain that we would top off our fuel and water tanks and then proceed through the Canal the next day. Late that afternoon with the help of two tugboats we pulled up to the fuel dock and started taking on bunker "C" fuel oil and fresh water. The next morning the Canal pilot and a squad of Army soldiers armed with machine guns came aboard. Two tugboats helped us away from the fuel dock and we started through the Panama Canal. I was on the flying bridge with the pilot, a helmsman, and a soldier who followed me around like my shadow with his machine gun at the ready. When asked why he did this he replied that he was under orders to shoot me if I gave any steering order to the helmsman or order to the engine room that would cause damage to the locks. The authorities were in constant fear that the locks would be sabotaged by some ship ramming the gates.

The Chief Mate had a crew on the bow and the Second Mate had a crew on the stern to handle the lines from the mules (large electric engines) that pulled the ship through the locks. The Panama Canal locks are a spectacular marvel of engineering. During the Canal transit the pilot is in charge. He would give me the speed and steering commands and I would see that they were done. The weather was hot with occasional showers. As the ship passed through the Gatun Cut muddy rain water turned to gold by the sun came cascading down the steep sides of the Cut making a spectacular sight. It took the best part of three watches to transit the Canal and it was dark by the time we anchored in Balboa harbor. The next morning a pilot and port officials came aboard and we got underway. The ship headed out of Balboa and the Captain received sealed orders. When the ship was clear of the harbor, the pilot and officials departed in the pilot boat. The Captain opened the orders and informed the Mates, the Chief Engineer, and the Navy Officer that the ship was ordered to proceed to some base in the Philippine Islands by way of the San Bernardino Straits.

PROCEEDING ALONE

As we departed Panama, another Liberty ship followed behind us making considerable smoke and when we were well clear of the land, they used their signal light to ask our destination. We responded that we were bound for the Philippine Islands. They replied that they were also bound for the Philippines and would tag along with us. When night fell Captain Hickey ordered a significant change of course so that we would lose the other ship. He said that two ships made too inviting a target. The other ship could give our position away if they continued to be careless and continued making too much smoke. Captain Hickey did not want to put his ship at risk because of another ship's carelessness. Since the night was dark with an overcast sky and we were showing no lights, the other ship was not aware that we had changed course. When dawn broke the other ship was nowhere in sight and we set the S S Patrick C. Boyle on the great circle track for the San Bernardino Straits.

The next day the Captain and the Chief Mate had a conference and the Captain told the Chief Mate that he would be staying in his cabin for the next few days. The Chief Mate was in charge and should not disturb him unless there was an emergency. The Captain had a few bottles of whisky he had to consume. Three days later he appeared in the Salon for breakfast. He was a little hung-over but alert enough to resume his duties. Being somewhat shocked by his behavior, I summoned up enough courage to ask the Captain why he had gone on a three day binge. He said that he had to lose himself in the bottle every so often. This was the only chance he would have for quite some time. As our ship proceeded closer to the combat area he would have to be sober and alert. He said that drinking whisky was the only way he could keep his sanity when he was sitting on ten thousand tons of high explosives in a European harbor while bombs were falling all around his ship. After several such situations, he was hooked on the bottle. He said he could control his need for alcohol and that he would not take another drink until his ship was in safe waters. To the best of my knowledge he remained sober throughout the rest of the voyage.

A few days after departing Balboa we three Mates noticed something strange about the Merchant crew. They always seemed to have an abundant supply of cigars. These they would smoke in the designated areas. More than once a sailor was seen to light up a cigar, take a few puffs and then toss it overboard. These were not cheap cigars. They were CORONA CORONA cigars that usually sold for a Dollar a piece when you could find them. We knew that Merchant sailors could not afford such extravagance and assumed that they must have broken into the P X supplies that were part of the cargo. The Chief Mate got out the cargo manifest and we examined it carefully. There was no record of cigars being part of the cargo. Finally the Chief Mate called the boatswain to his office and asked him where the crew was getting the cigars. He claimed in all innocence that he had no idea and it was a mystery to him as well. The next morning when the Chief Mate came off watch he found six boxes of CORONA CORONA cigars on his desk. He summoned the boatswain to his office again and asked him who put the cigars on his desk. The boatswain said that he had no idea who could have put them there or where they came from. The Chief Mate gave two boxes to the Second Mate and two boxes to me and kept two for himself. I put my two boxes away planning to send them to my father if and when the ship returned to the States. The Second Mate did likewise.

The Pacific Ocean was a strange body of water. The sea was smooth with a low swell and a rather oily surface appearance. The sky was hazy with low puffy clouds that resembled herds of sheep. The sun was unmercifully hot and the only breeze was that caused by the ship's movement through the water. At night when there was a moon the ocean sparkled. Visibility was unusually good which in spite of its beauty gave us some concern. A submarine would be able to see us at a great distance and that increased our chances of being torpedoed. Occasionally schools of tuna would be seen as well as pods of whales, but no other ships. Shipboard routine became boring. The armed guard officer kept his men busy maintaining the guns and instructing some designated merchant sailors in how to pass the ammunition. Because part of our cargo consisted of four thousand tons of aviation gasoline in fifty-five gallon drums, the ship had the odor of a gasoline station. Smoking on deck was forbidden and only allowed in designated areas. The Armed Guard Officer said he would shoot anyone he saw smoking on deck without any warning, and he meant it. The Captain posted a notice on the Ship's bulletin board which stated, "If this ship takes a hit from enemy action—find a parachute—it will be more useful to you than your life jacket."

After the first week on our voyage to the Philippines a shipboard crisis developed. The Navy Armed Guard sailors broke into the freezer locker and consumed all of the ice cream that had been put there for the entire voyage. The Merchant crew were incensed when they found out about the theft. They threatened to attack the Navy crew and teach them a lesson. Since the Merchant sailors out numbered the Navy boys by two to one, there is little doubt about what the result would be. The Chief Steward saved the day. He said that he had a recipe for making ice cream from canned evaporated milk and some other ingredients, and he had on board an old fashioned ice cream machine. This tub like machine required a great deal of tedious hand cranking to produce a couple of quarts of ice cream. The Armed Guard Officer decided that it would be suitable punishment for his crew to have them make enough ice cream to replace the amount that they had stolen. For several days there after the Navy sailors took turns at the hand crank to produce the replacement ice cream. The product was not as tasty as the commercially produced ice cream but it did satisfy the Merchant sailors, and a very serious confrontation was averted. The Armed Guard Officer took a more active control of his Navy gun crew. Every Saturday he set up a chair and some equipment on the aft part of the boat deck. One by one his crew would come to the boat deck and sit in the chair. The Officer would then proceed to give the man a haircut. He said that he had two reasons for doing this. It kept his gun crew looking shipshape, and it gave him practice in being a barber. He said that his father told him when he was young to have a trade as well as a profession. He was a lawyer by profession and by trade a barber. No matter how things developed after the war, he would always be able to make a living. Anyone else on board could get his hair cut by following the gun crew to the boat deck. Not everyone took advantage of this opportunity.

SILLY PRANKS

Seamen playing tricks and pranks on one another is quite common on a long and boring voyage. One day the Second Mate called me up to the bridge during the beginning of his afternoon watch. He asked if I had any fear of heights. When I answered no, he said that the Chief Radioman wanted someone to go up the after mast and clear a jam at the block for the antenna halyard. The radio antenna was stretched between a mast on the flying bridge and a small diameter mast extension on the after mast. I carefully climbed to the top of the aft radio mast and examined the halyard block. There was nothing wrong with the block and there was no jam. While I was climbing up the after mast, the Second Mate turned the ship into the wind. When I was at the top of the extended radio mast, the Second Assistant Engineer blew tubes. (It was customary to blow the soot off the boiler tubes with steam daily during the middle of the Second Assistant Engineer's watch.) I was totally covered with black sticky soot. Everyone had a good laugh while I headed for the shower to clean up.

That night I had my standby man allow the Second Mate to sleep a little later. That way he would not be able to relieve me till after midnight. I knew that the Second Assistant Engineer always sat right under the ventilator when he took his engine room watch. The cowl for this ventilator was on the flying bridge and it had an access door in it. The standby man had brought a pail of sea water to the flying bridge for me before he went off watch. After carefully searching the horizon for a sign of any other vessel, and not seeing any, I opened the access door on the ventilator cowl.

Peering down the ventilator shaft, I could see the Engineer seated on his chair in the engine room far below. I dumped the pail of water in the ventilator and closed the access door. When the Second Mate came on the bridge to relieve me the engine room phone began to ring. As the Second Mate picked up the phone, I told him to tell the Engineer that we had just taken a huge wave over the bridge. Now it was my turn to laugh.

CONSTIPATION

It is a known fact that seamen drink an inordinately large amount of coffee. During a four hour bridge watch a Mate would usually drink three or four cups of coffee. The helmsman was relieved at the wheel every hour and twenty minutes, and the relieving helmsman would always bring a fresh hot cup of coffee for the Mate on watch. As the weeks passed since the ship departed the States I noticed that the taste of the coffee became more and more rancid. Adding more canned evaporated milk and sugar did little to improve the flavor. What caused the rancid taste was hard to determine. Failure to clean the coffee pots adequately or a decline in the quality of the water in the ship's potable water tanks or both may have been the cause. The mess men began to add egg shells to the coffee grounds when they made a pot of coffee in an effort to improve the taste. There was little if any improvement. I switched to drinking tea instead of coffee. Although the tea was more palatable, it had another bad aspect. After drinking tea for a few days I became constipated. I went to the ship's pharmacist mate and asked him for a laxative. He gave me two brown pills and said these would solve my problem. A day later I went back to him and asked for a stronger laxative because the brown pills did not work. He then gave me three capsules and said these will act like a depth charge. Another day passed with no bowl movement. Now I started to worry that I might have a serious medical problem developing. After another consultation with the pharmacist mate he recommended that I stop drinking tea. He consulted his medical books and then gave me a small bottle of a liquid which he said was the most powerful laxative he had. This foul tasting liquid worked, and I went back to drinking the rancid tasting coffee.

THE ALBATROSS

One morning Captain Hickey came on the bridge and looked at the cargo on the fore deck. The olive drab vehicles, boxes, and crates were spattered with white bird dung. During the night a large albatross had landed on the fore mast cross tree and was still perched there. The Captain was greatly annoyed by the mess the bird had made and was still making. He said that he knew how to fix that bird and then left the bridge. A few minutes later he returned with a 38 revolver and started shooting at the bird. The Chief Mate, the Chief Engineer, and the Armed Guard Officer came on the bridge having been attracted by the sound of gun fire. When the Captain told them he was trying to shoot the albatross they went to their quarters to get their pistols. They returned quickly and the four of them lined up on the forward rail of the flying bridge like a firing squad and started shooting at the poor bird. I told them that they should not kill the albatross because it would put a curse on the ship. They were asked if they had ever read Tennyson's Rhyme of the Ancient Mariner. The four of them looked at me and laughed, and then they resumed their target practice.

The shooting went on for nearly an hour. To say the very least, they were terrible marksmen. They managed to chip a lot of paint off the fore mast cross tree before they were able to hit the bird with a fatal shot. Some of the crew gathered on the fore deck to watch the shooting match. A couple of the older seamen said that it was bad luck to kill a sea bird but nobody made any serious objection. I can only assume that the bird did not fly off because it was old and very sick. When the fatal shot hit the bird it tumbled down and landed on one of the large boxes on the deck. Two of the sailors from the group that had gathered to watch the shooting picked the bird up and spread its wings. The bird had a wingspan of at least seven feet. It was full of lice and rather emaciated and had actually been hit several times. They threw the bird over the side and no one except me thought about it again. I was sure that no good would come of this wanton destruction of the albatross.

CARELESS NAVIGATION

As we proceeded on our course navigation became a routine activity. The Second Mate would fix the ship's position at morning and evening twilight with star sights. After sunrise all three of us mates would take sun lines during the morning so that we could advance them to the noon Latitude line. Then at noon we would take the altitude of the sun with our sextants as it crossed the meridian. This gave us the Latitude at noon. Running the morning's sun lines up to the noon Latitude line gave us the exact noon position of the ship which was entered in the ship's log. As the days passed we started to take shortcuts with our noon calculations. One mate would calculate the sun's declination, another mate would calculate the equation of time, and another would calculate the other corrections to be applied to our observed altitudes. We would each use these calculations without checking them independently. This was not a good practice as we soon learned.

Our course took our ship through the southern part of the Marshall Islands, a group of thirty-two atolls and nearly nine hundred reefs lying between 5 and 15 degrees North Latitude, and 161 and 172 degrees East Longitude. The northern islands were held by the Japanese. As we neared these islands our noon position showed us to be about fifty miles too far to the south. The Captain was very annoyed and told us mates to pay closer attention to how the helmsmen were steering. Everyone assumed that the ship had been steered off course for several hours the previous night. A new course was set to put us back on track and our calculations indicated that we would not see any land until early the next morning. Much to our surprise, late that afternoon palm trees began to appear on the horizon ahead of us. We quickly went over our calculations for the noon position and discovered that we had not been fifty miles off our track at noon but were right where we were supposed to be. Our shortcut navigation procedure had caused the three of us to make the same error in determining the noon Latitude and the ship's position. The course alteration toward the north to put us back on track was actually leading us into the part of the Marshall Islands that were still in the hands of the Japanese. By the time we figured out what the error had been and where we actually were, there were palm trees on the horizon on each side of the ship.

The S S Patrick C. Boyle was steaming between two islands and the channel between them narrowed down to less than one half mile in width. These islands were part of the Wotje Atoll in the Marshall Islands, and according to the information we had, they were still held by the Japanese. The Captain had the signal for general quarters sounded and the guns were quickly manned and uncovered. The chart of the area showed that we could pass through the channel in a short period of time and be out in the ocean well clear of any other islands. The ship's guns were trained on the shoreline on each side of the ship and everyone in the armed guard and on the bridge wore a steel helmet in addition to a life jacket. As the ship got closer to the beaches with the green underbrush and palm trees in plain sight, we expected to be under fire. A Navy TBF airplane appeared and started to fly around us in very wide circles. The Navy airmen must have thought we were crazy to take our ship through that narrow channel and expose ourselves to the enemy. As we passed by the islands we could see no sign of the enemy. The white beaches along the shore line were devoid of any sign of life. They must have been well hidden and hunkered down thinking that we were an invading force. When the ship was well clear of the islands the plane flew off toward the south without any attempt to communicate with us. To say the least, we were very lucky. One well placed shot could have turned the S S Patrick C. Boyle into a giant fire ball.

THE BOMB

Once we were clear of the Marshall Islands normal shipboard routine resumed. Every few days the Armed Guard Officer would hold gunnery practice. Sometimes an empty 55 gallon drum would be thrown overboard and the gun crew would bang away at it with our three inch and our five inch guns. At other times a big black balloon would be inflated and released. Then the twenty millimeter guns would fire at it. On one of these exercises the young skinny crew mess man asked the Armed Guard Officer if he could have a turn with the twenty millimeter gun. Amid laughs by the Navy gun crew the Armed Guard Officer with a broad smile on his face told the mess man he could have a turn. By the time he got into the gun harness the balloon was almost out of range. The gun crew continued to laugh because they had been unable to hit the balloon when it was much closer. The kid took careful aim and fired one short burst. To everyone's surprise and consternation, a couple of seconds later the balloon exploded. Some of the armed guard sailors said, "A lucky shot, dumb luck." As the young mess man climbed out of the gun tub he said to the Officer, "I just wanted to see if I still had a good eye." It turned out that the mess man had made a couple of runs to Murmansk, and probably had more gunnery experience than the whole gun crew put together.

Our ship was getting close to the San Bernardino Straits and it was mid August and we were in the Philippine Sea. The Chief Radio Operator reported that he received a message that an Atom bomb had been dropped on Japan. None of us knew what an atom bomb was but there was much speculation that it was something much more devastating than the block busters we did know about. When we were within a day's time of making landfall in the Philippines we received a message by radio to return to Balboa in the Canal Zone. We put the ship about and proceeded on the reciprocal great circle track back to Balboa. It should be noted here that at this time while the S S Patrick C. Boyle was in the Philippine Sea the Navy's heavy cruiser USS Indianapolis was torpedoed by a Japanese submarine and sank. Hundreds of lives were lost in those shark infested waters. Had the Indianapolis been able to send an SOS on their radio, the S S Patrick C. Boyle and other ships in that Sea would have gone to the area of the sinking to rescue the survivors. Unfortunately, no radio message was sent, and ignorant of the tragedy we continued on our course. When we reached a position on the track just a few days from making landfall in Panama, we got another radio message directing us to proceed to our original destination. Accordingly the ship was turned around and headed back on the track to the San Bernardino Straits. Again when we were within a day of entering the San Bernardino Straits, the ship received another radio message instructing us to change course and proceed to the island of Eniwetok in the Marshall Islands. The ship was turned around again and set on a great circle track for Eniwetok.

A few days after this last change in destination we spotted a floating mine just after sunrise. It was an ugly black sphere just barely awash and the horns were quite visible. The ship's speed was reduced and the Armed Guard Officer ordered his crew to man the twenty millimeter guns. At a safe distance they opened fire on the mine trying to detonate it or to sink it. They should have called on the crew mess man to man one of the guns. The Navy gun crew were not able to detonate or sink the mine, so the ship resumed its course and speed. About eight hours later we encountered another Liberty Ship heavily loaded coming towards us on a reciprocal course. We communicated with each other by blinker light (we were operating under strict radio silence). They informed us that they were heading for the San Bernardino Straits, and we warned them of the mine we had passed eight hours ago. During the night, about eight hours later, the Chief Radio Operator reported that he just picked up an S O S call, and from the call sign, he was sure it was the ship we had passed earlier in the day. She had hit a mine or been torpedoed and was sinking. The ship in distress gave her Latitude and Longitude so we were fairly sure she had hit the mine we had failed to destroy. The Captain decided that since it would take at least sixteen hours to reach the sinking ship, we would keep on our course. He felt that since they had sent a distress call out on their radio, other Merchant and Naval ships closer to them would get to them before we could.

RAIN SQUALLS

One of the ship's two evaporators broke down and the supply of fresh water soon became critically short. The ship's boilers consumed a great deal of fresh water in the process of producing steam for the triple expansion engine. One evaporator alone could not keep up with the demands of the boilers. If more fresh water could not be found, it would probably be necessary to shut down one of the boilers. If that were to happen, the ship's speed would be reduced to about three or four knots. Fresh water washing was stopped for all hands and things were looking grim. Then Chief Mate Ciccosanti came up with a brilliant idea which he presented to the Captain and Chief Engineer. With their approval he had the boat deck thoroughly swept down and then had all but two of the scuppers plugged. To these two open scuppers fire hoses were attached and led to the water storage tanks. Next the Mates on watch were told to keep a lookout for any rain squalls. There were usually one or two rain squalls seen every day in these waters. When a rain squall was spotted we would steam toward it and once in it we would stop the ship and allow the boat deck to accumulate the rain water. It would usually take about two hours to fill the water tanks if the squall was heavy. With this technique the boilers were provided with enough fresh water for the ship to maintain its speed on the run to Eniwetok.

ENIWETOK

Upon reaching Eniwetok the ship went through a narrow pass and anchored in the center of a very large lagoon. Low lying land with palm trees could be seen on the horizon all around the ship. There were a few other ships at anchor some distance off. At the entrance pass to the lagoon there was a large tanker stranded high and dry on the reef. Judging by its condition it must have been there for some time. The water in the lagoon was unusually clear. Many of us decided to go for a swim and got into our swim trunks. It was great fun diving off the side of the ship and while under the water being able to see the whole length of the ship and the anchor chain disappearing in the deep blue water. There were only about a dozen of us swimming around for only a short time when we saw a launch approaching from the shore. A sailor on the bow of the launch was waving his tunic and shouting to us to get out of the water. When the launch came alongside we were informed that the lagoon was infested with sharks and barracuda. We were also told that four sailors had recently been killed by these predators while just wading waist deep off the beach. Needless to say, that ended the recreational swimming.

Just after noon a water barge and a fuel barge were brought alongside to replenish the ship. The engineers got the spare parts needed to repair the evaporator and started working on it right away. While standing on the flying bridge surveying the replenishment, the Second Mate and I noticed some of the merchant sailors hauling up a line from inside one of the ventilators to number three cargo hold. A wooden box was attached to the end of the line and this box was quickly transferred to the water barge alongside. A while later another box was hauled out of another ventilator and transferred to the water barge. We knew from the cargo plan that the cargo in number three hold where the boxes came from consisted only of vehicles in the tween deck and drums of gasoline in the lower hold. The sailors retrieved a couple of bags from the water barge and squirreled them away before the Second Mate and I got down to the main deck. Obviously there was some sort of barter exchange. The sailors refused to tell us what was in the bags and even denied having made any such exchange. The Navy crew on the water barge were even less cooperative, so we decided not to pursue the matter further.

WHITE LIGHTNING

The word was passed that we were going to depart Eniwetok at midnight. The transfer of fuel and water was completed just after dinner time and the ship settled down to a normal quiet routine. At 2300 the crew was roused out to get ready to get underway. I was on the bridge with the Captain and one of my able seamen as helmsman. The Captain and I noticed that the helmsman was stumbling around in a drunken stupor. The Chief Mate and the Second Mate reported to the Captain that the deck crew were all drunk. The Chief Engineer also reported that the black gang were all drunk and unfit to go on watch. The Chief Mate and the Second Mate got the anchor up, the Chief Engineer and the three Assistant Engineers manned the engine room, and I took the helm while the Captain conned the ship out of the Eniwetok lagoon. Only the licensed officers were able to man the ship. The unlicensed crew were all thoroughly intoxicated and unfit to stand any watches. The Captain was furious. By noon the ship returned to near normal operating condition although the crew was badly hung over. While I took the bridge watch the Captain and the other two mates began a search of the ship. They confiscated dozens of bottles and jars of a dirty gray-white alcoholic fluid. These containers were carried to the fantail where they were tossed overboard. Members of the crew not on watch stood around in small clusters watching through bloodshot eyes the disposal of their beverages and grumbling about how unfair it was. A further search of the engine room spaces revealed the source of the beverage in the fiddley above the boilers.

At the time the ship was stored for the voyage several wooden tubs of ground beef were placed in the freezer locker. This supplied the meat for hamburgers, meat loaf, meat pies, and creamed chip beef dishes. The crew saved some of these wood tubs when they were empty. They were cleaned, placed in the fiddley above the boilers, and filled with an assortment of potatoes, canned fruits, other vegetables, water and yeast. This mixture was allowed to ferment for several weeks. The unknown brew master checked the progress of brew until the proper level of alcohol content was achieved. In the meantime the crew saved all the bottles, jugs, and jars as their contents were consumed. Just prior to the ship's arrival at Eniwetok the brew master announced that the brew was ready for bottling. The crew strained the brew through some layers of cheese cloth and filled every available container with the dirty gray-white fluid. The evening before the ship's departure from Eniwetok, the crew members retired to their cabins and went on a drinking binge. By 2300 most of them were too intoxicated from drinking the white lightening to stand up. After their drinking binge most of the crew paid the price. They suffered from severe nausea and diarrhea for several days. Needless to say they got little sympathy from the ship's officers. As far as I know none of the Armed Guard sailors participated in the drinking binge. Their officer had them pretty well squared away by this time and it is doubtful that any of them would risk his displeasure.

THE LONG VOYAGE HOME

When the ship cleared the Eniwetok lagoon the Captain set a course for San Francisco. That was the destination spelled out in the sailing orders when the sealed envelope was opened. After a few days in the open ocean the shipboard routine returned to normal. Most of the sailors had recovered from their encounter with the beverage known as white lightning. A week or ten days had passed when word was received that the Japanese had surrendered. The War was over. However the radio reported that there were many Japanese units that were still active and did not believe that the War was over and that they had lost. We were advised to stay alert and to exercise every precaution. About a week before the ship was expected to arrive at San Francisco, a radio message was received directing the Armed Guard Officer to clear out the ship's ammunition lockers and to jettison the ammunition overboard. It took the Armed Guard sailors three days to complete the task of dumping all the ammunition overboard. To all of us on board this was proof positive that the war was over. Everyone in the Merchant crew was looking forward to getting paid off, leaving the ship, and returning home. The Armed Guard still had their enlistments to fulfill so they had no idea where they would be assigned.

The night before we were due to arrive at the Farallon Islands, the Pilot Station for San Francisco, the Captain joined me on the starboard wing of the flying bridge. It was an unusually beautiful night. There were patches of fog sitting like thick white clouds on the surface of the ocean which was so smooth that there was not even a ripple on the water. The cutwater and wake of the ship were a brilliant green caused by the marine life that luminesces when disturbed. The light given off by this marine life was so bright that it clearly showed the Captains face when he leaned over the rail. It was so bright that one could probably read a news paper by it. The ship came into an area of clear water after passing through one of the patches of fog. The Captain and I were looking to starboard when we saw three brilliant green streaks like three arrows heading right for the ship. They were spaced apart and each one a little further back than the one ahead. There was no time to turn the ship out of their path because they were too close. The Captain turned to me and said, "Hold on we are going to be hit!" We stared, almost fascinated, as the green streaks came straight at the side of the ship. Suddenly the streaks turned and ran parallel with the ship. They were dolphins, not torpedoes. The Captain laughed and said that those dolphins had taken a year off of his life.

SAN FRANCISCO

The next morning we picked up the pilot and proceeded into San Francisco Bay passing under the Golden Gate Bridge. The sun was shining and the city of San Francisco made a beautiful sight. As the ship sailed past Alcatraz Island and passed under the Oakland Bay Bridge, my thoughts returned to the albatross that had been so wantonly killed at the beginning of the voyage. Since leaving Balboa, the ship had been under way for seventy-two days with only a brief sixteen hour stop at Eniwetok Island. Killing that sea bird had placed a curse on the ship. Seventy-two days is an awfully long time to be confined to a ship at sea and the crew had been showing signs of unrest. The S S Patrick C. Boyle anchored in the southern part of San Francisco Bay, and the pilot was taken ashore by motor launch. A short time later the Port Captain for Boland and Cornelius, Captain Arthur Burke, came aboard with Army, Customs, Immigration, and other port officials. The ship was cleared and pratique was granted. Sea watches were broken but the ship remained at anchor. Mail for the ship's crew and Armed Guard was brought on board and passed out. The Purser gave those who wanted it a small withdrawal of money from the wages they had coming. Those who were not on watch were allowed to go ashore but were told to be back on board by 0800 the next morning because the ship was going to proceed up the San Joaquin River to the city of Stockton, California.

I went ashore with the Armed Guard Officer, the Second Engineer, and the Second Mate. It was my first visit to San Francisco and I was impressed. We went to a restaurant / night club called the Domino Club. While we were sitting at the bar waiting for a table, there were pretty waitresses in skimpy costumes walking around with trays of hors d'oeuvres for the patrons. It was a huge place with at least three floors for eating, drinking, and entertainment.

The food was excellent, and it was the first time I had ever been served sour dough bread. The Domino Club also boasted of having the world's largest collection of oil paintings of nudes. It may have been true because there were oil paintings on every bit of wall space. During dinner the Armed Guard Officer said that he had a girl friend in Stockton and that he would let her know we were coming there. He said he would see if she could arrange a sort of welcome home party for the ship's officers.

STOCKTON

The next day with most of the crew on board, the ship proceeded up the San Joaquin River and docked at the Army base pier in Stockton that evening. Soldiers were placed on guard at the gangway and the ship's company had to have passes to get off the ship. At 0800 the next morning gangs of longshoremen came aboard and rigged the ship's gear for working cargo. They off loaded the deck cargo first and then opened the ship' hatches. Cargo nets were secured between the ship and the pier at each of the five hatches to catch any cargo that might accidentally fall off a pallet or drop out of a sling.

It would take the best part of a week to discharge all of the cargo because the longshoremen only planned to work eight hours a day. The Armed Guard Officer came aboard with good news that evening. He said that his girl friend was going to throw a party at her house the next evening and that she would arrange to have enough of her girl friends there so each officer would have a partner to dance with. The Captain and the Chief Engineer said they would take care of the ship that night so all the mates and engineers could go to the party.

After supper the next day I left the ship with the other Mates and Engineers following the Armed Guard Officer in to town. We stopped at a liquor store and purchased a good quantity of alcoholic beverages and other things for the party. When we arrived at the girl friend's house, we were introduced to a group of lovely young ladies. Drinks were mixed and passed around. Music was provided by a record player with an automatic changer which was state of the art at that time. I paired off with an attractive girl named Sybil. We danced and talked as the evening wore on. Just as things were getting interesting, Sybil got a phone call. She apologized and said that her boyfriend had just gotten home and she had to leave. Naturally I was disappointed. Since I was the only one without a companion, I decided to return to the ship. After saying good by and thanking the hostess, I called a taxi to take me back to the ship. While waiting for the taxi, I went out to the kitchen and started to pour a drink. Roger McNeill was there and cautioned me to go easy on the booze. Like a jerk just to show off, I filled an eight ounce tumbler with whisky and drank it down. The taxi arrived and I headed back for the Ship. I have no memory of arriving back at the pier. The whisky had taken affect during the ride back, and I was stoned.

I awoke the next morning to the sound of my creaking cabin door as it was opened. Captain Hickey and the Chief Mate were looking in with big smiles on their faces. The Captain asked me how I felt, and I said fine as I started to sit up. Then I suddenly felt terribly sick. In my skivvies I rushed to the head and started to vomit. Returning to my room I noticed that my clothes were hung neatly over my chair. My feet were black and there were black foot prints on my cabin deck. The foot prints went up the bulkhead by the door, across the overhead and down the opposite bulkhead to my bunk. My memory was absolutely blank and I felt miserable. The Captain told me to take it easy and try to get back to sleep. The story I was later told about my return to the ship could not be refuted. They said that I climbed on board using the cargo net at number two hatch. I left my uniform jacket, shirt, tie, shoes, socks, and hat on top of the hatch and walked barefoot to my cabin. The main deck had been coated with a mixture of fish oil and lamp black that day. No one had any idea how my foot prints walked up the bulkhead and across the overhead to the bunk in my cabin. A full day passed before I could resume my duties, and it was a very long time before I could handle hard liquor again.

A MYSTERY SOLVED

One morning as the week wore on and much of the cargo had been discharged, a stevedore took me aside and said that he had some information for me. He then said that there were several F B I agents mixed in with his longshoremen. They were investigating the ship looking for something, but he did not know what it could be. I thanked him for the information and then went to Roger McNeill and told him what I had just learned. The two of us started to consider various possibilities and finally decided it must be the CORONA CORONA cigars that had been left in the Chief Mate's room at the beginning of the voyage. If we were caught with them we could be in a great deal of trouble. How to dispose of them without getting caught was an immediate problem. I came up with a novel solution. There were two five-inch brass shell casings in my room I had been saving to make into ashtrays. We emptied the boxes of cigars into the shell casings along with the smashed up boxes. Then the ends of the shell casings were bent over to trap the contents. When the longshoremen left the ship at the end of the day, Roger and I filled the shell casings with water to make sure they would not float, and then tossed the shell casings into the river on the off shore side of the ship. There was no way anyone could trace the cigar filled shell casings back to us. We breathed a sigh of relief and then waited to see what would develop.

We did not have to wait very long. The next morning while we were at breakfast in the salon, two men in business suits came in and introduced themselves to the Captain and said they were F B I agents. They asked if any of us Mates and Engineers knew of any contraband that had come aboard in New Orleans. Of course we claimed that we had no such information, and the F B I agents were asked what this was all about. They said that they had been investigating the possibility that members of our ship's crew had been involved in the theft of thousands of dollars worth of goods from a dockside warehouse in New Orleans. It seems that the theft occurred while the S S Patrick C. Boyle and another ship were loading cargo at the Paulene Street wharf. They said that a gang of men masquerading as longshoremen boldly walked past the warehouse guards and removed several cases of expensive cigars. The guards had assumed that the "longshoremen" were legitimate and performing a routine task. They had no idea on which ship, if any, the contraband had been loaded. The F B I had been conducting an investigation of this theft of Government property for the past two months, and were not able to determine where the stolen goods had gone. Both ships were suspect, but nothing could be proven. The Captain said that they were welcome to search everyone's quarters and any other parts of the ship they wanted to. They said that they had already searched the ship and thanked us for our cooperation and then they departed.

RICHMOND

When all the cargo had been discharged, the ship was moved to the Kaiser shipyard in Richmond for some repair work. San Francisco was some distance from Richmond, but could be reached by surface rail or bus. The Armed Guard was transferred from the ship to some Navy Base nearby. The Armed Guard Officer said that he had been ordered to return to New York and expected to be returned to civilian status shortly. The ship's Articles, the Contract between the Merchant Seamen and Officers and Boland & Cornelius representing the War Shipping Administration, were broken. A Shipping Commissioner and a Company Representative came aboard to pay off the crew. Most of them took their money and prepared to depart the ship with their belongings. Captain Burke, the Company's Port Captain, tried to talk them into signing on for another voyage but had little success. Of the unlicensed crew, only the chief cook, a Negro fellow, agreed to stay on. Captain Hickey said that he had to return home to New York. He had spent too much time away from his wife and daughter. Chief Mate Ciccosanti and Second Mate Roger McNeill wanted to return to New York to see their families and raise their licenses. I also wanted to go home and sit for my second mate's license. The thought of another long voyage so soon with new shipmates did not appeal to me. The Chief Engineer agreed to stay on for the next voyage because he was paying alimony to three ex-wives and a fourth was suing him for divorce. He just could not afford to go back to New York or to stay ashore. The other Engineers, the Purser, and the Radiomen all refused to stay on for another voyage.

During the next couple of days as people were departing the ship, Captain Burke appealed to them to make just one more voyage. He said that we had to do all we could to bring the "boys" home. It was our patriotic duty to keep the ships manned. Finally, Captain Burke made me an offer I could not refuse. He said that there was such a shortage of licensed officers he would have great difficulty finding a Second Mate. If I would sign on, he would have me assigned as Second Mate. This would allow me to get sea time as Second Mate with only a Third Mate's license. I would be able to by-pass the Second Mate's examination and sit directly for Chief Mate with just six months more sea time. I agreed to sign on for another voyage. As I was saying good-by to Roger McNeill he handed me a letter from Sibyl. He said that the letter had come to the ship before we departed Stockton and he had decided to withhold it from me until the ship had left. Roger said that he thought that Sibyl was just looking for a husband and I was far too innocent to recognize the danger. He had sized her up to be a gold digger of dubious moral character and that I would understand better when I had more worldly experience. Roger had adopted the role of "big brother" where I was concerned. The letter was kind of mushy from a girl who had only met me once for a couple of hours. Roger was right. I did not respond to Sibyl's invitation to date her.

Although there was considerable activity with repairmen, vendors, and officials around the ship, I felt rather lonely. My shipmates were gone. Roger McNeill, John Ciccosanti, and my mentor and teacher, Captain Peter Hickey had become close friends. There was little chance that I would ever see any of them again. The Chief Engineer borrowed fifty bucks from me and disappeared ashore. No doubt he was off chasing females around San Francisco. Roger thought that I was too inexperienced with women, and the Chief Engineer, foolishly, was too experienced with them. I was notified by mail that I had been promoted to the rank of Lieutenant Junior Grade (U. S. Maritime service). The extra half stripe was quickly added to my uniforms. A day or two later the new Captain and Chief Mate came on board. Captain Burke introduced them and said that the ship would be moved to a pier in Oakland or Alameda to load cargo as soon as the repair work was completed. The new Skipper, Captain Nils, was a short squat sour faced individual fifty plus years old with a brand new U. S. Coast Guard masters license. He had come up the "hawse pipe" and the S S Patrick C. Boyle was the first ship he was assigned to as Captain. Theodore Loos, the new Chief Mate, was a tall slender fellow about four years older than me and was a native of Staten Island, New York. He was a graduate of the Federal Maritime Academy at Kings Point so we had much in common. We were both "School Ship" boys and hit it off good right away. He called me "Art" and I called him "Ted."

Repair work on some of the ship's engine room machinery was moving along slowly. As long as the ship was in the shipyard there was no need to have a licensed Mate on board during the night when there was no work going on. This allowed Ted and me shore leave every evening. One afternoon Ted said that he was going to visit a couple of girls who had been classmates of his at City college. Ted had two or three years of college prior to becoming a Midshipman at Kings Point. He said that they were sharing an apartment in the Presidio area of San Francisco, and he invited me to come along. Naturally I accepted the invitation and the two of us proceeded to San Francisco by bus and trolley car. The young ladies had a nice apartment with a kitchen, dining/living room, two bedrooms and a bath. Introductions were made all around and the ladies served us cocktails as we became acquainted. One of Ted's classmates, Alice, a brunette, had a fiancee somewhere in the Pacific, and the other girl, Bonny, a blond, had a two year old daughter with her in the apartment. Her husband was a Naval Officer somewhere in the Orient and she had not seen him for nearly a year. The two girls were teachers at a private School. They had located in San Francisco so that they would be close by when their men came home from the war. Ted and I took them to a nice restaurant and spent a very pleasant evening dining with them. We agreed to meet again the next evening and go night clubbing in the "International Settlement," the "in" place in San Francisco. The lady in the adjacent apartment was always available to baby sit Bonny's little girl.

The next night Ted and I picked the girls up at their apartment and the four of us went to the infamous "International Settlement." We had dinner and then went dancing at two or three different night clubs. Since Alice was taller than I was, she would dance with Ted and Bonny would dance with me. Bonny had a bubbling, very friendly personality and seemed to enjoy being out on the town. She was a "fun" person to be with. We drank quite a bit and had a wonderful time. However the girls had to be home by midnight because they had to go to work the next day. Ted and I took the girls out to dinner and dancing every night for the next five or six evenings. The repair work on the ship was finally completed and the ship was moved to a pier in Alameda to load cargo. One evening Ted had to stay on board to supervise the cargo operations and he told me to go and visit the girls. Both girls had eaten their supper by the tine I got to their apartment. Alice said that she was not feeling well and was going to retire early. Bonny and I went out to a club nearby and had a few drinks. We returned to the apartment and Bonny told me to fix some drinks while she got into something more comfortable. Alice was in her bedroom asleep and the baby was asleep in her crib. Bonny called to me to bring the drinks into her bedroom so she could show me a painting she had there. She had changed into a rather revealing night gown. She took the drink and after sipping it put it down on a night stand. Then she put her arms around my neck and kissed me with some passion. Of course I responded as any young virile man would. However, before I lost all self control, I noticed the child in the crib and then I pulled back. I told Bonny that I was sorry and that no matter how much I wanted to make love to her I could not. She was a married woman and I would be the worst kind of scoundrel if I were to take advantage of her because her husband had been gone for so long a time. There was a long moment of embarrassed silence. I quickly got my coat and hat, and said "Good night" as I departed the apartment. I had preserved not only my personal honor, but hers as well.

A couple of days later Ted and I took the girls out to dinner again. After dinner we decided to go to the Top of the Mark, a rotating bar on the top of the Mark Hopkins hotel on Nob Hill. This unusual bar provided a panoramic view of San Francisco as the bar rotated. The four of us took the elevator up to the Top of the Mark and went to the entrance desk to request a table. The head waiter gave me a curious look and asked me to show him some identification. I produced my "Z" card which he examined carefully. With a slight smile on his face he said, "You can not come in here. You have to be at least twenty-one to be served an alcoholic beverage in this State, and you are under age." Both Alice and Bonny looked with some surprise at me, and Bonny started to laugh. I was terribly embarrassed, even ashamed. My blue uniform with one and a half gold stripes on each sleeve and my mustache failed to fool the head waiter. As we were returning to the street level in the elevator, Bonny said, "Art you really are a Boy Scout." We then went to the International Settlement where the clubs we visited had no problem serving me alcoholic drinks. Although Bonny was still friendly, there was an obvious change in her attitude and feelings towards me.

The loading of cargo was almost complete, and most of the new merchant crew were signed on. Captain Burke said that we would be sailing within the next two days. Our destination was Tacloban on Leyte Island in the Philippines. The cargo being loaded aboard was almost the same as the cargo we had discharged in Stockton just a couple of weeks ago. There was more than a little confusion with ships and cargoes following the surrender of the Japanese. Ted and I took the girls out to dinner for the last time the night before we were due to sail. We promised to keep in touch, but I never wrote any letters to Bonny nor did I ever receive any from her. The morning we were due to depart, Captain Burke brought a man aboard and said that he was being signed on as Second Mate. I felt that I had been tricked and told Captain Burke that I felt cheated. He said he was sorry but he had to accept this man because he had been assigned to the ship by the local office of the War Shipping Administration. He said that I would be held in high regard by the company, Boland and Cornelius, for my service and that in it would benefit me in the long run. This Second Mate was another Norwegian a few years older than Captain Nils and another graduate of the "hawse pipe." Although he seemed to be friendly, he was not the least bit impressive. I was resigned to making another voyage as Third Mate.

THE SECOND VOYAGE ON THE S S PATRICK C. BOYLE

As we were casting off from the pier I realized that this would be a different type of voyage. Captain Nils was arrogant, brusk to the point of being nasty, and showed only contempt for the Mates. The crew was an odd mixture. I had a young lanky "Okey" as one of my able seamen, and the other able seaman was a young Mexican lad as was the ordinary seaman. These two had not been across the border for very long. The rest of the deck crew was composed of both rather young men and a few who were older with more sea going experience. The most experienced of the able seamen was a short wiry red haired Australian about forty years old. The Second Engineer was a drunkard. The Purser was a very sophisticated fellow from San Francisco who had been a book keeper before going to sea. Since the war was over there was only one radio operator assigned to the ship.

An Army Captain was also carried as a "Super Cargo" to look after the cargo. The total compliment of people on board was forty four. There were four thousand tons of aviation gasoline in fifty five gallon steel drums stowed in the lower holds of one, three, four, and five hatches. Number two lower hold was full of supplies for the various Post Exchanges in the Philippines. The tween deck spaces were loaded with some ammunition in crates and boxes, various types of machinery in cases, and vehicles, trucks and jeeps. The vehicles had their gas tanks full and their electrical batteries hooked up. They were ready to be driven away as soon as they were off loaded. In number two tween deck a large ten wheeled tractor was located in the center of the hatch and secured with wire cables. Cased machinery was placed in the wings of this space. On the main deck there were trucks forward of the midship house, and large crates of aircraft wings aft of the house. All of this deck cargo was tied down with wire rope and chains.

A surprising discovery was made the first full day at sea. Second Mate Nielsen was ignorant of celestial navigation. He could not work up a simple sun line or even calculate the ship's latitude at noon, and star sights were out of the question. Someone must have taken the Coast Guard license examination for him. Or through bribery he was able to buy his Second Mate's license. In any event, as a navigator he was a complete fraud. This meant that the Chief Mate and I had to do the navigation work normally done by a Second Mate. We were both annoyed at the extra work imposed on us. Since the Captain and the Second Mate were countrymen — both Norwegians, the Captain thought that the Second Mate's short comings were no big thing. Captain Nils continued to show his contempt for Ted and me by passing numerous uncomplimentary remarks, usually during meal times. There was no doubt that he had a strong dislike and contempt for "School Ship Men."

ORGANIZATION

It is appropriate at this point to describe the normal organization of a peace time cargo ship ranging in size from five thousand to twenty thousand tons displacement. Such a merchant ship has three basic departments, the deck department, the engine department, and the stewards department. Each of these departments has a chief in charge, the Chief Mate is responsible for the deck department, the Chief Engineer is responsible for the engineering department, and the Chief Steward is responsible for the stewards department. These three chiefs are subservient to the Captain or Master who has overall responsibility for the safe and efficient operation of the ship. Below the Chief Mate there is usually a Second Mate and a

Third mate as well as a Boatswain, a Carpenter, six Able Seamen, and three Ordinary Seamen. The chain of command extends from the Captain to the Chief Mate then to the Second Mate and finally to the Third Mate and a Fourth Mate if one is carried on board. Under the Chief Engineer there is a First Assistant Engineer, a Second Assistant Engineer, a Third Assistant Engineer, three Oilers, three Firemen / Water tenders, three Wipers, an unlicensed Deck Engineer, and an Electrician if one is carried on board. The Chief Steward has two or three Cooks, three Utility Men, two Mess Men, and one Cabin Steward. Some Chief Engineers with over sized egos were inclined to believe that they were the second in the chain of command. In reality they fell behind the Third Mate in the chain of command. There were two other officers who reported only to the Captain. They were the Radio Operator who was responsible for radio communication, and the Purser who was essentially the Captain's secretary and book keeper.

THE STORM

One day as I stood my morning 0800 to 1200 watch I noticed that there were streaks of high cirrus clouds across the sky originating from one spot ahead on the horizon. We had been at sea for about a week. The sea was calm with the typical long low Pacific swell. The wind direction was constant but increasing in force with each passing hour. Barometric pressure was falling slowly and at a constant rate. When the Chief Mate relieved me I told him that the weather signs indicated that there could be a tropical storm developing ahead of us. Ted said that he would keep an eye on the weather signs. By the end of his watch the sky had become completely covered with a light haze. The wind had increased to a Beaufort force of three and there were waves with white caps. Wind direction had remained constant, and the swell had increased. The barometer was still falling at a constant rate. Ted and I were convinced that there was a storm brewing ahead of us. We called Captain Nils to the bridge and told him of our concerns and the weather signs we had been tracking for the past eight hours. With a very depreciating voice he said, "Vat do you school boys know about da vedder ? I bin going to sea for forty years und I forgot more about da vedder dan you vill ever know. Don't bodder me mit any more of dis nonsense." Then he strode off the bridge shaking his head and muttering, "Stupid school boys." The weather continued to deteriorate through the next three watches.

By the time I relieved the Second Mate at 0800 the next morning, the wind had increased to a Beaufort Force of five. The wind direction was still unchanged, and the barometer was still falling at a constant rate. Waves were running from about ten to fifteen feet in height, and the swell had become deeper. The ship was rolling easily at about fifteen degrees with a corkscrew motion. The sky was completely overcast. When Ted relieved me at 1200 we exchanged thoughts on the approaching storm. It seemed pointless to advise the Captain to change course and try to run away from the storm. Such advise would only bring more insulting comments from this arrogant bull headed Master. We decided to say nothing more and just let the Captain figure out the meaning of the weather signs. By the end of my second watch at midnight, the wind had reached gale force and the waves were running well over thirty feet. The ship was rolling heavily between twenty five and thirty degrees with each roll. Still Captain Nils made no attempt to change course and run from the storm. All the indications, unchanging wind direction, increasing wind force, the steady falling barometer, the increase in the size of the waves and swell meant that the ship was steaming toward the center or the eye of the storm. Sleeping was difficult with the heavy rolling of the ship. As the night wore on conditions continued to worsen.

Breakfast the next morning consisted of toast and coffee. It was impossible for the cooks to prepare any food because of the violent rolling. The engine revolutions had to be reduced because the propeller kept coming out of the water. When the propeller came out of the water the engine would over speed. This could cause damage to the engine and might even cause the propeller to spin off the shaft and be lost. The S S Patrick C. Boyle was caught in a Typhoon, and could barely make steerage way. When I came on to the lower bridge to take my morning watch, both of the other Mates, the Chief Engineer, and the Captain were there. They looked very concerned, especially the Captain. Mountainous seas were crashing over the ship. At times the whole fore deck would disappear beneath the turbulent water, and then the ship would rear up throwing tons of water and spray into the howling wind. The ship was rolling forty five degrees. It was impossible to stand up without holding on to a railing or some other fixed object. Books tumbled off their shelves, dishes, cups, glasses, and similar items slid of the tables and counter tops and smashed on the deck. Chairs and stools that were not tied down went crashing from side to side of the rooms they were in. Water sloshed out of the sinks and toilet bowls making some of the decks difficult and even dangerous to walk on. Some of the crew became sea sick while some others were showing signs of fear. The storm continued to worsen.

There was no doubt in anyone's mind that the ship was in danger of foundering for it was taking a terrible beating. Strange though it may seem, I felt no fear. Instead I had a feeling of exhilaration and fascination. The ferocity of the sea was exciting to behold. I made my way up to the flying bridge and clung to the railing in the starboard wing. It was like riding on a giant see-saw. I could almost touch the wave tops when the ship rolled to starboard. At one point I found myself looking up at the crest of a wave about to strike the ship. That wave must have been at least a hundred feet high. The wind driven spray felt like buckshot when it hit my face. Captain Nils called me to come back down to the lower bridge saying that I could be blown overboard if I stayed on the flying bridge. He was right, I was taking an unnecessary chance. During the afternoon watch as the five of us plus the helmsman were in the lower bridge the ship took an exceedingly steep roll. The wheel house clinometer showed a roll angle of fifty five degrees. The ship just hung there for a long moment and it looked like she would not recover. Then a wave caught her on the low side and she rolled to the other side, but this roll was not as steep. A loud thud was heard coming from one of the forward holds. The huge tractor in number two tween deck had parted the wires securing it and it was running free from one side of the tween deck to the other with each roll. This was bad. The size and weight of the tractor made it a formidable battering ram. With the ship rolling forty to fifty degrees, it would only be a matter of time before the tractor would smash through the side of the hull. First however it would have to smash through the cases of machinery stowed in the wings of the tween deck. It was those cases of machinery that saved the ship.

The next morning as a dismal dim dawn began to break, everyone was exhausted from a lack of sleep. Wind and seas were kept broad on the port bow by the almost heroic effort of the helmsman. Whoever was on the wheel was constantly fighting the seas. The large upright crates of aircraft wings on the aft deck acted much like a weather vane always trying to head the ship directly into the wind and seas. Reduced engine revolutions because of the heavy pitching gave barely enough force on the rudder to control the heading. If the ship were to broach or go broadside to the seas she would surely roll over, and if she went straight over the waves she would probably break in two. The atmosphere felt very oppressive, and the barometer gave the lowest reading I have ever seen. Unbelievably high waves kept battering the ship while the wind tore the tops off the waves and flung them at the ship like shrapnel. Cold sandwiches and coffee were the only food available for those who felt a desire to eat or drink anything. One seaman had an injured and possibly broken arm, another had a bad cut on his head, and everyone was bruised to some degree from constantly being knocked about by the severe rolling and pitching of the ship. Banging and screeching noises were still coming from number two hold where the tractor was still running free. After a couple of hours had passed the wind suddenly decreased to no wind at all. The waves were extremely high but confused. They seemed to have lost their direction. The ship rolled and pitched in an unpredictable manner. Overhead the sky became blue, but there were ugly dark storm scud clouds all around the horizon. The atmosphere was still very oppressive. The ship was actually in the eye of the Typhoon.

Respite from the wind was short lived. In less than an hour the wind hit the ship from the opposite direction like a sledge hammer. Wind and sea again had direction and were still furious. Now the helmsman fought to keep them broad on the starboard bow. The ship was moving out of the eye of the storm and away from it. The noise from number two hold stopped. It was assumed that the tractor had broken through the tween deck hatch and buried itself in the cargo of PX supplies in the lower hold. The ship continued to roll heavily but it was through the worst of the storm. Twenty four hours later the seas were lower and the wind was less than gale force. There was still a very heavy swell, but the Engineers were able to increase the ship's speed.

The barometer began to rise, a sure sign that we were getting away from the center of the Typhoon. Another day passed with the wind and the seas gradually decreasing. Even the swell became lower and the clouds started to break up. Full speed, eleven knots, was resumed. The S S Patrick C. Boyle had survived the worst Typhoon ever recorded in the Pacific. Later reports claimed that over three hundred ships of all types had been lost in that storm. Our arrogant, stubborn, Norwegian Captain had blundered our ship right through the center of that Typhoon. It could have easily been avoided if the Captain had not been too proud to listen to the advise of his "School Ship" Officers. Five days of misery and extreme danger could have been avoided as well as damage to our cargo. Still we were fortunate. None of the deck cargo was lost, although the two life rafts on the fore deck were carried away by the storm. The outside of the ship itself was cleaner than it had ever been. The storm had pressure washed every square inch of exposed surface and in some areas had even removed the paint.

Some credit is due the shipbuilders at the Fairfield Shipyard of the Bethlehem Steel Company in Baltimore, Maryland where the S S Patrick C. Boyle was built. Of the twenty seven hundred Liberty Ships built by various companies across the Nation, those built in the Fairfield Shipyard were the strongest and best built. Shell plates were riveted to the hull frames instead of being welded. No short cuts in manufacturing that compromised strength and safety were used. Other shipbuilders such as Kaiser Industries on the West Coast used welding almost exclusively in the construction of their ships. These ships were often referred to as "Kaiser's Coffins" because of their tendency to break apart in severe storms, especially when they were improperly loaded. The fact that the S S Patrick C. Boyle survived the Typhoon was due to the quality of its construction. There were some Liberty Ships of a lesser quality of construction that were lost in that storm. Naval vessels of various sizes reported severe damage. The total loss and damage resulting from this storm on both the land and the sea has probably never been adequately determined.

THE SHIP'S DOCTOR

Sometime during the early part of the voyage I had mentioned that I had worked for two months as an attendant in a psychiatric hospital in Central Islip on Long Island, New York. This was during the Summer vacation period between my junior and senior years in high school. Since the ship no longer carried a pharmacist mate, Captain Nils said that I was the only person on board with any hospital experience. Therefore he said that I was in charge of the sick bay. The sick bay was a cabin furnished with a single metal frame bed, a small desk, and several cabinets containing various medical supplies. There was also a sink with hot and cold water and a substantial basin. When one of the ship's company complained of a head ache or some minor cut, I would hand out some aspirin or clean and bandage the wound. The medical library consisted of a book with the title "The Ship's Medicine Chest And First Aid At Sea" provided by the United States Public Health Service War Shipping Administration. I took the role of ship's doctor seriously. It was fortunate for me and the crew that no one was seriously injured during the typhoon. The cuts were not severe and were easily treated, and it turned out that the seaman with the injured arm had a severe bruise but no broken bones.

THE PURPLE APPARITION

Shipboard routine returned to normal after the storm. The Filipino bedroom steward who was responsible for cleaning the officers cabins, making the beds, and providing clean linens and towels developed a problem. He had some sort of skin infection over his entire body that became more noticeable with the passage of time. His skin began to resemble the scaly hide of some sort of reptile. When these scaly bits of skin began flaking off we all became concerned that he could infect all of us. The Captain ordered the Chief Steward to assign the fellow to other duties and detail someone else to be cabin steward. Then the Captain turned to me and said that I had the responsibility of curing the fellow's infection. In order to determine the source of the infection, I interrogated the Filipino steward to find out where he could have picked up the infection. The book, The Ship's Medicine Chest, did not offer a clue as to what the infection was or how to treat it. The steward said that he had been swimming in water where there were many dead bodies on his last visit to the Philippine Islands which had been about two months ago. It was shortly after that time that he began to notice a rash developing on his legs. He had been treating it with some ointment that did little to stop the rash from spreading. Eventually it developed into his current condition of scales and cracked skin. No one on the ship had ever seen an infection like that before and I was left on my own to find a cure.

I took a bottle of green soap from the medical cabinet and gave it to the steward with instructions to go to the shower and wash his body thoroughly with it. He was told to go to the sick bay when he had finished washing. In the mean time I covered the sick bay bed with a rubber sheet, found some rubber gloves, and opened a box of cotton gauze. Then I opened a quart bottle of Gentian Violet, a very dark purple antiseptic fluid. I had seen this used to cure athlete's foot infections when I was on the training ship. When the steward reported to the sick bay I had him lay prone stark naked on the bed. Then I put on the rubber gloves, soaked a handful of gauze with the Gentian Violet, and proceeded to swab him from the soles of his feet to the top of his head. Every square inch of his body was soaked with the Gentian Violet. When he got off the bed and stood up, he was a horrible sight to behold. Anyone who had not been forewarned would jump with fright when they first set eyes on him. The steward, the purple apparition, roamed the ship in that condition for a few weeks. Eventually the purple color faded or wore off and his skin returned to its normal dark tan. However unconventional it may have been, my treatment worked for his infection was cured.

THE PHILIPPINES AT LAST

About two weeks after the Typhoon we made landfall in the gulf of Leyte and proceeded toward Tacloban on Leyte Island. A Navy Launch came alongside as the ship approached the anchorage area off Tacloban and handed up a package of instructions for the Captain. The S S Patrick C. Boyle was directed to go to a designated anchorage position on the outer perimeter of the anchorage area. A chart was provided which clearly identified the position. There were many other ships of all kinds in the anchorage. Squally weather developed with a strong wind on the ship's beam as the approach to the anchorage position was being made. As customary, I was on the flying bridge to assist the Captain in maneuvering the ship. Every time the Captain had the ship lined up to approach the position to drop the anchor, the wind would catch the high sheer of the forward part of the hull and cause the bow to fall off. The Captain made the approach with the engine going at dead slow speed and using small changes in rudder angle. When he started the third attempt to get to the position, I said, "Captain if you give the engine full ahead for a minute with the rudder hard over, she will hold her head and come right on to the position." He glared at me and shouted, "Get off my bridge — I don't take instruction from a God dammed Third Mate!" I left the flying bridge and went to the lower bridge. With some satisfaction I observed the Captain putting the engine on full ahead with the rudder hard over. The ship came right up to the desired position and the Chief Mate dropped the anchor. Part of the education Captain Hickey had given me dealt with maneuvering the ship in strong cross winds. I made a big mistake in trying to offer Captain Nils some helpful advice in maneuvering the ship. He was far too arrogant to accept any advise from a junior Officer. I felt very strongly that professionally, Captain Nils would not make a pimple on Captain Hickey's back side.

TACLOBAN

The ship was kept on the anchorage for the next few days. This allowed for some visits to the beach using the ship's motor lifeboat for transportation. The city of Tacloban which was located on a peninsula was not much of a town even for the Philippines. There were a couple of bars, but no restaurants. Although there had been considerable fighting in this area, there was relatively little battle damage to see. The Army had constructed a base on the end of the peninsula which included an out door movie theater. It was also possible to buy soft ice cream at the small commissary. Merchant seamen were allowed into this facility and the soldiers were generally friendly. The Navy had a larger base on the Island of Samar on the other side of the Gulf. The Navy Captain of the Port had his headquarters there and that was where most of the ship's business was conducted. The Military people in this area were in the process of liquidating much of the wartime material. Every day barges loaded with brand new jeeps, still in their knocked down crates, were moved to a relatively deep part of the Gulf where the jeeps would be dumped into the water. Other barges loaded with canned goods were also moved to this dumping ground for the same purpose. Filipino natives would take their out-rigger canoes to these dump sites and dive for the canned goods. Large piles of blankets and tent material were burned on the shore. Just off the beach there was a reef composed of a large number of landing craft that had been purposely stranded there. The sheer waste of perfectly good food, equipment, and other material was staggering. The Military used the excuse of not having the ships to transport this material back to the States, and that they were not allowed to sell it or give it to the local population. All they could do with it was to destroy it.

For the crew's recreation, the ship's carpenter constructed a sea sled from some of the wood dunnage we had on board. This was a device that resembled a door fitted with a bridle so that it could be towed behind the motor lifeboat. Hand ropes attached to the top end allowed a person to hold on while his feet were at the lower end. The motor lifeboat would tow the person around much like water skiers today. It was a lot of fun and everyone took turns being towed around at about seven knots. The water in our anchorage was murky and one could only see a few feet in it. One day while a bunch of us were swimming and cavorting in the water off the side of the ship, the noon call for lunch was sounded. Everyone scrambled up the companion ladder, and I was the last to get out of the water. I looked back and saw a large serpent like creature come to the surface just where we had been swimming. Neither its head nor its tail were visible. It had come to the surface and was now descending. The creature was about a foot in diameter and had alternate light gray and dark brown horizontal stripes about six or seven inches wide. It was not possible to tell how long the creature was. Judging by its diameter, it could have been fifteen to twenty feet in length. That ended the swimming and water sledding for the rest of our stay at the anchorage.

A day or two later the Army ordered the ship to be moved to a small port named Anibong on the other side of the peninsula some miles from Tacloban. This port consisted of a single pier and a couple of shed like buildings. On the land ward side of the pier there were open lots where a variety of items were stored. On one of these lots there were several dozen brand new jeeps parked in rows. They were all painted with the Army olive drab color and had the usual army symbols and numbers painted in white on their hoods. The Mates and Engineers began to speculate as to the possibility that these jeeps would also be dumped into Leyte Gulf. Our super cargo Army Officer passenger left the ship and we never saw him again. A young Army Lieutenant about my own age came aboard and announced that he was the Officer in charge of discharging our cargo. A short time later some trucks came down to the pier with native longshoremen to discharge the cargo. There was also a company of Filipino Army soldiers (Freedom Fighters) with these longshoremen. They were all wearing new khaki uniforms and were to act as guards to prevent any looting of the cargo. It took a couple of days to off load the deck cargo because the Filipino longshoremen were not very efficient or industrious. Once the deck cargo was removed, the five hatches to the cargo holds were opened.

When the hatch for number two hold was opened the scene in the tween deck space was unbelievable. The cases of machinery that had been stored in the wings of this deck were so badly smashed that it was not possible to tell what their contents had been. They had been reduced to piles of splintered wood and junk. The ten wheeled tractor unit had indeed gone through the hatch to the lower hold and buried itself in the cargo of Post Exchange supplies stowed there. An Army photographer and a couple of surveyors were brought on board to take pictures of the wreckage and estimate the amount of damage the cargo had suffered. When the Army surveyors departed, the Filipino Guards took over and immediately began looting the exposed cargo in number two lower hold. This was a perfect example of putting the foxes in charge of guarding the hen house. When I saw what was happening, I notified the Army Lieutenant in charge of the cargo operations and told him what was going on. He called a squad of U. S. Army M P 's on board to stop the looting. The Filipino Guards had taken uniform clothing, shirts, trousers, jackets, shoes, cartons of cigarettes, boxes of candy, tins of nuts, and similar items from the exposed cases and card board boxes. The Filipino longshoremen had also joined their countrymen in the looting. Some of this pilfered material was recovered as the Filipino Guards were expelled from the ship. I managed to snag a pair of Flight Officer's trousers from one of the Filipinos as he was trying to toss them to one of his buddies on the pier. They had quickly devised many different ways to get pilfered items off the ship. With the U. S. Army presence on board the rate of pilfering was significantly reduced.

While the cargo was being discharged at Anibong one of the Engineers proposed that the ship should have its own jeep. It just so happened that there was a lot full of brand new jeeps close to the pier. He reasoned that stealing one of them was justified since the Army was most likely planning to dump them in the Gulf anyway. One evening after the longshoremen and Guards had gone for the day, two of the Engineers and some of the crew pushed one of the jeeps on to the pier under the ship's cargo boom at number five hold. Slings were fitted to the jeep and it was hoisted aboard. It was then pushed to a place close to the stern house. A coat of gray paint was quickly applied and all traces of Army identification were removed. When the paint was sufficiently dry, a tarpaulin was thrown over the jeep. Our car thieves decided to wait for a couple of days to see if there would be any trouble from the Army. If the Army made any fuss about the jeep, they planned to claim no knowledge of how it got on board. Nothing was ever said by the Army or anyone else. The Engineers then said that they would need a drum of gasoline for the jeep. There was one drum of gasoline for the motor lifeboat, but much of that had been used up. At about that time the longshoremen started to unload our cargo of fifty five gallon drums of gasoline. Using chain slings with clamps they would unload the drums in clusters of four drums. I ordered the gang of longshoremen at number five hold to land one cluster of drums on the deck. One drum was removed from the cluster and rolled over to the stern house and turned upright. The short cluster was then landed on the pier. Within minutes the Army cargo Officer came storming down the deck to where I was standing. He was furious and accused me of stealing a drum of gasoline. I told him that his longshoremen had mistakenly discharged the ship's drum of lifeboat gasoline and I was merely replacing it with one from the cargo. The Army Officer accepted my response and said that I could only take that one drum and no more. Unfortunately after all that, the jeep was never used by any of our crew.

As the last of our cargo was being discharged, an Army truck came onto the pier. There were a dozen Japanese soldiers, prisoners of war, in the truck. An Army Officer came on board and told the Chief Mate that he could use the prisoners to do any work on the ship that he might want done. The prisoners would be available to work on the ship every day the ship was at the pier. The Chief Mate said that he would be pleased to find some work for them to do. The Japanese prisoners were marched aboard and formed a line on the forward main deck. They were a sorry looking group, small, thin framed, and very lean, almost emaciated. Their uniforms were faded and all signs of rank had been removed. They stood in line more or less at attention with their heads bowed and their arms hanging loosely at their sides. The Chief Mate, Ted, assigned three of the Japanese to the Chief Engineer to work in the engine room, and the remainder he gave to me to have them clean and paint the cargo holds. I took one of them and assigned him the task of washing and ironing the ship's Officers' clothes. The remaining eight Japanese were divided into two teams of four and put in charge of the boatswain and the ship's carpenter to clean and paint the holds. This was my first encounter with the Japanese. They were amazing. They turned to with great energy on any task they were given, and they never complained nor did they ask for any respite. In three days the Japanese assigned to the engine room painted the entire space from the fiddley skylight to the engine room floor plates. The Chief Engineer said that his engine room gang could not have done that much work in three months. The Japanese working in the holds swept them clean and managed to paint the tween deck spaces in all five hatches in the same time. One could only admire their extraordinary work ethic. Some of the Filipinos who were still doing odd jobs on board tried to abuse the Japanese when no one was looking. I put a quick stop to that nonsense. To me the Japanese were much better than any of the Filipinos I had encountered.

The pier at Anibong was five or six miles from the Army base at Tacloban. There was a road from Anibong that intersected the main road leading into Tacloban. No one from the ship was allowed to walk this road to Tacloban especially after sundown. The Filipinos had a bad habit of shooting at any stray Americans they saw walking along the road. To get into town one had to hitch a ride with an Army truck or other vehicle going that way or walk with an armed escort. Most of the truck drivers were very accommodating and would give anyone off the ship a ride as close to town as possible. One evening I decided to go into the Army base to see a movie and have some ice cream. A large tanker truck came by the pier and I hitched a ride. This vehicle had the largest wheels I had ever seen. I climbed up into the cab with the driver and asked him to drop me off at the street leading into Tacloban. It was dark by the time we reached the intersection with the main road into town. The driver pulled the vehicle over to the side of the road and stopped to let me off. It had become pretty dark. I opened the cab door thanked the driver and shouted "Geronimo" as I jumped down. The driver said good-by and put the tanker truck in gear to pull away. As I fell from the cab I passed the top of the wheel, the hub of the wheel, and the bottom of the wheel and I kept falling. Suddenly I found myself in muck up to my knees. In the dark I had jumped into an open sewer and the truck was gone. It took me several minutes to climb up the slimy side of the ditch to the road bed. In spite of the danger, I walked back to the ship as quickly as I could. The need for a shower and a change of clothes was over powering.

One day the Chief Mate, Ted, received a letter from home with information that a friend of his from college was in an Army Hospital in a town South and inland of the town of Palo on the Island of Leyte. He did some checking with the local Army people and learned that Palo was about fifteen miles from where we were. To get there it would be necessary to take the road from Tacloban that ran south along the shore of the Gulf of Leyte. At a point about ten miles from Tacloban there was a road that went inland from the coast road. The hospital was about four or five miles down this road. Ted asked me to go with him to visit his friend in the hospital. Right after breakfast one morning we hitched a ride on a truck from Anibong to the coast road that ran South from Tacloban. At the coast road intersection we hailed another truck heading South and hitched a ride. That truck dropped us off at the road running inland from Palo. There were no other trucks heading towards the hospital so we decided we could walk the four or five miles to the hospital. When we were about two miles down the road we heard what sounded like fire crackers going off. A little way further down the road, two soldiers stepped on to the road from the underbrush with their rifles at the ready. They asked us what we were doing there and where we were going. There were other soldiers hunkered down in the brush on both sides of the road. When we told them that we were trying to get to the hospital, they said we would get killed if we continued down the road. They and the rest of their company were in a fire fight with a gang of Filipino gorilla bandits between where we were and the hospital. The sound of firing became more intense and the soldiers advised us to go back the way we had come as quickly as we could. They were afraid that the bandits might come this way at any moment and try to over run their position. Ted and I trotted back to the coast road and as soon as we reached it we managed to hitch a ride on a truck heading for Tacloban. We decided not to try to go to the Hospital again.

The Captain finally got orders to take the S S Patrick C. Boyle to Manila and await further instructions. The ship was tentatively scheduled to be sent to Japan with a contingent of U. S. Army Soldiers. The hatches were covered, the cargo booms stowed in their cradles, and the ship was made ready for sea. When the Japanese soldiers were leaving the ship for the last time, they were thanked for the excellent work they had done. Cigarettes and candy were offered to them, but they politely declined to accept them. I asked the soldier who had been doing the laundry if I could take any letters to Japan for him and the other prisoners. In halting English he said no and explained that they were too ashamed to even let the people back home know that they were alive. These Japanese were strange people indeed. With sea watches set and all the crew on board, the lines were cast off and the S S Patrick C. Boyle left Anibong and headed North past the island of Samar. The inland passage was followed for a day and a night and late in the afternoon of the third day the ship arrived at Manila Bay. There were many ships at anchor in the bay, and over three hundred ships of all types sunk there. The S S Patrick C. Boyle dropped the anchor in the outer perimeter of the anchorage a couple of miles from the outer breakwater of Manila Harbor. Partially exposed superstructures and hulls of numerous sunken ships could be seen all across the harbor. They were Navy and Merchant ships of both Japan and the Allies, and they were a clear sign of the terrible battles that were fought there.

MANILA

Once the anchor was down and anchor watch established, the Captain ordered the motor lifeboat lowered. Some of the off watch crew requested shore liberty. They wanted to take in the night life of Manila. I was ordered to man the motor lifeboat and take them into the inner harbor of Manila and put them ashore. With my two Mexican sailors as boat crew, we loaded about a dozen of the ship's crew into the motor lifeboat and started for the shore. It was necessary to maneuver around many of the partially sunken hulks on the way in to Manila harbor. There was an outer breakwater and an inner breakwater protecting the piers in Manila harbor. After passing through these breakwaters, I headed the boat for the closest pier. This was a long finger pier and there were droppings of human excrement clinging to all the pier supporting structure from the apron of the pier to the water's edge. I moved the boat along the pier until it reached a camel adjacent to a ladder. The passengers were disembarked on to the camel from where they were able to climb the ladder to the road bed of the pier. By the time the last passenger was off the boat, the sun had set. Twilight in the tropics is usually very short. My Mexican crew men cast off the lines to the camel and we headed for the breakwater entrance. It was completely dark by the time we cleared the outer breakwater entrance. All of a sudden a wind and rain squall hit us like a sledge hammer. Very soon the waves began running six to eight feet in height and the rain became a tropical deluge. I had the two Mexican sailors put life jackets on, and I put one on myself. Neither of the Mexicans knew how to swim. The motor lifeboat began shipping water and soon the only things keeping the boat afloat were the flotation tanks under the thwarts. The boat was completely flooded. Lucky for us, the life boat's motor was in a watertight compartment, so it kept on running. With the two frightened Mexicans saying every prayer they knew in Spanish, I headed for our ship on the outer edge of the anchorage about two miles away. Water began flooding the engine compartment, and I was afraid the engine would flood out before we reached the ship. Just as I brought the boat under the boat falls of our ship, the motor quit running. We grabbed the falls and secured them to the bow and stern of the boat. The weight of water in the boat made it impossible to lift the boat out of the water, so we left it there and climbed aboard using the rat lines. That was one adventure I did not want to repeat.

A water taxi schedule was established using the motor lifeboat. Runs between the ship and the pier were made every four hours during daylight hours. I got ashore alone one day and walked all over the city of Manila. The city had suffered a great deal of damage from the fighting. There were piles of rubble and wrecked buildings everywhere. No serious attempt at cleaning up the city had been made. A river sliced through the city sepa-

The S S Patrick C. Boyle steaming into Manila Harbor,
December 1945

rating it into two major parts. The part on one side was obviously much older than the other. There was a temporary bridge built by the U. S. Army spanning the river. The old bridge had been destroyed. In the old part of the city there was a large stone fort built by the Spanish when they ruled the area. It had been converted to a municipal aquarium before the war, and the Japanese had converted it to a hospital during their occupation of Manila. It was also badly damaged from the fighting. As I walked through the interior corridors of the fort, I was appalled at what I saw. There were the twisted remains of steel beds, some with human skeletons in them, and a quantity of melted glass from the fish tanks. American soldiers must have put a flame thrower at one end of the corridor and turned the whole place into a crematorium. I prayed that those remains I saw in the beds had not been alive when that was done.

My walk through the city took me to an area where the Government buildings had been located. The Senate building had been of Greek / Roman design with stately columns in the front. Now it looked as if some giant had taken a club and bashed the front and roof into a pile of wreckage. All the Government buildings had been destroyed. The court yard area in front of the buildings was covered by gravel composed of steel shrapnel from exploded shells. There were many unexploded shells lying around everywhere. Parts of decomposed human bodies were scattered among the rubble. A shoe with a lower leg bone protruding from it and the top portion of a human skull still in a steel helmet were among the many grizzly sights. Broken weapons, machine guns, mortars, and rifles were rusting in the tropical heat all around the area. The sheer waste of war so apparent here made me feel rather depressed. Brave men in both armies had slaughtered each other and destroyed everything around them. I thanked God that I had not been forced to kill anyone or bring such destruction as I saw there.

A day or so later the Chief Mate, Third Engineer, and I went ashore and roamed down a main street of the city. We went into a bar, sat at a table and ordered some beer. There were several sailors in the bar. Most of them were off the cruiser USS Cleveland or some such warship that had recently arrived at Manila. At one end of the bar a group of these sailors were having a lot of fun. They had pinned a Filipino girl in a corner where they were removing her clothes. She was crying and begging them to stop. I stood up and said to my companions that we had to stop what was going on. Both of them grabbed me and pulled me down into my chair and told me to be quiet. Then they paid for our drinks and quickly hustled me out of the bar. They said that I had almost gotten them killed. Those sailors were a rough bunch and they had no use for Merchantmen like us. Any way the girl was a bar bimbo and not worth getting killed over. I do not know how the poor girl made out, or what the sailors did to her once they had removed all of her clothes.

Later that same day we were walking past a two story building near the river. The building was both a bar and a brothel. There were a lot of Army and Navy men in the building and the adjacent street. A fight broke out between a number of Army soldiers and Navy sailors, and they were throwing each other through the windows on both floors. Seeing this, my companions and I decided to head back to the pier and our ship's boat as quickly as we could. Army Military Police and Navy Shore Patrol units were converging on the building and the fighting as we left. Manila was a hot, dirty, untidy, and dangerous city. The next time we went ashore we spent our time at an Officers' Club on the outskirts of the city where the amenities were more appealing. The ship was shifted to a Navy pier near Cavite just south of Manila. Carpenters built some shed like structures on the aft main deck. These were to be used as latrines for soldiers we were supposed to take to Japan. Christmas 1945 found the ship still in Manila Bay. Finally two days after New Years we set sail for Japan without any soldiers on board.

JAPAN

The S S Patrick C. Boyle arrived in Tokyo Bay in mid January 1946, and anchored off the port city of Yokohama. I had just turned twenty one. The passage from Manila to Tokyo Bay was uneventful except for the weather. As the ship proceeded further North, the weather slowly became much colder. When we anchored in Tokyo Bay snow was falling and it was bitter cold. Shortly after our arrival a launch came alongside with a delegation of Army officials. They informed the Captain that the ship was to be turned over to a Japanese crew within four days. Our crew was told to pack their bags and be prepared to leave the ship for good. We were to be placed in temporary quarters ashore until arrangements could be made to repatriate us to the United States. This was a turn of events that none of us had anticipated. The Captain ordered the Purser to open the "slop chest" and divide the cigarettes evenly amongst the crew. I wound up with three cases of cigarettes, and each case contained fifty cartons. Japanese "bum boats" were alongside the ship buying everything they could. Clothing, candy, and cigarettes were the most sought after commodities. I sold my three cases of cigarettes to one of the "bum boats" for three hundred Yen per carton as many of the others of our crew did. I still had a dozen cartons in my cabin that I had acquired during the voyage. These I packed with my clothes and other personal items in preparation for the transfer to the quarters ashore.

The official rate of exchange was fifteen Yen to the dollar, and I had about forty five thousand Yen and the smallest note was a hundred Yen note. There was no way to exchange the Yen for dollars without getting into trouble. The military authorities were on the lookout for Americans involved in black market activities, and there was no way I could explain how I had acquired so much Japanese money. The Army provided launch service between the ship and the one useable pier left in Yokohama. One afternoon I went ashore with my roll of Yen intending to walk around the city to see what I could buy. At the head of the pier there was a jeep and four Army Military Police acting like customs guards. They had black arm bands with the letters "M P" on them and they looked very official. Some of my ship's crew did not sell their cigarettes to the bum boats. Instead they decided to take them ashore and sell them in the local black market where they would bring five hundred Yen per carton. I was wearing my blue uniform with the gold braid on my hat and the "M Ps" made no attempt to stop me as I walked off the pier, but the crewmen following me were stopped by them and searched. The cartons of cigarettes they were carrying were confiscated by the "M Ps", but they did not arrest or detain the crewmen. I wandered around the streets looking at the bombed out factories and warehouses, amazed at how clean everything was. There was no rubble or broken glass. One could have had a picnic on what remained of the floors in these buildings. The difference between Yokohama and Manila, two war torn cities, was like night and day. I felt at a loss. Here I had all this Japanese money and there was nothing to buy. Years later I realized that I had been standing on what I should have bought. As I continued my wandering I saw the same jeep with the Army "M Ps" driving by. They had removed the arm bands and were laughing uproariously. The back of their jeep was loaded with the cartons of cigarettes they had confiscated. Those phony "M Ps" had stolen those cigarettes from the unsuspecting crewmen who themselves were smuggling them ashore. I found a bar and enjoyed my first taste of Japanese beer before returning to the ship.

One night while I had the watch, one of my Mexican sailors fell overboard from the main deck while attending to the gangway. Without any hesitation, the red haired Australian able seaman who had been standing near by, dove into the frigid water to rescue him. He managed to pull the Mexican to the gangway platform where I was able to pull him from the water. I told the Aussie that his action was the bravest I had ever seen. He just shrugged and said that he knew the kid could not swim and he just could not let him drown. Later one of the other able seamen told me he had managed to locate his brother who was in the Army and stationed in Tokyo. In fact his brother was with a guard unit at the Japanese Army Arsenal in Tokyo. He said that he could get me any kind of gun I would want, so I asked him to get a sniper's rifle for me. The next day the able seaman handed me a Japanese sniper's rifle equipped with a bayonet.

Later that day I went ashore and managed to get on a train that took me from Yokohama to Tokyo. At an open air market I bought a pair of 6 x 30 binoculars with a leather case. I thought my father would like them for his visits to the race track. In the Imperial Hotel in Tokyo I found a jewelry shop where I purchased three semi precious stones with the intention of having them mounted in rings when I got home. They were a peridot, an amethyst, and a topaz. When I got back to the rail road station to return to Yokohama, I saw some young U.S. Army soldiers abusing some of the Japanese civilians. They would either prevent them from boarding a train or throw them off if they had already boarded. This was their way of showing how superior they were. These soldiers were newly arrived occupation soldiers and had never heard a shot fired in anger. Figuring these punks were ignorant of what my Officer's uniform really represented, I told them in as harsh a voice as I could muster, "Knock it off — that is an order! If you continue any more of that abuse I will see all of you in the brig." They were surprised and frightened by my outburst, and one of them said, "We were only having some fun, we ain't hurting anyone." The young punk soldiers left the station platform in a hurry.

I returned to Yokohama and the ship fully intending to go back to Tokyo the next day and do some more shopping. That never happened. The next day the whole ship's company was taken ashore for transport to an Army camp in the mountains. I never saw the S S Patrick C. Boyle again. At this time my pay was stopped as was everyone else's pay. Since we were no longer working on the ship, it was the Government's policy to discontinue our pay.

All the men from the S S Patrick C. Boyle were loaded into Army trucks along with their baggage and driven for several hours over rough roads to an Army camp in the mountains at a place called Sagami Harra. This had been a Japanese Army camp before the occupation. Now it was being run by the U.S. Army as a staging base for newly arriving occupation personnel and a holding pen for Merchant seamen awaiting transportation back to the States. The ship's Officers were assigned to a twenty man tent, and the unlicensed seamen were housed in wooden barracks. Everyone was given an Army cot, four wool blankets, a comforter, and a pillow. The tent was erected over a wooden platform and had a "Jerry stove" in the center. This stove looked like a beer keg with a stove pipe going straight up through the top of the tent. An Army Private showed us how to light the stove and where to get fuel oil for it. We had arrived late in the day and once we were settled in the tent, we were led to a mess hall and fed a meal "G I" style. The food was Luke warm to cold as was the coffee. Back in the tent we learned why we were given so many blankets. It was freezing cold. Even with the "Jerry stove" glowing cherry red it was impossible to get warm. In the morning we Merchantmen were placed on the end of the chow line and by the time we reached the steam table, the food was cold. It was almost impossible to tell what was being served to us. The congealed yellow mush was probably scrambled eggs, and the grayish white gooey stuff was probably chipped beef. Because we were still placed on the end of the chow line, the food served at lunch and dinner were equally bad, and served cold. We were restricted to the camp like prisoners of war, so there was no alternative to eating the food the Army provided. There was nothing else available.

The open "parade ground" between the tents and the barracks/mess hall was covered with a type of gravel composed of stones the size of base balls. It was very uncomfortable to walk on. There was one small wooden building that provided toilets, wash basins, and a couple of shower stalls. Sanitary conditions left much to be desired. One morning while I was shaving I made a comment to a soldier at the next basin that the accommodations at the camp were a far cry from what I had on my ship. The soldier replied that since I was a civilian, I should try to leave the camp and visit a resort town named Atami. He said that Atami was located on the sea coast some distance south of Yokohama, and was off limits to the Military. The soldier also said that there was a railroad station just a short distance from the camp's main gate. When I told my tent mates about what I had learned of this resort town, Atami, they insisted that I go and check it out. There was no telling when the Army would find transportation for us back to the States, but they were sure to give us a couple of days notice. Therefore it would be safe for me to leave the camp for two or three days. The next day, right after breakfast, I changed into my blue dress uniform, packed a small bag with my shaving kit, some clean skivvies, and a few other essentials for my exploratory visit to Atami. I walked boldly to the camp's main gate. The soldiers on guard duty saw my gold braid, came to attention and saluted me. I returned the salute and walked through the gate, and no one questioned my right to do so. From the gate I walked through the town to the rail road station and got on a train for Tokyo. It took about two hours to reach Tokyo. I was very much impressed with the Japanese rail system. The trains were all electric and the passenger cars were very comfortable by comparison to the Long Island Rail Road which I was used to.

The Tokyo rail road station was on a par with Grand Central or Pennsylvania Stations in New York. It was big and very busy. There were several Japanese in blue uniforms that I assumed were station attendants. I went to one after another asking each of them if they spoke English, and finally found one who did. I told him that I wanted to go to Atami and I needed help in getting a round trip ticket. He was very helpful. After getting a multi section ticket for me, he led me to a train platform and told me to let the next train go by, but to be sure to get on the second train, and to remember that I must change trains at a place called Kama Kura. Then he bowed and left the platform. A few minutes later a passenger train pulled in and passengers got on and off. Half an hour later another passenger train pulled in and I got on board. The train pulled away from the Tokyo station and I found myself sitting alone in the rear of a long passenger car with only about two dozen other passengers, all Japanese. As far as I could determine, I was the only person on the train who was not Japanese.

While the train was passing through the outskirts of Tokyo city I saw acres of concrete slabs that had been the foundations of houses. Nothing but bare desolation remained of what had once been a heavily populated area of the city. This was a part of Tokyo that had been fire bombed, and the ensuing fire storm had destroyed everything. When the train was free of the city and rolling through the country side, I called out, "Does anyone here speak English ?" All the passengers in the car turned to look at me and then started to talk amongst themselves. It occurred to me then that I might have made a big mistake calling attention to myself. After all they had just recently been at war with America and had suffered badly , and I was sitting alone wearing an American military uniform. A few minutes passed and a young man wearing a khaki uniform got up and walked back to where I was seated. He bowed and said in perfect English, "I speak English. How may I help you ?"

I told the young Japanese gentleman that I was going to Atami and that I had never been there before and I knew that I would have to change trains at Kama Kura. Since I could not read the Japanese train station signs, I would need to have someone tell me when the train reached Kama Kura. He responded that he was returning to his home in Atami and he would be pleased to guide me. I invited the Japanese fellow to take the seat next to me which he did. His khaki uniform had been stripped of all insignia so I asked him what he did during the war. He said that he had been a fighter pilot and had been stationed in Rabaul. When I said that I thought that all the Japanese Air Force in Rabaul had been destroyed, he smiled and said that they ran out of aircraft before they ran out of pilots. He had just been repatriated and was on his way home after a long absence. In turn I told him that I was a merchant ship's Officer, and my ship had just been given over to a Japanese crew. My old ship and several others with Japanese crews were to be used to repatriate Japanese soldiers from their outposts all over the Pacific. As the train continued on to Kama Kura, he pointed out things of interest and described their historical significance. I remember one huge stone Buddha carved into the side of a cliff that the train passed. When the train reached Kama Kura we got off and crossed to another platform where we boarded another train. It was just about sundown when the train reached Atami. When we got off the train he asked me where I planned to stay. I said that I hoped to find a hotel. My Japanese friend told me that there were three hotels in Atami. Two were European style and one was a Japanese style hotel. He said that he thought that I would like the Japanese style hotel and he would show me the way there.

After we had walked about a mile we came to a large three story wooden building laid out in the form of an open "U." That is, it had a center section with a wing extending from each side. The center of the "U" was beautifully landscaped with a large concrete dome in the middle. We walked up the curved drive to the main entrance of the Onyia Hotel. My Japanese companion removed his shoes and left them on the steps. I did likewise. We were met in the lobby by the hotel manager and my companion told him that I wanted a room for the next two nights. The manager did not speak any English. After a brief discussion with the manager, my companion said that everything was arranged and that the manager would see to my needs and would get me back to the train station when I was ready to leave. He then said that he hoped that I would enjoy my visit to Atami and started to leave.

I thanked him for his help and offered him a carton of cigarettes which I took from my bag. He said that he could not accept such a gift, because it was the custom in Japan to show a stranger the way without expecting any gratuity. I told him we had a dilemma, that it was the custom for Americans to show their appreciation to someone who has done them a favor by giving them a small gift. I would loose face if he did not accept my small gift. After some hesitation he accepted the carton of cigarettes, bowed politely and departed. The manager then motioned to me to follow him. He led me up two flights of stairs and along a corridor to a room with a balcony. The room was sparsely furnished in the Japanese style, and the balcony offered a view of the ocean and a hill covered with citrus fruit trees. The floor was covered with a tightly woven straw like material and was very comfortable to walk on. Light was provided by a single electric bulb. Two young maids entered the room carrying robes and slippers. They began to undress me and carefully folded each item of clothing as it was removed and placed in a cabinet. I made them stop when they reached my skivvies. A double robe was put on me as well as a pair of slippers. One of the maids placed a few lumps of charcoal in a tall ceramic vase, a hibachi, and lit them with a match. The charcoal began to glow and to throw off a remarkable amount of heat. Within a few minutes the room was toasty warm. The maids then prepared a bed for me. This bed consisted of two or three quilts placed on the floor and an oblong pillow filled with something resembling saw dust. When they were finished preparing my bed, the manager and the two maids bowed and left the room.

The time now was early evening, about eight or eight thirty. Since there were no chairs, I was sitting on the floor wandering what to do. It was too early to go to sleep, and I had failed to bring anything to read. A half hour had passed when there was a tap on the sliding door to my room. The door was opened slowly and the manager appeared. He bowed and then tried to communicate something to me which I did not understand. Finally he went through a performance in pantomime simulating taking a bath. I got the idea and nodded my agreement. The manager then led me down three flights of stairs to the basement of the building, and then down a long corridor. As we walked along the corridor I started to have some misgivings. Being the only non-Japanese person in the hotel and a recent enemy made me wonder where he was really taking me. At the end of the corridor there was a door that opened to a large dressing room. There were three or four Japanese men there getting dressed. They paid me no attention. The Manager indicated that I should place my robes and slippers in a basket and place them on a shelf. He then pointed to a very ornate chrome and glass door which I assumed led into the bath area. The door had an exquisite mermaid etched in the frosted glass. Completely nude I opened the door and went through. When the fog like steam caused by my opening the door cleared, I found myself standing about ten feet from three completely nude women. Embarrassed I beat a hasty retreat back into the dressing room. I thought that I had gone through the wrong door. The Japanese men in the dressing room realized my confusion and politely motioned for me to go back into the bath area. There was only the one door into the bath area, so I went back in.

Feeling very self-conscious, like the figure in "September Morn," I looked around the bath area. It was huge. There was a pool about seventy five feet in diameter surrounded by a wide esplanade along about three quarters of its circumference. On the far side there was a marble statue holding a vase from which hot water poured over a bed of rocks and into the pool. Roman columns spaced around the edge of the pool supported the dome shaped ceiling over the pool. On the side of the esplanade opposite the pool there were a series of six alcoves, which appeared to have been cut out of solid rock. In each of these alcoves there was an oblong pool about ten feet in the longer dimension. The temperature of the water in these pools ranged from near freezing to almost boiling. The water in the large pool was extremely hot. The walls, decks, ceilings, and pillars were all finished in mosaic tile duplicating an ancient Roman bath. There were about two dozen people in the bath most of whom were women. I proceeded quickly to the large pool and went down the steps until the water was waist deep. I was sure that I was scalding myself, but after a few minutes my body adjusted to the heat of the water. Unknowingly I had just committed a terrible boorish mistake. It is customary for one to wash his body thoroughly with soap and wash cloth, and then rinse off before entering the large pool. After an hour or so I left the pool and went into the dressing room. I toweled myself dry, put on my robes and slippers, and found my way back to my room. Soaking in the extremely hot water of the pool left me feeling more relaxed than I had ever experienced before. Sleep came on quickly.

The hotel manager solved the language problem for me the next morning. Just after sunrise he came to my room with a very pretty girl about eighteen years of age. She had studied some English in school and was able to act as my interpreter. Although her command of the English language was far from perfect, it was far better than my command of Japanese. Her name was Akami Sanie and she was a neophyte from the local brothel. She remained fairly close to me for the rest of my visit to Atami. This made locating good restaurants and ordering food and beverages much simpler. She showed me the various sights of the village and led me through the numerous shops selling all sorts of goods, clothing, ceramics, and art work. Occasionally one or two of her girl friends would join us as we toured through the village. There was much giggling and chatter between these girls and I found their company very pleasant. Having overcome my shyness, in the evening we spent some time in the hotel's Roman bath where I learned the proper protocols for bathing Japanese style. The procedure required me to sit on a milk stool while one or two girls washed me with soap and sponges. This was followed by a thorough rinsing with the girls pouring water over me from small wooden pails. They also washed themselves thoroughly as well. Then we proceeded to sit in the large pool and soak in the hot water for an hour or so. This utter luxury was a far cry from the dismal living conditions at the camp in Sagame Hara. The morning of my third day in Atami, I gathered the few items I had purchased, packed my bag, and bid the hotel manager farewell and paid my bill along with a generous gratuity. Akami led me to the railroad station and put on a very sad expression as I boarded the train. I gave her a generous payment for her time and assistance and told her that I would probably be returning with some of my friends in a few days. She came close to tears as the train pulled away. I could not help but think that the Japanese are an emotional people.

It was just past dinner time when I returned to the camp at Sagame Hara. My tent mates put me through the third degree. I told them all about the hotel and the sea side village of Atami. Word of my exploration spread to the adjacent tents. By the afternoon of the next day there was a group of about ten Mates and Engineers, mostly young men, who were eager to have me lead them to Atami. It took a couple of more days to square away our plans and to learn how much longer the Army planned to keep us in Japan. The word was that we were not likely to be repatriated to the States for at least two more weeks. The next morning those that were going to go to Atami with me started leaving the camp one or two at a time. We assembled at the railroad station and caught the train for Tokyo where we changed trains for Atami by way of Kama Kura. By the time we reached Atami it was early evening. I managed to heard the group to the Onyia Hotel with little difficulty.

The manager seemed pleased with the arrival of so many guests and assigned us rooms on the second floor in one wing of the hotel. I had explained the protocol for using the baths to my companions during our trip to Atami so they knew how to behave. When we went down to the baths I discovered that some other American seamen had also discovered Atami. A half dozen of them were in the Roman bath when my group arrived there. These other seamen were an uncouth lot and violated every principal of proper conduct. I noticed that there were very few Japanese in the bath. They had quietly evacuated the area when they saw how crude these seamen were. Their conduct was embarrassing to me. They were loud, course, and disrespectful towards the Japanese. Fortunately they had rooms in a different part of the hotel so we saw very little of them outside of the baths.

Two of my companions paid a visit to the local brothel the next morning and arranged to have all the available girls come to the hotel that evening. Some of my other companions located an adequate supply of beer and sake along with a variety of edible items. They also found a three piece band for the party being planned. As the sun was setting the girls and the band arrived. I inquired after Akami and one of the girls who could speak English told me that she was with another American at a different hotel. My disappointment must have been obvious because she said that she would tell Akami that I had returned. The party that developed was more like a fraternity house party than a Roman orgy. The band played a variety of Japanese songs which I found very pleasing. One song, China Night, was the Japanese equivalent of the German song Lily Marlane. Some of the girls acted out the meaning as they sang some of the songs such as the Coal Miners song. There was a great deal of laughing and singing and the band seemed to enjoy the party as much as we Americans did. This same scenario repeated itself for the next two nights.

I was at somewhat of a loss because Akami was not available. The girl who told Akami that I had returned to Atami reported that Akami was very unhappy that she could not get released from her commitment to the other American. She would much rather be with me. I could only imagine that fragile little girl being abused by the uncouth type of seamen that were staying at my hotel. The situation made me think of Puccini's Madam Butterfly and Franz Lehar's The Land Of Smiles. I was the American Officer and Akami was the Japanese maiden. The party was not as much fun without Akami. Although the other girls from the brothel were very pleasant, I just could not work up an interest in any of them. After three days I returned to the camp at Sagame Hara to learn if there was any word on when the Army was going to ship us out. Within three days the rest of the gang returned from Atami just in time to be informed that we would be leaving the camp in the next couple of days. I spent the remaining time slipping out of the camp to buy various souvenirs in the local town. Then one dreary day the Army told us to gather our gear and board a line of trucks which were to transport us to Yokohama.

The convoy of trucks reached Yokohama at about nine o'clock and proceeded on to the only working pier. The night was dark and cold with a light drizzle falling. There was a troop transport ship tied alongside the pier. This ship was the S S Marine Robin, a C-4 operated by the Grace Line. All the merchant seamen with their gear were discharged from the trucks and assembled in front of the ship. An Army Officer mounted a platform adjacent to the gangway and gave instructions over a loud speaker to the assembled seamen. He said that there were five hundred merchant seamen here and that there were five hundred bunks available on the ship. The only problem was that these bunks were spread throughout the ship. The merchant seamen should just go aboard and look for an empty bunk and claim it. There were already twenty-five hundred soldiers and seventy five Red Cross women on board. The merchant seamen were the last to board and the ship was due to sail at midnight. When I got on board I went down to the tween deck level and started walking forward through the mess deck and berthing areas. There were no empty bunks until I reached the fore peak compartment. This was a small space with five high pipe rack berths for about fifty people. The Army personnel in this compartment were mostly Second Lieutenants. There was one empty bunk on the bottom of one of the stacks of berths. Feeling exhausted I stowed my gear and climbed into this bunk.

FAREWELL JAPAN

Sometime after midnight the throb of the ship's engines and a prolonged blast of the ship's whistle awakened me. At last the ship was underway and heading for home. As the ship took the first swells after clearing the harbor all the loose crockery and similar items could be heard crashing to the decks. The rolling and pitching of the ship was normal but in the fore peak the corkscrew motion was much more pronounced. Within a short time one of the men in one of the bunks above me leaned over and vomited. He was soon joined by most of the other occupants of the compartment. There was soon a puddle of vomit sloshing across the deck as the ship worked through the sea way. The stench was overpowering. I had never been seasick before, but I soon started feeling sick. I got out of my bunk and put on my G I wind breaker and headed for the main deck ladder. When I reached the main deck there was a strong cold wind driving a mixture of rain and sleet into my face. In spite of the cold, the clean sea air was delicious. After a while I wandered down to the mess deck area. This was a large space furnished with narrow chest high tables set out in rows. Along one side there was a screened area housing a row of steam tables. There was no one else in this dimly lit space. The mess deck was located amidships so there was little feeling of the motion of the ship. I found a chair, propped it against a bulkhead, pulled my wind breaker up over my shoulders and fell fast asleep.

Suddenly I found myself on the deck sitting in the overturned chair. Looking up I saw this huge Army Sergeant standing over me with his hands on his hips and an angry scowl on his face. He had kicked the chair out from under me. In a high squeaky voice he demanded "Where have you been hiding for the past two days? I should have reported you AWOL." He then ordered me to get to work behind the steam tables and said that he was going to keep an eye on me. This was a stroke of good fortune. I mumbled some sorry type statement and went behind the steam tables. The soldiers there were setting up the steam tables for the breakfast meal. They looked at me and asked where I had come from since I was not a member of their company. Although I was dressed as they were in khaki pants, shirt, and G I shoes, I explained that I was part of the contingent of merchant seamen being repatriated. They laughed and said that I should tell their sergeant to go to hell. Instead, I told the soldiers that I would like to work with them behind the steam tables. They said it was fine with them. The missing man whose place I was taking was away gambling in one of the G I berthing compartments and was not expected to return to his steam table duties for the rest of the voyage. I noticed that these soldiers had held the rate of sergeant or corporal previously and their stripes had been removed from their uniforms. Steam table duty was probably a form of punishment for them. None the less they were a good natured lot and accepted me as one of them.

The first thing I noticed was that working behind the steam tables gave me access to the galley where food was prepared for both the troops and the higher rank (Captains, Majors, and higher) military and the civilian Red Cross women. The higher ranked people were fed a much better type of food in much more pleasant surroundings than those in the troop class category. Rank does have its privilege. Naturally we who worked the steam tables ate the better food. The routine for the troops was fairly simple. They would get out of their bunks in the morning and get on line to use the head (latrine). Next they would get in line for breakfast. At one end of the steam tables they would pick up a steel tray and utensils. Then they would proceed along the steam tables where the food, scrambled eggs, oatmeal, bacon, canned fruit, toast, and a beverage were placed on their trays. With their trays full they would proceed to one of the chest high tables, and standing up they would consume the food. When finished they would take their trays to a large garbage can, dump the leftover food, and place the empty trays and utensils on a counter at the scullery. Leaving the mess deck the troops would get on line again for the head. After using the head they would get on line for the noon meal following which they would get on line again for the head. The same procedure was followed for the evening meal. Needless to say with three thousand men in troop class the lines were very long and very slow. When the crew from the S S Patrick C. Boyle came through the line they were surprised to see me working behind the steam table and laughed at my situation.

I worked out a pretty good routine for myself. In the morning I would be in the mess deck before anyone else made an appearance. Then I would work with the soldiers setting up the steam tables and getting ready for the breakfast line. Before that line started through we had our breakfast, the choosiest items from the galley. Next there was clean up and set up for the lunch line. We ate our lunch before the lunch line started through. Afterwards again there was clean up and set up for the dinner line. Again we ate our dinner first, and it was not the same fare as that which was served to the troops. All of this effort was done in a leisurely way with frequent long breaks. When the clean up from the evening meal was finished, I would go to the fore peak compartment and catch a few hours sleep. At around two in the morning I would sneak back to the ship's crews' quarters and shave and take a shower in their head. At that hour of the day there was nobody roaming around the crews' quarters so I was never challenged. The crews' quarters and the engine room spaces were located in the stern of the ship and were essentially off limits to the troops. As far as the steam table detail was concerned we saw very little of the Sergeant in charge. He would make an appearance once or twice a day to make sure all of his men, including me, were present and working. This was how I survived the ten day voyage, troop class, from Yokohama to San Francisco.

There were some other things of interest encountered during the voyage. A few days out there was an announcement that the ship would be passing through a Tidal Wave. If the ship did pass through such a wave, there was no change in motion or other indication that it did so. I learned later that a tidal wave had its devastating effect only when the wave reaches the shallow waters around a land mass. The elite passengers berthed in the superstructure cabins were kept isolated by a company of marines who were the police force on board. They prevented any of the troop class passengers from entering the superstructure. However, there was one exception. Some of the Red Cross women went into business, the oldest profession. The word was passed that one could have his sexual needs assuaged for twenty dollars a session. Though I did not see it, there was reported to be an endless line of troops, policed by some of the marines, from the troop class area to some of the superstructure cabins. Considering the number of potential clients, those business women must have been millionaires when they got off the ship.

The ship reached the pilot station off the Farallon Islands in the morning and picked up the Pilot for San Francisco. This occurred just after breakfast was served. When the cleanup was completed I asked one of the soldiers to take a package ashore for me and mail it to my home. The package contained the sniper's rifle that I had acquired from the Tokyo Armory. He agreed to mail it for me and I gave him ten dollars to cover the cost. Then I went forward to the fore peak compartment and changed from my khaki G I clothes to my blue dress uniform. As the ship was proceeding through San Francisco Bay, I went back to the mess deck and entered the mess Sergeant's office. When he saw me in my uniform with the gold braid on my sleeves, he stood up behind his desk. I said to him, "As you were, I just stopped by to thank you for making this a very pleasant voyage for me." He brought both of his hands up to his cheeks and then muttered, "Oh my God, I thought you were one of my expletive soldiers." Wishing him good luck, I left the mess deck and returned to the fore peak compartment to gather my gear. The ship docked at a pier in Alemeda. The elite passengers disembarked first and quickly disappeared in some of the many cars, busses, and trucks lined up on the pier apron. Next the troops were disembarked and driven off in trucks to some Army camp. Then just about every available Customs agent in the Bay area formed a cordon around the ship. The last group, the merchant seamen were then disembarked. Each man and his belongings were thoroughly searched.

The Customs men confiscated anything that resembled military equipment or any item that had not been made in America. This included guns, swords, knives, some souvenirs, jewelry, and similar items. Many of the seamen had purchased very expensive heirloom Samari swords. There was a large pile of them alongside the gangway as the last of the seamen left the ship. I was one of the last to get off. As a Customs man was searching me and my belongings, I saw a large black limousine pull up close to the gangway. A chauffeur opened the door and a VIP type got out and went over to the pile of Samuri swords. He picked out two of the finest and then returned to his vehicle. My Customs man confiscated a bayonet, the 6 X 30 binoculars in a leather case, and a couple of Japanese battle flags that I had acquired in Japan. I argued with him over the binoculars but he was adamant that they were war booty. He probably kept them for himself. To this day I have no liking or respect for the men of the Customs Service. Like any bureaucratic organization, they will take advantage of anyone.

There were representatives from the various Unions and the Shipping Companies to meet the seamen being disembarked. When I was finally clear of Customs, I saw Captain Burke, the port Captain for my company, Boland and Cornelius. He was on hand to take care of the licensed officers. Rooms had been reserved for us in a small hotel in San Francisco and he had us transported there in a couple of taxi cabs. The Second Mate, the Second Assistant Engineer, and the Purser had homes in the local area and disappeared quickly. Captain Nils and Ted Loos, the Chief Mate, managed to get transportation to New York the next day. Captain Burke asked me to sign on as Third Mate on one of the company's ships due to sail out of Seattle. I declined and told him that I was going back to New York and sit for my Second Mate's License. My name was on a waiting list for a place on a civilian airplane to take me back to New York. After three or four days my name came up and I boarded an airplane one evening at the San Francisco airport for a flight to New York. The flight took about twelve hours with a two hour stop over in Omaha in the wee hours of the morning to refuel and exchange some passengers. Everyone had to get off the plane and go to the rather small and crowded waiting room. There were a good number of rather young women stretched out and trying to sleep on most of the seats in the waiting room. They must have been waiting to make connections to other destinations. My plane arrived in New York about mid morning on a Friday. After collecting my luggage, I took a taxi cab to the Long Island Rail Road station and boarded a train for Central Islip. Needless to say, my parents were happy to see me after so long an absence.

BOYHOOD TO MANHOOD

The foregoing covered some of my life's experiences from High School through the Maritime Academy and the end of my second voyage on the Liberty Ship S S Patrick C. Boyle. I returned home as a young man with a world of experience. It was a privilege to have sailed with some of the finest men that served in the wartime merchant service. There were also those in that service who left much to be desired. Captain Hickey was one of the best Masters I would ever sail with, and Captain Nils was at the other end of the spectrum. Our allies, the Filipinos, were somewhat of a disappointment. They were not as trustworthy as I had expected. Our enemy, the Japanese were a complete surprise. In all of my dealings with them I found them scrupulously honest, courteous, and industrious. They had good reason to hate an American like me, but they never showed any sign of dislike. The Soldiers who had fought them across the Pacific showed them some degree of respect. The new recruits recently sent to Japan as part of the Occupation Army showed only contempt for the Japanese. This was probably due to the four years of propaganda and hate they had been taught, and that they had never had to face the Japanese in actual combat. My impressions of people were completely changed.

That first weekend I spent pretty much at my parents home telling them of my adventures at sea and catching up on all that had happened in the home town since I had shipped out so many long months ago. It was mid March 1946 the War was over and many things had changed. My father's job in a defense plant had terminated and he had started a taxi business. James, my younger teenage brother worked with him as a taxi driver. My mother worked at the local psychiatric hospital and enjoyed her position as a charge attendant. Most of my high school buddies were gone from the local scene. I did get together with two of my high school classmates, Art Simms and Hugh Powers, on different days during the following week. Art had been in the Navy in the Pacific, and Hugh still had some college time to complete for his degree. Visits were made to my two Aunts and my cousins who lived about thirty miles away in the town of Hicksville. That first week home went by rather quickly.

On Monday of the following week I took the train from Central Islip to Manhattan to visit the office of the Boland and Cornelius Steamship Company, the company that operated the S S Patrick C. Boyle for the War Shipping Administration. Their office was located in a building at 19 Rector Street in the lower end of Manhattan Island. When I arrived at their office I introduced myself to the receptionist and made a request to see the port captain. She made a phone call and then ushered me into the main office and to the desk of Captain Beauvaise, the chief port captain for Boland and Cornelius. He was a corpulent man in his sixties. Rising from his chair he welcomed me with a broad smile and a hearty hand-shake. He said that he had been looking forward to meeting me and that Captain Burke had sent him a very complimentary report on me. After a few minutes of small talk he took me over to another part of the office and introduced me to Mr. Donald Woods, the operations manager, and Mr. Alonzo King, the assistant operations manager. They too greeted me with friendly handshakes.

An hour or so was spent in the Boland and Cornelius office with Mr. King and Captain Beauvaise. They told me that the company was cur-rently operating twenty six ships, mostly Liberty Ships. The company had just retired three old ships in the coastwise coal trade that were recently replaced with new colliers. The rest of the fleet were scattered over the world and some were just starting to carry Marshall Plan cargoes to Eu-rope. They asked me what my immediate plans were and I told them that I planned to enroll in the License Upgrade School and take the examina-tion for my second mate's license. Mr. King then asked me what my ulti-mate goal was. I pointed to Captain Beauvaise's chair and said that I wanted to occupy that chair some time in the future. The two of them laughed and said that was an impressive answer. They wished me good luck and said that I should come back to their office as soon as I was ready to ship out again.

My next stop was a visit to the License Upgrade School which was located in the Whitehall Building at the Battery in lower Manhattan. I signed up for the next class scheduled to start in the beginning of April. There was a substantial charge for the course but it was the prudent thing to do for a license examination. The class was set to run for about four weeks. I then went over to the U.S. Coast Guard License office in the

Customs House near the Battery and requested to be scheduled to take the license examination in May. Next I went back to the Long Island Rail Road station and purchased a commutation ticket for April and then figured what train I would have to take to get to the License Upgrade School by 0800 every morning. There was a train that departed Central Islip at close to 0600 that would allow me just enough time to get to the Whitehall Building in time for the class.

As the week wore on I started to feel rather bored. On a whim I decided to call Gloria to see if she were around and available. The call I placed to her home was answered by one of her sisters who informed me that Gloria was a student nurse at Roosevelt Hospital in Manhattan. The sister gave me a telephone number where I could reach her. That evening I called the number and after some time managed to get Gloria on the phone. She agreed to meet me for lunch the next day and told me where to pick her up at the hospital. I met her as planned. Gloria was still the beautiful petit blue eyed blond I remembered from high school and the graduation dance at Fort Schuyler. I took her to a nautical restaurant and bar called the Whaler. It was a very nice upscale place and I thought she would be impressed with it. We had a nice lunch and she declined any alcoholic beverages — still a faithful Methodist. During lunch Gloria let me know that she was not dating anyone and was committed to completing her nurse's training course. However she said that she usually went home every other weekend and would be available if I wanted to take her out. I explained that I was going to be rather busy for the next few weeks preparing for and taking the examination to raise my license, but that I would keep in touch with her and ask her out on those weekends when she was home.

In April the license upgrade classes started. I took the train in to Manhattan every morning and returned to Central Islip every evening. There was sufficient homework to keep me busy during the week day evenings. I would call Gloria once or twice a week to make plans to take her out on those weekends when she would be home. Once or twice I would meet her on a Friday evening in Manhattan on those weekends she was not going home and take her to dinner. This routine continued during the weeks I was attending the school. My relationship with Gloria was getting serious. On one of my evening rides home on the Long Island train I ran into Danny Greenberg, a fellow from town whom I had known for years. He had been a year or two below me in high school, and was now studying law at N Y U. Danny introduced me to his seat companion, Anita Soldo, an attractive brunette who was attending Queens College. I frequently found myself traveling home on the train with them. Anita got off the train in the town of Brentwood, one stop before Central Islip. Traveling home with Anita and Danny was very pleasant. We carried on interesting and intelligent conversations that made the time pass very quickly. I could not help comparing the bright, witty, sophisticated, and vivacious Anita with the quiet, reserved, and somewhat introverted Gloria.

When it came time for me to sit for the license examination I got a room in a hotel in Manhattan. It would have been extremely difficult to commute on the railroad and take the exam. Every free minute was devoted to cramming for the examination. Anyone who has ever taken a Coast Guard license examination in New York will attest to how difficult the examiners make it. There is no more nerve wracking or excruciating experience that I know of. The testing would start promptly at 0800. Once the examiners had given you a card of questions you could not leave your seat even to go to the head until all the questions had been completed and turned in. Each card usually had five questions that required a good deal of knowledge and effort to answer. Often the answer to one question was linked to the accuracy of the answer to the previous question. There was a one hour break for lunch, and most of the license candidates would go to the License Upgrade School during that period to review and analyze their answers with the instructors. Half the candidates sitting for Third Mate, Second Mate, and Chief Mate had failed the examinations they were taking by the third day of sitting. By the end of the week I had successfully completed the examination, and was told to return to the Customs House the following Monday to receive my new Second Mate's license.

That Monday morning I reported to the Customs House and received my Second Mate's license and went through the swearing in routine. From there I went directly to 19 Rector Street and the offices of the Boland and Cornelius Steamship Company. Mr. King said he was pleased to see me and that he had a second mate's berth available for me. I was amazed. Here the ink was not even dry on my Second Mate's license and I was being handed a berth as Second Mate. Mr. King was assigning me to one of the company's newest ships, the S S Pocahontas Seam. He said that he wanted me to do him a rather delicate favor. He wanted me to report to him on any dishonest transactions I might see the captain involved with.

I told him that I would not accept the job if I were expected to be a company spy. He said that he understood my position and respected me for it. However he asked if I would lie to cover up any wrong doings the captain might be involved in. I told him I would not lie nor would I participate in anything dishonest. It seems that the captain was suspected of passing on surreptitious charges to the company's account. Mr. King was satisfied with my position and gave me a letter of assignment to the S S Pocahontas Seam.

I left the Boland and Cornelius offices and proceeded by subway to a pier in Brooklyn where the ship was berthed. The S S Pocahontas Seam was a Liberty Ship hull with the engine room at the stern of the ship. She could carry eleven thousand tons of cargo, considerably more than the standard Liberty Ship. There was a mid ship house that had the quarters for the Captain, the three Mates, the Purser, and the Radio Operator. The Engineers, engine crew, deck crew, and stewards occupied quarters in the stern house. My cabin was spacious with a private head and two port-holes, one looking forward and one at the side. The Captain, a man in his fifties whose name I cannot remember, was a naturalized citizen from one of the Baltic countries. The Chief Mate, Taylor, was a graduate of Kings Point and about a year older than me. The Third Mate, Dixon, was also a Kings Pointer about my own age. Taylor impressed me as a surly arrogant type, whereas Dixon was friendly and pleasant. The Chief Engineer was a pleasant fellow about forty years of age, and the Assistant Engineers were all younger men. The ship was clean and sparkling. To say the least, I was impressed with this assignment.

S S Pocahontas Seam
Liberty Cargo Vessel, Boland & Cornelius

THE COASTWISE COLLIER RUN

The S S Pocahontas Seam was engaged in the coastwise coal trade. The ship would load eleven thousand tons of industrial coal in Hampton Roads and then steam to the Edison Company pier in Hunters Point in the Bronx borough of New York. After discharging the cargo the ship would return to Hampton Roads for another load. Then it would steam to Boston and discharge the cargo at the Everett Company pier. It would take a little over twenty four hours to make the run from Hampton Roads to New York, and a little over two days to make the run to Boston. Loading the coal would take between eight and ten hours. Discharging the coal would take between sixteen and twenty hours. A round trip from Hampton Roads to New York would take about five days with a one night lay over in New York and about seven days to Boston with a one night lay over. Third Mate Dixon and I developed a strong dislike for Chief Mate Taylor. He never missed an opportunity to stick one or the other of us with the loading and discharging of the cargo while he goofed off. When under way I had the twelve to four watch and Chief Mate Taylor had the four to eight watch. Every morning I would have my stand by man wake him at 0330 so he could get dressed and have a cup of coffee before relieving me at 0400. He would consistently relieve me from forty five minutes to an hour late. I would usually have to send the stand by man on his watch down to rouse him out a second or third time. Taylor would usually get up and get dressed and then jump back in his bunk and fall asleep. We almost came to blows when I told him I was going to put in for overtime every time he relieved me late. My threat did not stop him from continuing to relieve me late.

After four or five round trips to New York and Boston a new Captain was assigned to the ship. Captain Thomas came aboard and told the purser to pack his bags because he had his own purser. He then said that he had his own mates but they were not ready to join him yet, so we Mates could stay on for the time being. It seems that Captain Thomas came from Gwenn Island in Matthew's County, Virginia and had been sailing in the coastwise collier trade for many years. It was customary for the Matthew's County boys to dominate the coastwise collier trade to the exclusion of outsiders. Chief Mate Taylor came from a nearby Virginia county and he lost no time buttering up Captain Thomas. It was soon obvious that the Captain found Taylor acceptable, but even though Dixon and I were not Virginians, he made no attempt to replace us. I suspect that the home office warned Captain Thomas to be careful about replacing the Mates without cause. In the mean time Chief Mate Taylor became even more arrogant and obnoxious.

Since the S S Pocahontas Seam was in the coastwise coal trade with a quick turn around from port to port, it was almost impossible to keep a full crew on board. We were always sailing short handed. From week to week you never knew what kind of seamen you would be working with. On one occasion when the ship was departing the Hunters Point pier there were only three deck hands on board. The Chief Mate took two of them to the bow to handle the lines, and the third was sent to the wheel house. I was left to handle the stern lines alone, and there was only a single slow turning capstan on the stern. The ship was tied to the pier with two stern lines and one spring line all of which were made of eight inch Manila rope. Luckily I had the presence of mind to carry a fire ax aft with me when I went to the stern station. I managed to get the off shore stern line in with little difficulty. The pilot on the bridge then ordered me to take in the remaining stern line and hold the spring line. He used the stern spring line to warp the bow away from the pier. I had just gotten the stern line aboard when the pilot ordered me to cast off the spring line and bring it aboard. With the amount of tension on the spring line there was no way I could take it off the bitts and get a couple of turns around the capstan. My only choice was to sever the spring line at the chock with the fire ax, and that is just what I did. There was about one hundred and thirty feet of good eight inch Manila hawser left on the pier as the ship pulled away.

The makeup of the deck crew was different each time we left port. There were always two or three, and sometimes more who never got back to the ship at sailing time. They were either too drunk to wake up on time, or over slept in the local brothel. In each port there were new sailors reporting aboard from the union hall. One of these able seamen was a Navy Lieutenant, a former fighter pilot, on terminal leave who came aboard in Boston. To kill time he decided to ship out to make a few extra bucks. A teen age kid also signed on as an ordinary seaman and shared the same watch and room with this able seaman. This kid had extremely poor eyesight and appeared to have some sort of eye infection. In the two day run back to Hampton Roads the able seaman had developed a severe eye infection. Apparently the ordinary seaman had accidentally used the able seaman's towel and passed the infection on to him. Both of these men were dispatched to the hospital in Norfolk when the ship got into Hampton Roads. They were still there when the ship departed for New York. I never saw either of them again.

The ship's schedule put me in New York every other week for one over night and sometimes for two nights. Every other week I would take Gloria out for dinner and a movie either in New York or out on Long Island. My father always let me have the family car when I was home so it was easy to go out on a date. That routine continued through June and July of 1946. One evening in Manhattan Gloria and I were walking back to her quarters in Roosevelt Hospital after a pleasant dinner in a nice restaurant. We began talking about marriage. She said that she wanted to finish her nurse's training before getting married, and that she assumed that we were now engaged. I told her that we could go shopping for an engagement ring the next time we were both able to get time off during day time business hours. Gloria liked that idea very much. The next time my ship came into New York it was scheduled to lay over for five days to get some engine repair work done and start the annual Coast Guard inspection process. Since no night relief mates were available, we three mates had to take turns standing the night watches. On a Wednesday evening during this period, I brought Gloria aboard the ship for dinner and to show her around the ship. I introduced her to Captain Thomas and the other mates and engineers as my fiancee. After a very pleasant dinner, I escorted her back to her quarters at Roosevelt Hospital. I was scheduled to take the night watch on Thursday so I told her I would pick her up at the hospital Friday afternoon and escort her home to Central Islip.

As planned I met Gloria at the hospital and we caught the train for Central Islip. Feeling rather tired, I said very little as the train rattled on. After an hour or so Gloria in a rather defensive voice said, "Well I guess he told you." I just looked at her wondering what she was talking about, and replied, "Tell me about it." She said that Taylor had gone to her quarters the evening before and invited her to go out with him. He told her that I was on watch and that I would never know unless she told me. Then she said, "I went out with him, but nothing really happened." The way she said it made me look at her in a much different light. I could only imagine what "nothing really happened" meant. Although I was furious, I did my best not to show it. When we got off the train she asked if I was going to take her out that night. She must have suspected how angry I was. I told her that I would pick her up at about seven o'clock and we both went to our separate homes. Without a doubt, Taylor was a back stabbing louse, but what kind of girl was Gloria? My thoughts of marrying her were suddenly shipwrecked on a reef of doubts. I took Gloria out to dinner that night and a few subsequent nights when my ship was in port in New York. My feelings for her now were torn between desire and distrust. As a professional mariner I could not marry a woman I could not trust. I had heard too many horror stories of other men in my profession who had married unfaithful wives and suffered the torments of hell as a consequence.

During the latter half of July I developed an egg size lump close to the tail of my spine. It caused me no pain so I paid no attention to it. The last weekend in July the SS Pocahontas Seam was to lay over in New York to take on fuel and stores. The ship was anchored in the lower part of New York harbor. In the morning I took the water taxi ashore to get some new charts and the latest copies of the Notice To Mariners. On my return to the ship I felt the lump on my stern pop through the skin as I threw my leg over the bulwark while climbing aboard. I went to my cabin, dropped my trousers and skivvies and examined the lump. It was oozing a clear liquid so I cleaned it off and put a large band aid on it and got dressed. I told the Third Mate about the lump and that I was going ashore to see a doctor. The water taxi dropped me at the Battery and I went to the nearest phone booth and looked up the number of a doctor in the directory. I found the number for a Dr. Bermann with an office on Fortieth Street. I called that number and arranged to see the doctor within the hour. After a brief examination, Dr. Bermann told me that I had a pilonidal cyst and that it should be removed as soon as possible. He said that since I was a professional seaman that I should go the Marine Hospital on Staten Island and have the surgery done there. Dr. Bermann called the hospital and made arrangements for me to be treated there right away. I called the Boland and Cornelius office and told Mr. King about my problem and that I would be in the hospital for the next week or so. He told me not to worry and that he would get someone to take my place on the ship. He also said that he would make sure that my personal belongs were packed up and sent to my home.

That afternoon I arrived at the Marine Hospital on Staten Island and after an examination was placed in a semi private room in one of the wards. Surgery for my cyst was scheduled for the next morning. I phoned Gloria and told her where I was and that I would probably be in the hospital for at least a week. Then I phoned my parents and told them that I would be in the Marine Hospital for a week and that the operation was not anything serious. The surgery was performed the next morning and I spent the day in my room in a semi dazed condition. Removal of the cyst left a rather large open cut on my stern. The doctors said that the wound had to heal from the inside and that it would take a few weeks to heal completely. They gave me a rubber donut to use whenever I wanted to sit down. A couple of days later my parents came by to visit me and to see how I was doing. Dixon paid me a visit two or three days later. He said that he had packed my belongings and had them shipped to my parents home. Then he said that he had two surprises for me. One was that he had quit the ship because he could no longer stand Chief Mate Taylor. The other was that the Chief Engineer was in a room down the hall from mine. It seems that the Chief Engineer had a ruptured ulcer in his stomach and required immediate hospitalization and surgery. I spent several hours every day visiting with him and exchanging sea stories. Dixon said that he was staying with friends in Manhattan and that he would keep in touch with me. Curiously there was not even so much as a phone call from Gloria.

After eight days in the Marine Hospital the doctors released me to recuperate at home. They gave me a good supply of medicine and dressings to assure proper healing of the incision. The second day at home I got a phone call from Dixon. He had just signed on a ship scheduled to make a two month trip to the Mediterranean and they were in desperate need of a second mate. He had wanted to know if I would be interested in signing on. This was an opportunity for me to get away for a while so that I could sort out my thoughts regarding Gloria. I told Dixon that I would take the berth. He said that he would tell the company agent and that I should catch the next train to New York.

The S S Thomas Sim Lee, was a Liberty Ship and was at a pier in Brooklyn. The whole crew except for a second mate was signed on and the ship would leave as soon as I reported aboard. I packed my gear, said good by to my parents, and caught the next train to the city. Unable to reach Gloria by phone, I wrote her a short note telling her that I had to ship out on short notice and that I would be returning in about two months. It was after six o'clock in the evening when I finally reached the ship. The Shipping Commissioner had already left the ship after signing everyone on foreign articles. When I arrived the ship's lines had been singled up and there was a wooden ladder leaning against the side of the ship for me to get aboard. The docking pilot and the harbor pilot were aboard and two tug boats and line handlers were standing by. I was told that I would have to sign coastwise articles, but that I would be given the same rights and guarantees as the rest of the crew who were on foreign articles. The foreign article is a contract between the seaman and the company operating the ship. The seaman agrees to work on the ship for a period of at least twelve months, and the articles automatically terminate at the end of twelve months or when the ship returns to the port where they were signed. If the company exercises its option to terminate the articles in less than twelve months and in a different port, they are required to provide the seamen with wages and transportation back to the port where they were signed. A federal shipping commissioner must be present whenever a crew signs on foreign articles, or when the articles are terminated. Coastwise articles do not require a federal shipping commissioner and merely stipulate the position to be held by the seaman during the coastwise voyage. There are no guarantees on coastwise articles. The ship's agent representing the Atlantic Gulf and West Indies Line (AGWI Lines) departed the ship as soon as I had signed the coastwise articles. The ladder was thrown down, the lines were cast off, and the tug boats pulled the ship away from the pier. The ship was on her way to the port of New Orleans and the date was 8 August 1946.

THE S S THOMAS SIM LEE

The S S Thomas Sim Lee was a well worn War Shipping Administration Liberty Ship built in the Fairfield Yard of the Bethlehem Steel Company and operated by the AGWI Lines Steamship Company. The Captain was a sickly eighty five year old man who spent most of his time in his bunk. The Chief Mate was an energetic fellow in his late twenties and he essentially ran the ship. The ship was in ballast on the run down to New Orleans. It took eight days to get there and once there the ship tied up to the off shore side of a Russian freighter docked on the Algiers side of the river. This Russian ship had a large crew two thirds of whom were women. Anyone going ashore from the S S Thomas Sim Lee had to cross over the Russian ship. Some of our sailors tried to befriend some of the Russian women, especially the young and pretty ones. The girls were polite but would not fraternize. When they were asked how they liked America they had a stock answer which was, "America is nice but Russia is better." Whenever any of them went ashore they were always accompanied by one or two of the male members of the Russian crew. These girls seemed to have very limited wardrobes because they were always seen in the same dresses when they did go ashore. When the Russian Captain learned that our Captain was ill, he sent his female doctor over to see if she could do anything to help. The cold war had not started yet and this was a nice gesture of friendship. One evening the Russian Captain invited our crew over to his ship to have some tea and cakes and to see a movie. A tween deck space on the Russian ship had been set up as a makeshift theater. The story line of the film that was shown was about a circus and lavished an extreme amount of praise on Joseph Stalin. During the show one of the Russian stewards passed out Russian cigarettes to those of our crew who had accepted the invitation. These cigarettes were paper tubes only filled half way with tobacco. Although the Russians were friendly, they did not fraternize with any of our crew. After three days our ship was moved across the Mississippi River to a berth on the New Orleans side.

Two or three days later word came to the ship that AGWI Lines had canceled the voyage to the Mediterranean and was turning the ship back to the War Shipping Administration. The foreign articles were broken and everyone in the crew was given two weeks pay and money to cover the cost of returning to New York by bus, plane, or train. I was the only exception. Since I had been signed on under coastwise articles, I was not entitled to the severance pay and transportation money. AGWI Lines refused to honor the promises they made to me when I signed on in New York. Being a member of the Masters Mates and Pilots Union, I went to the Union office in New Orleans and asked them to lean upon AGWI Lines to make good on their promises. Captain Hansen, a naturalized Norwegian, was the head man in this Union office. After I explained my problem, he growled back at me, "Get to hell out of here and take your complaints to your own Local 88 in New York." Feeling totally frustrated, I left his office thinking that the dues I had been paying to the Masters

Mates and Pilots Union were a complete waste of money. When I returned to the ship, I found that everyone except a couple of the Engineers and the Third Mate Dixon had left the ship. He said that he had been waiting for me to return with him to New York. As I was just about finished packing my gear the port agent for the Isthmian Steamship Company came to my cabin and said that his company was taking over the ship. He asked both Dixon and me to stay on as part of the new crew and we agreed to do so. I was in no hurry to return to New York. The next day the Shipping Commissioner, the Isthmian Port Captain, and the new Master, Captain Howard, came aboard and a new crew, me included, signed on foreign articles for the next voyage of the S S Thomas Sim Lee.

Again the ship was scheduled to visit several ports in the Mediterranean Sea. Longshoremen began loading general break bulk cargo, and a fuel barge was brought alongside to top off the fuel tanks. When we were two days into the loading operation, the National Maritime Union (NMU) called a general strike. Our crew who were members of the NMU left the ship and all cargo operations came to a halt. The NMU set up picket lines around the entrance to the pier where the ship was berthed and did everything they could to prevent anyone from going on to the pier. The union was smart enough not to put any of our crew members on picket duty at our pier. Since there were no cooks on board, the officers would have to go ashore for their meals. Whenever the Mates or Engineers went ashore they would usually have to get a police escort to get back to the ship. The union pickets would make all manner of threats and they were mean enough to carry them out if the police were not there. It was especially dangerous to try to get back on the pier at night. There were fewer police present then and the pickets became much bolder. Two or three of them would try to rough up a single individual trying to get on the pier to return to the ship. If the officers tried to return in a group of three or four, the pickets would make a phone call to the union hall and a truck load of extra pickets would be rushed to the pier. This technique was employed by the union to restrict access to all the ships in the port. The strike was nation wide so all of the ships with NMU crews were tied up and idle. Ship operators and union officials argued and negotiated for almost four weeks before a settlement was reached. Cargo operations were resumed as soon as the pickets were removed and the crew returned aboard.

Two days after the NMU strike ended, the Masters Mates and Pilots Union (MM&P) called a general strike. Again everything came to a complete halt. Captain Hansen from the New Orleans MM&P Union hall came aboard and ordered all the Mates to leave the ship. I could not resist this opportunity to confront him. As belligerently as I could I said, "We have signed on foreign articles and cannot legally leave the ship. Any way I do not take orders from your Local Union Hall, you should remember that you told me that I should deal only with New York Local 88. Now get off this ship before I personally throw you off." Captain Hansen left the ship shaking his fist at me and threatening to get even. It was very satisfying to tell that arrogant square head where to go. I had written a letter to Gloria before the series of strikes began but she never bothered to reply. The MM&P strike lasted for about a week. When it ended cargo loading operations were resumed. A few days later the hatches were secured and covered, the Pilot came aboard, tug boats came alongside, and the ship cast off the mooring lines and pulled away from the pier. The Pilot was dropped off at the Southwest Pass Pilot Station and the ship finally started on the voyage to the Mediterranean.

THE FAR EAST RUN

The S S Thomas Sim Lee, hull number 921, was one of the older Liberty Ships and was in reasonably good condition. She had been built by Bethlehem steel in their Fairfield yard in Baltimore. Captain Howard was a short, slim, light haired man in his late forties or early fifties and was a native of Connecticut. The Chief Mate was a man from the Cayman Islands and a naturalized citizen. Dixon of course was the Third Mate. For the most part, the engineers were from East Coast states and were in their thirties. The one exception was the Second Engineer. He was a Greek national fifty plus years of age. The Radio Operator was a Texan about my own age. The Purser whose sir name was Polk was also my age. He claimed to be the great grandson of President Polk and had a superior attitude that was as offensive as it was comical. Although the NMU usually provided a checkerboard crew, this crew were all white men, and with a few exceptions were from the Gulf states of either Alabama, Louisiana, Mississippi, or Texas. One exception was a clean cut able seaman my own age from New Jersey whom I was lucky enough to have assigned to my watch. The NMU crew ranged in age from teenagers to men in their forties and were the scruffiest looking lot I had ever seen on a merchant ship. The first time I saw the chief cook he was staggering down the dock in a drunken stupor. For the next several months I do not recall ever seeing him sober. Where he got the booze is a mystery. There was almost a riot on board before the ship sailed because there were no black eyed peas in the galley stores. The company quickly complied with the demands of the crew and had several huge sacks of black eyed peas delivered to the ship. A kid seventeen years of age with red hair was assigned as messman for the officer's salon. He bragged that he was going to become a real seaman on this voyage. His idea of being a real seaman was to get a dose of the two most common venereal diseases, gonorrhea and syphilis. This was the compliment of the ship on the longest and most tedious voyage of my maritime career.

The trip Eastward across the Atlantic ocean was uneventful. As Second Mate and navigator I had the twelve to four watch. The Third Mate had the eight to twelve watch and the Chief Mate had the four to eight watch. Each of us stood two four hour watches in a twenty-four hour period. My watch crew consisted of two able seamen and one ordinary seaman. I would take morning and evening star sights at twilight regardless of what time it was. Even though I would be relieved at 0400, I often had to stay up until five or six o'clock to shoot the stars and calculate the ship's position. I would also take the morning and noon sights of the sun to determine the ship's noon position which was entered in the ship's log. The other two mates would also take morning and noon sun sights to verify the accuracy of the noon fix. The procedure was to take one or two angles of the sun between 0900 and 1000 to determine lines of position. Then at celestial noon, when the sun crossed the meridian, the angle of the sun above the horizon would be used to determine the latitude. By running the morning sun lines up to the noon latitude, a fairly accurate noon position for the ship could be fixed. If the moon and the planet Venus were visible during the day, their altitudes, angles above the horizon, could also be used to calculate additional lines of position. These lines of position could be combined with sun lines of position to establish a very accurate fix of the ship's position. This ritual of navigation cut into my time to sleep, and as a result I usually skipped breakfast in order to get more time in the sack. Since the cooks could not even prepare eggs that were palatable, skipping breakfast was not a great sacrifice.

CASABLANCA

Our first port of call was Casablanca in Morocco. This was my first encounter with a Muslim population. Although the city had a very definite French influence, it had all the attributes of a Muslim society that I found unattractive. The smells, the flies, the dirt, and the peddlers around the waterfront were not pleasant. There were some interesting buildings and market bazaars in the city. Any item you would try to purchase required a good deal of haggling to reach an acceptable price, and even then one would feel cheated. Although the officials and police were polite, the street Muslims presented a rather unfriendly attitude towards Americans. Fortunately the ship only stayed in Casablanca for two days to off load and load some general cargo. The next port was Algiers in French Algeria. Most of the officials there were French and relatively easy to deal with.

The Muslims who ran most of the shops were much like those in Casablanca. Algiers was quite a large city with many splendid buildings and parks. There was a huge bazaar called the Medina where anything could be purchased. Again the smells, the flies, the dirt, and the attitudes displayed by the street Muslims were less than pleasant. It took three days to load and discharge cargo, and then the ship departed for Tripoli, Libya.

As the ship proceeded along the North African coast a very scary situation developed. When the ship was rounding Cape Bon, Tunisia, it ran into a severe rain storm at noon time. I came on the bridge at about 1150 and looked at the chart in the chart room. Third mate Dixon had fixed the ship's position at 1130 and marked it on the chart. The course line laid out from that position appeared to take the ship well clear of the Isla Canni Reef. When I went into the wheel house to relieve Dixon the rain was so heavy it was not possible to even see the bow of the ship. I was surprised that the Captain was not on the bridge which is customary when the visibility is restricted. The engine room telegraph was not even on standby which is also customary. Third Mate Dixon said that the Captain was having his lunch and he did not think it was necessary to call him to the bridge for a mere rain squall. I put the engine room telegraph on standby and told Dixon to ask the Captain to come up to the bridge immediately. When Dixon left the bridge some inner sense made me feel uneasy so I changed the ship's course five more degrees to the left to allow more clearance past the reef. The rain was still coming down in torrents and after fifteen minutes the Captain was still not on the bridge. Suddenly the ship came out of the squall into bright sunlight. As the Captain came into the wheel house I walked out on the starboard wing of the bridge and looked aft. There just to the right of the ship's wake were the two huge rocks comprising the Isle of Canni reef. These buff colored rocks stood about three hundred feet above the surface of the water and did resemble a dog's canine teeth. Had I not made that course change, the S S Thomas Sim Lee would have piled up on those rocks. Needless to say, after that close call I could never trust Dixon's judgment or ability as a navigator again.

TRIPOLI

The next port of call was Tripoli, Libya. This port had a significant place in American history. In the seventeen hundreds and the early eighteen hundreds Tripoli was the major base of the Barbary pirates. They made a habit of preying on merchant ships and many European countries paid them tribute to allow their merchant vessels free passage in the Mediterranean Sea. When the Barbary pirates began preying on American merchant vessels, the United States government dispatched a squadron of ships from the fledgling U S Navy to teach the Barbary pirates a severe lesson in international diplomacy. It was a lesson well taught, and the United States became recognized as a nation to be treated with respect.

As the pilot was guiding the ship through Tripoli harbor toward our assigned berth I was at the stern with my crew to handle the mooring lines. That gave me an excellent position to view the construction of the commercial part of the port. The dock area was built over a great deal of rubble land fill. Much of this land fill appeared to be the remains of Roman columns, carved stone blocks, boulders, bricks, and rocks. A concrete apron had been build over this land fill and formed a substantial dock area. I wondered if some of that land fill were the remains of Carthage or some other ancient Roman ruin. Whatever the source of the land fill, I was sure that some of it came from a site or sites that should have been preserved for posterity.

Being on the edge of the Sahara desert, Tripoli or Tarabulus was somewhat more barren than Casablanca. It was also considerably smaller with a population of about one hundred thousand people. Most of these people were North African Arabs. There were a few Europeans who seemed to manage the cargo operations and did much of the intellectual heavy lifting. The Arab peddlers and tradesmen were even more obnoxious than those I encountered in Casablanca. There was no incentive to haggle with them over the purchase of some item because they had nothing that interested me. Cargo operations kept me busy during the day and I had no urge to go into the city after dark. Fortunately our stay there was only two days. The only regret I had leaving Tripoli was that there had been no opportunity to visit the sites of the Roman ruins in various areas around the harbor. The run along the Libyan coast to Egypt was uneventful.

ALEXANDRIA

The ship picked up a pilot outside Alexandria and entered the harbor, dropped the anchor, and lowered the gangway ladder. As the pilot departed, shore officials came aboard to clear the ship. Bum boats came alongside and a motley array of Egyptian peddlers and "businessmen" came aboard. When I went to my cabin I found two of these people sit-

ting on my settee and a third trying out my electric razor. When it comes
to sheer cheekiness, you would have to go a long way to beat an Egyptian.
These characters were trying to sell guided tours, trinkets, and souvenirs.
Peddlers were all over the ship. Anything that was not welded in place or
under lock and key just disappeared. After much effort the peddlers were
run off the ship and the gangway ladder was raised. It was necessary to
post sailors on the fore deck and the after deck to keep the peddlers from
climbing aboard by using ropes secured to grapnels. After a day or two at
anchor the ship went alongside a pier to work cargo. The British were still
somewhat in control of some of the commercial piers. A gang of German
war prisoners were brought aboard to discharge and load cargo. While
overseeing cargo operations, I struck up a conversation with one of the
prisoners, a man about thirty years of age. He had been an officer in the
German Africa Corps and spoke excellent English. It was obvious to me
that he was a well educated person and probably came from a good family.
He asked me when I thought the United States would go to war with
Russia. When I replied that the Russians were America's ally, he laughed
and said that I was very naive. Obviously he had a much more sophisticated understanding of modern history and politics than I did. It seems
that he had been captured at El-Alamein and had been a prisoner of the
British ever since. He said that the British treated him and the other prisoners well enough, but he had no idea when he would be returned to
Germany.

Alexandria was a large city with a population well over two million
people. Although there were some wealthy areas with impressive houses
and buildings, most of the city was sub standard compared to the average
American city. Many of the streets were wide and lined with shops selling
all manner of merchandise and very crowded during the daylight hours.
Buses, trucks, cars, taxis, horse or donkey drawn wagons, and push carts
were everywhere. As in the other Moslem cities I had visited, there was an
abundance of strange odors, dirt and flies. Alexandria also had an abundance of archeological and historical sites. The climate was warm, dry,
and pleasant, but most of the street people were unpleasant. There were
many young street urchins running around with shoe shine kits hustling
any non-Egyptian for business. After I just had my shoes shined by one of
them another asked if he could give me a shoe shine. When I declined he
stepped on the toe of one of my shoes with his bare heel and twisted it so
as to destroy the shine and scuff the leather of the shoe. He then ran off

shouting insults at me in Arabic. It was impossible to purchase anything without going through a process of haggling over the price. This seemed to be the standard procedure with the Moslem shopkeepers, peddlers, and taxi drivers. Some of our less than honest crewmen went into town to Mohammed Ali Square where the money changers had their sidewalk booths. There they changed a good deal of souvenir Confederate States of America paper dollars for Egyptian pounds. The Egyptian money changers were being cheated while they thought they were cheating the Americans on the rate of exchange. It is the only instance I know of where Americans got the best of the Egyptians.

One day I got off watch at 0800 and was not scheduled to go on watch again until midnight. The Radio Operator and I decided to spend the day visiting some of the sites of Alexandria. We went to the remains of a Roman bath called Pontis Pillar. While we were touring that site we met two American fellows from the embassy in Cairo. They invited us to go with them in their car to visit another historic site on the outskirts of the city, an ancient catacomb called Komo-Shu-Kaffa. This site was surrounded by a chain link fence and guarded by Egyptian soldiers. The embassy fellows parked the car outside the fence and hired the larger urchin of a group standing there to watch the car. The four of us entered the gate to the catacomb and paid the entrance fee. A couple of Egyptian soldiers approached us and asked us to surrender our cameras to them while we toured the catacomb. We refused to give up our cameras because we thought that we would never see them again. The soldiers just shrugged and walked away. The catacomb was a vertical well like shaft in the ground with a stairway carved into the side walls that spiraled down a hundred and fifty feet or more. At about every twenty feet of depth there were horizontal tunnels like the spokes of a wheel leading from the vertical shaft. These tunnels contained elaborate burial chambers. It was extremely interesting showing ancient Egyptian, Greek, and Roman art work in the different tombs. The four of us spent about two hours examining the tombs. The men from the embassy had done some research and were able to explain the significance of much of the art work we were seeing.

When we emerged from the catacomb there was an Egyptian Army officer and four soldiers waiting for us at the entrance. The officer, a lieutenant, told us that we were under arrest. They marched us around a low hill and up to a building on the top of the hill. There we were placed in a cell about twelve feet square with a narrow barred window and a heavy wooden door. For furniture the cell contained a rough wooden table, two benches, and two chairs. The soldiers confiscated our cameras before locking us in the cell. The embassy men said that this was probably a shakedown operation. We would be expected to give the soldiers a substantial bribe to release us. After about two hours an Egyptian Army Captain and two soldiers came into the cell and demanded to see our papers. The Radio Operator and I gave them our "Z" identification cards which they looked at with contempt. Then the embassy men handed the Captain their diplomatic passports. The Captain's dark countenance seemed to blanch when he looked at these documents. The embassy men said that the American embassy would raise hell over the treatment we had been shown and that someone would pay dearly for this. The Captain shouted some harsh orders at the soldiers and the three of them departed in haste. After locking the cell door, the Captain could be heard berating the soldiers as they went away down the passage. After an hour or so an Egyptian Army Colonel came into the cell with the Captain and the two soldiers and escorted the four of us to a large nicely furnished room. We were asked to be seated at a long table. The Colonel said that his soldiers had made a serious mistake and that we had been charged with espionage. This was now a diplomatic problem and that a General was on his way from Cairo to resolve the matter. They offered us coffee and soft drinks while we waited for the General to arrive. He arrived within an hour and convened an impromptu court to hear the charges. With sweat running down his cheeks the arresting Lieutenant gave his story to the General. The General, the Colonel, and the Captain interrogated the Lieutenant and spoke among themselves for several minutes. All this talk was in Arabic so we did not understand what was being said. However it appeared that the Lieutenant was in a heap of trouble.

The General informed us in English that the charges would be dropped, but that we would have to surrender the film from our cameras. He then asked the Radio Operator and me to step outside on to a balcony and wait there while he and the embassy men resolved the diplomatic issues. The Radio Operator and I were standing there alone looking down on a series if anti aircraft batteries that we had not been able to see before. I was tempted to reload my camera and take pictures of the guns to be mailed to the General after our ship had sailed, but I thought better of it. After a time we were joined with the embassy men and escorted to their car. They drove us back to the pier where our ship was berthed and told us that they were going to make a formal complaint. We thanked them for an interesting day and they invited us to visit them at the embassy in Cairo. The ship sailed for Port Said two days later and I never did get to see Cairo.

THE SUEZ CANAL

Port Said is at the Mediterranean Sea end of the Suez Canal. The ship was held up there for almost a day while a twelve ship convoy was assembled for the transit of the canal to the Red Sea. A long boat was landed on the fore deck and another long boat was landed on the aft deck using the ship's booms. Each of these boats had a four man Arab crew. A large wooden box fitted with a powerful search light was suspended over the bow and secured to the heavy bow davit. At night a man would be inside the box and he would train the beam of the search light on the navigation markers along the side of the canal. The Suez Canal is a sea level canal about one hundred miles long and about two hundred feet wide in the narrower parts. There are no locks, but there is a substantial tidal current in the canal. Ships travel through the canal in convoys. When an East bound convoy meets a West bound convoy, the one stemming the tide has to tie up to the bank to allow the other to pass. When it is necessary to tie up, the long boats are dropped in the water and their crews take hawsers from the bow and stern of the ship. They row the long boats to the bank of the canal and secure the hawsers to bollards located along the top of the bank. The banks are quite high in places. It took a full day to transit the canal from Port Said to the port of Suez. There was mostly barren desert on both sides of the canal. The town of Ismailia was located at the midway part of the canal. Mount Sinai dominated the horizon on the northern side of the canal. The long boats, the light box, and the pilot were dropped off at the port of Suez and the ship headed down the Red Sea. The original two month trip to the Mediterranean Sea was changed by the Isthmian Steamship Company. The S.S. Thomas Sim Lee was now dropping off and picking up cargo from port to port like a tramp steamer. Most of the food stores that had been taken aboard in New Orleans had been consumed by the time the ship reached Alexandria. The ship's chief steward and the local Egyptian agents restocked the ship with a food supply from various merchants in Alexandria. To say the least, this food was sub standard and often unpalatable.

The next port of call was Karachi, India. The passage through the Red

Sea and across the Arabian Gulf was hot, boring, and uneventful. The food served in the salon on board was awful. Beef stakes were so tough you would want a hack saw to cut them. The sugar in the sugar bowls was gray in color, not the normal white. Saltine crackers were infested with little brown bugs called weevils. Before eating one it was necessary to tap the edge of the cracker on the table to shake the bugs out of it. Potatoes were as small and round as golf balls and just about as hard. When you tried to stick a fork in one it would scoot across the plate. The second cook who was also the baker baked only one kind of bread. This bread was off white in color and appeared to be the baker's version of cracked wheat bread. It was fairly palatable and for many of us was the staple of our diet. One evening after supper I took a crumb of this bread and idly crushed it between my thumb and fore finger. To my surprise, instead of kernels of cracked wheat, I saw the tiny legs and body parts of the small brown bugs known as weevils. We were being fed cracked weevil bread, not cracked wheat bread. The cook was too lazy to even try to sift the weevils from the infested flour before making bread.

KARACHI

Karachi was a city of about three million people most of whom were Muslim. The city was spread out around both sides of the harbor. It was hot and untidy in places, and there were the strange unpleasant odors and flies that were so abundant in our previous ports of call. We were informed that there were significant political changes taking place in British India. The British were going to give India political independence, and the Indian subcontinent was in the process of separating into a Muslim nation and a Hindu nation. Border boundaries were being negotiated as was the date for the withdrawal of the British government and military forces. Fate had placed me in India at a time when history was being made. They use to say that the sun never sets on the British Empire, and here I was in India at twilight time for the world's greatest empire. Somehow I felt rather sad to see the jewel of the Empire revert to the control of the native politicians. I feared that British law, order, and sanitation would soon disappear. Our stay in Karachi was relatively short and most of the cargo operations were conducted during the daylight hours. The ship departed after four days and headed south down the coast of India to Bombay.

Every once in a while a person can be confronted with a problem they can not solve and are left feeling inadequate and perhaps guilty of not doing something to find a solution. On the morning of the day before the ship sailed I was confronted with such a problem. As I was standing by number four hatch observing the cargo being loaded, the gangway watchman approached me escorting a Nun and a very small boy. He told me that the Nun wanted to talk to the Captain or to one of the ship's officers. I told the Nun that the Captain was ashore and asked what I could do for her. The Nun was a young woman about twenty or twenty-five years of age. She was wearing a habit that was gray in color rather than black. With a voice that had a slight French or Italian accent she explained that she was from a Roman Catholic orphanage in Karachi. She was hoping that either I or the Captain would adopt the little boy and take him to America. The boy was about four years old and had been recently left at the orphanage when his mother died. There was no father and nothing indicating the boy's nationality. He had blond hair, blue eyes, and very fair skin. The Nun said that he was the only white child in the orphanage and she was afraid that he could not fit in with the other children. She feared for his ability to survive. In trying to find someone to take the child she was doing so without the knowledge or permission of those who were in charge of the orphanage. This small, thin Nun was showing more than a little courage in what she was trying to do.

The little boy said nothing and just kept looking down at the deck. I explained that rules and regulations as well as immigration laws would make it impossible for me or the Captain to take the boy. To do so would require going through the American Council's office and that it would take quite a while to process the paperwork. Also there was no guarantee that we would be allowed to take the boy. Furthermore the ship was scheduled to sail the next day. With a sad look on her face the Nun said that she understood and that she would try some of the British ships in the harbor. As she and boy were leaving the ship, I gave the Nun all the money I had in my pocket and wished her good luck in finding someone to take the boy out of India. Every once in a while I think of that poor little boy and wonder how he made out. There was probably more I could have done and should have done to help that child. The fact that I did not do more has always left me with a slight feeling of guilt.

BOMBAY

The harbor area of Bombay was large and part of it was a basin protected by locks because of the relatively large tidal range. The ship was berthed at a pier inside the basin. There were several other merchant vessels of various sizes berthed there, and most of them were flying the British flag. Bombay city was much larger and somewhat more cosmopolitan than Karachi. The population was about five million and was composed of a mixture of English, Hindu, Muslim, and other ethnic peoples. There were many fine buildings, houses, and parks. The Caste system was quite apparent. The population ranged from the very wealthy down to the lowly untouchable coolies. There were a large number of beggars on most of the back streets and many of them were unbelievably pathetic. Often they were small thin women with two or three small children clinging to them. On the main streets there were buses, cars, taxis, and rickshaws. The wealthier women wore fine garments called saris, and displayed a good deal of gold jewelry. Some wore a jewel on the side of their nose which was pierced as were their ears for ear rings. Coolies were the longshoremen who worked the cargo, and they appeared to own little more than the clothes on their backs. At night these coolies slept on the sidewalks of the streets around the piers. In spite of the abject poverty, there appeared to be very little crime. The police force was composed mostly of large impressive Sikhes who wore khaki uniforms and colorful turbans.

One afternoon I left the harbor area and went to a European club called Breach Kandi. After I had found a table and ordered a drink from the Indian waiter, a portly Englishman approached me. He gave me a stern look and said that this club was strictly for Europeans only. I had acquired a good tan during the voyage and he had assumed that I was at least part Indian. I told him that I was an American ship's officer and that I was just as much a Caucasian as he was. When he heard my accent he looked perplexed then shrugged and waddled back to the bar. The other Englishmen I encountered there were friendlier and apologetic for "Colonel" Blimp. After a couple of drinks, I left the club. While standing on a corner waiting for a bus to take me back to the harbor area, a fellow about my own age struck up a conversation. When he learned that I was an officer off one of the ships in the harbor, he told me that he was a lieutenant in the Royal Indian Navy. He said that he was going to the Indian Navy Officers Club in the harbor area and invited me to go along with him. I accepted his invitation. His name was Homi Driver and he did not have the rather dark complexion typical of most Indians. In fact his complexion was similar to my own. The Officer's Club was nicely furnished with a bar, a dining room, and a room with a couple of pool tables. Waiters served us drinks and we had an interesting conversation. The other officers in the club were a mixture of rather dark Indians and blond blue eyed Englishmen. For the most part they were all wearing British white tropical uniforms and ranged in rank from Ensigns to Commanders. Before I left the Officers Club, Homi asked if I would like to have dinner and take in a show with him and his fiancee the next evening. I told him that I would be delighted and he said that he would ask his fiancee to get one of her girl friends to go along as my date.

The following evening, wearing my white dress uniform, I met Homi and his fiancee as arranged at one of the hotels in town. His fiancee was a beautiful girl with very light skin and jet black hair. She wore a fashionable European style dress. Homi introduced me to his fiancee and her girl friend who was to be my date for the evening. The girl friend was as dark as any Indian woman and was wearing a green sari with gold and silver trim and jewelry that must have cost a king's ransom. We had an outstanding dinner at a very nice restaurant and then went to a theater to see an up to date English language film. My date was charming, well educated, and very interesting. I learned that Homi and the ladies were Parsees, or Zoroastrians, one of the minor religious ethnic groups in India. The Parcees came from ancient Persia and follow a religion of Sun worship. It was soon obvious that my companions were part of the upper class of Indian society. Both girls had been educated in England and were excited about the political changes happening in India. They felt that independence would be good, but they were a little apprehensive about the partition of India and the problems that would cause. I had only one more opportunity to spend an evening with my new friends. They made my visit to Bombay a very pleasant experience. While in Bombay I received mail from my parents and I was glad to learn that all was well at home. Although I had mailed letters to Gloria from each of the previous ports of call, there was no mail from her. I wondered if this could be an example of "out of sight, out of mind."

The ship departed Bombay and proceeded down the Indian coast bound for the port city of Colombo in Ceylon. On the way to Colombo some of the crew related their experiences while ashore in Bombay. They bragged about a part of the "Red Light District" called the "Cages." There prostitutes were available for one Rupee a throw. A Rupee is worth about twenty cents in U. S. money. Naturally some of the crew took advantage of such bargain prices. The salon mess man spent most of his time ashore at the "Cages." I cringed when I thought of him handling my food. Sure enough, half way to Colombo he developed the signs of having gonorrhea. He was well on his way to becoming a "real seaman" in accordance with his criteria. The Captain asked the Chief Steward to assign someone else to be the salon mess man, and to assign the infected mess man to duties that did not include any handling of food. This was just the beginning. Before the ship reached the pilot station for Colombo, five more of this illustrious crew developed the symptoms for gonorrhea or syphilis or both. One of this number was the new salon mess man and the Captain told the Chief Steward to provide another replacement. Food preparation on this voyage was bad at the start and became worse as the voyage wore on. That coupled with the possibility of picking up some vile disease from the food handlers made my meals less than a pleasant experience. The Captain assigned me the duty of treating the infected crewmen with the limited medical supplies carried in the ship's sick bay. The standard book, "Ships Medicine Chest And First Aid At Sea," provided the only guide for treating venereal disease. There was a small supply of penicillin and a somewhat larger supply of sulfa-thiazole for treating gonorrhea and syphilis. Every morning before lunch, I would line up my six patients and give each one of them a shot of penicillin in their backsides with a hypodermic needle. After a couple of days the symptoms of their infections disappeared, but I knew that they were still infected. Even though they were warned to be careful, some of them availed themselves of the pleasures provided by the prostitutes in the next port. The teenage mess man was one of them.

COLOMBO

Colombo was a much smaller city than Bombay and the largest city in Ceylon. It had a population of about a half a million people that were an almost fifty-fifty mixture of Hindu and Moslem. The harbor was small but well appointed with piers and facilities to repair ships. The ship spent three days in this port discharging and loading cargo. Several tons of tea as well as other cargo were loaded aboard. Ceylon is a source of a variety of precious and semiprecious jewels. These were available in great abundance in many of the shops in town. Most of the shops were run by Muslims and it was necessary to haggle over the price of any stone or piece of jewelry you wanted to buy. If the shop keeper thought you were a serious customer, he would ask you to sit at a table with him and discuss the value and the price of a jewel, a broach, or a ring. Tea or soft drinks were usually offered and you were expected to spend at least a half hour haggling over the price. It must have been a type of entertainment for the shop keepers. I bought a few stones and a couple of rings for gifts when I returned home. The ship's supply of penicillin was getting low and I knew that what little we had left would soon be exhausted. I was not able to get any more in Colombo. It just was not available. Knowing the careless attitude of this crew, there was no doubt in my mind that there would be additional cases of venereal disease needing treatment.

MADRAS

The ship departed Colombo and headed on a northerly course to Madras. When we arrived the pilot directed us to an anchorage where we remained to discharge and load cargo. Madras had a population of about two million people most of whom were Hindu. I did not get ashore there nor did most of the crew. The ship never went alongside a pier while we were in Madras. Instead barges were brought alongside by tug boats, and other boats brought out gangs of longshoremen. Every morning around 0700 the longshoremen would come aboard and a gang of them would form up by each of the ship's five hatches. They would stand around until their foremen told them to uncover the hatches and get the deck gear ready to work cargo. It was usually 0800 before cargo operations started. Loading from barges and discharging into barges was a slow process. With at least a hundred native longshoremen on board and an equal number working the barges, the ship seemed to be over run with Indians. Cabin doors and port holes had to be closed and locked to prevent pilferage of their contents. The daytime heat of the Indian sun turned the ship's living spaces into a sauna.

At the end of the first day of cargo operations, the Chief Engineer complained that all of the brass hose nozzles for the fire hoses at the deck fire stations were missing. Also the brass screw plugs for the sounding tubes were missing. There were two sounding tubes for each hatch that led from the main deck down to the "rose box" sump wells in the aft end of each lower hold. It seems that while the longshoremen were standing around on the main deck, they would use their toes to unscrew the brass plugs and then deftly hide them in their garments. The next morning I saw the Chief Engineer and one of his Assistant Engineers on the main deck just before the longshoremen came aboard. They had a blow torch and were applying considerable heat to the sounding tube plug at number three hatch. They joined me on the boat deck as the longshoremen came on board. We watched the mingling crowd as one of them sauntered over toward the heated sounding plug. He looked around and when he thought no one was watching, he stuck his big toe on the plug preparing to unscrew it. We were pleased to see him jump about three feet in the air and then go bouncing up the deck on one foot while holding the other in his hands and cursing loudly. The missing sounding tube plugs and fire hose nozzles were not replaced until the ship was clear of Madras and well out to sea.

CALCUTTA

From Madras the ship proceeded up the East coast of India in the Bay of Bengal to the mouth of the Hooghly river. We picked up a pilot and proceeded ninety miles up the Hooghly river to the city of Calcutta. The Hooghly river is about ten miles wide at its mouth and is one of the main tributaries of the Ganges river. Tidal effects are felt from its mouth to well over a hundred miles up stream. The color of the water in the river reminded me of the color of the water in the Delaware river back home, a dirty brown color. The ship went directly to one of the docks on the side of the river in Calcutta. As Second Mate my station was at the stern with a crew of four seamen when the ship was docking. While I was supervising the securing of mooring lines from the stern to the dock, one of the seamen called to me to look over the off shore side of the stern. There in the water just under the counter of the stern was a sight that I shall never forget. The body of a man, belly up was floating in the water swirling around in the wash of the propeller. His belly and testicles were swollen like balloons and his head and feet were submerged. His legs were bent is if he had been in a sitting position when he died. That was not all. Standing on his belly there was a huge black carrion crow pecking away at the belly. I cringed at the thought that the pecking of the crow might cause the swollen belly to explode. When the lines were secured I went to the bridge to report the dead man in the water to the Captain and the Pilot. The Pilot put his hand on my shoulder and said, "Son you are going to see many bodies in that river, there is hell to pay in India just now."

Calcutta was a city with a population of about five million people. There were many fine buildings and parks as well as an impressive monument to Queen Victoria. The main commercial street was Charinghi street where there were a variety of stores, office buildings, restaurants, and theaters. The native Indian population was composed of both Hindu and Moslem people. British troops and Indian police were maintaining law and order with some difficulty. The political partition of an independent India was in full swing and there was savage rivalry between the Hindus and Moslems. Gangs of either of these religions would prey upon single members of the other religion when they came upon them in the streets and beat them severely or even kill them. The situation became so bad that the British authorities declared a curfew and armored cars patrolled the streets after dark. One could walk along most of the city streets in relative safety in daylight hours, but wandering the streets at night time was dangerous. I only saw two kinds of birds in Calcutta. Black carrion crows were every where. There was also an abundance of gray brown vultures about the size of the pigeons that are found in many American cities. I could only imagine what these birds were feeding on. Cargo operations were slow and conducted only in daylight hours. The port agent said that the ship would probably be in Calcutta for three or four weeks. A rather macabre ritual developed with the ship's officers. In the early morning we would gather on the off shore side of the ship and count the number of dead bodies that were floating by with the out going tide. There were usually at least a half dozen bodies, the result of the previous nights religious fighting. After a half hour of body counting we would go into the ship's salon for the customary unpalatable breakfast.

One of the port officials recommended a couple of good restaurants to me. One restaurant named Firpos provided outstanding pastries as well as a fairly good cuisine. He also told me about the British and American Officers Club. This was a private club that was owned and operated by an English businessman. Membership was open to American and British officers including merchant ship officers. There was a small monthly fee for membership that I was more than happy to pay. The club was located in a nice building in the better part of Calcutta and had a bar, a lounge, and a beautiful dining room with a dance floor. Lunch and dinner were available daily in the dining room where the tables were served by a retinue of uniformed waiters. During the evening hours there were several hostesses in evening gowns who were available as dinner and dance partners. A ten piece orchestra provided dance music from seven PM till midnight. The hostesses were beautiful young polished Anglo-Indian women. Several were students at Calcutta University. They looked like European women and one would never think that they were half or part Indian. Apparently the Anglo-Indians were not fully accepted in the British/European society or the upper cast Indian society. Most were Christians if they professed any religion at all. They made entertaining dinner companions and pleasant dance partners—but that was all. As employees of the club they were there only to entertain the member officers. Any extracurricular hanky panky outside the club would result in their immediate disgrace and dismissal. The club was run in a very formal and proper manner. Most of the members were British Army officers with a few officers from the Naval and Merchant vessels in the port.

Shipboard routine required that I stand the four to midnight watch every third night. That left me free to have my supper at the club those other two evenings. I would usually arrive at the club at six o'clock and have a drink at the bar. Then I would have dinner in the dining room. If any of the hostesses were available, I would usually invite one or two of them to join me for dinner. After dinner the time was spent in pleasant conversation with a few drinks and dancing. One hostess named Penny could have been a stand in for the movie actress Ava Gardiner. She tried to teach me how to tango with some little success. The food served at the club was excellent and I usually ordered a steak with all the trimmings. It was a tremendous relief from the terrible food served on the ship. One evening after I had consumed a particularly delicious steak, I asked the waiter to give the cook my compliments. He left the table and a short time later returned to tell me that the cook appreciated my compliments and invited me to visit his galley. Out of curiosity and a desire to not offend the cook, I followed the waiter to the cook's domain. Cooking and food preparation was done in an open court yard behind the club building. The cook, a Muslim Indian, greeted me warmly and led me over to a large stove and oven made of buff colored bricks. There were iron grills on one end beneath which fiercely hot orange coals were burning. Several stakes were cooking on the grill. The coals were unusual. They were not wood or charcoal or any fuel I could recognize. I asked the cook what he was using for fuel. He said that he used dried cow dung and pointed to a large wooden box nearby which was half full of dried cow flops. He then went on to say that the fumes form the burning dung enhanced the flavor of the steaks. It occurred to me that it is not always wise to see how one's food is prepared. The method of preparing the steaks for the table did not deter me for I continued enjoying a good steak dinner every evening I was able to.

After three weeks of dining at the club I got to know most of the hostesses rather well. It was December 1946 and one of them, a girl named Brenda, invited me to spend Christmas with her and her family at their tea plantation in Darjeeling. Her father was a retired British Army Colonel and her mother was an Anglo-Indian. Brenda was a very attractive girl about nineteen years of age with light brown hair and blue eyes. She was a student at Calcutta University in her junior year. Brenda said that she had told her parents about me and that they were looking forward to meeting me. I could not help wandering if she had some long range plans for me. Although I was greatly tempted to accept her invitation, Darjeeling was a long way from Calcutta and sailing time for the ship was not far off. I thanked Brenda for the invitation and told her that I would be delighted to visit her home and meet her parents, but that it would be impossible for me to get enough time off my shipboard duties to do so. Seeing her disappointment, I promised to make every effort to visit her home in Darjeeling the next time my ship got to Calcutta.

One day about mid way through our stay in Calcutta, a harbor pilot came aboard and said that the ship would have to leave the dock and tie up between two buoys in the river. The mooring lines were cast off the dock and with the help of two tug boats, the ship was positioned between two buoys and secured to them with doubled up mooring lines. We were informed that a tidal bore was due to pass through Calcutta harbor later in the day. Just about at sundown we saw the water level along the shore line and the docks rise about twenty feet in less than two minutes. A tidal bore is a phenomenon found in certain rivers and estuaries around the world. It is an exceptionally high tidal wave that travels from the mouth of the river up stream to a point where it dissipates. Although tidal bores do not occur on a monthly basis, they can be predicted. It was necessary to pull our ship away from the dock because the rapid rise of the water level would have parted the mooring lines and resulted in damage to both the ship and the dock. The level of the river remained high for about a half an hour and then slowly subsided. There was some minor flooding on the opposite bank of the river but there was no appreciable damage because the tidal bore had been expected.

During one of my daytime wanderings along the streets of Calcutta window shopping and making an occasional purchase here and there, I was confronted by a Fakir with a monkey on his shoulder and accompanied by two attendants. The Fakir and his attendants wore turbans and white robes that were clean and better looking than the clothing of the usual street Indians. The Fakir told me that he would tell me my fortune for five Rupees. Without any warning, the monkey jumped on my shoulder. Alarmed and annoyed, I told the Fakir to get his monkey off of me and that I did not believe in fortune tellers. Somewhat angered by my response, the Fakir put his face close to mine and said, "I will tell you this much. You believe that you are going to marry a woman with blond hair, but that will not happen. You will marry a woman with dark hair." He then turned and walked away with his monkey and his two disciples. Later I had reason to think that perhaps the Fakir really could see into the future. I received mail from home, and wonder of wonders, there was also a letter from Gloria. That letter was disappointing to say the least. A six year old girl could have written a letter that made more sense. It rambled on for a page and a half and essentially said nothing. There was no indication that she missed me or that I had been away too long, and this was the girl that I was unofficially engaged to. I wrote letters to my parents, to Gloria, and to Anita, the college girl I had been introduced to on the Long Island Rail Road.

The ship took on a load of jute and jute products, cotton textiles, boxes of tea and similar general cargo. A day before Christmas, with a full load of cargo, the S S Thomas Sim Lee cast off the mooring lines at the dock in Calcutta and with a pilot on board headed down the Hooghly river. At last after a full month in Calcutta, we were heading home. The ship's laundry had been cleaned ashore prior to our departure. At the end of my evening watch on the first day out, I washed my face using one of the newly cleaned towels before hitting the sack. When I was awakened twenty minutes before four in the morning to take my next watch, my eyes were bloodshot with puss like mucous in the corners. My vision was so impaired that it would not be safe for me to take the watch. I alerted the Captain to my problem and he stood my watch with me. I bathed my eyes with boric acid every hour and was seriously worried that I might be going blind. There was no way of knowing what type of infection I had picked up from the towel. For the next three days the Captain stood my watches with me. On the third day my vision improved to the point where I could stand my watches alone. My eyes remained bloodshot for another week or so, but there seemed to be no lingering bad effects. That had been quite a scare.

We were unable to get any penicillin or other medicines for the ship's medicine chest before departing Calcutta. For treating the seamen with venereal diseases, I had only the remaining supply of sulfa-thiazole. There were now eight seamen with venereal disease infections. One of the younger of them had an unusual infection. He first reported that he had a chancre on his penis which was a sure sign of his having contracted syphilis. After a few days of treatment with sulfa-thiazole the chancre grew larger and went deeper into the flesh of his penis. Nothing worked to arrest the infection. The sore continued to grow larger and deeper. All that could be done was to put dressings on the lesion and put the seaman on restricted duty. There was nothing in the ship's medicine book that described or identified his infection. With only a brief stop in Suez on the schedule for the return voyage, there would be no professional medical treatment available until the ship reached New Orleans. By the time the ship reached New Orleans, the infection had eaten almost half way through the diameter of his penis.

One afternoon on the voyage home as I was taking an altitude of the sun with my sextant, my able seaman, Ted Ross, asked me how difficult it would be for him to learn navigation. He said that he would like to become a licensed ship's officer one day. Ross was always reliable and a good seaman. I loaned him some of my text books, *Duttons Practical Navigation*, *Farwells Rules Of the Road*, *Knights Modern Seamanship* and *The Merchant Officers Handbook*, and offered to tutor him through any of the subjects he found difficult. He studied diligently and required relatively little tutoring. I taught him how to use a sextant and recommended the subjects he should put extra effort into learning. I also told him that when he got back to New York he should enroll in one of the schools that prepare candidates for taking the license examination.

Since the Greek Second Engineer and I shared the same watch, we often spent some of our off watch hours discussing various topics. His English was not too good and most of the other officers avoided having long conversations with him. During one of our conversations he produced a photograph from his pocket and handed it to me. It was a picture of a very pretty young blond woman. He said that it was a picture of his daughter, and that he would like to have me meet her. She lived at his home in Greece, and had gone through the finest schools. Since I was single, he thought that I would make an ideal husband for her. That was quite a compliment and I told him that I would be pleased to meet her some time.

NEW ORLEANS AT LAST

It took almost seven weeks to make the passage from Calcutta to New Orleans. I continued treating the seamen with venereal diseases until the supply of sulfa-thiazole was exhausted. With the exception of the one seaman, most of the symptoms of the diseases these seamen had disappeared, but they were not cured. They were informed that they were still infected and contagious and that they should go to the Marine Hospital for treatment when we reached New Orleans. To the best of my knowledge, the only one who went immediately to the hospital was the one who had the huge open lesion on his penis. The ship docked in New Orleans on 17 February 1947, and sea watches were broken. As soon as the ship was cleared for the port, cargo operations were begun. Two days later a Federal Shipping Commissioner came aboard with agents from the Isthmian Line and the foreign articles were broken. Everyone was paid off for the voyage and most of the crew quickly disappeared. Ross made a point of thanking me for the help I had given him and said that he was going to New York and enroll in a license preparation school as soon as possible. The Third Mate, Dixon, said good by and that he was going home to Washington, D.C. My old friend, the Second Engineer, left as well and I never saw him again. The Chief Mate and I signed on coastwise articles and remained on board to oversee the discharge of the cargo. Longshoremen worked the cargo around the clock and completed discharging it in five days. At last during this time it was possible to go ashore and get some decent palatable food to eat and I took as many meals as I could ashore.

One morning during a break in discharging cargo, I went into the salon and poured myself a cup of coffee. When I was half way through the cup of coffee, two well dressed and attractive women came into the salon. Both of them were blondes and appeared to be in their early thirties. One of them introduced herself as Captain Howard's wife and said that the other woman was her sister. They were waiting for Captain Howard to return to the ship from the pier office. I poured a cup of coffee for each of them and refilled my cup. After a few minutes Mrs. Howard gave me a rather stern look and asked, "Did my husband have any women visitors on board when the ship was in India?" Both women looked at me expectantly awaiting my reply. The question was a complete surprise. I looked at Mrs. Howard for a full minute, then I replied, "Do you make a habit of asking such questions of Captain Howard's officers?" Before she could answer, I excused myself, placed my cup on the side board, and left the salon. The two of them looked somewhat disappointed and annoyed with my response. As I walked back out on to the main deck I could not help wondering what those two were up to. Captain Howard was a good decent man and here he had a wife that was looking for something she could use against him. Perhaps she was looking for some grounds to start a divorce action, or maybe she was just looking for some ammunition so that she could give him a bad time. It was obvious that her sister was there to cheer her on. I also wondered what Mrs. Howard had been up to while the Captain was away on a voyage for over six months. Had she been unfaithful herself, or was she just a conniving witch looking for alimony? Whatever the case might be, I felt sorry for Captain Howard, and realized even more so how important it was for a professional seaman to be careful choosing a partner for life.

GALVESTON AND HOUSTON

The Isthmian Line agents said that the ship was scheduled to sail immediately for Texas. There was still a shortage of licensed officers and they were unable to find a replacement for Dixon to fill the Third Mate's slot. However, they were able to fill the crew berths with seamen from the NMU hall. The Chief Mate and I had to stand watches of six hours on and six hours off on the run from New Orleans to Galveston. Shortly after the ship was moored to the pier in Galveston, Captain James Whitcomb Riley, the Isthmian Line port captain came aboard. He was officious to the point of rudeness and I took an immediate dislike of him. He informed us that the ship would load some cargo in Galveston and then proceed to Houston to top off the cargo. The crew would sign on foreign articles in Houston and sail from there to Europe. The hatches were opened and several thousand tons of sulfur were loaded aboard. Loading the sulfur took two days. The hatches were covered, a pilot came aboard, tug boats came alongside and the ship cast off from the pier. The run from Galveston up the ship canal to Houston took only a few hours. The ship tied up to a dock in the Houston harbor basin and the hatches were made ready to load more cargo. The port captain, Captain Riley was annoyed when I informed him that I was not going to sign on for the next voyage. I signed off the coastwise articles on 24 February and left the ship. I had been aboard the S.S. Thomas Sim Lee for seven months and could not stand the thought of signing on for another voyage. After seven months of rotten food, seamen with venereal diseases, swatting flies, and working in tropical heat, I was a mental basket case in need of rest and a change of scene. I made arrangements to fly home the next day and checked into a hotel for some much needed rest.

Arriving back home mid-week, I decided to take a day or two to unwind and get myself back on an even keel. I called Gloria's home to learn where she was and one of her sisters told me that she was now at a hospital in Greenwich, Connecticut and gave me a phone number for her. It was a Friday afternoon when I finally got Gloria on the phone and she was cool and evasive. She said that her duties kept her too busy to see anyone right now. The next day I called her number again and was informed that she had gone home for the weekend. When I called her home she answered the phone. I asked why she had not told me that she was going to be home for the weekend. She replied that what she did with her time was none of my business and that she did not wish to be bothered by any more phone calls from me. This response took me completely by surprise. I told her that I was sorry and that I did not realize that my phone calls were a bother to her, and that I would not bother her again. Her rather nasty attitude reminded me of how she often responded with a haughty disdainful attitude when I tried to start a conversation with her during our years in high school. Undoubtedly, Gloria had become involved with someone else while I was away for the past seven months, and probably felt that a quick brush off was the best way to handle me. That settled my dilemma with Gloria and I decided that I would leave her permanently in my wake. While in Calcutta I had purchased a silver compact in one of the better jewelry stores on Charinghi street and had it engraved with Gloria's initials. I wrapped it up with a short letter and mailed it to her. In the letter I told her that I would not bother her again and would like her to accept the compact as a farewell gift with my best wishes. That was the last communication I ever had with Gloria.

Some of my high school buddies were home and I spent a few days visiting with them. My parents and I made a trip to Philadelphia to visit with my uncle Jim and aunt Edith and my cousins. When we returned to Long Island, I learned that my classmates from Fort Schuyler, Dick Kadison and Bill Ryan were home again. I lost no time getting in touch with them and for the next week split my time visiting Dick in New York and Bill in Garden City. They were both back in school working to finish their under graduate degree programs. We spent many hours exchanging stories of our adventures since our graduation back in June of 1945. The Maritime

Commission was running a LORAN and RADAR school in Brooklyn that was available to licensed merchant marine officers free of charge. I signed up for that school and spent two weeks commuting from Central Islip on the Long Island railroad to attend the school. On several of my morning trips into the city I ran into Anita, the girl Danny had introduced me to many months ago. She would usually sit with me on the ride in, and we discussed various topics of interest. I asked her if Danny was still commuting and she said that because of class schedules she did not see him very often. Then I asked her if they were going steady, or did she have any other steady boyfriend. She said that Danny was just a friend and that she did go out with him occasionally as she did with other men. She had no serious attachments and was not looking for any. Anita also said that she worked part time at the Macys department store on 34th street in Manhattan.

One Friday as we were commuting on the train, I asked Anita if she would go out with me the following Saturday night and She said no. When I asked why not she said she already had a commitment. I asked her what one had to do to get a date with her. She replied that one would have to ask at least a week in advance. I asked her to reserve the next Saturday night for me, but she would not make a commitment. A few days later as we were riding on the train she agreed to go out with me, and I arranged to pick her up at Macys at six o'clock Saturday. Stupidly I waited for her at the wrong door and after a half an hour had passed, I figured that she had stood me up. As I was walking down the stairway to the subway station, I saw Anita heading for the other stairway to the subway. She thought that I had stood her up. I caught up with her and explained the mistake. A friend had recommended Zimmermans restaurant as a place to get a really good meal, so I took her there. It was a terrible mistake. The head waiter placed us at a table by the swinging doors to the kitchen. These doors kept banging throughout our dinner, and the dinner was as bad as its cost was outrageous. We went to a movie after the dinner and then I escorted her home to Brentwood. Feeling that the evening had been a disaster, I asked her if I could have another chance the next Saturday. To my surprise she said yes. This time I met her on time at the right exit. I had made reservations at the Town and Country Club, an up scale restaurant on Park avenue, and we had an excellent dinner. After dinner we went to see the Broadway show Sweethearts, for which I had previously purchased tickets. Later when I dropped her off at her home in Brentwood I knew that this date had been a success. Many evenings I would go up town after class and spend some time with Dick Kadison as I had before starting school. He introduced me to some of his friends and we often wound up at impromptu cocktail parties in one apartment or another. Two of his friends, Ira and his girlfriend Jane, became especially friendly, and I found myself in their company quite often. Some evenings we would visit various supper clubs in Greenwich Village.

THE NORTH ATLANTIC RUN

I made a call to Boland and Cornelius and spoke to Mr. King. He wanted to know what had happened to me, because I had been expected to return to Boland and Cornelius when I got out of the Hospital. After I brought Mr. King up to date on my Far East trip and the LORAN and RADAR school, he asked me to come into the office and see him when I finished school. When I visited the Boland and Cornelius office a week later I was welcomed like the Prodigal Son. Captain Beauvoise and Captain Burk were extremely cordial and Mr. King insisted on taking me to lunch. During lunch Mr. King informed me that he was preparing to put a team of officers together for a ship the company was getting ready to put into operation. He asked me to report to his office the next day for an assignment and said that he had a surprise for me. On the Monday morning following my completion of the LORAN and RADAR course I reported to the office of Boland and Cornelius and Mr. King. He told me that the company was outfitting and crewing the ship he had mentioned in Baltimore, Maryland for the European trade. The surprise was that the Chief Mate on this ship was to be my old friend John Ciccosanti. This was great news. Mr. King said that he was going to assign me as Second Mate, and that I should plan to report aboard the ship within a week. He said that he had not selected a Third Mate yet, and if I knew anyone looking for such a berth to bring him to the office. Mr. King said that he tried to crew the company's ships with competent men who were also compatible. As I left the companies office and was walking toward the subway station, I saw Ted Ross coming towards me. We shook hands and I asked him how things were going. He told me that he had just gotten his Third Mate's license. In a rather sad and hopeless voice he said that he thought it would be very hard to get a Third Mate's berth. I told him to come with me, and I took him to the Boland and Cornelius office and introduced him to Mr. King. Upon my recommendation, Mr. King gave Ross the assignment as Third Mate.

THE S S FRANCIS A. RETKA

The word was passed to my family and friends that I was shipping out again and would be gone for quite a while. About mid week, I reported aboard the S S Francis A. Retka in Baltimore. She was at a berth in the Todd shipyard. It was great seeing John (Chico) Ciccosanti again, and I filled him in on my adventures during my second voyage on the S S Patrick C. Boyle. The ship's boatswain and two seamen from the previous voyage's crew were still on board. The next day Chico left the ship and went into town to take care of some business and left me in charge. There was a commotion in the boatswain's cabin on the main deck. When I went to investigate I saw the boatswain on the deck with a bloody face. One of the able seamen, a big tough character, had just thrown several punches at the boatswain. In a drunken rage this seaman proceeded to walk down the companion way kicking out the escape panels on each of the cabin doors as he passed them. I ran after him and ordered him to stop. He turned on me, grabbed me by the front of my shirt and lifted me off my feet and against the bulkhead. As he pulled back his fist to hit me, I said, "Striking an officer gets you ten years in a federal pen and I will see you spend every minute of it." He put his fist down and released me while mouthing threats and curses about officers. The other seaman, a short fellow who was obviously his buddy joined him in making threats, and the two went into the crew's mess room. After seeing to the needs of the boatswain, I called the shipyard's security office on the shore phone and told them what had happened and that I needed help right away. Within minutes a patrol car pulled up to the gangway and two of the biggest uniformed guards I have ever seen came aboard. They asked where the trouble makers were, and when they confronted the big one, he was as meek as a lamb. He was a drunken bully and a coward to boot. They hand cuffed the pair and dragged them down to their patrol car, and told me they were taking them to the jail. I told them I would be along later to press charges. When Chico returned we assessed the damages and reported what had happened to the company agents. The next day I went to the court house with one of the agents. A Magistrate heard the charges against the two seamen. He ordered them to pay for the damages as well as a fine for disturbing the peace. They were then released and ordered not to go near the ship again.

Ted Ross reported aboard the following Monday as did the NMU crew. The company's agents, port captain, and the Shipping Commis-

S S Francis A. Retka
Hull No. 3091, Liberty Type Cargo Vessel, Boland & Cornelius

sioner came aboard the following day to process the signing of the foreign articles. The date was 15 April 1947. The S S Francis A. Retka, hull No. 3091, had just been given a fresh coat of paint. Unlike the battleship gray of the war time liberty ships, her hull was painted black, the superstructure was white, and the black smoke stack had the company's colors, bands of silver red and silver. She was one of the later built liberty ships and was in a relatively good condition. There was some concern expressed about the Second Mate from the previous voyage who was missing. He was a Norwegian who had been signed on to replace the American Second Mate when that fellow had to be rushed to a hospital in Norway with appendicitis. The last time the Norwegian was seen was when he went ashore one evening with the two seamen trouble makers. They had all just been paid off as the articles for the previous voyage were broken. Some of the Norwegian's belongings were still on board, and they were packed up and sent to the agent's office for disposition. The day after the signing of the articles for the next voyage, the ship was moved from the shipyard to the coal pier in Baltimore harbor. For the next three days a full cargo of industrial coal was loaded aboard. The fuel tanks were topped off, and stores for the voyage were brought aboard.

A docking pilot and a Chesapeake Bay pilot came aboard, the mooring lines were cast off, and two tug boats helped to get the ship away from the pier. The docking pilot departed with the tug boats, and the Bay pilot took over guiding the ship 150 miles down the Chesapeake bay. The pilot got off at the Cape Henry pilot station, and the S S Francis A. Retka was set on a course for Aarhus, Denmark. Unlike the crew of S S Thomas Sim Lee, this crew was a mixture of white, black, and oriental seamen. The First Assistant Engineer was a man in his late twenties with a happy-go lucky attitude. The other Assistant Engineers were also men under thirty years of age. Chico, the Chief Mate, predicted that this would be a good trip because we had Chinese cooks on board, and the Chief Steward was a no-nonsense man from Jamaica. Chico was right. The food on this ship was the best I had experienced thus far on a merchant ship. At supper one evening the Negro salon mess man served me a steak that was over done and almost too tough to cut. Seeing this, the Chief Steward grabbed the mess man by his ear and pulled him from the salon while telling him never to serve Mr. Murray a steak like that again. The Chief Steward kept everyone in his department on their toes, and he made sure that the living quarters were immaculate.

The passage to Aarhus was pleasant with good weather all the way. A pilot was picked up at the entrance of the Skagerak, and he guided the ship to the port of Aarhus on the East side of the Jutland peninsula. With the aid of two tug boats the ship was eased to a pier in Aarhus harbor and the mooring lines were made fast. Danish officials came aboard to clear the ship and grant pratique, the privilege of being allowed to go ashore. I went on the pier to read the ship's draft at the bow and the stern. This was done so that the amount of fuel consumed on the passage from Baltimore could be determined. As I was jotting down the draft at the stern on a note pad, an attractive girl, about nineteen or twenty years of age, came over to me on her bicycle. In perfect English, she said hello and asked where the ship had come from. I told her that we had come directly from Baltimore and then I asked her about Aarhus and what places of interest there were to visit. She said that most American seamen seemed to like the Moritza, a bar and restaurant in town, there were bathing beaches, and a modern museum on the outskirts of the city. Aarhus was the second largest city in Denmark with a population of about a half a million people. We exchanged names. She said that her name was Sonia Johansen. After our brief conversation, Sonia left the pier on her bicycle. When I went back on board the ship, I made a full report of my conversation with Sonia. Chico and the First Assistant Engineer decided that the three of us should pay a visit to the Moritza that evening. Longshoremen came aboard, the cargo hatches were opened, and the discharge of our cargo of coal was begun. The local ship's agents informed us that we would probably be in port for a week or more because the cargo would only be discharged during daylight hours.

After our evening meal, Chico, the Assistant Engineer, and I got a taxi at the head of the pier and went to the Moritza. The entrance way in the Moritza led to a ball room through a long bar with a row of tables opposite the bar. As we entered, I saw Sonia seated at one of the tables with two other young women. She beckoned us to come over and she introduced her two girl friends. After a round of drinks were served, the six of us went into the ball room sat at a table there. A band was playing popular music and we spent the evening dancing between rounds of drinks. We had a very pleasant evening, and before we left the Moritza, I made a date to meet Sonia there the next evening and have dinner with her. The following day after the cargo operations were shut down, I put on my shore side clothes and took a taxi to the Moritza. Sonia was waiting for me and I asked her to select a nice restaurant for dinner. She recommended a place called the Varna over looking the water. We took a taxi there and I found the Varna a very nice up scale place. During dinner a group of three musicians toured among the tables pausing at each table for a brief period while they played their songs. The dinner was excellent, and afterward Sonia and I walked along the beach in bright moon light. Sonia was not the least bit shy. She responded to my embrace and we kissed like long lost lovers. That evening seemed to end too soon as I dropped Sonia off at her home and then had the taxi return me to the ship. The watch schedule on the ship was set up so that each mate took a turn covering the midnight to eight watch. That allowed me to have two nights off in a row which I spent with Sonia. Most evenings we would have dinner at the Varna between eight and nine o'clock which is the customary European time for dinner. On one occasion during the day, Sonia took me on a walking tour of an out door museum which was a restored medieval Viking village. Another time we visited the castle which was the setting for Shakespeare's play, Hamlet Prince of Denmark. We also went to a bathing beach where the women bathers out numbered the men by at least twenty to one. Sonia went into the icy water which was far too cold for me, so I just reclined on the beach and took in the scenery. The ship's ten day stay in Aarhus ended when the last of the cargo was discharged. Sonia said that she would keep in touch with me and was looking forward to my return on the next voyage. She was on the pier waving good by as the tug boats pulled the ship away from the berth.

The ship departed Aarhus and set a course for the port of Narvik above the Arctic Circle in Norway. As the ship proceeded on a northerly course up the coast of Norway the daylight hours became longer each day. When the ship reached the mouth of the Ofoten Fjord, a pilot was taken aboard for the run up to Narvik. The scenery was spectacular. Snow capped mountains rose up from the water's edge several thousand feet into the sky. The depth of the water was over a thousand feet. At one point during our passage the pilot pointed to what appeared to be a house high up on the steep side of a mountain. He told us that it was the bridge house of a German freighter that a British destroyer had sunk during a raid on Narvik. The German crew and the prisoners they were carrying were taken off the ship before the British blew the ship up. When our ship reached the harbor of Narvik, the pilot guided us carefully to an anchorage area. This anchorage area was a shelf the edges of which fell off to a great depth. I

Second Mate Art Murray
S S Francis A. Retka

took a series of bearings and plotted them on the chart. When the pilot was satisfied that we were in position, he told the Chief Mate to drop the anchor. To our dismay and horror, the anchor hit the water and the chain ran out as usual, but it ran all the way out and over board. We lost the anchor and twenty shots of anchor chain because the ship was not on the shelf. Somewhat embarrassed, the pilot guided the ship further into the harbor and the second anchor was dropped this time on the shelf. A short time later port officials and the agent came aboard to clear the ship and grant pratique.

NARVIK

Narvik was a quaint little town with a few shops, a couple of restaurants, a fish processing plant, and a large pier. The pier had a large structure for handling the major export, iron ore. There was a rail line that ran from Sweden to carry the iron ore to the pier. After two days at anchor, the ship went alongside the pier and started to load iron ore. This ore was light gray in color, very heavy, and highly magnetic. It had to be loaded with great care in order to avoid buckling the tween decks in each hatch. A small pile of iron ore in the bottom of each hold and a smaller pile in each of the tween decks brought the ship down to her marks. Loading the ore took two and a half days. One day Ted and I took a walk into town to do some window shopping and have a look around. We struck up a conversation with two young women clerks in one of the stores. They agreed to meet us that evening and show us around Narvik. After supper Ted and I met the girls and went on a walking tour of the town. We stopped at a small eatery and had some pastries and coffee. At about eleven o'clock we escorted the girls to their home and the sun was still shining. It was June and we were above the Arctic Circle. We thanked the girls for the tour and returned to the ship. The closest thing to a sunset was when the sun dipped behind a mountain top for a few minutes. Before sailing, the Chinese cooks went to the local fish market and purchased the largest halibut I have ever seen. It took the two of them to carry it back to the ship for it must have weighed more than a hundred pounds. I had a halibut steak for supper every night on the return voyage to Baltimore.

The voyage back to Baltimore was uneventful. The ship picked up a pilot at the entrance to the Chesapeake Bay and proceeded to the Bethlehem Steel Plant pier in Sparrows Point, Baltimore. After the docking pilot and the tug boats had put the ship in a berth and departed, port officials came

Narvik, Norway, 0145 1 June 1947
The Land of the Midnight Sun

aboard, the ship was cleared, and pratique was granted. The hatches were opened so the cargo could be discharged. One of the engineers said that he knew of a great restaurant on Hanover street on the other side of Baltimore. That first day in port, Ted took the night watch and Chico, two engineers and I took a taxi from Sparrows Point to Rossiters restaurant on Hanover street. Rossiters was famous for delicious steaks served sizzling on steel plates. After dinner and a few drinks, the four of us took a taxi back to Sparrows Point. It was a little after ten o'clock when the taxi dropped us off at the entrance to the Bethlehem Steel Plant. We had to walk through the plant past the steel furnaces to get to the ship.

As I was in my cabin on the starboard side of the boat deck getting ready to turn in, I heard loud shouting and cursing coming from the Second Engineer's cabin on the port side. I left my cabin to see what was going on just in time to see one of the Wipers going down the ladder to the main deck. He had one hand over his forehead and blood was running down his face. The Second Engineer was standing at the top of the ladder with a five cell flash light in his hand and a look of rage on his face. The flash light was bent in a "U" shape. He said, "That commie punk burst into my cabin and threatened me so I wrapped this flash light around his head. He will think twice before he tries that again." The Captain, the Chief Mate, and the Chief Engineer arrived on the scene a moment later. The four of us got the Second Engineer to calm down and return to his cabin. After a few minutes had passed the Second Engineer told us what had happened and what had led up to the confrontation.

The Second Engineer was a devout Catholic and a vehement anti-Communist. The Wiper on his watch was a nineteen year old wise guy who was a dedicated communist. Recognizing the Second Engineer's religious and political convictions, this tall skinny kid spent the past voyage constantly tantalizing him with communist claptrap. He would draw a hammer and sickle on the Engineer's tools and tool box, write communist slogans on the engine room chalk board, and frequently "mouth-off" about the superiority of communism and ridiculed the Christian religion. The Second Engineer kept his temper and took all this abuse with a silent but growing wrath. Earlier this day the Second Engineer came upon a pile of communist propaganda publications that the Wiper had left on the engine room work bench. The Second Engineer gathered up these publications and tossed them in to the garbage can. That evening when the Wiper returned to the ship after spending some time in a local bar, he went looking for his publications. One of the men on watch in the engine room told the Wiper that the Second Engineer had thrown them away. The Wiper immediately went up to the boat deck level and burst into the Second Engineer's cabin and started to berate him. The Second Engineer jumped up from his seat, grabbed a five cell flash light from his desk, and struck the Wiper on the forehead with it. Stunned and bleeding the Wiper staggered down the ladder to the main deck where a couple of the seamen helped him in to the crew's mess room.

As more of the crew returned to the ship during the next half hour, they gathered in an angry crowd in and adjacent to the crew's mess room. One or two loud mouths began haranguing the mob to drag the Second Engineer from his cabin and give him a good beating. They were saying that what he had done to the poor kid Wiper had no justification. The shouts and threats became more menacing no doubt helped along by the booze most of them had been drinking while ashore. The Captain went to his office and returned to the Second Engineer's cabin with four thirty eight caliber pistols. He kept one and gave one to the Chief Engineer, the Chief Mate, and to me. Then he went to the top of the ladder and shouted down to the mob below, "Any of you who dare to come up on this deck will be shot. You had better disperse and go to your cabins." The security office of the Bethlehem Steel Company was informed of the trouble on board and they sent a carload of guards to the ship. The crew dispersed and someone took the Wiper to the hospital to get his head wound treated. With the danger of a confrontation over, the captain retrieved the pistols and returned them to the arms locker. The situation could have easily become a full scale mutiny. No charges were filed against the Second Engineer, and I never saw the Wiper again once the articles were broken.

The next day the company's agent and the Shipping Commissioner came aboard to break the foreign articles and pay off the crew. The iron ore was discharged in three days and the ship was shifted to the coal pier in Baltimore. Night mates were hired to cover the weekend watches, and on Friday, Chico went home to New York to spend a couple of days with his wife. Ted remained on board and I went home to Central Islip. I called Anita and made a date to take her out to dinner on Saturday evening. We had a very nice evening and I even worked up enough courage to kiss her good night when I returned her to her home. She impressed me as being superior in every way to any of the girls I had previously dated. I knew that there would be a lot of competition for her affection, and my profession would make it even more difficult. On Sunday both Chico and I returned to the ship in Baltimore. A new anchor and anchor chain was installed to replace the one we lost in Narvik. Another full load of industrial coal was taken aboard, a new crew signed on foreign articles before a shipping commissioner, and the ship departed Baltimore bound once again for Aarhus, Denmark.

When the ship was about half way across the Atlantic ocean, a message was received changing the destination from Aarhus to Malmo, Sweden. I sent a radiogram to Sonia telling her that I was sorry to report that the ship was going to Malmo instead of Aarhus. I thought that I would probably never see Sonia again. The ship arrived at Malmo on a Friday morning. As the ship was coming alongside the dock, much to my surprise, there was Sonia waving hello. As soon as the ship was cleared and pratique granted I went on the dock to Sonia. She told me that she had taken a room in a hotel in town for the weekend. When I asked her how she had managed to get to Malmo, she said that her father worked for the Danish railroad and had made the arrangements for her. I said that I would meet her at her hotel that evening as soon as the ship was finished working cargo for the day. That evening we had dinner at a very nice restaurant and made plans for touring Malmo the next day. Malmo was a city with a population of about a quarter of a million people. There were many interesting sights in this old city including a cathedral dating back to the fourteenth century. Cargo operations were shut down on the weekend so I was able to spend a good deal of time with Sonia. She had to return to her job in Aarhus on Monday, so we planned to meet in Copenhagen on the following Saturday if I could get the time off. Cargo operations went rather slowly and there was still a good deal of coal left on board when the longshoremen quit for the day on the following Friday.

One day two Norwegian detectives came aboard the ship and asked to interview the mates. They said that they were investigating the death and possible murder of the Norwegian Second Mate that had turned up missing prior to the previous voyage of the ship. A picture of the fellow showing him on a slab at the morgue in Baltimore was passed around. He had been found floating under a pier in Baltimore harbor. It had taken some time to identify him and notify the Norwegian authorities. We told the detectives that he was last seen going ashore with the two seamen who had given us so much trouble before they were dragged off the ship in hand cuffs. I felt that they were quite capable of robbing and murdering the

Norwegian Second Mate. Their names and identity "Z" card numbers were given to the detectives. I doubt that this obvious murder was ever resolved or that those who were responsible were ever brought to justice. The poor fellow left a wife and two children back home in Norway.

Chico, Ted, and I had worked out the shipboard watches so that I had the weekend off to visit with Sonia. Using cablegrams, arrangements were made to meet Sonia at the Copenhagen railroad station on Saturday afternoon. Leaving Ted on board, Chico, the Assistant Engineer, and I took the ferry from Malmo to Copenhagen on Saturday morning. It was about a three hour run over to Copenhagen so we decided to have lunch on board. During lunch the waiter served me a cold pleasant tasting liquor called aquavit. Every time I emptied the two ounce glass, the waiter would refill it. The ferry docked in Copenhagen just as we finished lunch. When I pushed back from the table to stand up, I discovered that I was paralyzed from the waist down. I was unable to move my legs. My two companions literally carried me down the gangway between them. We caught a taxi and went to the railroad station to pick up Sonia. By the time we reached the railroad station the paralysis had moved up from my waist to my head. I was intoxicated. Sonia was waiting for us at the station and the four of us took a taxi to Tivoly Park. It took quite a long while for the effects of the aquavit to wear off. After touring the park we went to the National Scala to have dinner and to see the acrobatic performance. From there we returned to the ferry terminal intending to return to Malmo with Sonia. Due to some immigration regulation, Sonia was not allowed to board the Ferry. It seems that there had to be at least a period of week between visits from Denmark and Sweden. Chico and the Engineer boarded the ferry and Sonia and I took a taxi to the Copenhagen airport. There we were able to get a flight to Malmo and there was no mention of a week being required between visits. After dropping Sonia at the same hotel and getting her squared away with a room, I returned to the ship. I was able to spend Sunday afternoon and evening with Sonia and on Monday she returned to Aarhus. We planned to see each other when the ship returned on the next voyage. Discharging the cargo was completed on Tuesday and the ship sailed the following morning.

Again the ship was heading for Narvik to pick up another load of iron ore. On the run through the Kattegat with a pilot on board, the ship nearly had a collision. The S S Francis A. Retka was on a parallel course with and a little distance behind a small coastal freighter on our right side.

Approaching on a reciprocal course head and head with the small freighter there was an American Victory Ship of the Moore McCormick line. The Victory ship turned to her right and the small freighter turned to her left, and the two ships sideswiped each other on their port sides. The Victory ship stopped her engines but continued turning to her right heading straight for our ship. Someone on the forecastle deck had the presence of mind to drop the anchors. The water was too deep for the anchors to hit the bottom, but their drag helped to take the way off the Victory ship. We missed a collision with the Victory ship by less than ten feet. The pilot and I both let out a sigh of relief at the near miss. I do not know how much damage either of those ships suffered, but as I looked aft, the Victory ship was alongside the small freighter apparently rendering some assistance.

The voyage up the coast of Norway was without any incident. A pilot was picked up at the entrance to the Ofoten Fjord and the ship proceeded to Narvik harbor. As before we anchored out for a couple of days and then went alongside the pier. One day at anchor I had the midnight to eight watch. At about two in the morning I was sitting in the salon having a cup of coffee when the First Assistant Engineer came in. He beckoned to me to follow him out on deck. Because we were so far above the Arctic Circle, the sun was still shining brightly. We walked forward to the number two hatch and both of us sat on the edge of the hatch. I asked him why he wanted me to come out on the main deck. He replied that he was concerned for my safety. The salon was located directly above the engine room boilers, and he thought that they were about to explode. I shot him an incredulous look. He said that he had just made a routine inspection of the engine room and found the Second Engineer, the Oiler, the Fireman/watertender, and the Wiper all sound asleep. The indicator on the steam pressure gauge was in the red sector showing that the pressure was dangerously high. When I asked why he had not awakened them, he replied that the Second Engineer was a useless sack of horse manure, and if the boilers did explode that would be the end of the Second Engineer's career and the industry would be rid of him. Luckily, one of the sleepers did wake up in time to open a valve and relieve the pressure. I could not help thinking that the First Assistant had a strange way of dealing with an unreliable subordinate.

During a lull in loading the cargo of iron ore, Ted and I went ashore and walked into the town. We went down to a small coffee shop by a ferry dock on the other side of Narvik. Several people were sitting there obviously waiting for the ferry boat. There was a tall slender blond girl about eighteen or nineteen with a family group. She wore no makeup, but she did not need any. She was strikingly beautiful. Ted kept looking at her and after a while leaned across out table and said, "Art I am in love." The ferry boat pulled into the pier and the waiting people walked on board. Just before the ferry boat cast off the lines, Ted grabbed my arm and pulled me with him onto the ferry boat. A half hour ride put us on the other side of the body of water at another ferry terminal. All the passengers including Ted and me boarded a bus. The bus carried us about five miles up a road that skirted around the side of a mountain. It stopped at a small village where the beautiful blond and her family got off. I suggested to Ted that he ask her for her name and address. He was too shy to do so. We got off the bus and watched the beautiful blond and her family get into a car and drive off. Ted was dejected. I was worried. We had to find our way back to Narvik pretty soon because the ship was near to completing the loading of the iron ore. Once loaded the ship would sail whether or not we were on board. Ted and I started walking down the mountain road toward the ferry terminal. Half way down the mountain road, a car that resembled a miniature model A Ford came along, and we were able to hitch a ride to the ferry pier. We arrived there just in time to catch the ferry boat back to Narvik. When we finally got to the loading pier, the ship was flying "Blue Peter" (International code flag for "P") from the main mast. That meant that the ship was going to depart within the hour. Ted's falling in love had almost caused us to miss the ship.

With a small pile of this very rich iron ore in each of the five holds and 'tween decks, the S S Francis A. Retka departed Narvik and set a course for Baltimore. The passage back to Baltimore was without any significant problems. The ship enjoyed rather good weather for the North Atlantic during the whole passage. It was Summer time and there were no storms. Upon arriving in Baltimore the ship went directly to a berth at the Bethlehem Steel Company plant in Sparrows Point. The Shipping Commissioner, port officials, and agents for Boland and Cornelius came aboard to clear the ship and break the foreign articles. Hatches were opened and discharge of the iron ore cargo was begun. The very next day the Shipping Commissioner and the ship's agents came aboard to sign the crew on a new set of foreign articles. Cargo operations were halted for the weekend and night mates were hired to look after the ship. We three mates were free to visit family and friends.

I arrived at home on Saturday and made a date to pick Anita up at her home at about seven o'clock. When I arrived at her house she invited me in to meet her parents. They were in the process of setting up their dining room table for an elaborate dinner. Anita's father said that he was about to have some business friends over for dinner and he invited me to stay and have dinner with them. The invitation was presented in a way that it made it difficult to refuse, so I accepted. Anita's parents and guests were very gracious and friendly, and the dinner was sumptuous by anyone's standards. After dinner Anita's father and his guests seemed very interested in the maritime industry and they asked a multitude of questions. It was obvious that they knew very little about the maritime industry. I spent well over an hour explaining the Marshall Plan, the types of cargos being carried, the tonnage capacity of a Liberty Ship, crew costs, the freight rates, and the turn around time between the East Coast of the United States and the various European ports. They were especially interested in the cost to charter a ship from the Maritime Commission and the going freight rate of $ 26.00 per ton for industrial coal. At that time industrial coal cost about $ 10.00 per ton at the pier. Anita's father was calculating the potential profit per voyage in his head and he and his friends seemed impressed. By the time this was over, it was too late to take Anita out. I had to return to Baltimore on Sunday, so I made a date to take Anita out the following weekend.

When all the iron ore was discharged, the ship was shifted to the coal pier and started loading another cargo of industrial coal. Night mates were only available for Saturday. Chico, Ted and I caught a flight from Baltimore to New York on Saturday afternoon. As the plane was on its way to New York, Chico looked at me and said that I should not be on this plane. He had scheduled me to take the watch on the ship on Sunday morning. Saturday evening I went to Anita's home as previously arranged. I had to tell her that I could not take her out because I had to catch a plane back to Baltimore that night. My visit was short, a little more than an hour. Anita told me that I had made quite a good impression on her father during my last visit. After we had spent that brief time together, I departed to catch a train to take me back to New York and the airport. Anita's family were amazed that anyone would travel from Baltimore to Long Island just to visit their daughter for less than an hour and then return to Baltimore. I did not bother to explain that it was the result of a mistake in scheduling watches for the ship.

Cargo operations went rather slowly so the ship was held in port over another weekend. This time I did not have the Sunday watch, so I went home to Central Islip on Friday. As I was walking home from the railroad station, a car pulled up beside me. It was Gloria's brother. He called me over and asked how things were going. I said that I was doing fine. He then asked me to get into his car and come home with him. Gloria was home for the weekend and he knew that she would be delighted to see me. I smiled and thanked him for the invitation, but told him that I did not think that it was a good idea. As we parted he said you have the phone number please give her a call. That was the last thing I intended to do. I could not help thinking that Gloria must have come home to lick her wounds after her latest love affair had gone sour. It would have been utter foolishness to get involved again with someone so fickle and untrustworthy. I had found another girl much more worthy of my love. Luckily I was able to take Anita out to dinner and a show on Saturday. While we were saying goodnight I asked her if she would ever consider marrying me. To my surprise she did not say no. Instead she replied that she would have to think about it. There was some other fellow named Charlie in her life who was also seeking her hand. I returned to the ship in Baltimore wondering how this would be resolved.

Fully loaded the ship departed Baltimore and headed down the Chesapeake Bay for Europe. However, on this voyage the ship was headed for Rouen, France rather than Denmark. I notified Sonia of the change in destination by radiogram but she did not reply. This voyage started out on a rather sour note. The Chief Engineer was arrogant and totally uncooperative. Before departing Baltimore, a dozen fifty-five gallon barrels of lubricating oil were landed on the after deck and placed around the sides of the stern house. Chico informed the Chief Engineer that he should have his people secure the barrels of lube oil for the voyage. Securing the barrels was the responsibility of the engine department, not the deck department. At first he refused, but after much argument, the Chief Engineer finally relented and had one of his engine room wipers tie the barrels to the hand railings with some quarter inch Manila line. Chico told him that the quarter inch line was insufficient, but the Chief Engineer refused to do any more.

A few days after the pilot was dropped off at Cape Henry, the ship ran into some very rough seas. With a full load of cargo the ship had relatively little freeboard, and the rough seas were washing over the main deck. One morning when the Chief Mate, Chico, came to the bridge at 0400 to relieve me, we heard some banging noises coming from the after deck. The barrels of lube oil had broken free of their lashings and were rolling around the after deck and bashing into the hatch coamings and deck machinery. If nothing were done, in a short time the barrels would damage the deck machinery. Chico had the Third Mate, Ted, called out to take the bridge watch. Then Chico and I put on rubber boots, and with fire axes in hand, proceeded to the after deck. Chico took the port side and I took the starboard side. We went out on the rolling deck with seas coming over and dodged the barrels rolling around the deck. As a barrel would roll past us we would hit it with the ax to let the oil pour out. It was a crazy scene with sea water and oil washing across the deck and the barrels crashing into each other and the deck machinery. To say the very least what we were doing was extremely dangerous. We could not order the seamen to put their lives at risk to save the deck machinery. That task was up to us, the Mates. Keeping our footing was extremely difficult, and there was the danger of being hit by one of the barrels, or being washed overboard. If either were to happen, it would mean death. When a barrel had spilled out enough oil to make it light enough to handle, Chico and I would join together and heave the barrel over the side. After an hour, soaked to the skin with sea water and oil, Chico and I tossed the last barrel over the side. Except for a few bruises, neither of us was seriously hurt. We had saved the deck machinery and survived the ordeal. Chico had the satisfaction of telling the Chief Engineer, "I told you what could happen." Still nasty, the Chief Engineer complained that he would have to order another supply of lube oil when the ship reached France.

During the passage to France, I told Chico and Ted about my new girl friend, Anita. They started kidding me about my short comings as a suitor, and decided that I would need their help. They demanded the right to review and censor my letters to Anita. When I finished writing a letter, it would be reviewed by each of them and duly revised. Parts would be deleted and additional sentences would be added. After their review I would rewrite the letter and of course modify most of their changes. This farce continued until the letters, about four of them, were submitted to the French mail system.

The S S Francis A. Retka entered the English Channel and proceeded to the port of Cherbourg on the Cap De La Hague, France. The ship docked there for a couple of days to await a berth space in Rouen, and to take on fuel. One afternoon Ted and I decided to take a walk around the town. It had been heavily damaged during the war and there were relics of the machines of war everywhere. Ted and I walked to the sea shore and wandered along below the cliffs where the Germans had installed rather elaborate gun emplacements. We came upon a pathway that led up the side of the cliff and decided to climb to the top. At the top there were the ruins of a chateau and just over the edge of the cliffs there were heavy concrete bunkers with the remnants of destroyed cannons. Walking along the path way past the chateau we came to a high chain link fence with a gate that was secured with a chain and a pad lock. We squeezed through the gate and when on the other side looked back. There was a large sign on the gate that stated in French, German, and English, "DANGER DO NOT PROCEED BEYOND THIS FENCE-AREA NOT CLEARED OF MINES." Ted and I had inadvertently just walked through a mine field.

The American ships that were docked in Cherbourg had crews that were predominately Negro. One night Chico, the First Assistant Engineer, And I went ashore and walked into a long bar with a rather large ballroom attached. We looked into the ballroom and saw a sea of Negroes with French girls drinking and dancing to the music of a rather loud band. The three of us returned to the corner of the bar close to the street door. We ordered some drinks and watched the raucous activities of the other patrons. After a while two Negroes came out of the ballroom and headed toward the street door carrying a third one between them who was protesting. As they passed us, the Engineer slapped the middle one on the back of his head who then started cursing and throwing punches at his two companions not realizing that it was the Engineer who had struck him. Within a couple of minutes they were joined by several others and a full scale brawl was soon underway. The three of us left the bar and crossed to the other side of the street. We stood there watching the brawl turn into a riot with many of the French girls running out of the bar screaming. A short time later several black van type trucks pulled up to the bar and disgorged dozens of French police armed with short black night sticks. They quickly restored law and order by simply grabbing a Negro, banging him over the head several times with a night stick, and then tossing him into the back of one of the trucks. In less than an hour the French police had subdued all the American Negro seamen and hauled them off to jail. I asked the Engineer why he had struck the Negro seaman and he replied that he just wanted to see what would happen. The Engineer was not only daring, he was dangerous.

A day or so later the ship was ordered to proceed to Rouen. The lines were cast off as soon as the pilot came aboard and the ship departed Cherbourg and headed into the Seine River Estuary. The trip up the river Seine was a beautiful passage. The river followed a cork screw path as it curved around low hills that seemed to be made of limestone. Occasionally the ship would pass a white limestone cliff face that seemed to have a home or living quarters carved into it. The French countryside was very appealing with farms and lush green pastures interspersed with patches of woodlands. As the ship approached Rouen there was a huge cathedral on a bluff above the city that dominated this river port. The population of Rouen was a little over one hundred thousand people. There were still many signs of the ravages of the recent war and it was obvious that there must have been considerable suffering. Our ship became one of more than twenty American ships in the port of Rouen. Again most of the seamen on these ships were American Negroes. The word was that these seamen would make an under the table pay off in the Union Halls to get assigned to a ship going to France. They seemed to have no problem pairing off with the French women and girls. Although Paris was only about seventy miles from Rouen, I had no incentive to visit the "City of Light." Rouen had been turned into a huge brothel and I felt that Paris could only be a larger version of the same.

During my off watch time I roamed around the city and visited the cathedral DeBonsejoures and other historic spots including the site where Joan of Arc was burned at the stake. Oddly this site was behind what appeared to be a fish market. One evening Chico, the First Assistant Engineer, and I walked to the outskirts of the city where a carnival had been set up. We stopped in front of a stall that was set up as a shooting gallery. There were several old small caliber rifles arranged on the counter. The First Assistant paid the proprietor and picked up one of the rifles. He then said that the targets were not worth his skill, whereupon he turned and aimed the rifle at a lamp light several hundred yards away. With one shot the light was destroyed. He quickly placed the rifle on the counter as the proprietor looked at him with amazement and consternation. The three of us quickly lost ourselves in the crowd. I began to think that going ashore with this Engineer could be dangerous. He seemed to have a penchant for taking unnecessary risks. It took almost two weeks to off load our cargo of industrial coal and we were into the last week of September. After a quick sweep down the ship departed Rouen and headed down the Seine River to the ocean. The pilot was dropped off and a course was set for the mouth of the Chesapeake Bay and Norfolk.

The S S Francis A. Retka was sailing in ballast. That is, it was empty and riding high with half of the propeller out of the water. In order to submerge more of the propeller, the lower holds of hatches four and five were flooded to the top of the shaft alley housing. Then to give the ship a better trim, the four deep tanks in the bottom of number one hatch were flooded. This was the customary way to ballast an empty Liberty Ship for an ocean passage. On the second day out dawn was just breaking during the last hour of my midnight to four watch. I noticed that the fore deck seemed to be going down hill all the way to the bow. I called the bow look out on the phone and asked him how close he was to the surface of the water. Although the sea was calm, he replied that there was some occasional spray coming over the bow and that the water's surface seemed to be very close. As Chico came into the wheel house to relieve me, I knew that we were in trouble. I called the engine room and asked the Second Engineer if he was still pumping water into the deep tanks. He replied that he was, and I asked him when he planned to stop filling the tanks. His reply was dumbfounding. He said that he was waiting for the bridge to inform him that water was flowing out of the overflow pipes on the main deck. I told him to stop pumping immediately, and then told Chico that I was sure that number one hold was flooded and that we were in danger of going down by the head.

Chico had his standby man wake the Third Mate, Ted, to take the bridge watch. When Ted came to the wheel house, Chico and I took flash lights and proceeded to the tabernacle for number one hatch. We opened the door and climbed down the ladder to the number one hatch tween deck. The water was knee deep there. The wood battens that line the sides of the hold had floated free of their clips and were floating on the surface of the water in a jumble of loose lumber. Chico and I climbed back up the ladder and went out on the main deck. Looking over the bow, I estimated that the ship had only about five feet of freeboard there. The freeboard should have been closer to twenty feet. Obviously the rubber gaskets for the large tank top covers were missing in several places. As the engineers kept pumping sea water into the deep tanks, the water flowed out and flooded number one hatch beyond the tween deck level. Had they kept on pumping, the ship would have sunk bow first without any chance to clear the life boats, or to get an SOS radio message off. It is likely that all hands would have been lost. Unbelievably the engineers had been pumping sea water into the deep tanks for two full days. Normally it would take less than half a day to fill all four deep tanks.

The ship was in an extremely dangerous condition with three holds, numbers one, four, and five flooded. With that much free surface the ship had little if any stability. The engineers were ordered to pump the water out of number one hold. When they started pumping the water out they ran into a problem. After pumping for a half hour or so the pumps were unable to pull any more water out of the hold. While all the wood battens were floating and rubbing together, they created a great deal of chafe which settled to the bottom of the hold. When the pumps started stripping the water, this chafe was pulled into the rose boxes from which the pumps were pulling the water and plugged the rose boxes up. The engineers had to resort to a very tedious process. They would pump water back into the rose boxes to blow away the chafe, and then reverse the process and start pumping water out until the rose boxes were plugged up again. The rose boxes had to be blown clear of chafe for about ten minutes after every half hour of pumping the water out. Aside from being labor intensive, this process was extremely slow in pumping the water out of number one hold. Nine days later when the ship finally docked in Norfolk, there was still four feet of water in number one lower hold above the deep tanks. We were unbelievably lucky. It was the first time in my experience that the Atlantic Ocean was a dead flat calm during the entire time of our passage from France to America, and this was at the usual height of the hurricane season. Had the ship encountered any rough seas, with her extremely low stability due to all the free surface in three of the five holds, she would have rolled over and sunk. Needless to say, this flooding only increased the existing animosity between the Chief Mate, Chico, and the Chief Engineer. Although he was extremely upset over the flooding and the danger to the ship, our Captain maintained a neutral position between the two. However, it was the Chief Engineer's instructions to his Assistant Engineers that resulted in the flooding of number one hold.

When the ship was about half way across the Atlantic Ocean, the Radio Operator handed me a radiogram addressed to me. As he did so he said that he could not understand the message and hoped that he had gotten it correctly. The message was from Anita and it read, "Charlie came,

I saw, you conquered. Love, Anita." This was great news. I was now engaged to Anita. When I told Chico and Ted they congratulated me and told me that it would not have happened without their help. They had a great time joking and kidding me about my love life. I sent Anita a reply by radiogram expressing how happy her message had made me and an approximate date for my return.

The ship picked up a pilot at the Cape Henry pilot station and went directly to a pier in Norfolk. We were tied up and secure before 0800. The date was 9 October 1947. As soon as Customs and Immigration cleared the ship, the Boland and Cornelius agents and Port Captain came aboard along with the Shipping Commissioner. While the crew was being paid off and the Articles terminated, the Chief Engineer took the Port Captain into his office and convinced him that Chico was responsible for the flooding of number one hold. Without giving Chico a chance to defend himself, or discussing the incident with the ship's Captain, the Port Captain told Chico that he was fired. Chico had a rather short fuse and instead of defending himself, he told the Port Captain to stick the ship in his ear. That evening when I saw Chico packing his gear to leave the ship, I asked him what had happened. When he told me what the Port Captain had done I decided to quit as well. Ted also quit. The next morning the three of us departed the ship and headed for New York. The Port Captain had to find three new mates to replace us. I thought that he might have more than a little explaining to do to the home office in New York. Chico and his family had an apartment in Brooklyn and Ted's parents had a house in Elizabeth City, New Jersey. I did manage to visit Chico and his wife a couple of times afterward, but I never saw Ted again. However I was informed a year or so later that Ted had fallen in love with and married Chico's sister.

When I got home I lost no time in calling Anita and made a date to see her. I picked her up at her home a day or two later and verified that she really was willing to marry me. We decided to tell her parents which we did the following evening. Anita's father and mother both seemed to be pleased with our engagement, especially since we agreed that we would not get married until after Anita finished college and had her teaching certificate. Her two brothers were also amenable to the idea of our getting married. My parents had no objection when I told them of our plans to marry. They had only met Anita a couple of times and they thought that she was a very nice girl. With regard to Anita's family, my mother said,

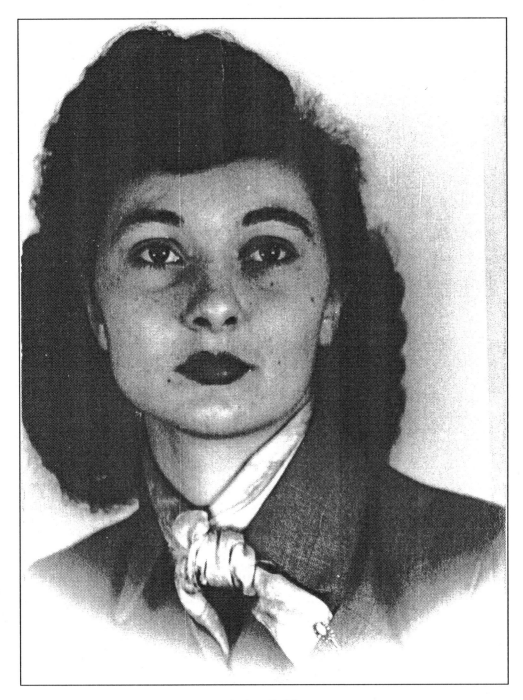

Anita Soldo
The girl I met on the Long Island Railroad.

"They are Italian, but nice Italians." Anita and I did not have any sort of formal engagement party. At that time we were both too busy. One evening while visiting at Anita's home we began talking about getting an engagement ring. Anita's father said that he had a friend that he commuted to New York with every day, and this friend worked for Tiffanies jewelry store. He said that if I wanted him to, he would ask his friend if he could get a diamond ring at a reasonably good price. I said that would be great and thanked him. A week or so later Anita's father took me aside and handed me a ring box containing a one and a quarter carat blue white diamond ring. He told me what the price was and that if I was satisfied, he would get my money to his friend. The next day I gave him an envelope with the money and a bottle of very good brandy to give to his friend with my thanks. The very next time I took Anita out I gave her the ring. She was pleased with it to say the very least.

During this same period of time many other things happened. On the Monday following my return home from Norfolk, I received a phone call from Mr. King. He said that I should come into the Boland and Cornelius office right away. I caught the next train in to the city and got to his office that afternoon. Mr. King lectured to me like a Dutch uncle and said that I had been wrong to quit the ship on such short notice. I then explained what had happened and how unjustly Chico had been treated. Mr. King said that he had suspected that something was not right and that he would investigate the matter further. Since it was near closing time for the office, he asked me to join him for dinner. I accepted and he took me to a very nice restaurant and we had an excellent meal. During dinner Mr. King told me that it would be a while before there would be another open berth for a Second Mate. However, he said the company was under contract with the Maritime Administration to prepare ships coming out of service for lay up in the national reserve fleet, and they were using Sullivan's Shipyard in Brooklyn to do this work. He said that he could keep me employed on a fairly steady basis if I were willing to work as a night mate on those ships. I said that I would like that and thanked him. He told me to report to the office the next morning for an assignment. I also told Mr. King that I planned to enroll in the License Upgrade School and sit for my Chief Mate's license. He said that was an excellent thing to do while waiting for my next berth to open up. At that time I did not realize that this was the beginning of the decline of the American Merchant Marine. A day or so later I asked Mr. King what he had decided to do about John

Ciccosanti. He said that he determined that the Port Captain had acted too hastily. The Chief Engineer had been fired and Chico had been asked to return to the company with apologies for what had happened. Unfortunately, Chico had already accepted a Chief Mate's berth on a ship operated by another company.

NIGHT MATE WORK

The opportunity of working as a night mate on the ships being laid up was excellent. The Coast Guard required that these ships have a licensed officer aboard at all times. This required having three mates for each ship with each mate taking an eight hour watch. The daytime mate would work from 0800 in the morning to 1600, then one night mate from 1600 to midnight, and another from midnight to 0800. The day mate ran the work gang cleaning out the storage lockers and stripping excess gear from the decks. Another gang worked in the machinery spaces under the supervision of an engineer. There were usually three or four ships in the shipyard all the time. It would normally take about a week to ten days to get a ship ready to be towed to the reserve fleet anchorage in the Hudson River above Yonkers. The night mates' work was very easy. All that was required was to tend the mooring lines as the tide changed and to keep the proper lights displayed. After four in the afternoon there was a uniformed civilian guard on the ship as well as a night mate. Most of my assignments were for the midnight to eight in the morning watch. For this work I was paid the day rate pay for a licensed mate. Most of the time the ship's power plants were secured and electrical power was supplied from the shore. The toughest part of the job was staying awake.

One night I was paired off with a rather chubby guard who kept insisting that I catch a few hours sleep. He said that he would call me if there were a need, and that he would check the mooring lines and lights every half hour. Being suspicious, I laid on the bunk in the Chief Mate's cabin and pretended to be asleep. Sure enough, a half hour later the guard came to the room and thinking that I was asleep, he walked away quietly. I waited for another half hour and then went down to the main deck very quietly. There I found the guard fast asleep on a bunk in the boatswain's cabin on the forward side of the mid ship house. Determined to teach this character a lesson, I quietly went up to the bridge deck. There I took one of the deep sea sounding leads, an item weighing about thirty pounds, from its rack and let it drop to the main deck. It struck the deck with a resounding noise just outside of the cabin where the guard was sleeping. Then I returned to the Mate's cabin and pretended to be asleep. Within a minute the guard rushed into the cabin and shook me. Sitting up I asked him what was wrong. He stammered out, "didn't you hear that bang?" I said no and asked him what it could have been. With a flashlight in his hand he started searching the main deck. I was sure he would not notice the sounding lead among all the clutter on the main deck, and I was also sure he would not sleep any more that night.

The routine of working as a night mate went on for several months. Some weeks I would work only two or three days, and other weeks I would work six or seven days. This gave me an opportunity to visit my friends as well as picking Anita up at Queens College once or twice a week and escorting her home. My buddy Dick Kadison had gone off to attend college in Chicago. Ira and Jane were back in New York and I was able to have dinner and socialize with them frequently. Sometimes Anita would be with me and we would go to some supper club as a foursome. Every once in a while Mr. King would invite me to have dinner with him. Life was good. One day I met Anita at her school to escort her home. As we were traveling East on the Long Island Railroad train, Anita was sitting by the window and I was by the isle in the middle of the car. The sun was streaming through the window and Anita's engagement ring reflected a rainbow of colors across the ceiling of the railroad car. It was less than a week since I had given her the ring. We both marveled at the way the ring reflected the sun light. As the train approached the Brentwood station we got up from our seats. Stepping into the isle I looked back and about six seats from where we were sitting there was Gloria. Our eyes locked for a moment but her face remained expressionless. Without any sign of recognition I turned quickly and escorted Anita off the forward end of the car. I was sure that Gloria was not there by accident. She must have seen us board the train in Jamaica Station and curiosity had gotten the best of her. Perhaps she thought that I was going all the way to Central Islip, and that I might start some sort of dialog with her when we got off the train. Whatever her intentions were is of no consequence because that was the last time I ever set eyes on Gloria.

Fall passed quickly into Winter and I was kept fairly well employed at Sullivans Shipyard. Early in December I learned that Chico was home for the holidays and I asked Anita to accompany me on a visit to the

Chiccosanties in Brooklyn. We caught a morning train from Brentwood to New York. The radio weather report called for snow flurries during the day which did not seem too ominous. When Anita and I emerged from the subway station in Brooklyn at about one that afternoon there was about four inches of snow on the sidewalk, and the snow was falling hard. It appeared that the snow flurries had become a snow storm. We would have to walk about three blocks to reach the Chiccosanties' apartment house. Not wanting to get stranded there, we decided to abort the visit and took the subway train back to the railroad station. It was necessary to go from Pennsylvania Station to Jamaica Station and change trains there for Brentwood. When we arrived at Jamaica Station the place was a mob scene. All the trains were delayed due to the snow storm which had actually become a blizzard. It was ten o'clock at night before Anita and I were able to get aboard a train for Brentwood. As the mob sorted itself out in the railroad car we found Anita's father. He had left his Manhattan office early and this was the first train he was able to catch. Anita and her father got off the train in Brentwood and the snow was knee deep and still falling. I continued on to Central Islip and my father was there to meet the train and drive me home. The snow plows were doing their best to keep the streets open and the snow stopped falling in the early hours of the next morning. When I woke up and looked out of my bedroom window the sun was shining on a beautiful Winter scene. After breakfast I borrowed the family car, a big Packard sedan, and drove over to Anita's house. Although the roads were not completely cleared of snow, with that car they were passable. Pulling up in front of Anita's house I beeped the horn to announce my arrival. I must have awakened everyone there. Anita and her Aunt Sue came to the door in their night clothes and looked at me with surprise and consternation. They were embarrassed because I had caught them with their hair still up in curlers. Anita did not want to come out and play in the snow so we agreed that I could pick her up later. Aunt Sue turned out to be quite a character. She was Anita's mother's younger sister and an uninhibited fun loving jokester. Although we had many a laugh, I think that Aunt Sue had some misgivings about Anita getting engaged to a professional seaman. It seems that she had been married to a seaman and it did not turn out well. This was going to cause me some serious problems in the future.

Christmas and New Year celebrations came and went, and in mid January I enrolled in the License Upgrade School. It was possible for me to attend the school during the day and pick up an occasional night mate assignment. I sat for the Chief Mate's license examination the third week of February. Four candidates including me began sitting for Chief Mate on a Monday morning. By noon on Wednesday, I was the only one of the four still sitting for the examination. The others had failed when they were less than half the way through. Without a doubt the examination for Chief Mate is by far the most difficult. There was one question on the examination that I found especially difficult. The question posed a hypothetical situation. "Your vessel is underway in a dense fog. You hear close aboard the fog signal of another vessel. What would you do?" The Navigation Rules state that when in fog only fog signals may be sounded. However there is also a special circumstances rule that might apply to this situation. Feeling that this was a trick question, I wrote out each of the rules that applied, the rule for sound signals, the two rules covering special circumstances, and the rule for the danger signal. In my answer I wrote that this was a special circumstances situation and that I would sound the danger signal as well as the sound signals for a vessel underway in fog.

My old buddy Dick Kadison had taught me, when we were Midshipmen, that the best way to pass a test on the Navigation Rules was to memorize them word for word. When the Coast Guard Examiners reviewed my answer, I could see that they were in a state of consternation. They kept going to the book shelf behind them to retrieve various books which they reviewed and discussed between themselves. Finally they called me to come to their table. My three page answer was in front of them. One of the Examiners then asked, "In a fog, what signals would you make?" Realizing what answer they wanted, I replied, "In a fog, only fog signals shall be made." They both nodded their heads and I was told to return to my table and continue with the examination. I finished the last questions on Friday, but I had to return the following Monday to take the Morse Code blinker light test. On Tuesday I went through the swearing in process and received my Chief Mate's License. Leaving the Customs House, I walked over to Trinity Church, went inside and said a prayer of thanks.

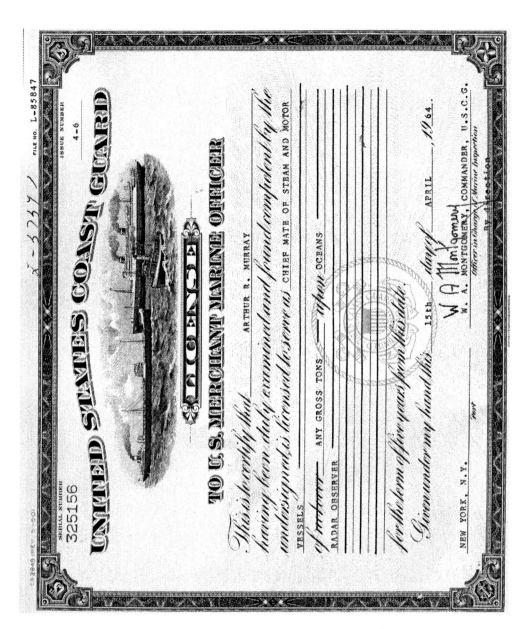

Chief Mate's License, 15 April 1964.

THE MEDITERRANEAN RUN

I left Trinity Church at Wall street and walked to 19 Rector street, the office of the Boland and Cornelius Steamship Company. There Mr. King congratulated me on getting my Chief Mate's License and said that the timing was perfect. He said that a company ship was due into Baltimore before the end of the week. The ship had been carrying grain to North European ports and iron ore on the return voyages during the winter months and the whole crew was getting off. Mr. King was assigning a new captain, new mates, and new engineers to this ship. He asked me if I would like to take the Chief Mate's berth. This was a surprise since the ink was not yet dry on my license. I accepted his offer with great pleasure. It was February 1948 and I had just reached the age of twenty three in January. With a twinkle in his eye, Mr. King informed me that I would be the youngest chief mate in the company's fleet of twenty six ships. He asked me to report to his office the following morning for my letter of assignment as Chief Mate on the S S Heywood Broun.

Leaving the Boland and Cornelius office I went to Queens College in Flushing to meet Anita and accompany her home on the Long Island Rail Road. Although she was pleased with my assignment as Chief Mate, she was somewhat unhappy with my having to ship out so soon. We spent a little time together that evening. The next morning I went to the Boland and Cornelius office and picked up my letter of assignment. Mr. King informed me that the ship had arrived in Baltimore and was discharging a cargo of iron ore at the Sparrows Point Bethlehem Steel plant. It was then to be shifted to a berth at the Camden piers in Baltimore. I returned home to pack my gear and get squared away for an absence of a few months. The next couple of days I spent as much time as possible with Anita and we had dinner with Ira And Jane in Manhattan on one of those evenings.

THE S S HEYWOOD BROUN

On Monday morning I caught a train from Central Islip to Penn Station and there caught another train to Baltimore. It was late afternoon when the taxi cab dropped me off at the Camden pier where the S S Haywood Broun was berthed. The cold overcast day tended to dampen my spirits as I walked down the pier towards the ship's gangway. I could see that the hull was badly rusted and showed the wear and tear of a winter in the North Atlantic. The main deck was in even worse shape. It was like walking on burnt toast as the layers of rust were crushed under my feet with each step I took. This ship had taken a terrible beating on its last voyage. Articles had been broken the previous week and most of the crew had already departed. When I got to the Chief Mate's cabin I found him packing the last of his gear. He was in a hurry to leave because he hoped to get home to his family in Boston that night. However he did take the time to show me the repair list he had put together and to point out some of the larger problems he was leaving me to deal with. One was that the fore peak had been flooded and was impossible to enter because of the debris that blocked the ladder below the entrance hatch. He told me that the Second Mate had been rushed to the hospital with a crushed pelvis when the ship docked. It seems that he had almost been swept overboard when a sea washed over the boat deck while he was trying to secure one of the life boats. A stanchion had caught him in the crotch as the water was washing him towards the edge of the boat deck. He was badly injured by the stanchion but it had saved his life. The boat however was lost. The Second Mate was taken to his cabin in great pain and all the available pain killers were exhausted before the ship was out of the storm.

Captain Burke, the company Port Captain, came aboard the next day with Captain Keenan, the new skipper. They expressed some concern over the sorry condition of the ship and told me that I had a lot of work ahead of me. Captain Keenan was a rather quiet man of slight build with a pleasant personality. He indicated that he was going to give me a free hand to square the ship away. The seamen to be assigned to the ship were to come out of the National Maritime Union (NMU) hall in Baltimore. From past experience I knew that this union could provide seamen who were reasonably good as well as some that were either incompetent or work avoiding trouble makers. Considering the task ahead of me, I determined to pick the deck crew very carefully. It was usually possible to spot a slacker from the NMU hall when they reported aboard. These types would report aboard in the morning and then say that they had to go back to their hotel to pick up their gear. They would leave immediately and not return to the ship until after working hours. That way they would pick up an extra day's pay without doing any work. I decided that I would send any seamen back to the NMU hall if they were not ready to go to work when they reported aboard. This was a big mistake. The first couple of days I sent at least six of these slackers back to the NMU hall. After that the NMU sent seamen who were ready to go to work the day they reported aboard. One of these ready to go to work able seamen was a fellow about thirty years of age named Jamie R. He had a full black beard that made him look like one of the characters pictured on a box of cough drops. The NMU had sent him to the ship to teach that "hard-nosed Chief Mate" a lesson.

It took better than a week to fill out the deck crew. Clean up work continued and stores were loaded for the next voyage. My boatswain and my ships carpenter were seasoned older seamen who had sailed on the ship on the previous voyage. They were good competent reliable seamen and probably the best that the NMU had to offer. The rest of the deck crew, six able seamen and three ordinary seamen, ranged in age from early twenties to fifty plus years of age. The Second Mate, Nottingham, reported aboard. He was a graduate of Kings Point with a rather gentlemanly manner and was a native of Baltimore. Before the end of the week the Third Mate, a big kid of Scandinavian background, reported aboard. I do not remember his name but he was a graduate of either the Maine or Massachusetts Maritime Academy. The new Chief Engineer was a man in his forties with an easy going personality. He had a very interesting background and had once been a card dealer in a New Orleans casino. The three Assistant Engineers were relatively young men. The rest of the black gang were typical of the types supplied by the NMU. They were a mixture of both black and white and consisted of three oilers, three firemen/water tenders, three wipers, and one deck engineer. The stewards department were also seamen from the NMU. The Chief Steward was a white man, the first and second cooks were black as well as the two mess men, and the two utility men. The cabin steward was white. The last to report aboard by the end of the week were the Radio Operator and the Purser. A Shipping Commissioner came aboard and the crew was signed on foreign articles. The company' agents informed the Captain that the ship was to proceed to Hampton Roads to load a cargo of coal. Just before the mooring lines were cast off and the gangway taken aboard, one of the able seamen, a short white haired man in his late fifties came to me with his bags packed. He said that he was not feeling well and was leaving the ship to go to see his doctor. There was no time to get a replacement for him from the Union hall, so the ship departed Baltimore short of one able seaman.

The ship reached Hampton Roads in the morning and anchored off the city of Hampton where several other ships were at anchor. The pilot went off in the pilot boat and the Captain had no idea when the ship would be ordered to the coal pier to load our cargo. The Captain decided to take a water taxi in to Norfolk to visit the agents office to learn when we would start loading. He and the Purser departed in a water taxi for Norfolk. When they were just out of sight another boat came alongside and a docking pilot came aboard. He asked for the Captain and said that the ship had to go to the coal pier right away. I informed the docking pilot that the Captain had gone to Norfolk and would not be back for a few hours. The docking pilot said that if the ship did not go to the coal pier right away he would have to go to the next ship in line. If he did so, it might be two or three days before the S S Haywood Broun would be able to go to the coal pier. He had presented me with a dilemma. I was a brand new Chief Mate and I barely knew Captain Keenan. How would he react if I took his ship from the anchorage to the coal pier while he was ashore? On the other hand if I did nothing, the ship would be delayed at the anchorage for a few days which would cost the company a good deal of money. The docking pilot stood there looking at me impatiently while I made up my mind.

I decided to risk the Captain's wrath. The worst he could do would be to fire me. I did not want the docking pilot or the other Mates to think that I lacked the self confidence or the courage to take the responsibility of moving the ship. I told the docking pilot that I would take the ship to the coal pier. The Chief Engineer was told to get the engine ready for maneuvering. The international "H" flag was run up indicating that there was a pilot on board. The Third Mate was told to have the boatswain get the deck crew to their stations for docking and to go forward with him to bring the anchor aboard. The Second Mate went aft to supervise the stern gang. About twenty minutes later the Third Mate signaled the bridge that the anchor was aweigh. I put the engine on slow ahead and gave the helmsman a course for the coal pier. Two tug boats came alongside and the docking pilot gave me and the tug boats maneuvering instructions to bring the ship alongside the pier. Every thing went smoothly and the ship was safely moored to the pier in less than a hour after leaving the anchorage. I rang up "finished with engines" and thanked the docking pilot for his help. Then I made the appropriate entries in the log book.

A short time after docking the crew uncovered the hatches and opened them. The loading foreman came aboard and said that he was ready to start loading the coal. After I completed a quick inspection of all five holds, I told the foreman to start loading. The Second and Third Mates were told to make sure the coal was distributed evenly in all the holds. There was only one large movable shoot that spewed the coal into the holds. As the loading began I went to the salon, poured myself a cup of coffee, and contemplated what I had just done. Moving the ship without the Captain being aboard could be a career buster. Two hours later Captain Keenan came aboard. He found me on the main deck watching the loading operation and asked me to come with him to his office. As I was following him I was wondering if he were going to order me off his ship. When we reached his office, in a voice that was too calm, he asked me to explain why I had taken it upon myself to move the ship to the coal pier. I repeated what the docking pilot has said to me, and explained the dilemma that put me in. There was no way I could contact him, and if I did not take the ship to the pier right away we would have had to wait at the anchorage for three or more days before we could go to the pier. Then I asked him what he would have wanted me to do. The Captain stood silently looking down at his desk for a few minutes. Then he looked at me and said, "You did the right thing, but you scared the hell out of me."

The Captain went on to tell me what had happened on his visit to the agent's office in Norfolk. When he got there he was informed that there were several ships at anchor in Hampton Roads waiting to go to the coal pier, and the agent did not know when the S S Haywood Broun was scheduled to start loading. The Captain then went back to the waterfront and got a water taxi to take him back to the ship. When he found that the ship was no longer at the anchorage, he assumed that it had either gone to the coal pier or had somehow been involved in an accident. He had the water taxi take him to the coal pier and was relieved to see his ship safely moored and loading cargo. Some time later he told me that he would never have expected a green Chief Mate to take such responsibility on his own shoulders. Had there been any sort of accident or mishap I would probably have lost my license.

Loading industrial coal continued through double shifts for two days. When the ship was down to her marks the loading foreman came to me and said that he had one more gondola carload of coal and he would like to load it aboard. It was night time and rather cold and the Underwriter's Inspector was nowhere to be seen. I told the loading foreman to go ahead and load his last gondola of coal. Sea watches had been set and the ship was to get underway as soon as the hatches were closed, covered, and battened down. The Bay Pilot was on board and the docking pilot and two tug boats were standing by. As the hatches were being covered the Underwriter's Inspector approached me on the main deck. Giving me a stern look he said that the ship was over her marks and we would not be able to sail until a sufficient amount of the coal were off loaded. This was very bad news. There was a pile of debris on the offshore side of each of the five cargo hatches. I reached into the pile nearest to me and pulled out a large chunk of iron ore. Handing the chunk of iron ore to the inspector and pointing to the piles of debris, I told him that there was at least a hundred tons of that garbage that would be tossed overboard as soon as the ship cleared the Chesapeake Bay. With some reluctance the Inspector signed off on the load allowing the ship to sail. Before the lines were cast off, the loading foreman put his head close to my ear and quietly told me that this was the largest load of coal he had ever been able to load on a liberty ship.

As the hatches were being covered I realized that we were still short one able seaman. There was no time to get a replacement from the NMU hall, so the ship departed the Hampton coal pier one seaman short in the deck department. I had to assign the ship's carpenter to standing sea watches in place of the old able seaman. This was annoying because it was not possible to get some of the repair work requiring a carpenter done during the voyage. As was customary, the NMU seamen held a meeting prior to the departure of the ship to elect the delegates for the deck, engine, and stewards departments. The duties of these delegates was to assure that the terms and conditions specified in the Union contract were carried out. They would take any grievances or problems to the appropriate department heads, the Chief Mate, the Chief Engineer, or the Chief Steward. Much to my surprise the deck delegate was a young clean cut kid, just out of the Navy, making his first trip as a merchant seaman. I should have been very apprehensive. This kid was too new to the NMU to even begin to understand the terms and conditions of the Union contract. When he came to me to announce that he was the deck delegate, I told him he had two choices. We could work on a "give and take" basis or we could go "strictly by the book." After conferring with his shipmates, he told me that they would prefer the "give and take" option.

The S.S. Heywood Broun was bound for La Spezia a sea port lying midway between Genoa and Leghorn in Italy. There was a great deal of work to be accomplished on the outbound voyage to get the cargo gear ready. Cargo previously carried in the ship had been loaded and discharged with shore side equipment, cranes, conveyors, and similar machinery. I had been informed that our cargo of coal would have to be off loaded with the ship's cargo gear in La Spezia. Since there had been little use of the ship's cargo gear for a long period of time, it had not been maintained properly and the North Atlantic had taken its toll. Some of the cargo whips (steel wire cables) had to be replaced and others had to be lubricated with heavy grease. Topping lifts for the cargo booms had to be lubricated and a few replaced with new wire cables. The cargo winches and fair lead blocks also needed cleaning and lubrication. Deep pitting rust was prevalent everywhere. Much of the ship's exterior had not seen a paint brush in over a year. During the day time watches I was able to have two seamen and the boatswain work on getting the cargo gear in shape. While not on a bridge watch, I turned to with them. The deck seamen were not too pleased with my working on deck with them. One surly ordinary seaman said that I had better watch myself, a falling shackle might hit me on the head. I looked him in the eyes and said, "Don't miss, because I will not." He got the message. With mostly good weather on the voyage to La Spezia, I was able to get the cargo gear in reasonably good shape by the time we arrived. The passage to La Spezia took about two weeks.

As the pilot was guiding the ship into La Spezia harbor I could see the wreckage left from the war. There were several sunken ships scattered about the harbor, and much of the dockside facilities were in disrepair. The city of La Spezia had a population of about one hundred and thirty thousand people. It was a major naval base for the Italian and German navies during the war and was a frequent target from land, air, and sea. The pilot informed us that there was wide spread unemployment and poverty in the area but that the situation was improving slowly. The ship went to a dock with a concrete apron and a single railroad track along the length of it. Our ship was the only American ship in the port. As soon as the ship was secured and pratique was granted sea watches were broken and the crew was put on day work routine. Gangs of longshoremen came aboard to open the hatches and rig the ship's gear for discharging the cargo and a steam locomotive pushed a line of gondola cars down the track alongside the ship. Within a couple of hours the longshoremen started discharging the coal into the railroad cars. Discharge operations were set to go from eight in the morning till four in the afternoon. It was a slow process and we estimated that it would take two to three weeks to off load all the cargo.

I had a conference with the deck delegate the first day the ship was in port. I told him that I wanted half the deck crew on board every day except Saturday and Sunday to put in a full eight hours of work. The other half of the deck crew could have the day off to enjoy whatever they chose to do ashore. The deck delegate was to make up a list of names of the men who would be aboard each day. It was left up to the deck crew to decide who would be on board each day and who would have the day off. I thought this was a very generous gesture on my part and the deck delegate seemed pleased with it. The next morning when I told the boatswain to turn the crew out to chip and paint and do other maintenance work he came back to inform me that only he and the carpenter were aboard. The rest of the deck crew had not returned to the ship. Later that day the deck delegate came aboard and I hastened to tell him that the deal I had made with the crew was off. Any one of the deck crew who was not ready to turn out and go to work at 0800 the next morning would be logged two days pay. This was the only punishment I could meet out to any seaman who refused to perform his duties. Pay withheld in this manner normally went into a fund for destitute seamen, not into the company's coffers. The deck delegate seemed to be a little embarrassed, but he just shrugged his shoulders and walked away. During the following days the deck crew were arrogant and refused to do any work on board. Jamie R. finally showed his hand. He was the ring leader and told the crew that my logging them two days pay for every day they failed to work would never stick. Only the boatswain and the carpenter were willing to work and I thanked them for their support. The thought of bringing this ship home in its present condition bothered me a great deal.

There was a constant parade of vendors, ship chandlers, merchants, and similar types coming aboard the ship. A hard hat diver and his teen age son approached me one day and asked if there were any odd jobs they could do for me. I took them on board and brought them forward to the fore peak. Opening the hatch, I showed them the tangled mess in the fore peak locker. Hawsers were wrapped around the ladder making access almost impossible. Cans of paint had been broached and the contents scattered over the jumble of spare parts and boatswain's supplies. I told them that I would pay them both the going wage rate if they would undertake the task of cleaning out the locker. They were pleased to get the work, and they worked diligently for a week cleaning out that locker. One day I observed the two of them tossing a large crate of brass pipe fittings and similar items overboard. They put a pile of cut up eight inch hawsers on the dock along with some of the other garbage. Then they sold the hawser pieces to an olive processor. It seems that the twine from the hawsers was used to make some sort of nets for crushing olives to make olive oil. When they finished cleaning the locker I thanked them and paid them off. A couple of days later I saw a small work boat anchored just off the ship's bow. There was the hard hat diver and his son salvaging some of the junk they had tossed from the ship. Laughing, I called down to them that they had been fooling me and throwing good junk overboard. They laughed and said that they would never do such a thing. A few days later the hard hat diver came aboard and gave me a German Navy 7X50 binocular and a watch with a damaged crystal. He said that he had salvaged them from a sunken ship in the harbor, and he thought that I might be able to use them. It was a nice gesture on his part and I thanked him. The binocular was badly out of parallax and in need of serious repair. The watch appeared to be a military type and either gold or gold plated. I thought it would be worth getting repaired when I returned home.

On the third of fourth day in port, the ship's agent asked me if there was any hard wood dunnage on board that I wanted to get rid of. He had a business acquaintance who was looking for some hard wood lumber. It just so happened that there were two large piles of dunnage in each of the five tween deck spaces. This was left over from the grain cargo carried on the previous voyage. A great deal of rough cut oak planks are used to build temporary hoppers for a cargo of bulk grain. This lumber had been carefully stacked in the tween decks and covered with tarpaulins before the cargo of coal was loaded for this voyage. I asked Captain Keenan if I could sell this dunnage. He said by all means sell it and the two of us can pocket the money. After examining the dunnage, the business man offered me five thousand dollars U.S. for the lot of it. That was a lot of money in those days and I accepted his offer. I went to the Captain and told him that I did not think it would be right for us to pocket the money. Instead, I wanted to use the money to hire some local laborers to get the ship fixed up and painted. Reluctantly the Captain yielded to my request. I then went to the ship's agent and told him what work I wanted to have done on the ship and that I had five thousand dollars to cover the cost. He was asked to hire the appropriate type of workmen to accomplish the work, and he said that he would be pleased to do so. There were a large number of men in La Spezia looking for work.

The boatswain and the carpenter were alerted to get chipping tools, brushes, paint, and other material ready for the workmen. Within a couple of days there were forty Italian workmen chipping, scaling, and painting all over the ship. The boatswain and the carpenter were run ragged providing instructions and materials for the workmen. Stages were rigged over the sides of the ship and workmen scaled the rust on the hull to bare metal all the way to the water line. Then a coat of red lead was applied followed by two coats of black paint. All the decks were scaled and painted. The midship house and the stern house were scaled and painted white. All the exterior wood doors were sanded and varnished. This work went on while the cargo was being discharged as well as when cargo operations were idle. The few of my lazy deck crew that occasionally came aboard looked at all this activity with indifference. I was getting the ship squared away without any of their help, and that gave me great satisfaction. The smoke stack was painted black and the company's insignia of a silver, red, and silver horizontal strip was applied. The masts and booms were painted a buff tan color and the shrouds were coated with white lead and tallow and the turnbuckles were painted black. The insides of the Gipsy heads on the cargo winches were painted white with a red dot at the axle. The appearance was striking. By the time the Italian workers were finished, there was not a square inch of the ships exterior that was not restored to a new or better than new appearance.

Anita's father had a business partner who had relatives in Genoa. Before I joined the ship, he had given me their address and suggested that I look them up if I got an opportunity. On one weekend while cargo operations were idle, I took a train to Genoa and called upon these people. They were most hospitable and insisted that I have dinner with them. After a sumptuous meal they took me around Genoa which I found to be a beautiful city with a large harbor and picturesque mountains rising on the land ward side. The city's graveyard was a most interesting place with a multitude of statues and mausoleums. There was a cathedral that had a large unexploded aerial bomb in the narthex. People said that it was God's miracle that it had not exploded. At the end of the day I caught the evening train back to La Spezia and was pleased that I had taken the time to visit Genoa and those gracious people.

The Chief Engineer had always been friendly during the voyage. One Saturday when there was no cargo activity on the ship, he came to my cabin and invited me to go ashore with him. He said that I had been working too hard and needed some relaxation. There was a nice hotel in town with a restaurant and bar that he had found, and he wanted me to go there with him and have a few drinks. I agreed and the two of us walked for several blocks along winding streets until we came to this hotel. We went into the bar and ordered some drinks. After we were there a short time two attractive young women came over to our table and sat down. Apparently the Engineer knew them because he introduced them to me as if they were old friends. Additional drinks were ordered. The women did not speak English very well, but we did manage to carry on a conversation with some difficulty. It was obvious that these young women were not from the choir of the local church nor were they candidates for the convent. After a couple of rounds of drinks, the Engineer said that he had reserved rooms upstairs in the hotel and that the four of us should go to the rooms. When we got upstairs the Engineer handed me a key and pointed to one of the rooms. He said that he would be in the room next door and then he and one of the women disappeared in the other room. The woman I was left with took my arm and escorted me into our room and closed the door. She turned the covers down on the bed and then started to take off her blouse. I motioned to her to stop and explained that I did not want to go to bed with her. At first she indicated that she was insulted. Then she questioned my sexual orientation. I assured her that I found her very attractive, but that I was a married man and would not cheat on my wife. This set up was a surprise to me and I did not want to offend the Engineer. She seemed to appreciate my situation, especially when I handed her twenty dollars. With a smile she sat on the bed and bounced up and down making the springs squeak. We sat in the room for about an hour making small talk until there was a knock on the door. The Engineer and his companion had finished their affair and the four of us returned to the bar. We had another round of drinks, bid the women farewell, and returned to the ship. The Engineer asked me how I enjoyed the company of the young woman, and I replied that she had been fine and I thanked him. A couple of days later he came to me and said that he was sorry he had put me through that encounter. He said that he had thought that he was doing me a favor and did not realize that I had such high moral reservations. I told him there was no need to apologize, that I knew his intentions were the best. It seems that when he saw his young woman a day or so later, she had told him about my reaction.

One night I was making the rounds of the ship. It was just before midnight. There was a commotion at the gangway and I went over to it to investigate. One of the black Wipers had come aboard drunk and in a very nasty mood. Apparently the Italians had been less than gracious to him ashore. He saw me and cursing white people, he whipped out a switch blade knife and lunged at me. I backed away as he tried to stab me in the stomach and I picked up a wooden hatch wedge to defend myself. As he stumbled towards me thrusting the knife at me, I warded off his thrusts with the hatch wedge. The Third Mate came up behind the Wiper and clamped the Wiper's arms to his sides in a bear hug. I knocked the knife from his hand and told the Third Mate to hold him there while I got some hand cuffs from my room. When I returned, two of my deck hands were there. As I started to put the hand cuffs on the Wiper they protested. I told the Third Mate to release the Wiper and told the seamen that they could take care of him. As one of the seamen approached the Wiper, he hit the seaman full in the face with a mighty blow knocking him to the deck. The seaman got up and said take that black bastard and hang him mate. Both of the seamen changed their minds about protecting the Wiper from me. I put a set of hand cuffs on each of his wrists and then the Third Mate and I dragged him back to the stern house. There I hand cuffed him to the overhead pipes in one of the rooms. He was left there completely immobile with his hands cuffed to the overhead pipes and his feet barely on the deck. In the wee hours of the morning I went back to the stern house to see how the Wiper was doing. He was half way sober and had vomited on himself. To say the least, he was much chastened. I took the cuffs off him and told him he could lose his seaman's papers and go to jail for what he had done. He begged me not to press charges and said that he would never misbehave again. I let it go at that figuring that hanging in hand cuffs for four hours was punishment enough.

In response to a request by Anita's father, I procured two wheels of Romano cheese. They were about eighteen inches in diameter and five inches thick and covered with a brown dust. I was told that they did not require refrigeration so I stowed them in my cabin in the bottom of my clothes locker. I also purchased a heavy brocade bed spread and a few other items from some of the vendors who were always coming to the ship with their wares. When the last of the cargo was off loaded, the longshoremen covered the hatches and swept the ship down before they went ashore. The booms and cargo gear were stowed for a sea passage. Sea watches were set at midnight and the next day the pilot came aboard and two tug boats came alongside. Before casting off the lines four Italian police came aboard and with the help of the Third Mate, a search of the ship was made for stowaways. They found four stowaways with their bags in the aft end of the shaft alley. These stowaways were arrested and hustled ashore. At last the lines were cast off and the ship steamed out of La Spezia harbor. After dropping the pilot, the ship steamed a few miles along the coast. The Captain ordered the engines stopped and a speed boat came along side the ship. The Purser and one of the seamen lowered half a dozen cases of cigarettes into the boat. The ship's engine was put on full ahead as the speed boat pulled away. The Captain and the Purser had made a little extra money for themselves.

The S S Heywood Broun was ordered to proceed in ballast to Charleston, South Carolina. Numbers four and five holds were flooded to the top of the shaft alley, and the deep tanks in number one hold were filled with sea water. This was the customary way to ballast the ship to keep the propeller immersed and the ship on an even keel. A day or so out, I called the deck delegate to my cabin and informed him that the seamen who had failed to report for work while we were in La Spezia were being logged two days pay for each day they did not work. These seamen averaged fifteen days each which meant that each of them would be docked thirty days pay. I had taken the time to enter their names in the ship's log book every work day the ship was in port. That way I was sure the fines would stick. A couple of days later the delegate informed me that Jamie R., the prime trouble maker, assured him that the logs would not be upheld. I told him to wait and see. The few tasks the deck hands were assigned on the homeward passage were done with deliberate slowness. Jamie R. was clean shaven by this time. The weather held good all the way back to the United States. One morning as I came off the four to eight watch I noticed a very disagreeable odor in my cabin. I traced the odor to my clothes locker. When I opened the locker door the smell was overpowering. One of the wheels of Romano cheese had gone bad. When the paper wrapping was pulled back, I could see that the center of the wheel had become very soft and mushy. There was nothing to do but toss it over the side. The remaining wheel appeared to be good and firm and eventually made it back to Brentwood.

I was on the bridge with the Captain when the pilot for Charleston came aboard. When he reached the bridge, he said to the Captain that he had brought a lot of liberty ships into Charleston but never one like this. "Your ship looks more like a yacht than a cargo ship," he said to the Captain. With some pride, the Captain replied that he had a very resourceful Chief Mate. Soon after the ship was docked and pratique granted, Captain Burke, the company's Port Captain, came aboard. Remembering how the ship looked when it departed Baltimore, he was amazed at how the ship looked now. When he spotted Jamie R., he asked if that man was aboard during the trip. He said that he was a trouble maker who had caused a great deal of trouble on other Boland and Cornelius ships. Had he seen him in Baltimore he would never have allowed him to sign on. I told him that Jamie R. had a full beard when he signed on in Baltimore. A short time later Captain Burke gave Captain Keenan and me the bad news. The company was turning the S S Heywood Broun back to the Maritime Commission, and she was due to be placed in the reserve fleet. He said that he had tried to get the home office to change their mind after he had seen the excellent condition of the ship. Captain Keenan said, "Art we should have put that money in our pockets. Nobody would have cared."

Voyage articles were broken on Friday, 30 April 1948. The Shipping Commissioner set up his books in the Officers' salon on the ship. The seamen lined up in the starboard companion way and entered the salon one at a time to sign off the articles in front of the Shipping Commissioner and receive the remainder of their wages for the voyage. The Port Captain and other company agents were there to handle the payment of the seamen's wages. When the deck crew were in line waiting their turns to sign off, Jamie R. went up and down the line urging them not to sign off. He insisted that if they refused to sign off their logged wages would be restored. Suddenly the young ex-navy deck delegate turned on him and said that he had listened to enough of his bull crap. Then he punched him in the face so hard that Jamie staggered back about ten feet and fell over backwards. The last one to enter the salon to sign off was Jamie. The Shipping Commissioner looked up at him and said that he understood that Jamie did not want to sign off. With that the Shipping Commissioner closed his books and told Jamie R. to come to his office on Monday if he wanted his pay. Shouting curses at everyone in the salon, Jamie R. left the salon and the ship.

Along with a couple of the engineers, the boatswain, and the carpenter, the company asked me to remain on board to get the ship ready for lay up. At about ten that night Jamie R. came back aboard and sheepishly asked me if he could stay on board till Monday morning. He was in bad shape. He had a black eye, a split lip, and numerous scratches and bruises. He had no money for food and no place to sleep. I told him he could use his old cabin as long as he did not cause any trouble. As he was departing Monday morning he thanked me for allowing him to stay aboard and said if he ever saw me on another ship he would not sign on. I replied that he need not worry about that, I would never let him sign on. That was the last I ever saw of Jamie R.

The small crew left to get the ship ready for the reserve fleet were put on coast wise articles. We slept on board, but because the galley was shut down, we had to go ashore for our meals. Captain Keenan's wife drove to Charleston from their home in New York to join him. One evening Captain Burke, Captain Keenan, Mrs. Keenan, and I went to Foley Beach, an amusement park not far from Charleston. There we had a nice dinner and tried several of the amusements. It took about ten days to inventory and sort out all the equipment and supplies. Some of this material remained aboard while other material was boxed for shipment to some government warehouse. The perishable goods, meats, canned vegetables, and other food stuffs were donated to the local Retired Seamen's Home. The work was completed on 11 May 1948 and we were all paid off. I thanked my boatswain and the carpenter for their support and loyalty and said my "good-byes" to the Captain and the Engineers. With a heavy heart I looked back at the S S Heywood Broun from the head of the pier for the last time. I knew that she was by far the best looking of the twenty seven hundred Liberty ships built for World War II.

The trip home to Central Islip was uneventful. My parents were glad to see me again, and I unpacked my gear in my old bedroom. No time was lost getting over to Brentwood to visit Anita. Her parents were pleased with the wheel of Romano cheese as was Anita with the things I brought for her. On the next Monday morning I went to the Boland and Cornelius company office in Manhattan. Mr. King invited me into his office and said that the report on how I had gotten the S S Heywood Broun in such great shape had impressed him and everyone in the office. He then proceeded to tell me that the head office in Buffalo, New York had decided to terminate their operations on blue water by the end of the year. The drop in the freight rates and the increased competition from foreign flag ships were making it difficult to make a profit on salt water. The company intended to continue operating their fleet of bulk carriers on the Great Lakes. My license was no good on the Great Lakes. They planned to lay up each of their salt water ships as the current cargo contracts were completed. Mr. King felt that it would be December before the last ship was turned back to the Maritime Commission. He assured me that he could keep me fairly constantly employed at the Sullivan Shipyard in Brooklyn through the Summer working as a night mate or a day mate getting the ships ready for the reserve fleet. He assigned me to start work as a night mate the very next day.

Working at Sullivan's Shipyard was great. The pay was good and the work was easy. I was able to spend a good deal of time with Anita and my friends in New York. Boland and Cornelius was under contract to prepare the ships of other companies as well as their own for the reserve fleet. Most of these were Liberty ships, but there were a few Victory ships, and some old merchant ships that had been built before the war. It was obvious that the American Merchant Marine was in a rapid decline. At the end of World War II there were at least four thousand merchant type ships under the American flag. How far the decline would go was hard to estimate. A large number of American ships were reflagged to foreign countries. Panama and Liberia were the most popular foreign flags for ships that were actually owned or controlled by American capital. In time Panama became the country with the largest number of registered ships. Foreign flag ships could pay their crews much lower wages than American flag ships. Some foreign flag ship's masters were paid less wages than an ordinary seaman on an American flag ship was paid. Foreign flag ships did not have to adhere to the strict safety regulations imposed by the U. S. Coast Guard. Overall they were much less expensive to operate and they could therefore show a profit even with the constantly declining freight rates.

THE M V AMIGA MIA

In July there was a lull in the number of ships coming into the Sullivan yard. I was informed that there would probably be no work for me for several weeks. While working in Sullivan's yard I would usually take my meals at a restaurant bar just outside the gate. In doing so I had established a friendly rapport with George, the bar tender. I told George that due to the slowdown in work, he would not be seeing me for the next several weeks. George asked me if I would be interested in a captain's job on a yacht. He said that the owner of a yacht in Sullivan's yard had told him that he was looking for a captain. I said that I would like to look into it, and George said that he would try to set up a meeting for me at noon the following day. True to his word, the next day George introduced me to a Mr. Jones, part owner of the yacht M V Amiga Mia. Mr. Jones was a short squat man about fifty years of age. He said that the other owner was a Ms Rose Martin, a sister of Glen L. Martin, an important man in the aviation industry. My credentials and experience were questioned and after some extended conversation, Mr. Jones asked if I would take the job as captain for $550.00 per month. That was pretty good money in those times so I accepted the job. Mr. Jones said that he had three engineers and three deck hands on board and still had to hire a couple of mates, a cook, and a steward. He then took me to the pier where the M V Amiga Mia was berthed and showed me around the vessel. I was asked to report aboard the next morning ready to go to work.

The next morning I reported aboard the yacht at about 0745 and Mr. Jones introduced me to the crew. They were all Scandinavians. The Chief Engineer was a short heavy fellow and his two assistants were taller, leaner, and younger. The two deck hands were also lean and young and about twenty five years of age. The Chief Engineer was a naturalized citizen and lived with his wife and children in Brooklyn. All the rest of the crew were aliens, and they ate and slept on board. The vessel was a partially converted navy picket boat eighty five feet in length. It had twin diesel engines and two generators. One generator ran off of one of the main engines and the other was driven by a small Buda diesel engine. The vessel's hull was double planked mahogany over oak frames and was sturdily built. There was a bridge with a wheel house and a chart room above the main deck which was planked with spruce wood. Below decks there were four cabins, two heads with showers, a well outfitted galley, a large dining salon, the engine room, and two storage rooms further aft to the stern. The deck hands were using scrapers to remove the remaining gray paint from the main deck. Mr. Jones told me that I was in charge and to do whatever was needed to get the vessel squared away. He said that he had open accounts with the local ship chandler and hardware stores and to charge whatever I needed to his account. It was obvious that there was a lot of work to be done to get this vessel squared away.

The next morning I rented an industrial type floor sander and set the deck hands to work sanding the main deck. Since the seams between the deck planks were filled with a tar like substance, I decided to put a coating of shellac on the deck and follow that with two coats of varnish. Several gallons of shellac, varnish, and paint as well as paint brushes and other material were gotten from the ship chandler and hardware store and charged to Mr. Jones's account. The rest of the week was spent varnishing and painting. The superstructure and hull were painted white and the wood doors and railings were varnished. The vessel started to look pretty good. About mid week Ms Martin made an appearance. She was at least a head taller than Mr. Jones and between forty and forty five years of age. Her manner was very business like. She informed me that the MV Amiga Mia was to make a good will tour of Central and South America representing the Armor Meat Company and the Shenley Whiskey Company. There were several investors in the project and they anticipated a good return on their investments. Ms Martin said that she planned to take investors and potential investors on day cruises aboard the MV Amiga Mia as soon as everything was ship shape and there was a full crew on board.

This Jones and Martin partnership was strange to say the least. It appeared to be strictly business. Jones appeared to have the responsibility of managing the yacht while Ms Martin handled the finances and negotiations with the investors. At some point early on, Mr. Jones had said that he had some experience in the merchant marine. He may have been a purser or part of the stewards department on some ship. It was obvious that he had little knowledge of seamanship and machinery. About half the time he never came near the boat. I assumed that he was perusing the business interests of the planned good will tour. Ms Martin's visits were even less frequent. She would make an appearance about once a week and only stay for a very short time. One day Mr. Jones came aboard the boat with an attractive woman about thirty years of age and introduced her as his wife. He asked me not to mention her visit to the yacht to Ms Martin because they did not like one another. The few times he did bring his wife to the boat Ms Martin was nowhere near. I asked Mr. Jones how I could get in touch with him if a need arose. He said that I should call Ms Martin and he gave me a telephone number for her. He said that she would know where he was and would be able to get a message to him. It seemed that he had no fixed address and he and his wife stayed in various hotels in Manhattan. This arrangement was getting more and more curious. I gave Mr. Jones my parents phone number and Anita's home phone number so he could contact me if there were a need.

During my second week as captain I hired a young fellow as my Chief Mate. He was a graduate of the Kings Point Merchant Marine Academy and had a Third Mate Oceans License. The following week, Mr. Jones brought a large burley Scandinavian man aboard and said that he was the Second Mate and that his name was Sven something-or-other. Sven was about forty years old and claimed to have been a tug boat captain with many years of experience. He claimed that he knew all the East Coast harbors intimately and that he was an expert in maneuvering vessels. Mr. Jones said that he had become acquainted with Sven in a bar and was impressed with his background and experience. Taking Mr. Jones aside, I told him that I would have liked to have reviewed Sven's credentials before he had been hired. I was told not to be concerned and that Sven would do all the maneuvering of the boat in, out, and around the harbors. This really annoyed me. Sven never posted his license in the wheel house as were mine and the Chief Mate's, even though I asked him to do so several times. Either he had no license, or he was ashamed of what ever license he had.

It did not take Sven very long to let the deck hands know that he thought that he should be the captain instead of me. Three or four days after Sven came aboard, the boat had to be shifted over to the fuel dock in a nearby yard. Sven took charge of the bridge and ran the boat over to the fueling dock. The MV Amiga Mia had a telegraph in the wheel house to give engine commands to the engineer in the engine room. With what I thought were excessive maneuvers, Sven managed to get the boat into position alongside the fuel dock, and the deck hands made her fast with the mooring lines. There was an oil barge moored to the dock several boat lengths astern of us. The engines were shut down and both fuel tanks were filled. Several five gallon cans of lubricating oil were also taken aboard. The diesel fuel and the lube oil were charged to Mr. Jones's account. When the fueling was completed, the engines were started and Sven again took command of the bridge. He told the deck hands to cast off the lines and then started backing the boat down. The boat backed along the dock much too fast. Sven put the engine telegraph on ahead on both engines, but the engines could not stop the boat fast enough to avoid ramming the stern of the boat into the bow of the barge moored astern. The engines were put in neutral and everyone ran to the stern to see how much damage had been done. The wood stern railing and the top part of the transom were pretty well smashed. However the damage was mostly cosmetic. I took control of the bridge and brought the boat back to its berth in Sullivan's yard. That was the end of the nonsense that Sven would do all the maneuvering when running in a harbor. His excuse for hitting the barge was that he had no experience with a twin engine boat that had an engine room telegraph.

The following week was spent repairing the damage to the stern. During the week, Ms Martin came aboard and told me to have the boat ready to take a group of guests for a day trip to the Mamaroneck Yacht Club on Saturday. She wanted the boat to be spotless and the crew to be in uniform. On Saturday morning a chef and a waiter came aboard with a good deal of fancy food and beverages and proceeded to set up the galley and the salon. A while later an accordion player came aboard. He was to provide music for the outing. The deck hands and the engineers were wearing clean blue jeans. The Chief Mate and I were wearing our dress white uniforms with the choke collars and epaulets. The Second Mate wore a white short sleeve shirt with a black tie and white duck trousers. The waiter, the chef, and the musician were wearing white jackets and black trousers. All things considered, the boat and the crew looked rather impressive. The guests began arriving around noon time and Ms Martin and Mr. Jones were at the gangway to greet them and show them aboard. By one o'clock there were twelve guests on board, and Ms Martin told me to get the boat underway. Food and drinks were being served on the main deck and the musician was playing his accordion as the boat pulled away from the pier.

The passage up the East River and into Long Island Sound to Mamaroneck was pleasant and uneventful. We docked at the yacht club and everyone except the crew went into the club for dinner. There was plenty of food on board for the crew and I forbade any of them to drink any alcoholic beverages. The return trip to Sullivan's yard was also uneventful and we arrived at our berth a little after midnight.

This Saturday cruise became a regular routine. We would visit yacht clubs in Larchmont and Oyster Bay as well as Mamaroneck. I was allowed to take Anita on one of these trips, and she did not enjoy it at all. The water was a little rough that day and Anita became terribly sea sick. There was usually a different mix of guests on these trips as Jones and Martin were acquiring more investors in their venture. One guest who made at least three of these trips was a Mr. Tosti. He would spend a lot of time on the bridge with me while we were underway telling me stories of rum running during the days of prohibition. He owned and operated a restaurant, the Rainbow Room, in Manhattan. Mr. Tosti's wife and attractive nineteen year old, and very sophisticated, daughter usually accompanied him on these outings. Sometimes Miss Tosti would come into the wheel house and asked to be shown how to steer the boat. She was being a bit of a coquette, but I maintained a strictly business attitude as was proper for the captain. Mr. Tosti became one of these investors. I do not know how much he invested, but I was led to believe that the investors were putting between ten and twenty thousand dollars each into the venture. I do not know how many investors put money into the venture, nor what rewards and guarantees they were promised by Jones and Martin.

Once in a while Ms Martin would come aboard and give the alien crewmen some money. They usually got twenty or thirty dollars and they had to sign a book she carried with her. They were expecting to get their remaining wages in a lump sum at the end of the proposed voyage. The Mates, the Chief Engineer and I were paid our monthly wages in cash at the end of the month. The Chief Engineer disappeared at the end of the first month and I was told that he had shipped out. A replacement for him was never hired. The two remaining engineers were aliens and were not licensed engineers. Towards the end of August Jones and Martin had a lot of food stores delivered to the boat. A thousand pounds of dressed meat was stored in the freezer. Canned goods filled the lockers, and crates of fresh vegetables were stored in the aft lazarett. The vegetables worried me and I told Ms Martin and Mr. Jones that they would not keep very long in the heat of August. There was no way to cool the lazarett and there was no where else to store the vegetables on board. They brushed off my warnings and told me not to worry about the vegetables. Although they said nothing, I was sure they were planning to depart Sullivan's yard very soon. In any event, they were not advertising any plans to depart soon. Where they might order me to take the boat was a question, although they had previously mentioned that the rest of the conversion work on the MV Amiga Mia might be done sometime later in one of the ports in the Gulf of Mexico. Charts for the East Coast, the Gulf Coast, and Central America had been acquired and stored in the chart room during the previous weeks.

Following the pattern of the previous Saturdays, guests came aboard for another day cruise. This group was smaller than usual. Only seven guests, including the Tostis, came aboard. There was no musician this time, but the cook and the waiter had been part of the crew for the past week. Ms Martin told me to take the boat to Atlantic City. This was a much longer run than the runs we used to make to Long Island Sound, and it was twilight by the time we entered the boat basin in Atlantic City. The boat was moored at one of the piers and Ms Martin, Mr. Jones, and the guests left the boat and headed for one of the fancy hotels for dinner and entertainment. At about one o'clock in the morning, Mr. Jones, Ms Martin, and Miss Tosti returned to the boat. I asked Mr. Jones where the rest of his party were and he replied that they had taken a limousine back to New York. He then told me to get the boat underway for New Orleans. I woke the crew and told them that we were going to get underway and that sea watches were set. The mates and engineers were told that we were heading for Florida. Once away from the pier, I turned the bridge over to the Second Mate to take the boat out of the harbor. I went down on the main deck to help the Chief Mate and make sure all the mooring lines and loose gear were properly stored for a sea passage.

Atlantic City's large hotels and boardwalk are located on a peninsula that runs parallel to the New Jersey coast. The boat basin lies behind this peninsula and at its northern end opens to an estuary leading to the open Atlantic Ocean. The channel from the boat basin runs close to the shore line of the peninsula. To exit the boat basin, a vessel would normally head in a northerly direction till it reaches the end of the peninsula. Then it would make a right turn and staying close to the shore line, head on an easterly course out into the ocean. At the point where a vessel would make the turn there was a fairway buoy with a white light flashing the Morse code letter "A." To seaward there was another buoy with a quick flashing white light marking an extensive bar. Further to seaward there was another quick flashing white lighted buoy marking a wreck. As the boat reached the fairway buoy and Sven was making the turn towards the ocean, he lined the boat up with the quick flashing buoys. Seeing this I called to him from the main deck to turn the boat closer to the shore line. He called back that he was following the channel markers, and then put both engines full ahead. I raced up to the bridge but got there too late. Sven ran the MV Amiga Mia hard up on the bar. I put both engines on stop, and told Sven to get out of my sight. He quickly disappeared below. His expert knowledge of all the ports on the East coast was sorely lacking where Atlantic City was concerned.

With the boat hard aground, the owners came up on the bridge and wanted to know what had happened. I told them that the hot shot Second Mate that they had hired had ignored my orders and as a result ran us up on the bar. They asked what I intended to do and whether the Coast Guard should be called for assistance, to which I replied no — I was going to try to refloat the vessel without any outside help. The engineers were instructed to check the bilge fore and aft to determine if there was any structural damage to the hull. The Chief Mate was told to take soundings off the stern to determine if the propellers were in the sand or were clear. A short time later one of the engineers reported that the boat was taking on water but that the pumps were keeping up with it. The Chief Mate reported that as near as he could determine the propellers were touching the sand but were not buried in it. The engineers were told to stand by the engines and to respond to the engine room telegraph smartly. Making sure that the rudders were amidships, I put both engines on slow astern. The propellers were turning smoothly so I put both engines on full astern. The boat did not budge. Then I alternated putting one engine on full astern for a couple of minutes while the other engine was on stop. After about twenty minutes, the boat began to slowly back off the bar. It took almost an hour to get the boat completely off the bar and floating freely. She was still taking on water and the owners asked whether or not we would have to return to the harbor for repair. Since the pumps were keeping up with the inflow of water, I told them that I was going to continue to head out to sea. I felt that the double planked hull would work itself to close the opened seams and stop the flooding. A few hours later, the engineers reported that the boat had stopped taking on water. The hull had sealed itself.

Sea watches were set and I plotted a southerly course running outside in the ocean. The Second mate had the eight to twelve watch, the Chief Mate had the twelve to four watch and I had the four to eight watch. I had no charts or reliable knowledge of the ICW and therefore chose not to run inside. The course was set to keep the boat from five to twenty miles off the coast depending on the contour of the coast line and the offshore shoals. It was estimated that the boat would round Cape Hatteras and Diamond Shoals during the night. I left instructions in the Night Order Book for the mate on watch to call me when Diamond Shoals Light Ship was bearing four points on the starboard bow. This should have occurred at about midnight. I woke up at three in the morning and was surprised that I had not been called sooner. Going to the bridge, I asked the Chief Mate what time he had passed Diamond Shoals Light Ship. He replied that he never saw the Light Ship and that he had no idea of our position. The depth sounder was showing that the boat was in very deep water, and a short time later it was showing no bottom. The boat was beyond the continental shelf. Dawn broke on a gray sky and a rough sea with a heavy swell. A heavily laden tanker was seen on a northerly course to the shore ward side of our boat. It was obvious that the boat was a great deal further to seaward than it should have been. Something must have gone wrong with the boat's compass, or someone was steering the wrong course for several hours.

At about nine o'clock in the morning the sun was high enough above the horizon for me to take its altitude with my sextant and work out a line of position. Fortunately the boat was equipped with a good chronometer, and I had made a habit of taking a time tick every day to check its accuracy. My calculations showed that the boat was over fifty miles off shore. Using the sun as a reference, I headed the boat in a westerly direction and instructed the mates to carefully monitor the depth sounder and scan the horizon ahead for any sight of land. It was obvious that the steering compass had acquired a substantial error. This compass had always been accurate with less than a couple of degrees of deviation on any magnetic heading. What could have caused it to go so far off was a mystery. During the late afternoon a radio tower was spotted on the horizon at about four points on the starboard bow. A couple of hours later a buoy was sighted, and then another. Once we came up close to the buoy I was able to identify it and where we were. The Amiga Mia was at the sea buoy for the Cape Fear River. After examining the chart for the area carefully, the mag-

174 *The Smooth Log*

netic bearing from the sea buoy to another buoy was determined. I lined up the boat on this range bearing and went through the procedure of "swinging ship" to determine the compass deviation on various headings. The deviation on a southerly heading was found to be about forty five degrees East. While the helmsman was steering South (180 degrees) on the steering compass, the boat was actually making a course of East South East (135 degrees). Knowing the deviation of the compass, I was able to set a reasonably reliable course from the Cape Fear River sea buoy to Florida.

At eight o'clock that evening Sven, the Second Mate, came on the bridge to relieve me. I showed him the vessels dead reckoning position on the chart and gave him the course to steer and the speed we were making. As I was entering my watch report in the log book, I noticed Sven propping what appeared to be an attaché case on the compass binnacle. Then he opened the upper part of one side of the attaché case and exposed the dial and controls of a radio. He carefully tuned in a station until he could hear the music clearly. The speaker of this attaché case type portable radio was hard against one of the two quadrantal spheres on the compass binnacle. I asked Sven in a quiet voice if he made a habit of playing his radio while he was steering the boat. He replied that he did and that he liked to listen to music while steering the boat. It made his four hour wheel watch pass much more quickly. A radio speaker has a very strong magnet. The speaker magnet of Sven's radio had magnetized the soft iron quadrantal sphere and had caused the severe deviation in the magnetic compass. Holding my temper in check, I told Sven what he had done, and that if I ever saw that radio in the wheel house again, I would throw it over the side. It occurred to me that if Sven had magnetized the quadrantal sphere on the other side of the binnacle, the Amiga Mia would probably have run up on Diamond Shoals, the grave yard of ships. The owners had stuck me with this arrogant dung head and there was little I could do about it. I was more convinced than ever that this clown had no license, knew little about navigation, and had lied grossly to the owners about his expertise and experience.

During the morning on the following day the engineers reported that the main generator which ran off one of the main engines, had burned out and they could not repair it. The only electric power was now being supplied by the generator that was powered by a small independent Buda diesel engine. The owners were informed that we would have to put into the nearest port which had the facilities to repair the generator. Checking our position on the chart, the nearest suitable port was Charleston, South Carolina. The vessel's course was changed for Charleston, and we arrived there in the late afternoon. The Charleston Yacht Club allowed the Amiga Mia to berth at one of its piers. Arrangements were made to have repairmen on board the following morning to repair the generator. That evening I went ashore and called Mr. King at his home number. I wanted him to know that I had taken the Amiga Mia as far as Charleston and also to find out if there was any change in the work load at Sullivan's yard. He said that he was glad that I had called and that I should get off that vessel and return to New York right away. He said that I could be in a great deal of trouble. There were several suppliers including Sullivan's yard who were looking for the owners of the MV Amiga Mia. They had left New York without paying any of their bills and there was a substantial amount of money owed for berthing, fuel, food stores, supplies, repair, and maintenance of the MV Amiga Mia. Furthermore, after checking around, Mr. King had learned that Ms Rose L. Martin was in reality Rosie Cohen. He was unable to learn whether Mr. Jones was using his real name or an alias.

After my conversation with Mr. King, I was in a bit of a quandary as to what I should do. A day or so after he hired me, Mr. Jones or whatever his name was, told me that he had gone to the Customs House in Manhattan and entered my name as captain of the MV Amiga Mia in the Coast Guard vessel registration file. As the official Captain of the MV Amiga Mia, I could be held liable for all those debts. Mr. King also said that he could put me to work in Sullivan's yard as night mate as soon as I returned to New York. The smart thing would be to get off the boat and get back to New York as quickly as I could. On the other hand, I was owed a month's wages at this time and I was sure the owners would refuse to pay me if I quit. Furthermore I felt some responsibility for my crew since I was sure that they did not have a clue as to what was going on. I phoned Anita and gave her an account of everything that had occurred since departing Sullivan's yard, but I did not tell her about the information I had received from Mr. King. There was still the question of the many investors in the "good will tour of Latin America by the MV Amiga Mia." What was their responsibility or liability? If the owners of the boat were running some sort of scam on them, would I also be held liable for the money they had invested? I wrestled with the problem all night and finally decided to take the boat as far as Florida. That would give me a couple of days to work out how I would handle the problem of dealing with these crooks. The origi-

nal voyage plan to New Orleans included pulling into Stuart, and taking
the St. Lucie Canal, Lake Okeechobee, and the Caloosahatchee River across
Florida to Fort Myers and the Gulf of Mexico.

The next morning the repairmen came aboard and completed repairing the generator by mid afternoon. The lines were cast off and the MV
Amiga Mia headed out to sea while it was still light. A course was set for
Stuart, Florida. Morning broke on a flat calm sea and the sun promised to
be as hot as it had been for the past week. The cook came to me and said
that a good deal of the fresh vegetables stored in aft lazarette were going
bad and starting to smell equally bad. I told him to get the mess man and
the deck hands to work passing the crates of vegetables up on the aft deck
one at a time. Then they were to sort through each crate and toss the
spoiled or rotten vegetables overboard and salvage whatever was good.
There was soon a trail of oranges, apples, bananas, lettuce, carrots, potatoes, pears, and peaches in the vessel's wake. Rosie Martin or Coen was a
late riser. It was usually ten in the morning and at least two cups of coffee
before she came on deck and was civil enough to talk to. This morning she
came aft and seeing all the vegetables floating in our wake, asked me what
I thought I was doing. I told her that I had warned her about bringing
such a large amount of fresh vegetables aboard in this hot weather, and
that I was trying to salvage what I could. She bellowed that it was my fault
and that the cost of the spoiled vegetables would be deducted from my
wages. I replied, "Madam you are not going to deduct anything from my
wages." Whereupon she screamed that I was fired. I said, "Madam you
can not fire a Captain at sea. As far as you and this crew are concerned I
am God almighty on this vessel." Then I called to the bridge, "Bring this
vessel about and put her on the reciprocal course." Sven looked confused,
so I shouted in as stern a voice as I could, " Do it now!" Sheepishly Sven
did as he was ordered and brought the vessel about. The crew stood there
with their mouths open aghast at what was taking place. Then I looked at
Rosie Martin or Coen and said, "This vessel is going back to New York,
there are several people there looking for you." In a red faced rage she
went below.

On my way to the bridge I passed by the skylight over the salon. I
could hear Rosie ranting to Mr. Jones about what had just transpired on
deck. I heard him say, "Put that gun away, he is right, you can not fire a
captain at sea." He then said, "Let me see if I can reason with him." As a
precaution, I went on the bridge and took out the flare pistol. I put a

round in the pistol and then stuck the pistol in my belt. Giving Sven a very stern look I said, "If you fail or refuse to obey any of my orders I will consider it as mutiny and you will suffer the consequences." The big buffoon looked distressed and said, "You are the Captain, no argument from me." A short time later Mr. Jones came into the wheel house and asked me to come with him to the salon. He said that he wanted to resolve the controversy and return the vessel to a course for Florida. With some apprehension, I went into the salon and took a seat at the table. Mr. Jones and Rosie were seated across from me. Mr Jones asked me why I was heading the boat back to New York. In a sarcastic tone I told him that I knew that they had skipped out without paying their bills, and that I was going to give them a chance to square their accounts. Rosie stood up and reaching across the table she slapped me across the face as hard as she could. I stood up with my hand on the flare pistol and said, "You do that again and I will have you put in irons and locked in your cabin until this tub gets back to New York." The look on my face must have frightened her because she sat down and looked cowed. Mr. Jones then asked what it would take for me to relinquish command of the vessel. I replied that I wanted my wages in full plus two hundred dollars transportation money back to New York in my hand and in cash. Then and only then would I take the boat into Jacksonville and turn over command to whom so ever they wished. Rosie objected, but Mr. Jones agreed and said that he would get the money together.

I packed my belongings and returned to the bridge with them. It took only a few minutes to plot a course for Jacksonville. After an hour or so, Mr. Jones came up on the bridge and handed me the money that I had demanded whereupon I had the vessel's course changed to a heading for Jacksonville. I called the crew together and told them what was happening, and advised them to get off the boat with me in Jacksonville. The Chief Mate said that he could not turn down the chance to become captain and that he was going to stay on. The rest of the crew said that they had too much time invested in this venture to give it up at this time. A few of them expressed regret that I was getting off. It was well into the night when the boat entered Jacksonville harbor, and I guided the boat a good distance into the harbor until I found docking space at an old empty unlighted lumber pier. The boat was brought alongside the pier and made fast. I gathered my belongings, shook hands in farewell to the crew and turned over command to the Chief Mate. It was about ten o'clock when I stepped on to the pier in complete darkness because there were no lights. I walked up to the roadway at the head of the pier. The lights of the city of Jacksonville were a good distance off to my right. To my left there were the lights of a service station about a half a mile away. I turned to the left and walked to the service station. There was a telephone booth there and I called the Jacksonville air port and made a reservation for the next flight to New York which was at midnight. The airport clerk that I made the reservation with told me that a limousine would pick me up at the Roosevelt Hotel at about eleven o'clock. I made another call for a taxi cab, and a half hour later I was having a drink at the bar in the Roosevelt Hotel while waiting for the limousine to the airport. At last I was free of the MV Amiga Mia, but little did I know that my troubles were just beginning.

I did not arrive at my parents home in Central Islip until the next morning. Being somewhat exhausted, I took a long nap and did not come alive until late in the afternoon. My mother told me that she had received a couple of phone calls recently from some man who was looking for me, and she had told him that she did not know where I was. He never gave his name or a phone number where he could be reached. A call was placed to Mr. King at Boland and Cornelius and an appointment to visit the office the next day was made. Mr. King asked me where the MV Amiga Mia was bound and I told him it was bound for New Orleans. He said that he was going to pass that information on to the manager at Sullivan's yard. That evening I had a date with Anita and gave her the story of my adventures taking the MV Amiga Mia from Brooklyn to Jacksonville. Curiously, Anita's mother said that she had received a couple of phone calls from a man who wanted to speak with me. When she told him that she did not know where I was, he would hang up without giving his name. I had no idea who this mystery man could be. The next day I took the train into Manhattan and went immediately to the Customs House. There I checked the vessel registration files for the registration of the MV Amiga Mia. When I located that document I was pleased to find that it showed Mr. Jones as the official captain. He had lied when he told me that he had my name entered on the document as the captain. This was good news because I could not be held liable for all the unpaid bills and debts owed by the MV Amiga Mia. Next I went to the Boland and Cornelius office and Mr. King invited me to have lunch with him. During lunch I told him of all the misadventures with the MV Amiga Mia, and that the vessels

Coast Guard document did not show me as ever having been the captain. After lunch we returned to his office and he assigned me as night mate on one of the ships in Sullivan's yard.

The rest of the week was spent working as night mate at Sullivan's yard and commuting home to Central Islip. Anita was very busy with her school work at Queen's College so I did not see her because our time schedules were out of phase. We did make a date to go out on Saturday night when she would be home. My assignment at Sullivan's yard was completed and there would be no work for me until the following week. That evening when I arrived at her home I was met at the door by Anita and her father. She was in tears as she handed her engagement ring to me, and her father told me to get off his property and never to go near his daughter again, and that I was a despicable two-timing scoundrel. I was taken completely by surprise and wholly dumbfounded. I had no idea what had brought this on. The following day, Sunday, I called Anita's home and her mother answered the phone. In a very harsh voice she told me that Anita never wanted to see me or talk to me again. On Monday I reported to the Boland and Cornelius office and got another assignment as night mate on a ship in Sullivan's yard. I knew that Anita worked at Macy's department store on Saturdays and I planned to seek her out there and find out what had gone so wrong with our engagement. Macy's was a very large store taking up a whole square block in Manhattan, and had about eight active floors. When I got to the store I knew that I might have a problem. Anita was on the "Flying Squad" of part time employees and could be assigned anywhere in the store. I went to the personnel office and asked the woman in charge of the "Flying Squad" where Anita had been assigned. She gave me a very curious look and said that she was not allowed to give out such information. I thanked her and said I would just have to find her the hard way. I started in the basement floor and visited every counter, and then took the escalator to the next floor and visited every counter. An hour later at the top floor, I had completed my search of all the floors with no success. Dejected I started taking the escalators down to the lower floors and from the escalator between the third and fourth floors I spotted Anita at one of the third floor counters.

As I approached Anita she was surprised to see me. I told her that we had to talk and she agreed to meet me when she got off work. We met in a coffee shop a couple of hours later, and I asked her what had happened. Anita, cold and teary eyed, told me that the mystery caller had told her mother that I had been staying at the Bravoort Hotel with my wife for the past two and a half months and had skipped out without paying the bill. The mystery man was the manager of the hotel and was most unpleasant on the phone. Anita's mother had given one of the letters I had written to Anita to her Aunt Sue, who lived in Manhattan, and asked her to check out the Bravoort Hotel. Aunt Sue had reported back that the manager had described me fairly well as the person he knew as Mr. Murray and that the signature on the hotel's register was identical to my signature on Anita's letter. I protested that it was not true and that I did not even know where the Bravoort Hotel was. Anita was not convinced. The evidence against me was overwhelming. She had to believe her Aunt Sue because Aunt Sue had nothing against me and had always admired me. Anita and I parted on that note. I was very angry and completely frustrated. How could such an accusation be made against me and why? I did not know how I would be able to resolve this situation. My engagement was broken and my reputation ruined.

The following Monday morning I visited the Boland and Cornelius office and told Mr. King about my broken engagement and the accusations made against me. He was very sympathetic and advised me to see an attorney and take some action against the Bravoort Hotel. When I told him that I did not know any lawyer in New York, Mr. King said that he would arrange an appointment for me with his lawyer. After a few minutes on the phone, Mr. King said that I had an appointment with his lawyer that afternoon and he gave me the name of the lawyer and the address of the law firm. This law firm had offices in a building just a few blocks away. After having lunch with Mr. King, I strolled around lower Manhattan until the time of the appointment. The law firm's offices were very impressive. The lawyer Mr. King referred me to was very cordial and invited me into a conference room where there was another lawyer and a secretary to take notes. I told them all the gory details of my broken engagement, the accusations, and the involvement of the Bravoort Hotel. They responded that I had a perfect case to sue the hotel for deformation of character. I had been defamed and as a consequence had suffered damages. With my concurrence they would institute a suit against the hotel for $ 250,000. They said that they would take this case on a contingency basis, and that their law firm would get one third of the settlement, however much that might be. I told them to start the action and I signed the necessary papers for them to do so.

The night mate work was starting to phase out. At lunch one day Mr. King confided that he too would be looking for another job by the end of the year when the last of the ships was to be turned back to the Maritime Commission. By chance I met one of my former classmates and he informed me that the New York State Maritime Academy was inviting all of its wartime graduates to come back to the school and complete the courses for a college degree. The tuition would be free, and the only costs would be for text books, subsistence, and similar things. I remembered receiving some notice of this from the Academy many weeks ago, but I had put it aside because of my involvement with the MV Amiga Mia. Now this was too good an opportunity to pass up. The first day I had free I went to Fort Schuyler in the Bronx and applied for enrollment in the Post Diploma (PD) program. I was accepted and informed that classes were scheduled to start the following week. After completing the enrollment procedure I caught the bus that would take me from Fort Schuyler to the subway station in Westchester Square. Another fellow got on the bus and asked if I had signed up for the PD program. When I told him that I had, he said that he had also and introduced himself. His name was Lou Piccoli and he was a graduate of the U.S. Maritime Academy. He was overjoyed that he had been allowed to enroll in the PD program at New York Maritime. As we were riding along, he asked if I would be interested in sharing living quarters with him in order to keep the costs down. I said sure and that we could get together the following day and look for a place close to Fort Schuyler. My problems with Anita and our broken engagement were far from over, but at least I would be close enough to try to set things straight. I still had no idea how the hotel had gotten my name and were pursuing me to pay bills someone else had run up.

Lou and I found a place just outside the entrance gate to Fort Schuyler. It was a concrete block building that was part of a marina. The building had a dirt floor, and a stove and a kitchen sink, an enclosed shower and toilet, and a heater. It was ruggedly grim, but the rental price was cheap. Another PD named Fitzgerald asked to join us and share these quarters. Lou and I agreed and then each of us raided our parents homes for some old beds, chairs, lamps, book cases, clothing lockers, and a couple of tables. These rough quarters were quite serviceable by the time our first classes started. As PD's we attended classes with the Midshipmen. However, we wore civilian clothes while the Midshipmen had to wear uniforms. It was an odd situation. As was the custom, the Midshipmen would snap to attention when the uniformed instructor entered the class room while we, PD civilians, remained seated. There were usually eight to a dozen PD students in each class. One day an instructor wearing the uniform of a Navy Commander asked the PD students why they did not stand when he entered the classroom. One older PD responded that a person with the rank of a Navy Captain, even though he was in civilian clothing, did not have to stand at attention for a mere Commander. The rest of the PD students just chuckled at the response. That instructor never brought that subject up again.

STOLEN IDENTITY

The next Saturday I went once again to Macy's and located Anita. She was mellowing but insisted that she would not see me behind her parents backs, and she was still inclined to think that I had been cheating on her. I convinced her that we should go to the Bravoort Hotel together and confront the manager. The Bravoort was located on the lower end of Fifth Avenue, and it was only a short subway ride to get to it. The two of us walked into the hotel lobby and I asked the clerk to call the manager out. A minute or so later a short stout man came out of the office and introduced himself as the manager, and asked what I wanted. I told him that I was Arthur Murray, the man he had been looking for. He looked shocked and put his hands up to his cheeks while shaking his head. Beads of perspiration broke out on his forehead and he said, "No, no this cannot be. The Mr. Murray I am looking for is short like me and older than you." The manager had a slight French accent, and kept repeating that there must be some mistake. When asked to do so, he produced the hotel register and opened it to the page where someone had signed it with my name. It was obvious that it was not in my hand writing. I asked him to describe more fully the Mr. Murray he knew and his wife. From the description he gave, it could only have been Mr. Jones of the MV Amiga Mia and the woman he had introduced as his wife.

Anita was now convinced that I was innocent, and she could not understand why or how her aunt Sue could say that it was I who had stayed in that hotel with some woman. I asked how it was possible for someone to run up such a large bill and leave the hotel without paying it. The manager said that the man using my name told him that he and his wife would be staying at the hotel for four or five months. They put meals as well as laundry bills on their account. The last couple of days they were there, they sent all of their clothing out to the cleaners. Then the day that they disappeared, they went to the cleaners and picked up all clothing they had sent out a day or so before. The hotel was stuck with a substantial bill. Jones had given the hotel two phone numbers where he could be reached. The phone numbers were those of my parents and Anita's. I knew that Jones and Martin were crooks, but I was amazed at how really rotten Jones could be. Although he did not say so, the manager must have been contacted by the lawyers who were representing me. He was extremely apologetic and offered to give me a letter exonerating me of any wrong doing. As Anita and I were leaving, he followed us all the way to the street apologizing for his mistake and saying that the hotel should not be held responsible. I thought that at last this smear on my honesty and my character was erased. Anita was happy again and could not wait to get home so she could tell her parents how wrong they had been.

I phoned Anita the next day, Sunday, to see how her parents had reacted. Luckily, Anita answered the phone. She was still distressed because her parents were not convinced of my innocence. They did not accept what she told them about the hotel manager having made such a terrible mistake and how it had come about. As far as they were concerned, I had bribed the manager to tell her that story. Aunt Sue had done a very good job of destroying my credibility. A short time later Anita's father accompanied by her older brother and another man I did not know appeared at my parents home. He was furious and told me very forcefully never to go near his daughter again if I valued my life. His visit was short, but I got the message. I returned to New York and met Ira and Jane for dinner. They were very sympathetic but could not offer any solution for my dilemma. On Monday classes were resumed. The week dragged on till Friday. I had borrowed my father's car for the weekend and I picked Anita up at a school in Manhasset where she was a student teacher. We both agreed that this situation could not go on. Anita suggested that we elope and I agreed. I called Ira and Jane and they agreed to meet us at a restaurant in Greenwich Village that evening. During dinner we told Ira and Jane that we were going to elope and drive to Elkton, Maryland that evening. There was a popular belief that people could get married in Elkton without the customary three day waiting period. At first Ira and Jane seemed willing to go with us, but as the evening wore on they changed their minds. Anita and I were on our own. I purchased a pair of gold wedding rings for an outrageous price at a jewelry store that I found open even at that late hour. It was close to ten o'clock at night. Then Anita and I started out for Elkton.

SCHOOL AND TYING THE GORDIAN KNOT

As Anita and I were driving south to Elkton she told me that her decision to elope with me was not made on the spur of the moment. She said that she had thought it through for the past few days. There was a small Franciscan Chapel on 32nd Street a short distance form Macy's department store. Anita had been visiting this Chapel a few times since our engagement had been broken. After our visit to the Bravort Hotel and her parents continued intransigence she felt that she was in a hopeless situation. On her next visit to the Chapel she asked for an audience with one of the monks. A young priest took her aside and sat down with her to listen to her problem. She told the priest the whole sordid story and said that she did not know what to do. He listened to her patiently and then asked her, "How old are you?" She replied, "I am twenty one." He then asked, "Do you truly love this man?" She responded, "Yes I do very much, but I also love and respect my parents." The priest then quoted a verse from the bible about growing up and leaving your mother and father. He then told her if you truly want to marry this man you do not have a problem. She should get married where ever she could, and if she could not get married in the "Church," she should come back to him and he would marry her in the "Church." With that he wished her well and God's speed. It was that monk who broke the stalemate and convinced Anita to marry me in spite of the feelings of her parents.

We took route one south and it was slow going. The sun was coming up when we reached Elkton. I asked a service station operator for directions to a chapel where people could get married. He laughed and said that I had seen too many old movies. There haven't been any quick marriage chapels in Elkton for the past ten years. He advised us to go to the City Hall in Baltimore where I would have a better chance to work something out. We stopped at a diner and had breakfast, and I fortified myself with several cups of coffee. Then we proceeded on to Baltimore. I found a place to park the car fairly close to the City Hall. It was now about ten in the morning. We located the license clerk's counter and approached it with hope. The clerk was a pleasant man of slight build and about fifty years of age. I explained that we wanted a license to get married right away. He said that there was a mandatory three day waiting period in Maryland. Seeing our distress he said that he was very sorry but there was nothing he could do. Dejected, Anita and I walked into the large spacious part of the City Hall building. Anita was desperate and about to start crying. I was equally upset and wondering what to do next.

As we were trying to decide what to do, a tall thin man about thirty years of age approached us. He said, "Excuse me, you seem to be in some sort of trouble. I am an attorney and perhaps I can help you out." I told him that we had eloped and that it was essential that we get married to-day. He then said that he could get the license for us and that he would need $ 75.00 to do it. As I gave him the $ 75.00 I could see the clerk watching us from behind his counter. The attorney told us to wait where we were and he turned and went over to the license clerk. We could see the two of them arguing for about five minutes. The attorney came back to us and as he handed me the $ 75.00, he said the clerk would not budge. I decided to approach the license clerk again. When we reached the counter, the clerk said, "You young folks should watch out for legal sharks like that one. I would not give that leech the right time." I said to the clerk that I was sure every law has one or more loop holes in it, and there must be some loop hole in your Maryland three day waiting period law. He replied that there was an exception for military men that was passed during the war and it had not yet been rescinded. It was too bad that I was not a soldier or a sailor on active duty, for if I were, he could help me. I took my "Z" card out of my wallet and handed it to him and said, "I am an active licensed officer in the merchant marine will that count?" He looked at the card carefully, and handing it back to me, he said, "It may be stretching the law, but I will take a chance and issue you a license to get married."

I thanked him and paid the license fee. The clerk then asked what church we would like to use for the wedding service. I replied that we were not familiar with any church in Baltimore and would just like to have a Justice of the Peace perform the service. He informed us that in Maryland you had to be married by clergy, no Justice of the Peace had the authority to perform a marriage ceremony. Then he asked what faith we were. Anita replied that she was a Roman Catholic, and I said that I was a Methodist. Smiling, the clerk said that we would no doubt be married in the Catholic Church. He then asked if we would like him to set up a time and place with a Catholic church in Baltimore, and we replied that we would appreciate it. Retreating to a phone some distance behind his counter, he spent a few minutes conversing with someone. The clerk returned to the counter and informed us that we had an appointment with a Father Dugan at six o'clock in the rectory of the Baltimore Cathedral. Thanking him, I handed him a twenty dollar bill to show my appreciation for his help. He handed it back to me and said, "You keep it son, you will need it a lot more than I will." Occasionally a person is fortunate enough to meet truly decent people. This clerk was one of those and one of the nicest strangers I have ever encountered. He saw the distress Anita and I were in and he went out of his way to help us.

Leaving the City Hall, Anita and I went to a restaurant and had some lunch. It occurred to me that we had left New York in such haste, that we only had the clothes we were wearing. After lunch we went to the Hub department store and spent a few hours shopping for clothes. Anita bought a suit and skirt, a hat, under garments, shoes, and pajamas. I bought a couple of shirts and a couple of sets of skivvies and socks. Then we went to the Biltmore Hotel and reserved a room. A little before six o'clock we arrived at the rectory of the Baltimore Cathedral. Father Dugan, a relatively young priest, cordially ushered us into a parlor like room, and said he would join us there shortly. After about ten minutes, he came into the room and we told him of our elopement and our wish to be married. He took Anita aside to hear her confession, and later jokingly asked if I wanted him to hear my confession. Of course, I declined. The priest then called another young couple into the room and introduced them to us. He said that they had agreed to stand up for us. Father Dugan then performed the ritual of the marriage ceremony. Anita and I were married. He then prepared the appropriate documents for us certifying our marriage and wished us well in our future together. We left the rectory and went to a restaurant and had a quiet dinner. Afterward we went to the hotel, and Anita sent a telegram to her parents telling them that we were married. I also phoned my parents and told them that Anita and I had gotten married in Baltimore.

We returned to New York the next day and got a room at the Algonquin Hotel in Manhattan. I was running low on money, so I made a visit to the Seaman's Bank and drew out enough to carry us through the next couple of weeks. Anita phoned her parents while I was at the bank, and they insisted on seeing her the next day. They arranged for a meeting at the Drake Hotel at ten o'clock in the morning. Knowing that her parents were very angry with me, I did not look forward to the impending confrontation. Before we left our hotel that morning, I went to a phone booth and looked up the phone number of the police station closest to the Drake Hotel. I then gave a very detailed account of my situation and my apprehension that there might be considerable trouble to the desk sergeant who took my call. The desk sergeant asked for my description and Anita's description and what we would be wearing. He said that he would have a plain clothes detective there to take care of any trouble that might occur. As Anita and I entered the lobby of the Drake Hotel, a large man in a brown suite gave me wave of his hand and a wink. I assumed that he was the detective. When Anita and I entered an anti room where her parents, her older brother, and another man were seated, the detective stood by the entrance way trying to look disinterested. This other man was the one I was most concerned about. He resembled a gorilla with a shave and a suite. I was sure his knuckles would drag on the floor if he stood up. After each one took turns telling me what a low life louse, snake, rat, and coward I was, the other man said, "You better treat my cousin good or I will come looking for you." That was Anita's cousin, Jimmy Romano. Obviously a man one would not be wise to antagonize. I said nothing, and after a few minutes we left the Drake Hotel with Anita in tears. I was glad to get that meeting behind us and that there was nothing more than harsh words thrown at me.

The following morning I went to visit the attorneys who were preparing my suit against the Bravoort Hotel. I told them that Anita and I had eloped and that we were now legally married. The attorneys looked disappointed and half heartedly congratulated me and wished me luck. They said that I no longer had a case against the hotel, and told me to tell my bride that I had thrown away $ 160,000 in order to marry her. Next I went to the Boland and Cornelius office on Rector street and told Mr. King that Anita and I had eloped and had gotten married in Baltimore. He wished us well and said that he would like to take us out to dinner some evening soon. The company was still in the process of turning their ships back to the Maritime Commission, and Mr. King said the office would probably be closed by the end of the year. However, he said he would do his best to get some night mate assignments for me as often as he could. Mr. King thought that my returning to school was a good thing to do. He said that the future of the American merchant marine did not look too good. There were too many foreign flag companies acquiring American ships and then competing with the American flag ships for the available cargo. This was driving the freight rates down making it much more difficult for American companies to make a profit and stay in business. Boland and Cornelius decided to quit operating ships on salt water when the freight rate for industrial coal fell below $13.00 per ton. To further exacerbate the problem, our short sighted self serving politicians began clamoring for an end to subsidies for American flag vessels so they could compete with the foreign flag operators.

The next problem Anita and I had to face was finding a place to live. We could not stay in the hotel for an extended period because it would have been far too expensive. I wanted to at least complete the semester at the Fort and Anita had to complete her student teaching program and get her teaching credentials. We decided that it would be best to find a place somewhere in Flushing or the Bay Side part of the Borough of Queens. That would put us equal distances to the Fort and the school on Long Island. We searched the papers for available apartments or houses for rent. With the horde of men coming out of the services and looking for places to live and start their own families, there were few places available for rent. More critical however was the fact that ex-servicemen were given preference for housing. As a civilian merchant mariner I was not eligible. The lying politicians had decided to cancel all the promises they had made to the merchant seamen when they needed them. They knew that merchant seamen did not generally vote, but that the servicemen returning to civilian life would vote. My dislike of and contempt for career politicians increased even more. The few places Anita and I found were totally unacceptable. We finally decided to take a place in Whitestone on a temporary basis. This place consisted of a very large room on the second floor of a house in a residential area. There was a screen divider to separate the bedroom space from a makeshift dining area. There was a private bathroom, but the kitchen had to be shared with another renter. It was outrageously expensive, but it was close to bus transportation that made it possible for us to go to our separate schools.

I returned the car to my father and that left us with the need to buy a car for ourselves. Automobiles were in short supply because of the demand for them. To get a new car one had to go on a waiting list. Used cars were extremely expensive. For the first few weeks of our marriage Anita and I relied on public transportation to get around. I had missed a week of school and had a lot of work to catch up on. My parents came to visit us one evening in our one room apartment and had dinner with us. They were very supportive. A couple of weeks later Anita told me that one of her classmates had told her about his aunt who was looking for someone to rent her house. The aunt's husband was an army captain and was assigned to a post in Japan. We went to visit the aunt, Mrs Malazzo, and she said that she was going to join her husband and was going to leave for Japan in about four weeks. Her house was the end unit of a row house with two stories and a cellar. She was sufficiently impressed with us to suggest that we move in to her house at the end of our one month's rent of the apartment. It would mean sharing the house with her for about a week. She was renting it to us furnished, but there was one other stipulation. We would have to take care of her dog. Since her house was located in the part of Flushing that bordered on Whitestone, the location was ideal for Anita and me. The address was 2212, 169th street. We accepted her offer and moved in at the end of the month. During that period I managed to find a car we could afford. It was a 1939 Willies/Graham sedan. About ten days later Mrs Malazzo was in the process of leaving. Unfortunately we had never settled on the amount of money she wanted for the rent. On the day Mrs Malazzo was to leave she hit me with the price of the rent she wanted. It was much larger than I had expected, and I wanted to turn it down. She would not negotiate a lower cost and when I balked, she started to cry and fuss saying that I was letting her down. Anita said that we had no choice and had to accept her demands. Foolishly I acquiesced. We were now stuck with a rent I knew we could not afford.

My school work was very demanding, and the occasional night mate assignments I got helped with paying the bills. However with both of us going to school and the high rent we had to pay, my bank account was shrinking rapidly. Two months went by and Anita and I decided to sub let part of the house to another couple in order to reduce our costs. A recently returned soldier and his German war bride moved in with us and I charged them half the amount we were paying in rent. They stayed only for a month until the soldier was able to get housing under the military preferential program. Another couple of months went by before we got another couple. They were young like us and had a new born baby. The husband worked for a furniture company in Flushing and his wife stayed at home to take care of the baby. They were good natured and we got along fine. There was one problem however. The mother had a bad habit of leaving the front door open when she had the baby outside for fresh air. It was winter time and the cost of heating the house became excessive. The mother did not care because I had to pay the fuel bill. After a few months they found a more suitable place and moved on. We had the house all to ourselves again, and decided that sub renting was not something we wanted to continue doing.

Some of my classmates made a habit of visiting our place frequently. They enjoyed the opportunity to relax and enjoy a good meal with us once in a while. One of my classmates, Bill Ryan, got us interested in the Alumni Association and we spent an occasional evening there helping to get the mail out. These sessions were called "stamp licking parties." Another married couple, Joe and Patricia Betz, were a part of the group of younger people helping at the Alumni office. Joe was also a classmate. He had taken the marine engineering program while we were at the Academy, and had gone on active duty in the Navy when we graduated. Like me, he too had returned to the Academy to take advantage of the Post Diploma degree program. Joe and I were the only PD students from our class who were married. Anita and Patricia took an immediate liking to each other, and the four of us soon became life long friends. Once in a while Mr. King would invite Anita and me to have dinner with him in Manhattan. He was a bachelor and it was obvious that he enjoyed our company. We also saw Ira and Jane on occasion, and when my buddy Dick Kadison came home from college in Chicago for a couple of weeks we visited with him. I taught Anita how to drive an automobile, and when she got her license she was able to visit her parents with less difficulty.

One Saturday as I was walking from the subway station to Sullivan's yard to do a weekend assignment as a night mate, I met one of the Norwegian seamen who had been on the MV Amiga Mia. I was surprised to see him and I asked him what he was doing back in Brooklyn. He should have been on his way to Central America with the boat. The story he told me verified my opinion that Jones and Martin/Cohen were the worst kind of crooks. He said that a few minutes after I got off the boat, Mr. Jones got off and walked up the darkened pier to the roadway. He returned a short time later and said to Rosie Martin/Cohen, "I could not find him." It must have been me he was referring to, and he probably intended to retrieve the money they had given me. The seaman then said that they waited until daybreak before leaving the pier. They proceeded to Stuart and crossed Florida via Lake Okeechobee and out into the Gulf of Mexico. The boat encountered some severe storms crossing to New Orleans, and took quite a beating. The crewmen were exhausted by the time the boat made it up the Mississippi River to New Orleans.

The evening of the day they docked in New Orleans, Rosie Martin/ Cohen gave each of the crew twenty dollars and told them to have a night on the town. She and Mr. Jones would stay aboard and look after the boat. After their rough passage, the whole crew went ashore happy to have a chance to see and enjoy the town. Later that night when the crew returned to the pier, the MV Amiga Mia was gone. They were all left stranded in New Orleans with only the money they had left after their night on the town and the clothing they were wearing. The crewmen went their separate ways, some looking for local employment and others looking for a way to get back to New York. It seems that when the crew was out of sight, Mr. Jones and Rosie Martin/Cohen moved the boat across the river to Algiers with the help of a couple of men they had hired earlier. There they took on fuel and provisions and hired additional men to fill out the crew. As soon as they had all they needed, they departed for Galveston, Texas. Miss Tosti was still with them. They probably kept her with them because she was an attractive young woman and made them look more legitimate. None of the original crew got any of the wages they were owed. Since the seamen and engineers were aliens, and probably illegal aliens, they could not go to the authorities for redress. If they did so, they would be deported. It is likewise doubtful that the Chief Mate and the Second Mate got any of the wages they were owed. Rosie Martin/Cohen and her partner were shrewd unscrupulous operators.

On a Friday evening a few weeks after my meeting with the Norwegian seaman, I decided to take Anita out to dinner in Manhattan. We went to the Rainbow restaurant, the one that Mr. Tosti owned. As we entered, Mrs Tosti recognized me. With a look of surprise she put both of her hands to her cheeks and said, "You are alive, I thought that you were dead." After Anita and I were seated at a table, she sat down with us and explained her surprise at seeing me alive. She related that a few days after the MV Amiga Mia arrived in Galvaston, the local Sheriff came aboard with a court order and seized the vessel. The people in New York who were owed so much money had caught up with the MV Amiga Mia. Rosie was furious, and she blamed me for tipping off the people in New York as to where she and the MV Amiga Mia were. Then a day or so later Rosie and Miss Tosti were in a waterfront bar where two tough men joined them. Rosie had arranged to meet these men there. At this meeting Rosie hired these men to seek me out and put my lights out permanently. They were paid half of their fee then, with the understanding that they would be paid the other half when the job was done. Miss Tosti was certainly familiar with hit men considering her father's background, and was sure that these two men were professionals. When her daughter returned home and told her all about the happenings in Galvaston, Mrs Tosti assumed that the hit men had fulfilled their contract. I believe the slick con woman, Rosie Martin/Cohen, was taken by another pair of slick con men. As far as I know, no such hit men ever came looking for me. However, after what Mrs Tosti told me, I began to look over my shoulder much more frequently. I heard some time later that the MV Amiga Mia was sold at auction, and that Rosie Martin/Cohen had some shill bidding on it for her. As to what ever happened after that, I have no knowledge. I also believe that the investors lost all the money they had invested in the bogus venture. However I doubt that Mr. Tosti lost his investment if he actually made one. With his background and the people he knew from the days of prohibition, cheating him would be a life threatening risk.

Towards the end of December I got a night mate assignment on the last of the Boland and Cornelius ships to be taken out of service. The ship was berthed at the Brewer Dry-dock Company pier on Staten Island. When I reported aboard to relieve the day mate, I discovered that it was a dead ship. That is, there was no power on board, and there is nothing colder than a dead ship in the winter time. In order to keep from freezing, a coal fire was kept burning in one of the stoves in the galley. Kerosene lanterns were placed at critical places to provide some light. My relief mate came aboard a little before midnight, and it turned out to be my old skipper on the S.S. Haywood Broun, Patty Keenan. We greeted each other like long lost friends. As we huddled close to the stove in the galley, we brought each other up to date on what we had been doing since leaving the S.S. Haywood Broun in Charleston. While we were talking a large black rat jumped up on the galley table and sat there looking at us rather forlornly. Captain Keenan pulled a sandwich out of a bag he was carrying and unwrapped it. He then broke off a substantial piece and gave it to the rat. It was consumed immediately, and the rat was given another piece. The three of us must have made a strange scene. Captain Keenan and I talking quietly and the rat sitting there eating the Captain's sandwich like some household pet. It was now Sunday morning, and the ship was scheduled to be towed up the Hudson River to join the reserve fleet in a day or so. As I was leaving the ship, the Captain and I wished each other a merry Christmas and expressed hopes of sailing together again some day.

Before Boland and Cornelius closed their office in January 1949, Mr. King wrote a very nice letter to me. As the acting operations manager he thanked me for my loyalty and dedication to the company and praised my professional competence while expressing regret that the company was closing its doors and he would not be able to offer me another assignment to a ship. This letter was better than any of the letters of recommendation I had received from the captains I had sailed with. A month or so later Mr. King took a position with the State Department. They sent him to Korea to help that nation start its own merchant marine. He had introduced us to his sister Vera and asked that we look in on her once in a while. She also lived in Manhattan and worked in some downtown office. Mr. King wanted us to keep in touch with him and said that he expected to return to the States in about two years. Anita did some student teaching at a school in Glenwood Landing out on Long Island, and then became a full time teacher there. Those first two semesters as a PD student were very busy. However, my bank account was deflating much too fast, and even with Anita working, I would not be able to return to school in the Fall without more money coming in. I decided that I would have to find a ship and go back to sea for a while to get enough money ahead to be able to return to school. My classmates who had gone on active duty with the Navy were subsidized in school by the G. I. Bill. Those clever lying politicians made sure that there was no similar bill for the men who served in the merchant marine during the war.

It was now June 1949, and the decline of the American merchant marine soon became obvious to me. I started making the rounds of the various steam ship company offices in Manhattan. The usual procedure was to enter an office and ask to see the operations manager, and to tell the receptionist that I was looking for a job as a mate. Sometimes I would be asked to fill out an employment application and wait until the company called me. Other times I would get to speak with someone in the operations department. The response was usually that there were no openings at this time, but that they would keep my application on file and call me when an opening occurred. I made a habit of including Mr. King's letter with the application forms I submitted. Because of the time traveling between these offices and the waiting time to see someone, it was possible on average to only visit three shipping company offices each day. When I went into the office of the United Fruit Company, Captain Day, the operations manager invited me into his office. He said that he had no job to offer me, but since he was also a graduate of the New York Maritime Academy he wanted to assure me personally that he would call me if any mate's job opened up. By the end of my first week of looking for a job I became very discouraged. There were more licensed deck officers looking for work than there were jobs available.

The next week of looking for a job was equally discouraging until Friday. On that day I went into the offices of the Farrell Line. After filling out the usual application form and submitting it to the receptionist, I was asked to remain while the senior Port Captain reviewed it. About a half hour later I was invited into the office of Captain Sullivan. This tall lean white haired man shook my hand and asked me to take a seat, then said that he was impressed with my record. After I answered several questions about my shipboard experiences and schooling, Captain Sullivan asked me if I would accept a position as a Third Mate. I said that I would be delighted to do so. He then said that I should return to his office the following Monday and that he was going to assign me to the S.S. African Star as Third Mate. The S.S. African Star carried four mates, but only the Second, Third, and Fourth Mates were watch standers. The Chief Mate was on a day routine and did not stand watches. The S.S. African Star was a C-3 class vessel and was assigned to the run from New York and U. S. East Coast ports to South and East African ports. The turn around time for this run was about three months. Anita received the news of my getting a job with the Farrell Line with mixed emotions. She was glad that I had found a ship, but distressed that the voyage and my time away from her would be so long.

THE AFRICAN RUN

The next week I reported aboard the S.S. African Star, and on 20 June 1949, I was signed on foreign articles as Third Mate. I had been told that I would need to have a complete set of uniforms. This ship carried twelve passengers as well as cargo and was operated on a very formal basis. The master was Captain Jonathan M. Wainwright V, son of the famous General Wainwright who surrendered to the Japanese on Corregidor. Arthur Renahan, a tall pleasant fellow was the Chief Mate. The Second Mate was a fellow named Albert Boerum and he had a rather superior, standoffish attitude. The Fourth Mate was a friendly fellow named Patrick McDonough. They were all graduates of the U. S. Merchant Marine Academy. Other officers included a Chief Engineer, three Assistant Engineers, a Radio Operator, a Purser, and a Chief Steward. The unlicensed crew consisted of a boatswain, a carpenter, a deck engineer, six able seamen, three ordinary seamen, a ship's electrician, three each oilers, firemen, wipers, and three each cooks, stewards, and utility men. There were also two Midshipmen from the U. S. Merchant Marine Academy, one each for the deck, and the engine departments. All of the crew were white, except for a few Negro stewards. The ship itself was immaculate. All the bridge and boat deck railings had teak wood caps and all the decks were painted. There was no rust to be seen anywhere. The door to my port side cabin was opposite the door to the passengers lounge across the companion way. There were six spacious and luxurious passenger cabins. The S S African Star was by far the nicest ship I had ever been assigned to, and the ship's officers were always in proper uniform and were shown the proper respect by the crew as well as the shore side people.

A few days after the articles were signed the S S African Star set sail for Capetown with a full load of cargo and twelve passengers. The passengers included a company official with his wife and two children, a teen age girl and a boy eight or nine years of age. There were also three couples going on vacation, and a doctor and a business man returning to South Africa.

S S African Star
C-3 Passenger/Cargo Vessel, Farrell Line

Six Brahma bulls were carried on the aft deck in specially constructed pens. The officers took their meals with the passengers in the dining salon, and there was a separate lounge with a bar for the passengers. A half hour before each meal was served, a steward would walk along the companion way past the lounge and the passengers cabins continuously sounding a chime or gong. The stewards wore white jackets and black trousers with a blue stripe down each leg. The Mates wore khaki, navy blue, or white uniforms, and the seamen always wore clean shirts and trousers, usually khaki, when on bridge duty. This ship was run like a passenger liner.

I had the twelve to four watch, the Second Mate had the four to eight watch, and the Fourth Mate had the eight to twelve watch. Second Mate Boerum always seemed a little testy around me. It may have been due to the fact that he was sailing as Second Mate on a Second Mate's license, while I was sailing as Third Mate with a Chief Mate's license. Fourth Mate McDonough had a Third Mate's license. The Chief Mate Renahan had a Chief Mate's license. Rumor had it that Mr. Boerum was dating one of the Farrell girls. He kept a picture of her in a prominent place in his cabin.

The run to Capetown was smooth sailing all the way. From the time the New York pilot was dropped off till the time the pilot for Capetown was picked up, the ship never experienced any foul weather. The deck crew were a relatively young happy pleasant bunch, and the boatswain, a man in his late fifties, was like a father to these seamen.

When the ship reached warmer waters, the deck crew built a makeshift swimming pool on number four hatch using wood dunnage and canvass tarpaulins. They filled it with sea water and it was used by both the crew and some of the passengers. As was the custom, the crew held homage to King Neptune with a raucous party when the ship crossed the equator. Some of the passengers, especially the teen age girl, joined in the fun and games. Everyone had a great time.

One morning at 0400 as we were changing watches the New York Marine Operator was picked up on the ship's VHF radio. The ship was in the Caribbean Sea, and the VHF radio usually only had a line of sight range. However, the atmospheric conditions allowed the New York Marine Operator to come in loud and clear. I took the VHF radio's microphone and gave the New York Marine Operator my home phone number and placed a call. I woke Anita up in the wee hours of the morning. She was surprised and delighted to get the call but after a couple of minutes our voices faded away as the atmospheric conditions changed with the approaching dawn. The Radio Operator explained the phenomenon had something to do with bouncing radio waves off the ionosphere. In any event there was only a minimum charge for the call because we were unable to give the Marine Operator the ship's position. Another pleasant thing developed during this passage. Every afternoon when I got off watch at four o'clock, I would go to my cabin and rest for a while before dinner. My cabin door was kept ajar by a hook to provide better ventilation. From four to five o'clock the passengers were served cocktails in the passenger's lounge. Every afternoon I would see a steward's arm reach through my door and deposit a highball on my desk. All things considered, the passage to Capetown was very pleasant.

As the ship approached the Cape of Good Hope, it encountered a noticeable swell a day or two before land was sighted. These were known as the Cape Rollers. Late one afternoon land came into sight on the horizon and as we approached deserted rocky hills became visible. The ship ran parallel to the coast line as the Cape of Good Hope was approached. During my night watch on the bridge I saw a cluster of bright lights in one spot on the otherwise dark shoreline. The chart of that part of the coast indicated that there were no towns or any industry there. Captain Wainwright came into the wheel house, and I asked him if those lights indicated a town or a settlement. He said no, and that actually those lights represented a great tragedy. A Captain making his last voyage before retiring from the sea had been assigned to a brand new ship making its first voyage to South and East Africa. During a very dark night, the Third Officer made a navigational error and ran the ship aground on that desolate rocky coast. The ship was a total loss. The lights on the shore were those of a salvage company recovering what cargo could be removed.

Capetown made a beautiful sight as we approached it from the sea. There were white or light colored buildings and an abundance of trees and other greenery with Table Mountain and Lions Rump forming a background along the horizon. A pilot boat brought the pilot out to the ship, and with the pilot on board the ship proceeded into Capetown harbor. The harbor was protected by a long breakwater that had a road way along its entire length. Entering the harbor, the ship had to pass close to the breakwater and people standing there could be clearly heard shouting welcome. I was told that one of our seamen was married to a South African girl and that she and her family were probably part of that crowd. As soon as the ship was moored to a pier and pratique was granted, the company agents came aboard with mail and various documents. Sea watches were not broken and cargo operations were started right away. We were due to sail the following afternoon.

I had several letters from Anita and my mother so I went to my cabin to read them. A letter from my mother said that she had written to her cousin, Jimmy Taylor, who lived in Capetown, and had informed him that I would be arriving there on the S S African Star. I had just finished the letter when the gangway watchman knocked on my door and said that there was a couple on the dock asking to see me. It turned out to be Jimmy Taylor and his wife. Jimmy Taylor was a short heavy set man in his late fifties, and his wife was a slender red haired woman at least a head taller than he was. I invited them aboard and the steward served them coffee and cake in the dining salon. Later I took them on a tour of the bridge. Jimmy Taylor just nodded as I explained the use of each piece of equipment on the bridge. When we walked out to the wing of the bridge, he put his hand on the dogger and said, "On my ship I had them install a platform so that I could see over the dogger."

"Your ship?" I asked.

He replied, "Yes, I had command of His Majesty's Ship XXXXX, a frigate." Jimmy Taylor had led me down the garden path and then sand bagged me. I had no idea that he had been a senior officer in His Majesty's Navy. He and his wife invited me to visit their home that evening, but circumstances would not allow me to do so. With my watch duties and the ship sailing the next day, I could not accept their invitation to visit them ashore.

The next afternoon the ship departed Capetown and set a course for Durban. The run up the coast of Natal, East Africa to Durban was uneventful. Durban was the major seaport for South Africa and had a population of about three quarters of a million people, whereas Capetown had a population of at least a million people. Durban harbor was a land locked lagoon with an entrance to the Indian Ocean. The city was quite impressive and very clean with many large buildings, stores, and restaurants. This was the port for disembarking our passengers. The last of these to leave was the doctor. He was met by a Mr. And Mrs. Foster and they asked to be given a tour of the ship. As they were leaving, Mrs. Foster said that she was having a welcome home party for the doctor at her house, and she invited the Captain and the ship's officers to attend. McDonough, two of the Engineers, the Radio Operator and I accepted her invitation. The others declined with thanks, because they already had other engagements. The next evening Mr. Foster picked us up at the gangway and drove us to his home. It was a large house in a residential area of Durban. There was quite a large crowd at the welcome home party, and there was an abundance of food and drinks for everyone. Mr. Foster was a former jockey and well known all over South Africa.

During the party Mrs. Grace Foster was especially attentive to me, and introduced me to her daughter and several others of her friends. As the evening wore on she told me that her daughter, who was about twenty years old, was the product of a previous marriage. She had been married to a sea going Scott named Murray and the marriage did not work out. They had divorced after only a few years. This was probably the reason she took such an interest in me. However it was soon obvious that the Murray she had been married to was not related to me in any way. Mrs. Foster invited me to attend another party the following evening. This dinner party was being held at an upscale place called the Athelone Gardens. I do not know if she had invited anyone else from the ship, for I was the only one of the ship's company at this dinner party. All together there were about a dozen people at this party including the doctor. An excellent roast beef dinner was served by Indian waiters while an orchestra played dance music in the background. The Athelone Gardens was a large elegant place with both an inside and an outside dining area in a garden setting. Our party was seated at a long table in the outside area. The other guests were very friendly and made my evening very enjoyable. After the dinner and an hour or two of cocktails, Harry Foster drove me back to the ship. When he learned that I would be on watch the next evening, he invited me to have dinner at his home the following evening and said that he would pick me up at eight o'clock. It was customary to have dinner at about nine o'clock in the evening in South Africa. I spent another pleasant evening with the Fosters. Grace was a born and bred South African with a Boer and English background. She owned a small tea house restaurant in downtown Durban. Harry was an Englishman who had emigrated to South Africa as a young man and made quite a name for himself as a jockey. He then went on to training and breeding race horses. Grace was a full head taller than Harry and they made an odd looking couple. They had obviously taken a liking to me and went out of their way to make my visit to Durban enjoyable.

The officers of the S S African Star
(L to R) Mr. Sabadosh, Captain Wainwright, Mr. Boerum,
Mr. Murray, Mr. McDonough

The ship stayed in Durban for six days and then departed for Lourenco Marques in Mozambique. The trip North up the East Coast of Africa was uneventful. We pulled into the harbor of Lourenco Marques in the late afternoon, and with the aid of a pilot went to a dock. Sea watches were not broken and the ship remained in port for only about eight hours. Lourenco Marques was a clean picturesque city with many impressive buildings. The city had a population of about three quarters of a million people. Unfortunately, I did not get an opportunity to go ashore to sample the shops and the local atmosphere. After discharging and loading some general cargo, the ship received instructions to proceed on up the coast of Mozambique to the port of Beira. Again the run up the coast of Mozambique was uneventful. After steaming a little less than two days, the ship entered an estuary whose waters were muddy brown and proceeded to an anchorage off the city of Beira. The few deep water docks were already occupied by other ships and there were four or five additional ships at anchor waiting their turn to go to a dock. Port agents informed Captain Wainwright that it would be about four weeks before dock space would be available for the S S African Star.

Four weeks swinging on the hook was not something we wanted to do. Sea watches were broken and the crew went on day work. This gave the Chief Mate an excellent opportunity to get a lot of painting and other maintenance work accomplished. A card table was set up in the wheel house and a game of monopoly was started with the off watch officers playing. That game went on for a full three weeks with different people playing in teams around the clock. Three times a day after each meal, the mess men would dump the garbage off the stern. Large black sharks would gather off the stern usually a good half hour before the garbage was dumped. We could see their fins and part of their backs as they swarmed around waiting for their meal. The muddy water made it impossible to see their whole bodies, but we could tell that they were big and dangerous. One day the Chief Engineer asked to have the draft read so that he could determine how much fuel oil had been consumed since the ship left Durban. I was on deck watch that day so it was up to me to read the draft. With the help of the Second Mate and the Fourth Mate a boatswain's chair was rigged and I was lowered over the stern to a position where I could see the draft marks. The number of feet the stern was down was called up to the Second Mate and he recorded it on a pad. Next these two mates lowered me over the bow so I could read the draft forward. I called the draft reading to them and then said haul me up. Instead of raising me up, they lowered me more. As the chair reached the surface of the water, I stood up and started to climb up the rope. When I had climbed up several feet, they lowered the rope more putting me back too close to the water's surface. All I could think of was those big black sharks. There was about a two knot current running and the anchor chain entered the water about a hundred feet ahead of my position. My arms were getting tired from hanging on the rope and I was about to let go and try to swim to the anchor chain when they started to haul the rope up. When I reached the gunnel of the forecastle deck, the two jokesters ran aft and hid from me. That practical joke could have cost me my life.

By the middle of the second week at anchor boredom set in. I asked one of the ship's agents who had come aboard if it were possible to go on a safari inland for a couple of days. He said that he would ask some people in town and let me know. Returning to the ship the next day, he informed me that he had found two professional hunters who would be willing to take a small group on a safari. With the Captain's permission, six of us, the Fourth Mate, the Second Engineer, the Radio Operator, the two Midshipmen, and I arranged to go on a picture taking safari. The stewards department prepared food for three days for us and with that and a good supply of drinking water and sodas, we went ashore one morning and joined our guides. The guides were professional elephant hunters and were a strange pair. The older one was a rugged out door type and the younger one small and slight of build. He was obviously more polished and better educated. His name was Basil Laconides, and I learned later that he was the author of a book on African game. The agent made the introductions and the guides said that they would take us to a game preserve known as the Gorongrossa Plain. It would take a full day to get there, and they had two Fargo pickup trucks for transportation. The charge was about thirty-five dollars apiece which was very reasonable.

We piled our provisions in the backs of the two trucks and then with one of our party in the cab with the driver and two in the back of each truck we started out for the Gorongrossa Plain. The trucks drove out of the town of Biera and passed through a few miles of farm land. The hard surfaced road soon gave out to a dirt road. From the farm land we entered a forested area with many low overhanging tree limbs. Our guides warned us to duck low and avoid getting close to these limbs. They said that there were two types of snakes that were often in these tree limbs, the green

Basil Laconedes, a native boy, and Art Murray.
A native village in Mozambique, on the
way to the Gorongrossa Game Preserve.

mamba and the black mamba. The green mamba would be hard to see, and the black mamba was a larger and more aggressive reptile. Both are deadly. Few ever survive a bite from either of them. About three hours into this woodland we came to a native village of straw and wattle huts. Our guides stopped the trucks and conversed with the village elders for a while. One of the natives offered us fresh cut papaya. These were the largest papaya I had ever seen and they were deliciously sweet and juicy. Our journey continued on for a few more hours and suddenly the forest was behind us and we were on a vast plain dotted with clumps of brush and trees. The earth was black with a sparse covering of yellow straw like grass. In the distance ahead of us there was a concrete building with a palm thatch roof. That was our destination. We had reached the Gorongrossa Plain.

The two trucks pulled up to the side of the concrete building and parked. All of us got off and began transferring our gear into the building. There was one large room with three smaller rooms and a lavatory room. There were no doors to any of these rooms. The large room was furnished with a wooden table and five or six chairs. There were also four wicker chairs with large fan like backs. The smaller rooms were furnished with three single wood frame beds with cord or rope net lacing and no mattresses. They were reasonably comfortable with a blanket spread over the netting. The windows were open with no screening or other means to keep flying insects out. Our guides said that there would not be too many flies or mosquitos around because this was the dry season. However there were large black ants running around everywhere. We ate a Spartan meal of bread, canned meat, and fruit preserves and washed it down with Coca-Cola as the sun was setting. The guides set up a kerosene lantern and advised us to bed down early. We were told to sleep in our clothes and to keep our socks on. As I was sitting in one of the wing back wicker chairs to take my shoes off, I leaned back and felt something crawling on the back of my neck. Thinking it was one of the large back ants, I reached back to brush it off. Suddenly I felt a sting on the back of my neck that was many times more severe than any bee sting I had ever experienced. I jumped out of the chair and turned around to find that I had been stung by a scorpion. It was cream colored, about three inches long, and resembled a miniature lobster. I took one of my shoes and knocked it to the floor, and then beat it to a pulp. The pain in the back of my neck was severe and spiked up with every beat of my heart. Basil, the guide, said that the scorpion

(L to R) Loren Sahud, Art Murray, Basil Laconedes

sting though painful was not lethal, and that the pain would probably be much less by sunrise. He then warned us to be sure and shake out our shoes before putting them on in the morning. Basil said that scorpions and spiders were primarily night hunters and had a habit of hiding inside shoes and boots as the night was ending.

Morning came with a bright sun and a cloudless sky. Twilight was brief. Our party came alive slowly. After a breakfast of bread, crackers, and Coca-Cola we packed up our gear and loaded the trucks. Some of us had a few mosquito bites, but we were not worried about Malaria. We had been taking Atabrin pills daily since leaving Durban. Atabrin made one's skin become somewhat yellow, but it protected one against contracting Malaria. With the trucks loaded, we started out on the Gorongrossa plain looking for animals to photograph. We came upon a large herd grazing on the grass. The herd consisted of antelope, gnus, springbok, wildebeest, zebras, and other grazing animals. They were mixed together and not grouped by species. We were able to get quite close to them. After we had taken several photographs, our guides told us to get back in the trucks and hold on tight. They then maneuvered the trucks closer to the herd and honked their horns. This noise was strange to the grazing animals and it spooked them. With a large zebra in the lead, the whole herd stampeded. Our guides got their trucks about thirty feet behind the lead zebra and followed him just like the rest of the stampeding animals. Some were galloping so close to the truck that we could almost reach out and touch them. It was obvious that the stampeding animals had no idea what they were running away from. To them our trucks were just two more stampeding animals. After running for about ten or fifteen minutes, the herd began to slow down and finally stop running. Without much concern they resumed grazing while our trucks moved away. The animals did give our trucks a wide berth but they did not show much fear. To them our trucks were just strange animals that should be avoided but not feared.

Our guides drove us some distance to a small lake and stopped the trucks so that we could get off. I was amazed to see hippopotami, ducks, geese, and other water fowl in the water with huge crocodiles. The crocodiles were either sunning themselves on the bank or lying motionless in the water with most of their bodies submerged. The guides warned us that though these crocodiles appeared docile, they were extremely dangerous. They told us that the crocodile can run very fast on his stubby legs for a short distance. They will sometimes knock their prey into the water by slamming them with their tails when the prey gets too close to them. Once the prey is in the water the crocodile will kill it and stick it in the mud on the bottom and leave it there for a time to ripen. A little distance from the edge of the lake there were some termite castles. These were tower like mounds of sun hardened mud and clay and were as hard as sandstone. They stood six to eight feet high and were four to five feet thick. The guides warned us that lions would often sleep in the shade of these termite mounds. They said that if we should come upon a snoozing lion we should not run, but rather back away slowly. Lions are usually wary of humans, but if we were to run, a lion might just give chase. Both of our guides carried a shotgun with them as we walked around. They said that a shotgun is the only weapon that will stop a charging lion.

As I was walking past a termite mound with Basil I saw the skeleton of a good size fish. Basil explained that during the monsoon season the Gorongossa plain becomes a very large lake with an average depth of three to four feet. When the monsoon season, about three months, passes, the lake begins to dry up leaving several small lakes and ponds like the one we were now visiting. The wild animals migrate to higher ground during the monsoon and return when the waters recede. As we continued walking, Basil grabbed my arm in mid-stride and told me to stop. There just one step in front of me was a puff adder. It was a short rather fat reptile and appeared to have been sleeping. The pattern of colors on its skin allowed it to blend in with the yellow grass. Had I taken another step I would have stepped on it and would have probably been bitten by it. The puff adder is a venomous snake and its bite can be fatal. I backed away as the puff adder moved off sluggishly in the opposite direction. Continuing our walk, Basil and I came upon the bones of an antelope that had been a recent kill. There was little left after the vultures and ants were finished with it.

After walking around the lake for a couple of hours we returned to the trucks. Our guides said that they would try to find the most dangerous animal in Africa for us. That animal they said was the African buffalo. They travel in small herds usually numbering less than eight to ten animals. We began driving from one clump of trees to another looking for the African buffalo. These clumps consisted of four or five green thorny trees with thick underbrush beneath their limbs. As we continued our search we noticed a rain squall moving across the plain in our direction. When it was close, those of us in the backs of the trucks pulled canvass covers over our heads. The rain fell in a torrent for ten minutes or so and then moved off. Suddenly the trucks became bogged down. The black earth turned into a liquid puree and the wheels of the trucks sank down in it to the level of their axles. Our guides told us not to be concerned because the sun would bake the earth hard again in about a half hour. They were right. In thirty minutes or less the hot sun had baked the ground dry again. A few minutes of rocking back and forth and spinning the wheels had both trucks up and running on hard ground. Our search continued until our guides spotted a small herd of buffalo in the shade of a clump of trees.

Approaching the trees we saw that the herd consisted of three large animals and three that were slightly smaller. They were black with thick horns on the tops of their heads that curved around to the front of their heads. The guides told us to stay inside the trucks and to hold on tight because they might have to move the trucks out quickly. We were told that the African buffalo was very aggressive and inclined to charge at any animal that posed a threat to them. After we had taken several pictures, our guides moved the trucks backwards slowly towards the herd. As we got closer, the largest of the buffalo turned towards us, snorted and put his head down. The guides took this as a sign to shift gears and get ready to get out of there. With the big bull buffalo in the lead the whole herd charged at the trucks. Our guides got the trucks rolling and shifted into high gear quickly. The trucks were soon going about thirty miles an hour and the buffalo were keeping up. We must have gone a good quarter of a mile before the buffalo began to slow down and give up the chase. I asked Basil what the buffalo would have done if one of the trucks had stalled. He replied that the buffalo would have turned it into a pile of junk in short order. They are powerful, mean, and extremely dangerous. Knowledgeable people give them a wide berth.

Our picture taking safari continued until the sun got low on the horizon. Returning to the concrete huts, we had a leisurely meal and settled in for the night. There was practically no twilight. The sun set and the darkness of night came on quickly. We sat around listening to the guides telling of their adventures hunting elephants. They hunted them for the ivory, but the flesh was given to the natives for food. The natives would dry the meat for storage by placing stripes of it on wood racks and allowing the sun to bake it dry. Basil said that he was going to give up elephant hunting. He felt that the herds were being decimated and that the wild African elephant could soon become extinct. They were being slaughtered to such an extent that the market price for ivory was becoming too low to make the effort profitable. There was also extensive poaching in the game preserves not only for elephants, but for other types of game. Basil was concerned that with the proliferation of fire arms in the hands of the natives, the wanton slaughter of Africa's wild life would soon be out of control. At heart he was a conservationist.

When the sun came up the following morning we had our usual Spartan breakfast and then policed the concrete huts so that they would be clean for the next visitors. Our gear was stowed in the trucks, and at about mid morning we started the long ride back to Biera. The return trip went rather quickly and we arrived back at our guides compound in the afternoon. I gave each of our guides an extra twenty dollars and thanked them for taking us on such an interesting and exciting adventure. Before our party started back to the waterfront, Basil asked me to hang back. When my shipmates had departed, Basil took me to a locked shed where he and his partner stored their ivory. He unlocked the shed door, went inside, and came out with a pair of ivory tusks each one about a yard in length. Basil said that he wanted me to have them as a souvenir of the safari. He appreciated my organizing and motivating my shipmates to go on the safari and giving him and his partner a chance to earn some extra money. I accepted his gift with many thanks.

I invited both guides to come out to the ship the following day and have dinner on board. Basil came out to the ship, but his partner had left Biera on a business trip and could not make it. During dinner and while he was being shown around the ship, Basil seemed rather shy. It may have been the first time he had ever been aboard such a well found vessel. A few days later Basil took me on a tour of Biera and we visited some of his friends who had some captured wild animals. One of these animals was a caged leopard that had a very nasty disposition. Another of his friends had a baby elephant that had been orphaned when its mother was killed. It was still a suckling and appeared to be very hungry. The people who had the poor thing were not able to feed it. When I returned to the ship I asked the Chief Steward if he had enough canned milk on board to feed the baby elephant for a few days. He agreed to let me have as much as he could spare. The following day I went ashore and with Basil sought out the man who had the baby elephant. When we got to his place we were informed that the elephant had died. That news made me feel rather sad for several days. What I would have been able to do with the poor thing I do not know.

After four weeks swinging on the anchor, the S S African Star went alongside a dock in Biera. Gangs of native longshoremen came aboard and opened the hatches. Cargo operations were begun immediately, and were scheduled to run around the clock. Other ships had come into the port and were required to wait at anchor for their turn to go alongside a dock. Biera was a major port for Rhodesia as well as Mozambique and was therefore a very busy port. There were railroad tracks running along the dock and a variety of flatbed and gondola type rail cars were brought alongside the ship. Once the general cargo for Biera was discharged, we began loading hides, hardwood logs, and copper ingots. I had the four to midnight watch overseeing the loading of the cargo. The ship's cargo gear had to be used to discharge and load all the cargo. The stevedore foremen knew what they were doing and the native longshoremen were reasonably good at their work. However they were nowhere near as efficient as the longshoremen in Brooklyn, New York. With all five hatches working simultaneously, I was kept fairly busy going from hatch to hatch and keeping the stowage plan up to date.

During the night time cargo operations I had two exciting and frightening experiences. The native gang foreman at each hatch made a habit of putting one or more fishing lines out on the off shore side of the ship. Every once in a while they would catch a fish that weighed one or two pounds. The foreman at number three hatch was rather old and somewhat frail in appearance. One night as I came to number three hatch I saw him struggling with his fishing line. He appeared to have caught a very heavy fish and was having difficulty hauling it aboard. Since the cargo lights were aimed at the hatch opening, the deck and bulwark on the off shore side were in a very dark shadow. Seeing the old man pulling in his fishing line with such difficulty, I went over to the bulwark and began helping him pull the line in. The fish he had hooked must have weighed fifty to seventy-five pounds. Finally we got it over the bulwark and on to the deck. The fish turned out to be an eel about ten feet long with a head like a very large police dog and teeth to match. It was angry and snapping at us. The old man ran up the deck towards the forecastle, and I scrambled up the ladder to the boat deck. The eel slithered about the deck looking for some way to get back in the water. It created quite a commotion on the deck with the native longshoremen scurrying to get away from it. Finally a more courageous native grabbed a piece of two by four lumber and beat the eel to death. When calm returned to the deck, the old man and one of the longshoremen carried the eel off the ship. I do not know if it eventually wound up in the old man's cooking pot.

A night or two later we were loading copper ingots in number two hold. These ingots measured about two feet square and were about three inches thick. They were loaded into the ship's hold by the use of rope slings each containing eight to ten slabs. Each of the slabs were separated by pieces of wood. Longshoremen in the lower hold would remove the slabs from the sling and stack them by hand. It was a slow labor intensive process. The loading process was proceeding well when there was a sudden commotion in the lower hold. Some longshoremen were hurriedly climbing up the ladders to the main deck, while others were scrambling up the wooden battens on the sides of the hull. I went to the hatch foreman and asked him what all the excitement was about. He said that a very deadly snake had come aboard with a sling load of ingots. The ingots had been stacked on the pier side during the daylight hours to facilitate loading them aboard at night. Apparently the snake had slid in between two of the ingots in one of the stacks to avoid the heat of the sun. The stackers in the lower hold were startled and terrified when they lifted one of the ingots and discovered the snake. After much jabbering in their native tongue, one of the native longshoremen took a wooden club and climbed back down into the lower hold. He located the snake which was black and about six feet in length. Jumping around to avoid the snake's strikes, he managed to bash its head with the club. He then proceeded to smash the snake's head to a pulp. The hatch foreman said that the snake was either a cobra or a mamba. Either one is deadly and both are plentiful in Mozambique. Many of us were concerned that there may have been some more snakes brought aboard with the cargo that had not been detected.

With cargo operations close to completion, I made one more visit to Basil's home and purchased a python skin about eighteen feet in length from him. The skin had not been tanned, and was rolled in a tight bundle and had a slightly disagreeable odor. I thought that I could get it tanned when I got back to New York. When the last of the cargo was loaded, the hatches were covered, and the ship departed the port of Biera. A course was set for Durban and on the voyage south the port of Loernco Marks was by-passed. Three days later we arrived at the beautiful port city of Durban. Mr. Foster appeared at the dock shortly after the mooring lines were secured and invited me to have dinner with him and Mrs. Foster that evening. I accepted his invitation and enjoyed a very pleasant dinner with the Fosters and another couple from Johannesburg who were visiting them. This couple had been at the Foster's home on my first visit and that was more than six weeks ago. It seems that when people visit friends and relatives in South Africa they stay for an extended period of time. This visit to Durban was rather short and the ship sailed three days later.

On our voyage south down the coast of Natal the next port of call was East London. This was a small tidy city of about thirty six thousand people. The surrounding countryside was very much like a parched desert. Even though the city was located on the shore of the Indian Ocean, there appeared to be little rain fall inland. The ship tied up at a dock in the afternoon and made ready to load some cargo. Loading cargo was done only during the daylight hours so we had to spend another full day in port. We sailed the next morning bound for the city of Port Elizabeth. The distance was less than one hundred and fifty miles, so we steamed at a reduced speed in order to make our arrival in daylight. Upon arrival I found Port Elizabeth to be another clean tidy city with a population of about three hundred and sixty thousand people. The ship went right to a dock and started loading cargo an hour or so after the lines were secured. Later in the afternoon when I got off watch I went into town to see some of the city and browse around the shops.

While I was in a jewelry store purchasing an interesting looking desk clock, the owner asked me if I was off the American ship that had come into the port that day. When I told him that I was the Third Officer, he said that he had something that I might be interested in. He then produced a diamond bracelet and said that it was part of an estate he was disposing of for a friend. The largest diamond was about two carats and the others tapered off in size towards the ends of the bracelet. Since this was a special sale he said that I could have it for eight hundred dollars. He also suggested that it would be easy for me to smuggle it ashore when the ship returned to the States. I told him that I would think his offer over and that the ship was not due to sail until tomorrow. At dinner on board that evening, I told Captain Wainwright about the diamond bracelet offer. He warned me to be careful and that some less than honest jewelers would take advantage of a naive sailor. They would sell diamonds of low quality to an unsuspecting sailor at what would seem to be an extremely low price. Then they would inform the U. S. Customs agents to be on the lookout for that sailor when the ship reached the States. The jeweler would then receive a handsome reward from the U. S. Customs after the sailor was apprehended trying to smuggle the diamonds ashore. My conversation with the Captain convinced me that the possible gain did not justify taking such a risk. I did not even bother to go ashore again before the ship sailed.

The next morning the ship sailed for Capetown. The run was a little over four hundred miles so we arrived in Capetown in the late afternoon. Sea watches were not broken because there was just a small amount of cargo to be loaded. Cargo operations began early the next morning. A few tons of frozen lobster tails in wooden cases were loaded in the ship's cold locker. The agent allowed the ship's officers to buy some of the cases of frozen lobster tails. I bought two cases of lobster tails, about twenty pounds each, for two South African Pounds (about $ 10.50). About five million dollars worth of gold ingots were brought aboard and stored in the forepeake locker. A sturdy steel bar was welded across the locker doors to prevent anyone from getting to the gold. As the gold was being loaded aboard, one of the guards jokingly said I could have one of the ingots if I could pick it up. Each ingot weighed about four hundred pounds. By mid afternoon all the ships hatches and lockers were secured and the ship was ready to depart. As we were pulling away from the dock there were several pretty South African girls waving farewell to our sailors.

The next port of call was Walvis Bay in South West Africa. It took about two and a half days steaming the seven hundred plus miles to reach the entrance to Walvis Bay. Since the S S African Star was fairly heavily loaded it was necessary to wait for high tide before trying to enter the harbor. Even then the ship's bottom scrapped over the bar going into the harbor. Since the pilot advised that there was not enough depth of water at the dock, the ship had to anchor in the harbor. I had never seen a more desolate place. There was a single long concrete dock with a couple of long low warehouse sheds adjacent to it. No trees or greenery of any kind were visible — just a sandy desert stretching to the horizon. A short time after we anchored, a small tug boat brought a barge along side. Half a dozen natives were aboard the barge to off load the cargo. One of these natives was an albino Negro. The poor fellow had to keep his head and body covered to keep from being burned by the sun. The cargo consisted of a hundred or more bales of karakul skins. These were the skins of unborn lambs and were used to make very expensive women's coats. Because of their high value they were treated as special cargo. Each bale had to be examined and counted as it was stowed in a special locker in number one hold. The loading was completed in a few hours and the ship was ready to depart on the next high tide. Once clear of the Walvis Bay harbor, the S S African Star was put on the great circle course for the West Indies.

It seems appropriate at this point in my narrative that I recount my impressions of Africa and the people I met there. Without exception everyone I encountered in South Africa and Mozambique appeared to have a genuine admiration and affection for America and Americans. There was no sign of the dire poverty and shortage of food that was so prevalent in India and some of the Muslim countries I had visited in the past. Apartheid was the social norm in South Africa and to a lesser degree in Mozambique. The Caucasians were generally better off economically than the nonwhite portion of the population. The nonwhite population of South Africa in descending order on the social scale consisted of Asiatic Indians (Muslim and Hindu), Chinese, Half-castes, and full blood Negroes. The Indians and Chinese were shopkeepers, waiters, and blue collar tradesmen. The few half-castes I ran into were usually clerks in some business or government office. The only noticeable friction or animosity I saw was primarily between the Indian store keepers and the Negroes whom the Whites referred to as Kaffers. There had recently been some rioting in Durban between the majority Kaffers and the minority Indian shop keepers. Police and troops had to be called out to keep the native Kaffers from slaughtering the Indians whom they accused of always cheating them. However, for the most part I found the cities in Africa to be neat, clean, sanitary, orderly, and free of crime. Although the South Africans were always friendly, I was afraid that might soon change. It seems that the Black Caucus in the U.S. Congress was offended by the apartheid policy of the South African Government, and they introduced various sanctions against that government. With so much for them to worry about at home, I do not understand why they felt they must meddle in the affairs of another country. Although there was little social intercourse between the Whites and the Nonwhites, they did get along, and no one appeared to be going hungry.

The S S African Star steamed from Walvis Bay to Port of Spain, Trinidad. As usual the weather during our passage across the South Atlantic was beautiful with never a storm or a rough day. The ship entered the harbor at Port of Spain in the late afternoon and anchored. The lush green hills with white houses scattered about a little distance off were a pleasant sight to behold. Again sea watches were not broken. A tug boat brought an oil

barge alongside the ship and refueling operations were begun. Some fresh
stores were brought aboard to replenish the galley supplies. The Captain
and the Purser had to take care of some ship's business and were the only
people to go ashore. During the night while I was on watch, a Negro
fellow paddled up to the companion ladder in a canoe fitted with an out
rigger. I went down the ladder to find out what he wanted. All he was
wearing was an old straw hat and a pair of tattered shorts. He said that he
had some souvenirs to sell and asked if there was anything I might be
interested in buying. Half jokingly I asked him if he had any shrunken
heads. With the look of a man gravely insulted, he sat up erect and said in
a most disdainful voice, "Sir, we are civilized people in these islands."
Then he turned his canoe about and slowly paddled off into the night. I
have to admit that I felt a little bit ashamed of myself. By dawn the fueling
was completed and the oil barge was towed away. A few hours later the
anchor was pulled up and the ship steamed out of the harbor and set a
course for New York.

It took about five days to steam from Port of Spain to New York. It was
late afternoon on 20 September 1949 when we arrived and the ship went
right to the company pier in Brooklyn. Anita was there to meet the ship,
and after being away for three months, it was great to be home again. As
soon as pratique was granted, I met with her briefly on the pier and then
went back on board to help get the ship ready to discharge cargo. Company regulations would not allow Anita to go on board the ship, so she
had to wait on the pier for me. As soon as I got off watch an hour or so
later, we drove to our rented house in Whitestone and I caught up on all
that had been happening while I was away. Anita had gotten a teaching
job in a school in Glenwood Landing out on Long Island and was very
pleased with it. With the two of us now making an income, our financial
situation was much improved. Anita asked me to visit her class and tell
them all about Africa. I arranged to get a day off and went with her to her
school. Although it was only a fourth grade class, the kids were smart and
asked some really profound questions. Later Anita introduced me to Mr.
Keesler, the principal. She had gotten his permission to store my two cases
of frozen lobster tails in the school's refrigerator. He mentioned that he
loved lobster tail and I told him to help himself to them. That turned out
to be a mistake. Two weeks later there were only half a dozen lobster tails
left from the two twenty pound cases. Mr. Keesler had an enormous appetite and more gall than self control.

The S S African Star remained in New York for less than a week discharging and loading cargo. The Second Mate Boerum took off for Boston to sit for his Chief Mates license. He was reluctant to sit for it in New York where the examiners were the toughest in the Country. I was asked to take the Second Mate's position until he returned. During the day Anita went off to her school and I went to Brooklyn to work on the ship. The evenings we had to ourselves. Saturday and Sunday we spent visiting some of our friends, and we managed to get in a short visit to my parents. Late one afternoon I was overseeing the discharging of the bales of karakul skins we had loaded in Walvis Bay. Longshoremen were in the habit of using a hand held hook while handling cargo. I told the two longshoremen who were to work in the lower hold to leave their hooks up on deck. One of them slipped by me with his hook. Looking down into the hold from the main deck, I saw this longshoreman dig his hook into one of the bales of karakul skins. Furious with him, I told him to stick the hook in his belt and get out of the hold. We exchanged some nasty words and he began climbing out of the hold threatening to put his hook into me. I had no weapon to defend myself, and I could not afford to show fear and retreat. As he was climbing up the ladder from the lower hold, I was busy unscrewing the brass hose nozzle from the hose at the adjacent fire station. When the longshoreman climbed over the hatch combing on to the main deck, I was standing there with an eighteen inch brass hose nozzle in my hand. He looked at my brass club and decided that I could do him more harm that he could do to me. I ordered him off the ship and walked behind him to the gangway to make sure he did get off. The rest of the longshoremen returned to discharging the bales and none of them dared to use a hook.

Mid-week the ship set sail coastwise to pick up additional cargo. Philadelphia, Baltimore, and Charleston were ports of call. While we were in Philadelphia I visited my Uncle Jim and Aunt Edith. Although they were pleased to see me, they declined my invitation to visit the ship. After Charleston the ship returned to New York to complete the loading of cargo. On the coastwise passages, the Fourth Mate, McDonough asked me to stand his watch with him whenever the ship encountered heavy traffic. He had no confidence in maneuvering the ship when there were several other vessels close at hand. Rounding Cape Hatteras and approaching New York harbor with a dozen other ships going in different directions at different speeds can be a very nerve wracking experience. The ship remained in New York for another two days during which time Mr. Boerum returned. He lost no time in showing me his brand new Chief Mate's license, and letting me know that he was now my professional equal. He resumed his position as Second Mate and I reverted to the position of Third Mate. The radioman, Loren Sahud, and the Chief mate, Arthur Renahan, took the next voyage off. A new radioman and Chief mate came aboard as replacements. The new radioman was a quiet somewhat introverted fellow. The new Chief Mate was a burly fellow in his early fifties. Foreign articles were signed on 29 September 1949 and the next day sea watches were set and the ship departed New York bound for Cape town, South Africa. Turn around time had been a little more than ten days.

With a full load of cargo, twelve passengers, and a pilot aboard, the S S African Star cast off her lines and with the help of two tug boats headed for the open sea. The pilot was dropped off at the Sandy Hook Pilot Station and a course was set for the Windward Passage. Once through the Windward Passage, a great circle course was set for Cape Town, South Africa. Among our passengers there was a Catholic Priest and a Brother sharing the same cabin. Father Oakes was a widower in his early fifties who had just entered the priesthood, and Brother John was an Irishman. They were on their way to some remote area in Africa to tend to the needs of the natives. Father Oakes was a pleasant fellow who enjoyed a joke and was quick to laugh. He had an automobile in one of the ship's holds that he was taking to Africa. One of the Mates suggested that the Bishop of his area in Africa would probably confiscate the automobile because Father Oakes belonged to an order whose priests took an oath of poverty. Father Oakes responded that should that happen there would be an ecclesiastical funeral.

When the ship was just a few days from reaching Cape Town, the radio operator brought a radiogram to my cabin. As he handed it to me he said that he regretted having to do so. It was a short massage from Anita informing me that my father had died. I was suddenly overcome with grief and concern for my mother. Here I was at sea thousands of miles away when I should at home to help her through this tragedy. The radioman had taken the leave to inform the Captain and he in turn told the Chief Mate to take my next watch. Father Oakes came into my cabin and sat with me for a couple of hours. We talked about my father and I must admit that his quiet words were most comforting. I knew that Anita would be there to help and comfort my mother. Because I had no other information, I assumed that my father must have suffered a fatal heart attack.

During the next twenty four hours just about everyone on board expressed their regrets over my loss. I missed only one four hour watch and was back on duty when my next watch came up. I sent radiograms to both my mother and Anita expressing my sorrow and regrets for not being there.

When the mail came aboard in Cape Town, I learned that my father's death had been caused by a Long Island Railroad train. He had been crossing the tracks at an unguarded crossing during a heavy rain storm. Both he and the passenger in his taxi were killed by the impact with the train. My mother's letter indicated that she was all right and that Anita had been there to help her with the arrangements for my father. He had been buried in the National Cemetery at Pine Lawn on Long Island. Anita's letter gave me more details and assured me that there was nothing for me to worry about. The mail put my mind at ease. Even so, I knew that I would have to leave the S S African Star when it returned to New York. There were bound to be many loose ends to clear up, and it was my duty to take care of them.

Our stay in Cape Town was short as usual. I was unable to make contact with the Taylors because they were on holiday in England. After two days the ship proceeded on to Durban. The Fosters visited the ship soon after our arrival and invited me to visit their home as soon as I could get off. It was late December and we were into Christmas week. The Fosters asked me to have Christmas dinner with them. They were planning a dinner with a dozen or more guests. Mr. Foster said that he would pick me up at a popular dinner theater in down town Durban at about six o'clock in the evening the day of the dinner party. That day I went ashore with the Third Engineer early in the afternoon, and the two of us went to the dinner theater to have a drink or two. We sat at a table in the dining area and ordered drinks. A short distance away there was a table with eight or ten people having a party. These were obviously people from a nearby office building and this was the last working day before the Christmas break. They were a mixture of well dressed young men and women. One of this group was a very attractive blond in her early twenties. About every fifteen or twenty minutes she would leave the group and walk past our table on her way to the powder room. The group were consuming a good deal of adult beverages. The second time she passed our table she paused by us and said hello. On her third pass she stooped and asked if we were Yanks. We told her that we were from the American ship and exchanged names. When she returned from the powder room she took a seat at our table. Her group at their table continued partying and paid no attention to her joining us. We ordered another round of drinks. She said that she was a secretary, that she was unattached, and that she liked Americans. She also said that she had no plans for the evening and that she would be pleased to spend it with me if I had no other plans. I responded that I was waiting for Mr. Foster to pick me up and thanked her for the invitation. She seemed impressed and said that everyone in Durban knew Mr. Foster. Then she turned her attention to the Third Engineer who said that he would be delighted to spend the evening with her. As it turned out she was leaving Durban the following day to spend Christmas with her family in a town some distance away.

Mr. Foster arrived right on time to pick me up. We drove to his home where most of the guests had already arrived and the party was well underway. I was introduced to everyone and handed a cocktail. After an hour or so of small talk everyone was ushered into the dining room and seated for dinner. The main course was roast mutton with all the trimmings. There was much animated conversation during dinner and I answered a multitude of questions about America and the maritime industry. Following the main course and several glasses of wine the Christmas pudding was brought to the table. After everyone had been served a substantial piece of the pudding, our hostess invited them to begin eating it. All eyes seemed to turn to me as I put my fork into my piece of pudding and brought it to my mouth. As I began to chew the pudding I bit down on something very hard. Trying not to seem uncouth, I brought my napkin to my mouth and tried to remove the hard object as unobtrusively as possible. Mrs. Foster asked me if there was something wrong with the pudding. I replied that I had found something hard and thought that I should not swallow it. She then said that I should put the object in my plate to determine what it was. When I did so I was surprised to discover that the object was a silver coin. At that point everyone at the table began to laugh. I was informed that I was very lucky and that I would have good luck during the new year. It was the custom in South Africa to add some silver coins to the Christmas pudding, and anyone finding one in his serving of pudding would be blessed with good fortune. At about ten o'clock I thanked the Fosters for a very enjoyable evening and said my good-byes to the other guests. Mr. Foster was kind enough to drive me back to the ship.

Once back on board the ship, while walking down the companion way to my cabin, I passed the Third Engineer's cabin. I tapped quietly on his door to see if he was still awake. He opened his door and when I asked him how he had fared with the blond secretary, he opened the door wider and pointed to his berth. There she was under a sheet with a smile on her face. As I excused myself and turned away, he whispered in my ear, "You have no idea what you missed." That may be I thought, but he was a single man and I was not. It would be inappropriate for me to infer that many South African women were promiscuous. They were just more sexually liberated and open than American women. The young women who dated our crewmen were more like the groupies who follow the national baseball and football teams back in the United States. These wholesome good looking girls were store clerks and office workers who liked Americans and enjoyed their company. The South African ports were without doubt the best liberty ports for young American merchant seamen. Unlike the Asian and European ports that I had visited, I never heard anyone talk about prostitutes being available in any of these South African ports.

The following narrative may seem a little off color, but it should serve to further describe the social attitude and mores of both the ship's crew and the young ladies of South Africa. The S S African Star was a happy ship. As a matter of fact, I believe it was the happiest ship I ever sailed on. Most of the deck crew were young clean cut white American men. The boatswain was a gray haired man in his late fifties, slight of stature, and blessed with an easy going personality. The seamen liked and respected him as if he were a benevolent uncle. In turn he was a considerate and tolerant leader and instructor. Many of the deck crew referred to him as either "Boats" or "Pops." One evening a few of the deck hands invited the boatswain to go ashore with them to attend a party they had set up. They had arranged to have one of their young lady friends be his companion at this party. As the evening wore on this young lady provided "Boats" with the pleasures that only a woman can provide for a man. This considerate and generous act did not involve the exchange of any money. Instead it was an act of pure kindness and respect and demonstrated the nature of the regard and affection these young ladies had for our sailors. When one of the men on my watch told me about the party I gained a better understanding of what made South Africa such an inviting destination for our seamen and why most of them were homesteaders on this ship.

A few days after Christmas the ship departed Durban bound for Lorenco Marks in Mozambique. Again our stay in Lorenco Marks was brief. After a day or two the ship sailed for Biera. The voyage up the coast was uneventful and the ship anchored in the harbor of Biera to wait for berth space at the dock. Three or four days later dock space became available and the ship went alongside. My safari guide Basil was off on a trip to Rhodesia so I was unable to see him. One evening I went ashore with the Radio Operator to take in a movie at the only theater in Biera. We stopped off in a bar to have a beer or two before going to the movie. The quiet reserved Radio Operator ordered a whisky with his beer which surprised me. Along with the beer the bartender served each of us a small bowl of steamed cockles and a plate of prawns. The prawns were huge, and we ate them and the cockles with a dash of hot sauce. After the second round of drinks, the Radio Operator directed some nasty and belligerent remarks towards me. This sudden change in personality caught me off guard. It seemed that he wanted to provoke a fight. I had done nothing nor had I said anything to cause him to act this way. He also made some nasty remarks to the bar tender. I told the Radio Operator that he could go to the movie by himself and that I was returning to the ship. I had no intention of getting into an altercation ashore with this nut case. The next morning at breakfast he was friendly and his usual quiet self. I resolved to avoid going ashore with him in the future. Apparently when he had a few drinks he wanted to have a fight with anyone nearby.

The ship chandler informed the Chief Steward that he had a source of fresh vegetables that were grown without the use of human waste fertilizer. The Steward ordered a substantial supply, and for the first time in several weeks we were served fresh salads with our meals. Twenty four hours later the first signs of trouble appeared. Everyone on board began to suffer from diarrhea. Our fresh vegetables were contaminated and we all had a form of dysentery. It got worse each day. Working on deck monitoring the cargo operations became more and more difficult. The ship's Purser who had a few years of medical school gave everyone some medicine to relieve the distress but for the most of us it had little effect. The ship's carpenter who was a big portly man became so weak he could not get out of his bunk. Anything I ate went right through me. When I drank a glass of water I had to be close to a head because in five minutes or less I would have to pass it out. I lost my appetite and started losing weight. The tropical heat of Biera only made the problem worse. Somehow we managed to discharge and load the cargo. After ten days the diarrhea began to diminish and my appetite began to return. My body weight was down to less than one hundred pounds. Clothing hung on my emaciated frame like a loose tent, and although mentally alert, I felt physically weak.

When the ship finally departed Biera, a course was set for Durban. On the first day out the Third Assistant Engineer complained of having severe stomach pains. The ship's Purser examined him and determined that he had a ruptured appendix. It was fortunate that the Purser had some medical training and was able to accurately diagnose the Engineer's ailment. Any other Purser might have just given him some medicine for an upset stomach, and he would certainly have died. It was obvious that the Engineer had to get to a hospital as soon as possible. The closest port with a decent hospital was Lorenco Marks. The port agent was contacted by radio and asked to make arrangements to get the Engineer to the hospital. The ship changed course for Lorenco Marks. In the mean time ice packs were applied to the Engineers stomach and the Purser gave him a shot of penicillin to ward off the possible spread of infection. About half a day later the S S African Star steamed into the estuary leading to the harbor of Lorenco Marks. A motor launch came alongside and the Engineer was transferred to the launch while the ship was still underway. A bag of his personal belongings went along with him because it was obvious he would be returning to the States by some other means. Once the transfer was completed, the ship returned to a course for Durban.

Shortly after we docked in Durban the Fosters came to the ship and invited me to visit their home again. They had really adopted me. I had dinner at there home one evening, and dined out with them at the Athelone Gardens on another evening. One afternoon the Second Engineer and I took a two mile walk along the shore line south of Durban. We went to visit the whaling factory. Small hunter ships would seek out and kill the whales near the Antarctic waters. When they had four or five whales they would tow them to the whaling station for processing. The operation was something to behold. A dead whale would be hauled up a ramp from the water's edge on to a large wooden platform. Men with very sharp knives secured to long poles would then make an incision along the entire length of the whale's underside. This would release the animals entrails and other internal organs which would flow out and engulf some of the men up to their chests. Large slabs of blubber and flesh were then cut free and hauled off to huge cooking vats where the oil was boiled off. The stench from the blood, guts, and fumes from the oil rendering was so over powering that the Engineer got sick to his stomach. Some of the whales laying in the water by the ramp had large chunks missing from their tails. Others had circular scars on their skin about a foot in diameter. A foreman told us

The Haul Out Ramp at the Whale Processing Plant
Durban, Union of South Africa

that big sharks would feed on the dead whales as they were being towed from the hunting grounds. That accounted for the missing chunks. The circular scars were found only on the sperm whales. It seems that the sperm whale feeds on the giant squid, and the scars were caused by the suckers on the squid's tentacles. Judging by the size of the scars, those squid must be immense. We managed to buy about a dozen whales teeth from the foreman before we started the long walk back to Durban.

There was a rather unique practice between the ships that visited the South African ports. The captains and sometimes the officers of those ships would visit each others ships. There were ships of the Union Castle Line and the Pacific and Orient Line, two British companies, ships of a Dutch line, and ships of the Farrell Line and the Robin Line, two American companies. All of these ships carried at least twelve passengers and some carried many more. Their gangways were always open and visitors were welcome to come aboard. The friendly good natured intercourse between these ships flying the flags of different nations was in sharp contrast to what one would find in the ports of Europe and America. Perhaps the pleasant Mediterranean type climate of South Africa and the friendly attitude of the South African people made the difference.

The last evening before the ship left Durban was spent with the Fosters at their home. I told them that I would be leaving the ship for personal reasons when it got back to New York, and that I did not know if I would be able to return to South Africa again in the near future. I gave them an open invitation to visit my home if or when they were to visit the United States. They said that they hoped to be able to do so one day. When it came time for me to return to the ship, they gave me a farewell present. It was a genuine antique knobkerry, a Zulu war club. Mrs. Foster's family were part of the old Dutch settlers of South Africa, called Afrikaans or Yarpies, and this club had been in her family for many years. It was taken in battle from a slain Zulu by one of her ancestors. That particular battle is remembered as a national holiday in South Africa, Ding Gongs Day, or the Battle of Blood River. It was the significant battle that established the supremacy of the Boer settlers over the Blacks. There is a striking contrast between the settlement of the American West and the settlement of South Africa by the Boers. South Africa was once known as the Republiek Van Suid Afrika. I hesitated accepting such a family heirloom, but they insisted and asked me to be sure and keep in touch with them.

On the voyage south to Cape Town, the ship visited the ports of East

London and Port Elizabeth. While in Port Elizabeth, the Second Engineer and I visited the Snake Park, one of the largest parks devoted only to snakes. In the open area of the park there was a sunken rectangle with a moat running around the side walls. The sunken area was about three feet below grade and the moat created an island about a quarter acre in size. This island contained a variety of plants and several formations of rocks which served as a habitat for several species of snakes. A Negro game keeper wearing a khaki uniform and knee high boots walked among these snakes with impunity. I asked him if I could hold one of the snakes and he obliged me by handing me a jet black python. This snake was about ten or twelve feet long and weighed about forty pounds. It was quite tame and quickly wound itself about me as if I were a tree. The snake had a relatively small head considering the size of its body. After the Second Engineer had taken some pictures of me with the snake, I handed it back to the game keeper with my thanks.

Again the ship remained in Cape Town for only three days. I took the opportunity to walk around the city one evening and had a nice dinner at a very nice restaurant, the name of which I believe was the Delmonico. The ship departed Cape Town in the early afternoon. As it went slowly past the wide breakwater, there were the wife of the ship's electrician and her two brothers with their guitars. They were playing and singing a famous South African song, the Sari Marier. The sounds of their singing carried clearly over the small expanse of water to the ship. It was a farewell I shall never forget. As the beautiful city of Cape Town, Table mountain, and Lions Rump faded in our wake, I was overcome with a feeling of sadness. I was sure that I would never see South Africa again.

The voyage across the South Atlantic and into the Caribbean Sea was smooth and uneventful. Once again the ship pulled into Port Of Spain, Trinidad to take on fuel. The Captain, the Purser, and the Radio Operator went ashore to take care of some ship's business. I have no idea what the Radio Operator had to go ashore for, but when he returned to the ship alone, he was intoxicated. The fueling operation was almost complete when the Captain and the Purser returned. Within a few minutes the Radio Operator began an unprovoked argument with the Captain. When the Captain ordered him to go to his room and stay there until he sobered up, the Radio Operator became extremely abusive and threatened do the Captain physical harm. Since the Captain was much bigger and stronger, any physical attack would have had rather bad results for the Radio Operator. Realizing that the Radio Operator was insane, the Chief Mate and

*Art Murray and friend at the Serpentine Park,
Port Elizabeth, Union of South Africa.*

the Second Mate subdued him and shackled him with hand cuffs. Then they dragged him to the tabernacle house by number three hatch and locked him in there. When the fueling was completed, the oil barge was taken away by a tug boat. The anchor was hauled up, and with a pilot aboard, the S S African Star left Port Of Spain. Once clear of the port, the pilot was transferred to the pilot boat and the ship set a course for New York via Mona Pass. All the while the Radio Operator continued to shout threats and curses at the top of his lungs from the tabernacle house. It was obvious that he would become mentally unstable whenever he consumed alcohol. Perhaps I was at fault for not telling the Captain of my experience with the Radio Operator when I went ashore with him in Biera. The Radio Operator was released from his confinement the following day and returned to his duties. However the Captain informed him that he would not sail on any Farrell Line ship again, and told him that he should get medical or psychiatric help for his problem.

At this point in this narrative it seems appropriate that I include some information on what has developed in Africa in the years following my two voyages there. This narrative is being written during the years 2001, 2002, and 2003. During the intervening years since 1950 there were many political upheavals affecting Africa. Elitist liberals in Europe and America carried on a constant drumbeat calling for the liberation of the colonial areas of Africa, an end of Apartheid, and giving the Negro populations political power. The communists of Soviet Russia, China, and other socialist nations fomented civil unrest and revolution in many parts of Africa. Tremendous quantities of fire arms and ammunition were made available to Black revolutionary organizations. Our Congressional Black Caucus and numerous loud mouthed political leaders in the United States kept the pressure on to destroy any political control of Africa by Europeans and any other White people. The bloody uprising of the Mau Mau in Kenya eventually led to the British turning over political control of that colony to the native politicians. They also surrendered Rhodesia and did everything they could to undermine the government of Ian Smith who tried to help the white farmers maintain ownership and control of their farms. The Belgians pulled out of the Congo, and The French pulled out of French West Africa. The Portuguese gave up both Angola in the West and Mozambique in the East of Africa. What followed was anarchy, civil war, and famine.

Many of the European colonies in Africa encompassed the lands of different tribal populations. Once the law and order control of the Europeans was removed, these different tribal populations began fighting with each other for control of the various resources, territory, and to settle old scores. Religious differences resulted in other conflicts. Negroes of the Muslim persuasion fought Negroes of the Christian and other religious persuasions. Slaughter of unbelievably ferocity occurred across Africa. The expulsion and murder of the White farmers in many areas resulted in famine. Rhodesia which once produced abundant crops and exported food to other countries was unable to feed its own population. The Negro revolutionaries who took over the farms were unable or unwilling to make them productive. AIDS and other diseases have ravaged Sub-Sahara Africa since the White and European control was overthrown. Most of the Negro political leaders who emerged as the leaders of these newly freed nations turned out to be buffoons or charlatans or both. The United States and some of the more prosperous European nations lavished billions and billions of dollars in various types of aid on these new African nations. Much of that money found its way into Swiss bank accounts of the political and military leaders of these African Nations. The rest was squandered on foolish projects and internecine warfare.

Perhaps the policies imposed on the native Negro peoples by the European and White rulers was the root cause of the political upheaval and revolutionary changes in Africa. Much of the hatred of the Whites was fomented by communists agents and activists. How beneficial these changes have been for the native Negro populations is questionable. Before there was little or no hunger. Now there is famine in many parts of Africa. Before there was law and order. Now there is widespread lawlessness. Before there was sanitation and reasonably good health and medical care. Now disease has reached epidemic proportions in many parts of Sub-Sahara Africa. White farmers have been murdered or driven off their farms, and many of those who survived have emigrated to other countries. The Blacks who took over their farms do not have the skills or the motivation to make them productive. While their leaders live lavishly, the future of the native Negro populations looks bleak. Perhaps in a few decades Negro leaders who can bring law and order to their nations will emerge, and perhaps they will be able to restore an economy that can support their people.

I left the S S African Star after its return to New York and the voyage articles were broken. Although I thought that I was taking a leave of absence from the Farrell Line, it turned out that other personal obligations negated that. I learned that my father had been killed by a train at an unguarded crossing in Central Islip. He had been driving a passenger to the railroad station and crossed the tracks during a very heavy rain storm. The train that struck his vehicle failed to blow its whistle as it approached the crossing. Both my father and his passenger were killed by the impact and the resulting fire. My mother had hired a lawyer in Bayshore to represent her interests. This lawyer turned out to be as phony and incompetent a scoundrel as one could find. Unfortunately, the lawyer who normally handled my father's affairs was representing the relatives of the woman who was killed with my father. After my first meeting with my mother's lawyer I advised her to get rid of him and let me find one for her that could better represent her. She did not take my advice. Her lawyer had made all sorts of claims that he could get a good settlement from the Long Island Railroad because he used to represent them. This raised a warning flag in my mind.

A couple of weeks after my return, my mother phoned me one evening. She said that her lawyer had informed her that he had reached a settlement with the Long Island Railroad and that she would net eight hundred dollars after his fee was paid. She was in tears. He had told her that she had to accept their settlement. It was that or nothing. I phoned her lawyer the next day and told him that I thought the settlement was totally inadequate. He responded in a very nasty voice that I should keep my nose out of it, and that my mother was his client, not me. Before I could take any action to get another lawyer, my mother accepted the settlement. It did not even begin to cover the costs. My mother dutifully paid all my father's outstanding debts, and in so doing deflated her meager bank account. One scoundrel who ran a service station gave my mother a substantial bill for fuel and services he claimed my father owed him. A week or so later my mother found a copy of the same bill in my father's papers. It was marked "Paid in Full." When my mother confronted the service station owner, he returned her money with a rather red face. It took a few weeks to clear up my father's business affairs. The taxi business was over. My mother continued with her job in the local hospital. My brother took my father's death very hard. With no job and no prospects, some time later, he enlisted in the Army.

SCHOOL AND WORKING ASHORE

Anita and I were still renting the house in Whitestone and Anita was still teaching at the school in Glenwood Landing out on Long Island. I decided to stay ashore for a while to be sure my mother would be all right and able to be adjusted to living without my father. She was made of very strong stuff and adjusted to the changed situation very well. The house on Brightside Avenue was given up for an apartment over a grocery store on Main Street in Central Islip. My mother continued working at the State Hospital and soon began going out with some of the other widows she knew from work. Anita and I decided to trade in our old Willies automobile for a new car. After some searching we settled on a Studebaker starlight coupe. It was a very impressive looking machine with a torpedo nose and a wrap around rear window. It made traveling out to Brentwood and Central Islip much easier. Anita would visit her parents and I would visit my mother. I was still persona-non-grata with Anita's parents, but a thaw was developing.

Finding a job ashore was not easy. There was still a flood of service men returning to civilian life while most of the defense factories were no longer needed to produce war material and many found converting to producing peace time goods difficult if not impossible. The job market was tight to say the least, and Ex-GI's were given preference for the few jobs that were open. As a professional merchant seaman I was considered a civilian. One evening Anita and I were having dinner with Mr. King's sister, Vera. He was still in Korea and we felt it would be proper to see her once in a while. During dinner we discussed the problems with the job market. Vera said that she had a friend who was a marketing manager for Bristol Laboratories, a pharmaceutical company, and that he was looking for a sales representative. She said that she would arrange a meeting with him for me. A few days later I received a telephone call from this manager inviting me to visit his office in Manhattan to see if a position as a salesman would be suitable for me and his company. The meeting went very well. The manager explained that he was looking for someone to cover a territory ranging from western Pennsylvania across all of northern Ohio. The two major products to be sold were penicillin and streptomycin. The customers were only hospitals and drug store chains. The manager felt that my use of penicillin on shipboard treating seamen, and my limited experience working in the Central Islip State Hospital were sufficient for me to be a salesman for his company. He offered me the position, and I accepted it. He also recommended that I read a couple of particular books on antibiotics so that I would have a better understanding of the products I would be selling. Arrangements were made for me to visit the Bristol Labs plant in Buffalo, New York to get a briefing and indoctrination on what a salesman would have to do.

Anita's school was on Spring break so she was able to have a few days free to go with me on my indoctrination at Bristol Labs. In our new Studebaker we drove from New York to Buffalo, a distance of about 500 miles. Anita insisted on driving the whole distance. She was pretty tired when we finally arrived in Buffalo and checked into our hotel. The next day we got the VIP tour of Bristol Labs and quite an education in how penicillin is produced. I was introduced to several of the scientists who developed the production processes and to the man who would be my immediate manager. The following day was spent being instructed in the technical procedures for selling penicillin and streptomycin. The territory assigned to me was western Pennsylvania and northern Ohio with a small corner of West Virginia thrown in. I was informed that there had not been a representative of Bristol Labs in that area for several years. It was suggested that I should use Pittsburgh as home base and plan a route from there that would allow me to cover half the territory in one week and the second half the next week. Bristol Labs put me on a moderate salary which was to be enhanced by the addition of a percent of the sales I made. All travel expenses were to be covered and I was advised to stay in the better hotels and to eat my meals in the better restaurants. It was a company policy to maintain a good image of their salesmen. I was given a copy of Golds Medical dictionary, a price list book, and a large carton of samples of the company's products. After a round of hand shakes and good wishes I departed Bristol Labs. Now I was on my own to start a new career in pharmaceutical sales. Anita and I drove back to Whitestone. We left Buffalo without ever visiting Niagara Falls.

Back in Whitestone Anita made arrangements to commute to school with one of the teachers at her school. The next Monday morning I drove the Studebaker to Pittsburgh and checked into a hotel. The following day I found a one room furnished apartment in Mckeesport on the north side of Pittsburgh. This was to be my operations base. Pittsburgh was an industrial city with steel plants being the major businesses. There was a tremendous amount of soot in the air all the time. I had to change my shirts twice a day because the collars and cuffs would become grimy in a couple of hours. On my first foray I headed for the northern part of the territory. A small farming community hospital in Beaver Falls was my first stop. Amazingly they had no doctor on hand nor a pharmacist on duty. It seemed that the doctor spent most of his time on house calls, and did hospital rounds only twice a day. There was a chief nurse in charge and apparently there were only a few patients in the hospital. When I asked the nurse how much penicillin she had in the pharmacy she replied that she had no idea. She invited me to look over her supply room and to see if there was any there. It turned out that there was none. I asked her how she would normally get the medicines she needed. She replied that the doctor would prescribe what was needed and that the local drug store would send the medicines over to the hospital. Most of this hospital's patients were maternity cases or farm type injuries. I recommended that she should have a supply of penicillin on hand at all times. After reviewing the various types of penicillin products I had available she selected the one that would be most convenient for her. This was a package item which contained a pre-loaded syringe with 100,000 units of penicillin, the most expensive of my product types. She ordered a hundred of them and I gave her four or five from my sample kit to tide her over. I felt that this was a successful visit because I had provided a much needed service and made a profitable sale.

As I continued on this first round of hospital visits there were several encounters with people that opened my eyes to what can best be described as opportunistic personalities. In one hospital in Akron there was a female pharmacist who was twenty five to thirty years of age. She was not altogether unattractive, but she was no raving beauty. She listened to my sales pitch for about five minutes. Then she had one of her own. She had a rule of not giving a pharmaceutical salesman any business until she had gotten to know him better. Knowing her better required dinner in an upscale restaurant, theater, and some night clubbing. She was obviously a free spirit looking for a free ride, and perhaps more. Needless to say, I did not make any sales at her hospital. At another hospital on my route the doctor in charge of purchases wanted me to give him a fairly large supply of the various antibiotic items I had as samples. It was obvious that he intended to sell them himself and make a good deal of money. For example, Bristol Labs would sell a vial of 100,000 units of penicillin for as little as eleven cents. The pharmacists and doctors would charge anything from one dollar to five dollars for that same vile depending on the circumstances of how they were dispensing it. Although I had a fairly large supply of samples, I declined to give him any while claiming that I had none with me. Again there was no sale.

My itinerary took me to Cleveland. There all the Cleveland hospitals purchased their medicines through one central purchasing agency. This was a very wise business arrangement for them. Because of the very large volume of any such purchases they were able to negotiate the most favorable price for any item. I made my sales pitch to one of their agents and then quoted the lowest price I could offer on my products. A vial of 100,000 units of penicillin had a price ranging from twenty five cents to just eleven cents. A similar range in price also applied to streptomycin, although the bottom price was much higher than the bottom price of penicillin. The agent said that my offer would be compared to that of other companies, and if mine were the lower he would process an order for Bristol Labs. That was the best I could do. Continuing on I visited a few more hospitals in various cities and towns before returning to Pittsburgh. Due to the distance between the various hospitals and the time each visit consumed, I was usually only able to visit one hospital a day. Occasionally if there were more than one hospital in a given city or town I could make two or three sales visits. In one large hospital the doctor in charge of training asked me to make a verbal presentation to his group of interns. He wanted me to explain the uses of penicillin and streptomycin and the various forms in which it could be administered. Apparently this was something that a "Detailer," a pharmaceutical salesman, was expected to do. Accordingly I spent an hour or more lecturing to a dozen interns and answering their many questions. It must have gone well because I got a moderately good order for some of my products.

The routine of the traveling salesman continued for about two months. It was the loneliest experience of my life. Every other weekend I would fly home from Pittsburgh to New York to spend some time with Anita. The money was good, but I did not like the life I was leading. On my last foray into northern Ohio, either by chance or design, I found myself trailing one day behind the salesman for Merc Labs. We were on the same itinerary and he was beating me badly by selling penicillin for a price that was lower than I could offer. The irony of this was that Merc got their penicillin from Bristol Labs. I called my manager but he would not authorize me to go below the prices in my price book. On the return leg of this sales route I managed to get to the Veteran's Hospital in Stubensville ahead of the Merc salesman. I was able to get the pharmacist there to place the largest order for my products that I had ever been able to do before. A day or so later I was calling on the Catholic Hospital in McKeesport, Pa. After cooling my heels for almost an hour, the pharmacist, a skinny shrewish nun, met me in the lobby. I had barely introduced myself when she let loose a barrage of nasty comments such as how dare I request to speak to her and waste her time. She had no use for salesman generally, and only purchased what pharmaceuticals she needed from the Merc salesman. I was told in no uncertain terms that I was not to bother her again. Before departing I said to this witch, "Madam, when salesmen like me stop calling on you, your Merc salesman will be able to charge you whatever he pleases and you will not know whether or not you are being cheated." That evening I spoke to my manager and informed him that he would have to get another salesman for this territory. I cleared out of my one room apartment and drove home to Whitestone the next day. Thus ended my short and unhappy career as a traveling salesman.

Back home once again I decided to return to school and complete the degree program. The Spring semester at the New York State Maritime College was almost over. In order to avoid wasting the Summer months I enrolled in Queens College for their Summer semester program. I signed up for two courses worth three credits each. After some searching I found a night time job at the Lily Tulip Cup factory somewhere in Queens. I was placed on the midnight to eight in the morning shift running four machines simultaneously producing wax paper cups. The work demanded my full attention. If one of the four machines was ignored for only a few seconds, there would be paper cups spewing out all over the place. At eight in the morning another worker would replace me and the machines continued to stamp out paper cups without any interruption. When I got back home to Whitestone Anita would have breakfast ready. After a quick meal I would prepare whatever homework was required for that day's classes. A couple of hours later I would drive over to Queens College, attend one class, eat a brown bag lunch, and attend the second class. Then in the early afternoon I would return to Whitestone and catch a few hours sleep. This was followed by supper and some homework. Then a little after eleven at night I would drive over to the Lily Tulip Cup factory. This work, school, sleep grind continued for two months. I completed both courses with a 'B' average, which was not bad for a student who was sleep walking part of the time.

I continued working at the Lily Tulip Cup factory until the Fall semester classes started at the New York State Maritime College. It would not be possible to take a full semester load of classes and continue the factory job. By chance I ran into an old instructor from one of the Maritime Administration classes I had taken a couple of years before. He informed me that there was a job for a Second Mate available with the New York City Department of Public Works. That department operated four tank vessels that carried sewage sludge from the different processing plants around the city out to a dump site five miles southeast of Ambrose Light Ship. Losing no time I applied for the job and got it. I was scheduled to do three night trips during the week days and two day trips during the weekend. This worked out very well with my schedule of classes, and I had ample time to devote to the required studies. After my classes I would usually go home to study and have dinner. Then some time in the late evening Anita would drive me to the plant where the vessel I was assigned to would be loaded and ready to depart. She would be informed of the approximate return time of the vessel so she could pick me up.

These tank vessels were about two hundred and fifty feet in length and carried a cargo of fifteen hundred cubic yards of sludge. The bridge house, crew quarters, and engine room were in the stern, and the vessel had twin screws and diesel engines. In spite of the cargo, these vessels were clean and rather smart looking. The crew consisted of a Captain, a Chief Mate, a Second Mate, three Engineers, and three Able Seamen. The Captain had the pilotage endorsement for New York harbor on his license. When docking or undocking I would have the wheel while the Captain gave the maneuvering instructions, and the Chief mate would be on the main deck with the seamen handling the mooring lines. Once clear of the dock one of the seamen would take the wheel and the Captain would stand the bridge watch to the Narrows. Then either the Chief Mate or I would take the bridge watch and con the ship out to the dump site.

The ship was configured with a double hull. The inner hull was separated into six tank compartments that contained the cargo. When the ship reached the dump site the speed was reduced to slow ahead and the ship was turned into the wind. The seamen would then turn the hand wheels on the main deck that opened the bell valves on the bottoms of the tanks. This would allow the sludge to pour through large open pipes between the tanks and the bottom of the ship. Fifteen hundred cubic yards of sludge could be dumped in about a quarter of an hour. Although the specific gravity of the sludge was much more than that of sea water, the dumping would leave a brown discoloration of the water in the ship's wake. This could stretch for a quarter of a mile or more. Once the dump was completed the ship would head back into New York harbor with one of the Mates taking the bridge con. Each of the four vessels operated by the Department of Public Works made two trips a day to the dump site. The vessels were loaded at the sewage plants by plant personnel just like any tanker at a petrochemical plant.

My position as a Second Mate required me to rotate between two or three of the tankers. Some times I would go out on the MV Coney Island, and at other times I would go out on the MV Tallmans Island or the MV Wards Island. The Captain of the MV Coney Island was a good natured likable man of fifty plus years. He suggested that I should bring Anita along on one of our night cruises and he would also bring his wife. We chose a night when there was a full moon and good weather. Anita and the Captain's wife enjoyed the moonlight cruise on the MV Coney Island. Although Anita claims otherwise, there was only the sweet salty breeze of the ocean to smell. We always made sure to turn the vessel into the wind when dumping the cargo and then made a very wide turn when leaving the area to return to the harbor.

THE ALUMNI DINNER DANCE

During this period of time the annual dinner dance for the NYSMC Alumni Association was held at the Hotel Victoria in Manhattan. Joe and Patricia Betz went with Anita and me to this affair. It was well attended by many of our classmates with their dates. Joe and I were the only married men of our class at this dinner dance. One of our classmates, Bill Ryan, who was also President of the Alumni Association at this time, had reserved a suite of rooms at the hotel. He invited his classmates to join him there to continue the party when the dance was over. Everyone was having a good time as the evening wore on. Near the end of the evening

Patricia Betz asked me to dance a polka with her. By that time of the evening my lack of adequate sleep and one too many highballs had caught up with me. Under ordinary circumstances I would never dance the polka. Starting to dance the polka with Pat Betz is the last thing I remember of this Alumni dinner dance. What happened there after was reported to me by Anita, Patricia, and Joe.

When the last dance tune played by the orchestra was finished most of the class of '45 went up to Bill Ryan's suite for cocktails and conversation. Once we all got there the party continued. I already had more to drink than I should have and still one of my classmates gave me a rather strong highball. Shortly after drinking this, I got up from the chair I was sitting in and fell flat on my face. Anita then announced that I had drunk too much and she was going to take me home. She, Patricia and Joe then went to the coat room to retrieve our coats. While they were gone my classmates carried me to the bed room and laid me out with my arms crossed over my chest and the Gideon Bible in my hands. The girls then placed their corsages around me and added some candles at the sides of the bed. When Anita, Patricia, and Joe returned with our coats, my classmates and their dates were holding an impromptu wake for me. Anita was not amused.

With some difficulty, Anita, Patricia, and Joe got me down to the all night coffee shop and poured a few cups of black coffee into me. After a while I became semi-conscious and Anita informed me that they were going to take me home. I informed them that I was scheduled to report aboard the MV Coney Island at Wards Island for an 0800 departure and I insisted that I had to go to the ship. The three of them finally gave in and took me to the ship. It was early in the morning and there was no one on board. They got me on board and into a bunk in one of the cabins. I fell fast asleep. As a precaution, Anita removed my tie and took my wristwatch, my wallet, my ring, and tie clasp before leaving the ship. A few hours later I awoke still somewhat dazed to the sound of the diesel engines. Looking out the port hole I saw the United Nations Building going by. With all of my valuables gone my first thought was that I had been rolled and dumped on some ship. Then I realized where I was. I doused my face with cold water and came awake enough to take my turn on the bridge. The Captain and First Mate joked about finding me asleep in the cabin when they and the rest of the crew came aboard, and that they decided to let me sleep while they got the ship underway. They were glad to see that I was able to resume my duties taking the ship out and back. A few days later Anita received a condolence card from Bill Ryan. It read, "Hallilula He Has Risen." Everyone had a good laugh at my expense and I vowed never to allow demon rum to do that to me again.

BAKING A BETTER CAKE

One evening Anita and I had an impromptu gathering at our Flushing residence. Pat and Joe Betz, and another of my classmates, Ed Muhleman were visiting us. After a couple of rounds of cocktails Ed informed us that his girl friend who worked for an advertising agency had a problem. Her firm was planning an advertising campaign for their customer, General Mills. The Betty Crocker Division was coming out with a new product, a make and bake package cake mix. They were looking for a married sailor who with his wife would be the focal point of the advertising campaign. The girl friend had asked Ed to find a suitable married sailor and he did not have a clue where he could find such a couple. Joe and I suggested that we were married and we were both sailors of a sort. Although we were both officers, we went to sea which is what sailors do. Pat, Joe, Anita, and I told Ed that we would be available if his girl friend thought we would be suitable. Ed said that he would see what his girl friend might think of using us.

Unable to find anyone else, Ed's girl friend contacted Joe and me and asked us if we would allow our pictures to be used in her firm's advertising campaign. We agreed and she asked us to visit her firm's office in Manhattan with our wives one evening a few days later. Joe and I were to be in our dress uniforms. As agreed the four of us arrived at the firm's offices at about five o'clock and were ushered into an elaborate adjacent kitchen facility by Ed's girl friend. She introduced us to a couple of executives and a professional nutritionist. This group then proceeded to lay out the plan for the advertising campaign. Joe and I were to bake a cake using the new Betty Crocker cake mix, and Pat and Anita were to bake equivalent cakes from scratch. The professional nutritionist would then judge which cakes were the best, the scratch cakes or the mix cakes. It took about two hours to go through the process of mixing batter and baking the cakes. When the cakes were finished the nutritionist sampled each of them. Surprise, surprise, she found that the cakes made from the Betty Crocker cake mix were superior to the cakes made by Pat and Anita from scratch.

Following the cake baking contest, we were taken to an adjacent photography studio. Pictures of Pat and Joe holding a cake between them

Sailor Beats Mate

were taken. Then similar pictures of Anita and I were taken. The executives said that the most suitable of the pictures would be used in their campaign. They planned to use a lead in of, "SAILOR BEATS MATE" followed with an account of the contest. After signing legal releases for the use of our pictures, each of us was given ten dollars and a couple of packages of Betty Crocker cake mix. As we were leaving the firm's offices, the nutritionist confided to Anita that her scratch cake was really better, but she was required to claim the mix cake was better. After leaving the advertising firm's offices, the four of us went down to Greenwich Village and had an excellent dinner in one of the better restaurants. Weeks later the Betty Crocker advertisements began appearing in various magazines and news papers. A picture of Anita and I was a prominent part of the ad. During the following couple of months I received letters from different parts of the world from four or five of my classmates who had seen the advertisement in various magazines.

THE MENTAL HOSPITAL

I continued working on the "honey" boats till the start of the next semester at Fort Schuyler. It soon became obvious that my schedule of classes would make it very difficult if not impossible for me to continue working on the New York DPW tankers. Quite by accident I heard that the Creedmore State Psychiatric Hospital in Queens had some openings for psychiatric aids. I went there and applied for a job. My previous experience as an attendant in the Central Islip Psychiatric Hospital (while still in high school) was enough to get me a job at Creedmore. I was assigned the job as the floating relief psychiatric aid in the admissions building at Creedmore Hospital. The admissions building had four floors with each floor devoted to a particular category of mental illness. A new patient would be examined and evaluated by the doctors and then assigned to the appropriate floor. There they would receive an initial regimen of treatment and evaluation. Some would be released to their families after a month or two and others would be transferred to one of the other buildings for long term treatment or permanent internment.

Each floor of the admissions building had two wings, one for male patients and one for female patients. The wings were separated by a dining hall. Meals were served for the female patients first and then the dining hall was cleared so that the male patients could be served. There was no mingling of male and female patients allowed. Each wing had a recreation room and each patient had a private bed room. The bedrooms were small and contained a single bed, a small table, and a chair. A communal washroom and toilet facility, one for male and one for female, was available on each floor in each wing for the use of the patients. There was also an office with a desk, a filing cabinet and a couple of chairs for the staff. As a rule there were two eight-hour shifts at night with only one psychiatric aid on duty from four in the afternoon to midnight, and then from midnight to eight in the morning for each floor of each wing. There was also one registered nurse on night duty to cover all four floors. Each wing held about twenty patients.

This job was ideal for me. I would report to the hospital at four in the afternoon and go to my pre-assigned floor and relieve the day aids. The patients would be given their evening meal from five to six o'clock by a staff from the main kitchen. They would then be ushered into the recreation room and remain there until eight o'clock. Then the patients were directed to their rooms to turn in for the night. By nine o'clock they were all bedded down and I would make a tour down the hallway every half hour and check each room to be sure everything was all right. Between these tours I would sit in the office and study in preparation for the next day's classes. At midnight I would be relieved by another aid and I would go home for a night's sleep. In the morning I would have breakfast with Anita after which we would go our separate ways. Anita would commute to her school in Glenwood Landing and I would commute to Fort Schuyler. We would swap the use of our car and take turns with a car pool as circumstances required. The work at Creedmore State Hospital was easy and it gave me a good three hours every night to do my studies. I was able to do as well as those of my fellow classmates who did not have to hold down a job because they were going to school on the GI Bill. Working at Creedmore got me through my last semester at Fort Schuyler. In June 1951 my program of study was complete and I received my Bachelor's Degree from the New York State Maritime College.

THE BANANA BOAT

Having completed my studies, the next problem was to choose a career path. Anita wanted me to find a job that would keep me ashore. I was torn between looking for another ship and looking for a job ashore. Shore side jobs for new college graduates were scarce because of the flood of new college graduates produced by the G I Bill. I gave Creedmore Hospital two weeks notice and quit my job as a psychiatric aid. Through the Masters Mates and Pilots Union hall I got an assignment to a ship operated by the Grace Line. This was as a relief for the Fourth Mate who was taking the next trip off for vacation. The ship was the S S Santa Anna, a flush deck C-2, on a voyage to Central America with a four week turn around. This ship carried five Mates. A Chief Mate on day work, three watch standing Mates, and a cargo Mate also on day work. On this ship the Fourth Mate stood what would normally be the Third Mate's watch on a ship with three Mates. Anita did not object to this assignment since I would only be making one trip as a relief Mate and would be on this ship for a only month or less.

I joined the ship at the Grace Line pier near 23 Rd street in the North River and met the other Mates. They all seemed to be a friendly good natured lot and I anticipated a pleasant voyage. That was until I was introduced to Captain Sigord Kopang, the Master of the S S Santa Anna. He was a small man of slight build in his sixties, and an old country Norwegian. My first impression was that he had little regard for junior officers. Since all of the deck officers and most of the engineering officers had Naval Reserve Commissions, the S S Santa Anna flew the Naval Reserve flag, an eagle with wings spread on a dark blue background. The ship itself was well found, clean, and had a reasonably good stewards department. The deck crew were mainly Latino types with little or no command of the English language. There were only two able seamen who were white Americans. This problem of language did cause me some difficulties, and had it not been for my limited knowledge of Spanish, the voyage would have been a disaster.

The S S Santa Anna loaded some cargo in New York and then went coastwise to Philadelphia to load more cargo. Most of this cargo was "break-bulk" and much of it was strapped to pallets. As we were departing New York on my morning watch I had my first encounter with Captain Kopang's temper. My Latino ordinary seaman was given the task of putting up the flags. These flags included the National ensign, the Pilot flag, the Grace Line house flag, and the Naval Reserve flag. As the ship was steaming through the harbor the captain walked out of the wheel house to the wing of the bridge. He came back into the wheel house and I could see his neck turning red much like the red fluid rising in a thermometer. With a scowl on his face he looked at me and asked, "Mister have you ever seen a crow flying up side down?" I replied, "No sir." Then he exploded shouting,

"Vell mister you have one flying from the after mast now!" My ordinary seaman had carelessly hoisted the Naval Reserve flag up side down. I called the ordinary seaman to the bridge and dispatched him to quickly reverse the Naval Reserve flag. The captain was fuming, the pilot was smiling, and I felt like a chastised school boy.

My next incident with the captain occurred as the S.S. Santa Anna was heading up the Delaware River towards Philadelphia with a pilot aboard. I had the bridge watch. As the ship was approaching a bend in the river I looked across the flat lands and saw a cruiser heading down stream from the Philadelphia Navy Yard. This cruiser had a tug boat at the bow and another at the stern. Judging from the amount of red lead patches, it was obvious that this cruiser was not in commission and was probably being towed to a scrap yard or a berth in the reserve fleet. The captain came into the wheel house and saw the cruiser now approaching us from dead ahead. He looked at the cruiser then back to me several times. I could see the red color rising on the back of his neck and I knew he was getting ready to explode. When the cruiser was less than a quarter of a mile from us he exploded. Turning towards me he shouted, "Mister don't you believe in dipping the flag to a passing warship?" In a calm voice I replied, "Captain I do not believe we are required to dip the flag to a warship that is not in commission. There will be no one on board to respond to the courtesy."

"How do you know that?" he shouted. I replied, "That warship is a cruiser under tow, spattered with red lead, and she is not flying any flags." With that he turned and stomped out of the wheel house. The pilot shook his head and smiled at me. That evening I had a talk with the Second Mate. I asked him if the Captain treated all the Mates the way he was treating me. He replied that the Captain had a habit of riding the junior Mate hard, and I should not take it personally. That was probably the reason why the Fourth Mate whom I was replacing had gone on vacation.

The ship departed the United States and headed for Venezuela. During my eight to twelve evening watch the Captain would occasionally come out of his quarters and walk through the wheel house. He usually wore a seedy looking bath robe and slippers with the heels crushed down. This caused the slippers to go clomp, clomp, clomp as he walked from wing to wing of the bridge. It was obvious that he was looking for something to complain about and when he said anything to me it was never complimentary or pleasant. I got used to this and it kept me alert trying to anticipate and correct anything he might find fault with.

Our first port of call was a small back water named Los Cocos where we off loaded some of our general cargo. It was a hot, humid, and unpleasant place. Several of our crew returned to the ship late at night after shore leave so drunk on the cheap rum that they could hardly walk. Luckily the ship stayed there less than forty-eight hours. The next port was La Guaira, the port for Caracas, a much larger place with some fairly decent restaurants and hotels. I went ashore with one of the Engineers and enjoyed a couple of beers in one of the hotel bars. The ship off loaded a good deal of the remaining cargo there and departed after two days. Proceeding East and South along the coast of Venezuela, we put in to Carupano, another small port. The remainder of our general cargo was off loaded there. The ship, now empty, was scheduled to proceed to Saint Marc in Haiti. We departed Carupano at night on my watch. As we dropped the pilot and set course for Saint Marc the Captain was on the wing of the bridge watching the pilot boat depart. I quickly took departure bearings and plotted them on the chart. The Captain came into the wheel house and stood there alternately looking at the fading lights of Carupano and back at me. Finally he exploded, "Vell mister, are you going to vait until you are out of sight of land to take the departure bearings?" In a calm voice I replied, "Sir, they are plotted on the chart and departure time was noted as 2130." With a scowl he strode into the chart room and after a couple of minutes left the chart room and bridge without any further comment. I felt great satisfaction knowing that this time I was one step ahead of the Old Man.

Saint Marc could hardly qualify as a port for large ships. There were no docks. The S S Santa Anna was maneuvered close to the beach and both anchors were dropped. The stern was then turned toward the beach and two mooring lines were taken to the shore by some natives in a row boat. These lines were made fast to a couple of large trees and then pulled taught. This was how the ship was moored to load cargo. Sea watches (four hours on, eight hours off) were maintained and after the formality of clearing the ship with the port officials, several boats loaded with native long-shoremen and bundles of bamboo poles came alongside to get the ship ready to load bananas. The ship had five holds with deck hatches and side ports. All of these were opened. The native longshoremen began building stages with bamboo and ropes. When these were completed they began rowing out long boats loaded with stalks of bananas. The natives formed human conveyor belts to pass the bananas from the boats to the holds through the side ports and down through the hatches. Down in the holds the stalks of bananas were placed on hooks on varnished boards running fore and aft in each hold. As one row was filled, varnished wood battens were put in place by the native longshoremen and another row was started. The battens secured the bananas and prevented the bananas from banging into one another. This was rather slow labor intensive work. All the while they were loading the bananas, the natives were singing and chanting in Creole French. It was like a scene from some Hollywood movie. I found their singing very pleasant and regretted not having any means of record-ing it. Their singing reminded me of the Jamaican Banana Boat song made famous by Harry Bellefonte.

The loading continued from about eight in the morning till midnight. During daylight hours there were three Mates overseeing the stowage of the bananas, but at night there was only one Mate on duty. I had the duty from 0800 to noon and 1600 to midnight. The work required that the Mates had to go from hold to hold continually to make sure the battens were put in place properly and that all the stalks of bananas were hung correctly. Without the help of the other Mates the work was exhausting on the 1600 to midnight shift. One evening at about ten o'clock as I climbed out of number three hold and started aft toward number four hold, the Captain called down to me from the boat deck. He said, "Mister the crew are coming aboard my ship with booze, put a stop to it!" I replied that I could not oversee the stowage of the cargo and watch the gangway at the same time. He then bellowed, "I don't vont any booze on my ship!" Just then a boat came alongside the gangway and half a dozen crewmen came up to the main deck. Each of them carried one or two bottles of rum

S S Santa Ana
C-2 Cargo Ship, Grace Line

aboard. As each man steeped off the gangway I said, "Captain's orders," and confiscated the rum and placed the bottles on the bulwark railing. The crewmen stood around me arguing and grumbling. I knew the Captain was still standing on the deck above watching but saying nothing. A few minutes later another boat came alongside and the Captain's steward came up the gangway with a case of rum in his hands. As he reached the main deck I took the case of rum from him saying, "I will take that."

He protested, "This case of rum is for the Captain."

I replied, "Don't lie to me. The Captain would not forbid the crew to bring any rum aboard and then order a case of rum for himself." Upon saying this I dropped the case of rum into the water along with the bottles that were lining the bulwark railing. The next thing I heard was the clump, clump, clump of the Captain's slippers and the slamming of the door as he went into his quarters. This time I was "one up" on the Old Man. The crewmen laughed and went off to their quarters and I resumed my work with the cargo of bananas. I heard nothing more about booze from the Captain. However I must note that the local distillery produced an excellent quality of rum and a one liter bottle cost about fifty cents.

Saint Marc was an old town with unpaved streets, no electricity, and buildings that could best be described as shabby. The population was about nine thousand people and as far as I could see was mostly Negro. The only white people I saw were a couple who paid a brief visit to the ship. They were European or possibly American and either owned or managed the banana plantation that provided the cargo for the ship. Their visit was so brief that I never had an opportunity to talk to them. On a cliff high above Saint Marc there was an old abandoned French fort. After the noon meal one afternoon one the Engineers and I went ashore and hired two native boys to guide us up to the fort. After a long walk on a narrow and twisting trail up the face of the cliff we came out on a flat area with the fort overlooking the town and the harbor. The fort was in a bad state of disrepair and must have been left abandoned since the slaves revolted over two centuries ago. The cannons had been tumbled from the walls and were lying in the dirt outside of the walls of the fort. These cannons were quite large and measured about twelve feet in length. Although they were covered with rust and some moss, they appeared to be in good shape. There were also several large iron cannon balls about six inches in diameter lying about. Since I could not figure any way to get one or two of these cannons down to the ship, I had to satisfy myself with a cannon ball as a souvenir. It was not without difficulty that I carried one of these cannon balls down the cliff trail and back to the ship.

Finally the ship had a full load of bananas. The stages were dismantled. The side ports were closed and secured for sea. The deck hatches were closed and covered. I estimated that we had about five thousand tons of green bananas on board. Contrary to the stories I had heard about banana boats being over run with poisonous snakes and spiders, there was no sign of any such vermin in the cargo. The mooring lines were brought on board, the anchors were hauled up, and the ship departed Saint Marc on a beautiful tropical afternoon. A course was set through the Windward Passage, through the Bahama Islands, and directly for New York. The run to New York took four days. Captain Kopang's visits to the bridge while I was on watch became less and less frequent. The last day of the voyage I packed my belongings and was ready to leave the ship as soon as possible. Shortly after the ship docked at the Grace Line pier sea watches were broken and the crew was paid off. I said good by to a couple of the Mates and Engineers. A Grace Line Port Captain came to my cabin and asked if I were going to sign on for the next trip. He seemed surprised when I said that I had signed on as a relief mate for only one trip. He said that the home office thought that I was going to stay on the ship as one of the permanent officers, and seemed genuinely disappointed when I told him I was planning to leave the ship as soon as I could. Shortly after the Port Captain left my cabin, the Chief Mate came in and asked me to reconsider and sign on for the next voyage. He said that Captain Kopang's feelings were hurt when he was told that I was getting off, and that the Captain liked me and wanted me to stay. I told him that I could not sign on for the next voyage because I had promised my wife that I would only make the one voyage. Actually I was surprised that Captain Kopang wanted me to stay. I know that I did not make a good whipping boy, and maybe this had impressed him favorably.

CHANGING ADDRESSES

When I got home Anita informed me that the Malazzos were coming home from Japan soon and we would have to find somewhere else to live. As luck would have it, Patricia and Joe Betz had a friend who had an apartment available in their house in Queens. Anita and I were introduced to Harry and Jean Madonna and they were pleased to rent the apartment to us. The apartment was on the top floor and consisted of a living room, a bed room, a kitchen, and a bath room. All of these rooms were small, but adequate for our needs. However, the walls and woodwork of the apartment were in need of a new coat of paint. Anita and I along with some of our friends spent the week before we moved in painting the apartment. We bought furniture, some new and some recycled to furnish the apartment and settled in. The Madonnas were pleasant people to deal with and the apartment was quite comfortable. However in less than a month we were moving to another apartment.

Anita was teaching school in Glenwood Landing. When we were informed that the Malazzos were coming home Anita applied for an apartment in Glenwood Landing. This was in a three story building that had been a school and had been converted to an apartment house when a new school building was opened. It was a short distance from the new school where Anita was teaching. There was a waiting list for these apartments and it was assumed that it would be a long time before one would become available. We were surprised when the owners told Anita that one was available a couple of weeks after we had moved into the Madonna's apartment. This was also a small apartment on the top floor of the building consisting of a living room, bed room, bath room, and an efficiency kitchen which was little more than an oversize closet. We gladly accepted the offer of this apartment. Although the Madonnas were sorry to see us go, they said that they would have no difficulty finding someone to rent their newly painted apartment. We hired some professional movers to transfer our furniture form the apartment in Queens to the apartment in Glenwood Landing. Everything went well and we settled in with no difficulty.

SEARCHING FOR A JOB

While we were moving into the Madonna's apartment I had been putting my applications in several different business concerns looking for a shore job. The job market was tight. I was competing with thousands of new college graduates produced by the GI Bill. After the second or third week of looking, Joe Betz suggested that I try the New York Naval Shipyard in Brooklyn where he was employed as a machine shop foreman. He said that they had openings in their engineering section. I visited their employment office and got an interview with a less than pleasant bureaucrat. After reviewing my application and my college transcript, he offered me a position as a low level GS 5 naval architect. Not realizing that he was low-balling me and that I could have negotiated for a higher GS rating, I accepted his offer. All of this happened on a Wednesday and I was told to report to the shipyard security office on the following Monday for processing. Anita was delighted to learn that I had secured a shore side job with a prestigious title in spite of the low grade and equivalent low pay. As fate would have it, I got a call on Thursday evening from the Panama Railroad Line. They offered me a position as Third Mate on the S S Cristobal. I had submitted an application to them at the same time that the MM&P Union had assigned me to the S S Santa Anna. Applying for a job with the Panama Railroad Line had been a shot in the dark because they never had any openings. They operated three passenger ships that ran between New York and Cristobal, Panama and each ship was on a three week turn around. Jobs on these ships were considered to be the best in the entire maritime industry.

THE NEW YORK NAVAL SHIPYARD

I was delighted with the offer from the Panama Railroad Line. Anita and I discussed the potential benefits of both of the available jobs. Anita felt that the Naval Shipyard job offered the best potential for a career path, and she did not want to face a life where her husband would be absent most of the time. I had to agree with the soundness of her argument. I decided to decline the Panama Railroad Line's offer and to take the job at the Naval Shipyard. Friday morning I called the Panama Railroad Line office and thanked them for the offer but told them that I could not accept it due to another commitment. The following Monday morning I reported to the Naval Shipyard in Brooklyn and was processed in. The employment office assigned me to the Compartment and Access group in the engineering and naval architecture section. The head of this section was a fellow named Ruperto Ruiz and my immediate supervisor was a Mr. Rosquist. There were about a dozen men in this group. Abe Rosenblum was the group checker and an amiable man. After being introduced to the men in the group, I was given a drawing table and a set of drafting tools and then indoctrinated in the work and procedures the group was involved with. The work consisted mostly with modifying existing design drawings for the modifications of the aircraft carriers.

Four or five of the men in the group were recently discharged Army types who had been hired on the preferential policies set up for ex-GIs. They did not have college degrees or other advanced education and only limited drafting experience. Two of the younger men were graduates of Manhattan College and had degrees in city planning. The rest were a collection of low level draftsmen. The section was working on the conversion of three aircraft carriers, the CV 18, CV 19 and CV 20. One of them was the USS Oriskaney. Our group had to modify the drawings for the layout and location of the various compartments on these ships. As a drawing was revised it would be passed on to Abe Rosenblum to be checked for accuracy and then to Mr. Rosquist for approval. The output of work by this group was unbelievably poor. Within a week it became obvious that my work output was far superior to that of the other men in the group. Abe Rosenblum informed me that only he, Mr. Rosquist, and I had any formal education in naval architecture. He could not understand why I had been given such a low GS rating. One of the older draftsmen always had his head down and appeared to be working diligently when actually he was sound asleep. Midmorning one day he fell off his stool and broke his arm. This put him out of business for a few weeks. The two Manhattan College boys spent most of their time playing a game called "Battleship." They sat one behind the other and could be heard quietly calling letters of the alphabet and numbers to each other. The other men were equally slow or ineffective.

After about two months I became fed up with my low GS5 status especially since I discovered that two other classmates of mine were working in another engineering group as GS7s. I went to Ruperto Ruiz and told him that I felt that I should have a higher GS rating. He said that there was nothing he could do now, but he expected that there would be some announcements coming out of Washington soon for higher GS ratings. He said that he would let know when they came out so that I could apply for a higher grade. After a couple of more months went by, I approached Mr. Ruiz again, and he said that the announcements would be out within the next two months. When two more months had passed I went to Mr. Ruiz again and told him that I was going to start looking for a job elsewhere. He reached into a desk drawer and handed me a published announcement, saying that it had just been released. He asked me not to show it to anyone else and to fill out the application and send it to the designated address in Washington DC. The announcement was for a GS7 Naval Architect position, and I lost no time in filling it out and sending it in. I confided to Abe that I had submitted the application for a GS7 rating and he wished me good luck.

My life became a rather steady routine. Anita and I would get up early in the morning, have breakfast, and then I would drive to the railroad station and catch the commuter train to Jamaica. From the Jamaica station I would take a subway train to Brooklyn, and from there walk four or five blocks to the Navy yard. Part of this walk took me through a new complex of high rise public housing apartments. During the ten months I worked at the Navy yard I watched these buildings slowly deteriorate from modern appealing structures to trash-laden, untidy slums. The people who occupied the buildings were low income or welfare recipients and were a mixture of both white and black people. This was a clear example of the old saying, "You can take the people out of the slums, but you can not take the slums out of the people." I could not help feeling sorry for the decent people who were trapped in that complex with the White and Black trash that were turning it into a slum. Crime also increased with the deterioration of the buildings. This to me was a casual lesson in the social sciences or how the best efforts of the do gooders often become a tremendous waste of tax dollars.

Abe Rosenblum became quite friendly, and it seemed that he and I were carrying a major part of the work load for the group. I got along well with the other men in the group, and they were pleased to be able to pass the more complicated work to me. One day two men in dark three piece suits came into our section and spoke to Mr. Ruiz. When Mr. Ruiz pointed out one of the Manhattan College boys drawing tables, they marched quickly over to it. They told the Manhattan College boy to gather his personal belongings together and then marched him out of the room. He appeared to be under arrest, and none or us had a clew as to what he had done wrong. Since the Cold War was in full swing, we assumed that he had been in violation of some security rule. Perhaps he was a card carrying Communist or a member of some sort of subversive organization. What ever his problem was, none of us in the group were ever able to find out, and none of us ever saw him again. The remaining Manhattan College boy was distressed because he no longer had anyone with whom to play "Battleship."

Every few weeks I would go to Mr. Ruiz and ask him if there had been any reply from Washington. He would always say there was nothing new and that I should be patient because these things usually took a long time. The personnel records offices were located on the floor above the floor I was working on. When a couple of more months had gone by, I went up to the floor with the personnel records offices. I managed to find the clerk who had charge of the records for the engineering section. This clerk was a friendly chubby woman about fifty years of age. When I asked her if there was any information on my application for an advancement in grade, she said that she was not authorized or allowed to give out that type of information. She listened to my story with a sympathetic ear and agreed that my application should have been processed months ago. Then she said that she would check into the status of my application discretely, and that I should come back in two days. When I returned to her desk two days later she looked at me with some apprehension. She said that I would have to promise not to tell anyone where I got the information she was about to divulge. When I agreed, she told me that my promotion had been approved over three months ago and that Mr. Ruiz had been sitting on it. I thanked her and assured her that I would not tell anyone how I found out. To say the very least, I was furious at the way the deceitful Ruperto Ruiz was stringing me along.

I decided that I could not work for Ruperto Ruiz any longer. Coincidental with this revelation, Anita informed me that she was pregnant. We had a long discussion about the situation at the Navy yard, and Anita agreed that I should not have to work under such a scoundrel. Anyway I would have to get a better paying job because, being pregnant, Anita would have to leave her teaching job. My Navy yard salary was too low for us to maintain a decent living standard. When Anita's father learned that she was pregnant, he offered to let us buy the model house in his building development at what it cost him. This was an excellent opportunity for us to get a house of our own and we accepted his offer gratefully. With the help of Anita's father we were able to get a mortgage on this house. We were also able to buy the adjacent lot which had a fine stand of trees. The property was in the town of Islip and located just south of Montauk highway in an up scale community. The move from our apartment in Glenwood Landing to our new house in Islip went very well. It was at the time of year when Anita's school was closing for the summer vacation and Anita terminated her teaching position. I began commuting on the Long Island Rail Road between Islip and Jamaica and usually had only standing room on the train. It took a little over two hours to commute between Islip and the Navy yard.

Anita and I agreed that the only way I could make enough money to carry the cost of a house would be for me to go back to sea. We were having dinner with Mr. King one evening, and we told him that Anita was pregnant, and that I was looking for another seagoing job. He told us that job openings on ships were becoming scarce and that the MM&P Union had most of the available jobs tied up. Shipping companies could only hire new Mates through the Union and it would probably take several months to get a ship through the Union hall. At this time Mr. King was working in a management position at National Bulk Carriers, but this company's large fleet of ships were all foreign flag, either Liberian or

Panamanian. Mr. King said that he would make some phone calls and see what he could turn up for me. True to his word, Mr. King called me a couple of nights later and informed me that he had arranged for me to meet with a Captain Weaver at the Isbrandtsen Line office at 26 Broadway in lower Manhattan. He gave me Captain Weaver's phone number and said that I should call him and arrange a time to meet with him.

I called Captain Weaver the next morning and arranged to meet him the following day. Instead of reporting for work at the Navy yard that day I went directly to the Isbrandtsen Line office. My meeting with Captain Weaver was very cordial. He was the Isbrandtsen Line's Port Captain and an old friend of Mr. King's. He said that Mr. King had told him of my service record with the Boland and Cornelius Line and praised me as one of the best ship's officers he knew. Captain Weaver said that he would like to assign me to one of Isbrandtsen's ten ships right then, but he could not do so because of the MM&P Union agreement. However he had a plan to get around the Union if I were willing to go along with it. The plan was to have the Isbrandtsen Line hire me as part of their office staff. After about three months they could then transfer me to the marine division and assign me to a ship. I agreed to give his plan a try and he then took me to meet the head of the Isbrandtsen Line's claims department, Walter Isbrandtsen. Hans Isbrandtsen, the owner of the company, had two sons, Jacob and Walter, and a daughter. He and both of his sons were directly involved with the operation of the company. Apparently Walter had been briefed about me before my initial meeting with Captain Weaver. He welcomed me aboard warmly and said that it would be good for his division to have a claims analyst with shipboard experience. They offered me a salary that was somewhat higher than my Navy yard salary, and I accepted. It was a Friday and I told them that I would resign my job at the Navy yard and would be ready to start work with them in two weeks.

That weekend I prepared a letter of resignation from my Navy Yard job giving them two weeks notice. Upon reporting to work the following Monday morning, I went to Mr. Ruiz's office to submit the letter. His deputy, Mr. Castellano, informed me that Mr. Ruiz was in Washington DC and would not be in the office for the rest of the week. I handed him my letter of resignation and asked him to open it and read it. From my drawing table I could see Mr. Castellano talking on the phone and he seemed quite concerned. A short time later he called me over to his desk. He said that he had just spoken with Mr. Ruiz and that Mr. Ruiz was distressed over my resignation. Mr. Castellano was told to ask me to re-consider and to tell me that I would be promoted to a GS7 grade as soon as Mr. Ruiz returned from Washington. I told him to tell Mr. Ruiz that I would not change my decision to resign and that he had two weeks to find a replacement for me. Mr. Rosquist and Abe expressed regret at my resignation. When I told Abe that I had found out that Mr. Ruiz had been sitting on my promotion for over three months he said that he understood why I was quitting. He would quit too if he had somewhere else to go. On my last Friday there Mr. Rosquist, Abe, and some of the men in the group took me to a local bar for a couple of rounds of farewell drinks. The following Monday morning I reported to my new boss, Walter Isbrandtsen, at 26 Broadway in Manhattan. This was now July 1952.

THE AROUND THE WORLD SERVICE

The Isbrandtesn Line's claims department was located in a large rectangular room with about eight desks set up for claims analysts and with one larger desk for Walter Isbrandtsen at one end of the room. The ceiling of the room was two stories high. Half way up one wall there was railing running the full length of the wall and forming the edge of a gallery floor. On this floor there were several desks occupied by female typists. This was the typing pool and was in the charge of a skinny old harpy who kept a tight reign on the typists. When one of the claims analysts needed to have a letter prepared he would call the old harpy and request a stenographer. Within a few minutes a prim young woman would appear at his desk with a pad and pencil ready to take dictation. When finished taking notes she would return to the pool. A half hour later she would return to the analyst's desk with the typed letter and envelop for his review. If the analyst found the letter satisfactory, he would pass it on to Walter Isbrandtsen for final review and signature. This procedure kept a tight control on company claims department correspondence and made for a very efficient use of manpower. The work schedule was for a six day week. From Monday to Friday the work was from eight in the morning to five in the afternoon. On Saturdays the work was from eight o'clock to noon.

I was introduced to the seven analysts in the room and one of them, Mr. Menken, a man in his forties, was assigned to instruct me in the work I would be doing. He acted as my mentor and told me quite a lot of the history of the Isbrandtsen Line. When ever there was damage to cargo carried on one of the company's ships, either the shipper or the consignee would submit a damage claim. Paying damage claims was a significant expense to a cost conscious company like Isbrandtsen. Therefore each claim was carefully reviewed to ascertain what, if any, responsibility the company had, and what would be a reasonable or acceptable amount of money to pay to settle the claim. Often the claimed damage would be covered by insurance of one form or another. Sometimes the claim would be referred

258

to the company's lawyers for resolution. If the company had to pay out a significant sum of money for damage to some cargo, the Master and Chief Mate of the ship involved could expect a most disagreeable letter or sometimes a visit from Walter Isbrandtsen. With my shipboard cargo handling experience, I could usually review a damage claim and ascertain the extent of a ship's culpability. After a couple of weeks the other claims analysts were coming to me for specific information on how a particular type of cargo was handled and stowed on a ship.

The Isbrandtsen Line was unique among American flag shipping companies. Hans Isbrandtsen was an old country Dane and he ran his company with an iron hand. There were ten ships in the fleet, six on the around the world service and four on the North European service. The house flag was the international "M," a white Saint Andrew's Cross on a blue background, and this flag was painted on all of the ships' smoke stacks. Freight rates for North Atlantic shipping were set by a conference of the shipping companies of the various countries engaged in the North Atlantic trade. The Isbrandtsen Line advertised a freight rate that was always ten percent below the conference rate. This assured that Isbrandtsen ships would always have cargo to carry. Payment for freight would be accepted in the currency of any country. If a surplus of a particular currency posed a problem with conversion, Hans Isbrandtsen would purchase some commodity in the country of that currency and then carry it in his ships and then sell it where ever he could. In this regard he was a true merchant and ship operator. To him an empty ship was intolerable.

The Isbrandtsen Company was also in the coffee business. They processed, packaged, and sold a brand of coffee under their own name, Isbrandtsen's 26, and Isbrandtsen's Owner's Preferred. It was available in several grocery store chains along the Eastern seaboard. How they got into the coffee business was typical of how Hans Isbrandtsen operated. Shortly after the Japanese attacked Pearl Harbor a Japanese army was marching down the Maylay peninsula and attacking Singapore. There was an empty Isbrandtsen ship at a dock in Singapore at that time. The Captain contacted the New York office by radio and asked for instructions. Hans Isbrandtsen asked the Captain what commodity was in the dock's warehouse. The Captain replied that the warehouse was full of bagged coffee beans. He was told to load the coffee in his ship and set sail for New York as quickly as he could. Two months later this ship with a full load of coffee dropped anchor in New York harbor having successfully eluded enemy submarines in both the Pacific and Atlantic oceans. In spite of anticipated shortages of coffee because of the war, the local coffee company barons got together and offered Hans Isbrandtsen a ridiculously low price for his ship load of coffee. Those coffee barons were trying to hustle the wrong man. Hans Isbrandtsen managed to find an old coffee processing plant that was for sale. He bought the plant, had it refurbished, and began processing, packaging, and selling his own brand of coffee.

After a few weeks I found myself having lunch on a regular basis in a nearby coffee shop with two or three other men who worked for other shipping companies in down town Manhattan. During lunch we would exchange sea stories. One of these stories concerned Captain Weaver. He had been involved in a very serious situation. On a ship he was Captain of there had been a fight between the mates and some of the stewards. A Negro cook had been beating one of the mates with his fists and was completely out of control. Captain Weaver came on the scene with a pistol in his hand and ordered the cook subdued and placed in hand cuffs. A couple of the mates managed to get a cuff on one of the cook's hands, whereupon he broke free and attacked the Captain. The cook lashed out at the Captain with the handcuffs on his one hand. Captain Weaver fired one shot at the cook killing him instantly. When the ship returned to a US Port, the National Maritime Union crewmen with the support of union officials accused Captain Weaver of murder. He was tried in a Federal court twice and both times the trial resulted in a hung jury. Even though Captain Weaver was not found guilty of murder he could not go to sea again. The National Maritime Union threatened to boycott and tie up any ship he might be assigned to. He was essentially beached and fortunate that Isbrandtsen gave him a position as a port captain.

A short time after starting my claims analyst job, I was asked to be the company's stand by mate. Although New York was the home port for all of the Isbrandtsen ships, they would go coastwise to other ports, Philadelphia, Baltimore, Norfolk, Charleston, and Savannah to load and discharge cargo. Occasionally one of the Mates on these ships would have to take some time off for personal or medical reasons. If a company ship were due to sail coastwise on a Friday and needed a relief mate on short notice, I would be called to fill that berth. The company expected me to have my license with me at all times and to be willing to jump on a ship without advanced notice. Since I was already an employee of the company there was no need for the company to go through the MM&P Union.

The first time I was called upon for this special duty was quite an eye opener. On a Friday afternoon in late July Walter Isbrandtsen got a call from the marine department informing him that they needed a relief mate for a company ship due to sail that evening for Philadelphia. He asked me if I could take the assignment. When I said yes, he told me to clear my desk, take my license, and report as soon as possible to the S S Flying Spray at pier 29 in Brooklyn. I called Anita and told her that I would be sailing to Philadelphia and would be gone for a day or so. An hour later I reported aboard the S S Flying Spray and was informed that I would be taking the Third Mate's position. I was introduced to Captain Aarhus the Master and an old country Dane. The ship departed pier 29 a couple of hours later for the run down the coast to Philadelphia. All I had with me were the clothes on my back. While on my eight to twelve watch, the ship ran into a heavy rain storm. As was customary in limited visibility, I called the Captain to the bridge. I put the engine telegraph on stand by and was examining the radar display when the Captain entered the wheel house. A torrential rain was falling. The Captain said to me, "I like my mates in da ving." I told him that I did not have any foul weather gear and he repeated, "I like my mates in da ving." Without further comment, I left the wheel house and stood the rest of my watch on the starboard wing of the bridge in a deluge. There I could see or hear nothing and I was soaked to the skin within minutes. When I got off my watch I went to my cabin and stripped off all my soaking wet cloths. I hung them in the fiddley above the boilers to dry out. The ship docked in Philadelphia in the early afternoon on Saturday and I was told that I was not needed any further and could return to New York. Once again I had been subjected to the whims of a very nasty Scandinavian skipper. I left the pier where the ship had docked and walked towards Broad Street and the nearest subway station. On the way I passed a dry cleaner's store and stopped there briefly to have my badly wrinkled suit pressed. At the Philadelphia Pennsylvania Rail Road station I caught a train to New York and then another to Islip and home.

After the experience on the S S Flying Spray I kept a small bag at my desk packed with some essential clothing and toilet articles. About every two or three weeks I would be called upon on a Friday afternoon to ride one of the company's ships as a relief mate. Some of these relief assignments would be for three or four days, and one of them was a two week coastwise trip. One of these sudden assignments placed me in a very awkward situation. As I was walking down pier 29 to join the S S Flying Cloud, I recognized a man walking toward me. It was my first Captain, Pete Hickey. Greeting him warmly and shaking his hand I said, "I am glad to see that you are the Captain of this ship, it will be great sailing with you again." With an embarrassed look he responded, "I am not the Skipper, I am sailing as an AB." I was surprised and told him that we would talk later aboard the ship. An hour or so later sea watches were set and the ship departed the pier and started the run to Philadelphia. As fate would have it, Pete Hickey was one of the Able Seamen assigned to my watch. Here was a man who had taken the time to teach me ship handling and seamanship when I was a green Third Mate. He had probably forgotten more about seamanship than I would ever know. Now he was just an AB on my watch. I felt embarrassed and sick at heart. During the run to Philadelphia he told me that he had lost his Captain's license and could only sail as an AB. It seems that on the last ship he was Master of, the Third Mate had run the ship aground on the Isle Of Pines, Cuba. At the time this happened, Captain Hickey was asleep in his bunk intoxicated. The Coast Guard found both Captain Hickey and the Third Mate guilty of dereliction of duty and revoked their licenses. Since then he had been shipping out as an AB. Because of his alcoholism his wife had divorced him and he had lost everything he had owned. His wartime years running ship loads of high explosive munitions across the Atlantic to European ports under constant enemy action gave him nothing but a dependency on the bottle. Captain Hickey was just another unrecognized hero and a casualty of World War II. When the S S Flying Cloud returned to New York, I took Captain Hickey out to dinner and we talked at length about old times. That was the last time I saw him. He deserved a better fate than the one he had been handed by a fickle and unappreciative Government run by selfish self serving politicians. I can't help but wonder how many patriotic heroic merchant seamen were used, abused, and abandoned by the professional politicians who run the government to benefit themselves and their cronies.

There were other unusual characteristics peculiar to the Isbrandtsen Company. The Isbrandtsens' had a large farm in Bayshore on Long Island only five or six miles from Islip. This farm extended from many acres on the North side of Montauk Highway across to the South side all the way to the Great South Bay. Much of it was planted with hay to support a small heard of prime cattle. There was a mansion type farmhouse on the farm which was the residence of Walter Isbrandtsen and his family. One day Walter asked for volunteers to report to the farm the next day to gather in the hay. About half a dozen men from the office force including me spent the next two days pitching hay on the farm. It was pleasant out door work and only a few miles from my home. Another incident caught my attention. There was an extremely attractive receptionist in the entrance lobby at 26 Broadway, and there were usually a few young men hanging around her desk. One noon time as I was passing through the lobby on my way to lunch I saw this receptionist weeping as she was cleaning out her desk. Apparently Hans Isbrandtsen had noticed how this very pretty receptionist attracted the young men away from their work. He had a simple though ruthless solution for this distraction. The receptionist was dismissed with two weeks pay, and replaced by a very efficient old, skinny, and unattractive female.

THE S S SAXON

At the end of October 1952 I was told that I would be given an assignment as Second Mate to a ship on the North Atlantic run. I cleared my claims department work and got ready to ship out. On 6 November 1952 I traveled to Philadelphia and reported aboard the S S Saxon, a tired old Liberty Ship. The Master, Captain Peters, was a slender man about six feet tall with a swarthy complexion and a pock marked face. He was an easy going and pleasant person as was the Chief Mate. The Third Mate was a couple of years younger than me and went by the nick name Scooby. The Chief Engineer was an older Swedish man of short stature and with a very nervous personality. The three Assistant Engineers were in their late twenties or early thirties. There was a Radio Operator about my own age, but no Purser. The ship loaded a partial cargo in Philadelphia and then sailed down the coast to Charleston. The S S Saxon then returned to New York to top off the load of general cargo. Foreign articles were signed on 13 November and the next day the ship sailed for Germany.

The North Atlantic is usually a miserable body of water in the late Fall and Winter, and it was no exception on this crossing. The heavy seas held our speed to an average of nine knots. Some days the ship made eleven knots and on other days made barely six knots. As usual I had the twelve to four watch. Occasionally the Captain would come into the lower bridge wheel house a little after midnight and spend a half hour or more telling me of some of his experiences. One night he came into the wheel house with a yellow legal pad in his hands. There were several pages turned over and there were names written on each line. The Captain told me that he had been spending most of the evening writing down the names of all the women he had made love to. He said that he had written the names of three hundred and twenty women on the pad thus far and that there were at least a hundred more whose names he could not remember. I thought he was kidding me and I told him so. He said that he was quite serious and was worried that his memory was beginning to fail. This tall tail was unbelievable, or so I thought until the ship docked in Bremerhaven.

The ship beat its way across the North Atlantic through Pentland Firth at the North of Scotland and into the North Sea. The passage through Pentland Firth was an unusual experience. Tidal currents there run as high as ten knots. With a favorable tidal current the ship made twenty knots over the ground as it passed through Pentland Firth. There was no improvement in the weather as the ship proceeded across the relatively shallow North Sea to the Wesser River. The ship was shrouded in dense fog as it made its way into the mouth of the Wesser River. Navigation was done only by radio direction finder and fathometer. Among his other accomplishments, Captain Peters was an excellent navigator. For more than an hour of anxious navigating, he maneuvered the ship at slow speed through the dense fog and following some instinct or sixth sense, he ordered the engine to be stopped and the anchor dropped. Once the ship was riding securely on the anchor, I left the bridge and walked up to the bow. Through the dense fog I heard voices speaking in the gutteral German language just ahead. This was followed by the sound of bells and gongs being rung by other ships at anchor. When the fog began to lift I was amazed to find that we were anchored just a ship's length off the stern of a very large German freighter. That was the source of the voices that I had heard earlier. Had the Captain not stopped the ship and anchored where he did, we would have collided with that ship. When the fog finally cleared there were several other ships seen at anchor ahead of us.

The next morning port officials came aboard and cleared the ship for entry into Bremerhaven. A pilot came aboard before noon and with the help of two tug boats maneuvered the ship into the locks for the port of Bremerhaven. The ship was secured to the side of the lock while the water level was raised to that of the harbor. While secured there about two dozen young women came to the side of the ship and asked for the Captain. After exchanging greetings he invited them aboard. The ship then moved to a berth in the harbor. The Chief Mate set about getting the hatches open and ready to discharge cargo. I went down on the dock and recorded the draft of the ship at the bow and the stern. Then I went to the bridge wheel house to make the log book entries. Just off the wheel house the door to the Captain's office was open as was the door to his adjacent cabin. There were women everywhere. When I informed the Captain that the ship was about to start discharging the cargo he told me to take it easy. Then he said that I should select a couple of the young women and take them to my cabin. I thanked him for his generous offer but declined. These women were all very attractive and apparently knew the Captain from his previous visits to Germany. This confirmed the Captain's claim to having made love to a multitude of women. Somehow he had a tremendous attraction for women, and I was duly impressed.

The Captain went ashore that afternoon with the women and some of the seamen. Before leaving the ship he gave the Chief Mate a list of bars he would be visiting during the evening. He said that any of the ship's company who might need some money could look for him in one of those establishments. During a conversation with the company's agent that day, I was informed that Franz Lehar's operetta, "The Land Of Smiles" was being performed at the new State Theater in Bremerhaven. Since I did not have to go on watch until midnight, I decided to see this performance. The State Theater was an impressive building and had been built after the war. The performance of "The Land Of Smiles" was outstanding. It was without a doubt the most pleasant evening I spent in Germany during this voyage.

After two days in Bremerhaven the ship proceeded up the Wesser River to the port of Bremen. This city had been severely damaged during the war. On one terrible night a thousand plane raid destroyed a large area of the city and over twenty thousand civilians perished. I took a walk through the devastated area one afternoon and was appalled. There were just piles of bricks and rubble where houses had once stood. Women and children, young and old, could not escape the bombs raining down on them. How the masterminds of war can justify the wanton destruction of civilian populations is beyond my ability to understand. It was obvious that it would be a long time before this monument to unlimited air bombardment would be erased. As I continued my walk into the part of Bremen that was still pretty much intact, I noticed that the people on the streets seemed to be lacking the signs of affluence one would see in an American city. Everything seemed rather drab. There was also an odor of burning soft coal or peat that permeated the atmosphere. As darkness fell I stepped into a noisy, smoky, dimly lit bar for a beer, and noticed many young women offering their time and talents to the numerous American seamen there. The economics of post war Germany required some compromises with normal morality.

After about three days all of the cargo for Bremen was discharged. The hatches were then covered and the ship departed for Belgium. Two days later we were secured to a dock in the port of Antwerp. Again several attractive young women appeared at the side of the ship looking for our Captain. The man must have been an amorous legend in his own time. Antwerp showed very little signs of the recent war. It was a busy bustling city and the people on the streets appeared to be moderately well off. There was one street, Skipper Straza, that seemed to be the favorite destination for the American seamen. It was a wide street lined on both sides with bars, restaurants, shops, and houses that provided other amenities. Again the Captain left word on board that during the evening he could be found in the Coney Island Bar, the Robot Bar, or two or three other similar establishments on Skipper Straza. Any of our crew who needed some money could seek him out in one of these places and make a small draw against his wages. The Captain would make note of these outlays on the back of a book of matches or any other scrap of paper he might have in his pocket. How he was able to keep a proper account of these transactions was a mystery. Somehow he did manage to keep it straight and the crewmen appreciated his willingness to cover their needs in such an informal manner. Antwerp was a great town for night life and our crew took full advantage of everything it had to offer.

The S S Saxon spent about five days in Antwerp taking on a load of general cargo. An oil barge was brought along side and our fuel tanks were topped off with bunker-C fuel oil for the voyage home. When the ship cleared Belgium and the English Channel, the Captain set a course on the high circle back to New York. It was just a couple of days before Christmas in December 1952. The weather was terrible. The ship ran into a North Atlantic gale. Because of the increase in radio traffic during the Christmas and New Year period, the radio operator was unable to keep up with current communications. In spite of the foul weather the ship's Steward and the cooks provided a very nice Christmas dinner for the ship's company. The day after Christmas as I came off my morning watch I experienced rather severe stomach cramps which lasted well into the afternoon. I thought they were the result of my eating too much of the rich food provided the day before. A week or so later, the Radio Operator congratulated me and handed me a radiogram informing me that I became the father of a healthy baby boy on 26 December. This was really wonderful news even though it was so late. I had to wonder what really was the cause of the stomach cramps I had the day after Christmas.

There is more than one great circle track across the North Atlantic between Europe and America. The high track is the northern most track and is the shortest in miles but it takes one to the higher latitudes. Normally most ships will take a more southern route across the Atlantic in winter time in order to avoid the bad weather and rough seas of the northern route. Captain Peach decided to take a chance on the weather in the hope of getting across in fewer days. North Atlantic gales in January are legendary. This crossing was no exception. When the ship reached the higher latitudes it was well out of the Gulf Stream. The water temperature was about thirty degrees. The almost constant spray and precipitation coated all the external surfaces with a film of ice. A four hour watch on the bridge was pure agony. It was impossible to keep warm even though I wore my long johns and my bridge coat. The heavy rolling and pitching of the ship made it even more miserable. As I came off watch at 0400 one morning I was walking along the starboard main deck passageway past the crew's head. Suddenly the ship took a heavy roll to starboard and I heard a shout of consternation coming from the head. When I looked in I saw one of the firemen standing with his trousers around his ankles and his lower torso dripping water. Apparently when the ship took the heavy roll the surface of the sea water outside of the ship was twenty or thirty feet higher than the toilet seat he had been sitting on. The flapper valve on the discharge end of the sewer pipe must have stuck open and the reverse of gravity caused a gusher of frigid water to literally blow him off the toilet. He was not a happy sailor. However, that was not the only problem we had with the frigid water.

One day while the ship was still struggling through the frigid waters, just as the noon meal was to be served, the Chief Engineer came into the saloon very distraught and informed the Captain that the ship was almost out of fuel. He said that there was only enough fuel in the settling tanks for about two day's steaming. The Captain said that it was impossible because we had taken on a full load of fuel before leaving Antwerp. The

Chief Engineer said that he had personally sounded all the fuel tanks and they were empty. He could offer no explanation except to say that the fuel supplier in Antwerp had somehow short changed the ship. Running out of fuel put the ship in an extremely serious situation. The Captain informed the home office of our plight by radio. A short time later the home office informed the Captain that they were making arrangements for a salvage tug to leave Saint Johns, Newfoundland and rendezvous with us in mid ocean. The tug would then tow our ship back to Saint Johns. Both the Captain and the Chief Engineer were extremely concerned. This situation could cost them their jobs and perhaps even their licenses. Everyone was concerned. The North Atlantic is no place to run out of fuel in the winter time.

However, Lady Luck decided to smile on the S S Saxon. The very next day the ship entered the Gulf Stream and its warmer water. The surface of the sea changed from a dull gray blue color to a clear deep violet blue typical of the Gulf Stream. Several hours later the Chief Engineer reported that he suddenly had plenty of fuel in the fuel tanks. The Captain got off a quick radio message to cancel the salvage tug. The reason for the fuel problem was almost laughable. Bunker-C fuel has the consistency of heavy creosote and it must be heated to make it thin enough to flow through pipes. Fuel tanks on liberty ships have coils of steam pipes in them to warm the bunker-C fuel oil. These steam pipes on the S S Saxon had rotted away so there was no heat in the tanks to warm the fuel oil. As the ship was rolling in the heavy seas, the fuel oil congealed in the outer ends of the tanks away from the sounding pipes. That was why the tanks were showing empty when the Chief Engineer sounded them. Once the ship's hull was exposed to the warmer water of the Gulf Stream, the fuel oil melted and flowed evenly across the tanks. Had the ship not entered the Gulf Stream when it did there would have been hell to pay all around. The rest of the voyage was uneventful. When the ship finally docked in New York, the articles were broken and the crew were paid off. I left the ship and went home to Anita and my brand new son. A few days later the S S Saxon sailed on her next voyage without me.

THE WAYBILL SYSTEM

After a couple of happy days at home getting acquainted with my new son and our collie dog Bruce, I got a call from Walter Isbrandtsen to report to him at 26 Broadway the next morning. When I reported in at the office Walter greeted me warmly and said that he had a special task for me to do on my next voyage, and that would be as Second Mate on the S S Flying Cloud. The Isbrandtsen Line was introducing a new method of tracking cargo consignments from origination to destination. This was the Waybill System. It consisted of a multi-page document that would go with each consignment of cargo on the ship's manifest. At each stage of the shipping process a page of the Waybill document would be filled out describing the condition of the consignment and any changes to its condition. It would start with one page being sent to the home office when the consignment was accepted by the company for shipment. Another page would be submitted when the consignment arrived at the pier or ship for loading. When the consignment was off loaded at its destination port another page would be annotated and sent to the home office. The last page would be completed and sent to the home office when the consignment had been delivered to or accepted by the consignee. This procedure would give the claims department a complete and accurate history of the transport of a consignment of cargo while it was in the custody of the Isbrandtsen Line and would give them better control of liability for any damage claims against such cargo. The Waybill would be an additional document that went along with the Bill of Lading for each consignment of cargo. My special task was to explain the introduction and use of the Waybill system to the company's agents in each port of call on the around the world service. The agents in the Northern European ports would be instructed by someone else. This was just another example of how the Isbrandtsen Company got things done at minimal or no extra costs.

On 6 January 1953 I signed on as Second Mate on the S S Flying Cloud in New York. After a coastwise run to Norfolk, Baltimore, and Philadelphia, the ship returned to New York to top off the cargo and take on twelve passengers. The ship was scheduled to shift from the Army Base pier in Brooklyn over to Staten Island to load the last few items of cargo. In spite of the Company's rules, the Captain said that the Chief Mate and I could have our wives on board the evening the ship moved over to Staten Island. Both Anita and the Chief Mate's wife came aboard the ship just after the evening meal was served. Fortunately they had both eaten before they came aboard. Shifting the ship to a pier on Staten Island took a little over an hour. Anita watched the activity of undocking and docking from the boat deck with the passengers who had come aboard earlier in the day. Afterward she spent my off watch hours with me in my cabin. In the morning at breakfast in the salon, Anita ordered her favorite, eggs over easy and sausage, from the menu with anticipation. When the salon mess man served it to her she was greatly disappointed. The eggs were watery, the sausage had a greenish tint, and the flavor left much to be desired. She said, "This is awful." I replied, "This food is fresh now. You should see what it will be like two months from now." Anita said that she would prepare a "care package" of food for me to take on my next voyage. Until now she had no idea how bad shipboard food could be. She and the Chief Mate's wife went ashore at noon and took the ferry boat back to Brooklyn.

THE SOUTH AFRICANS

A situation was developing prior to my signing the S S Flying Cloud. Since my last visit to Durban, South Africa, Anita and I had been exchanging letters occasionally with my South African friends Harry and Grace Foster. During my run to Europe on the S S Saxon the Fosters informed us that they planned to visit New York in the early Spring and would like to accept my offer to visit us. Of course Anita and I wrote to them and said that we would be pleased to have them as our guests. There was only one serious problem. I would probably be away at sea when the Fosters came to the United States. Knowing how well the Fosters treated me during my visits to Durban, Anita said that she would do her best to be a good hostess during my absence. This was an additional burden on Anita. With a new car, a new house, and a new baby to look after, her available time would be stretched to the limit. I felt terrible about leaving Anita to host and entertain people she had never met, but there was no decent way to discourage the Fosters from coming. With courage and optimism Anita assured me that she could manage to entertain the Fosters for the few days they would be visiting. I had forgotten that when South Africans visit someone the visit lasts for more that a couple of days. Such visits last for a few weeks and the Fosters' visit was no exception.

Sometime in late March the Fosters arrived in New York by ship. Anita was at the pier to greet them and to drive them with their baggage to our home in Islip. The fifty mile ride to our home impressed them very much. The highways and parkways crowded with cars and trucks of every description took them by surprise. There was no such density of vehicles in the streets and roadways of Durban. The first day of their visit was somewhat awkward. Our house had only three bedrooms. One bedroom was ours, one was set up as a nursery, and the other was our guest room. The guest room was furnished with a single double bed, two night stands, a large dresser, and a couple of chairs. Grace Foster informed Anita that she and Harry usually slept in separate beds. Anita said that she was sorry that there was only the double bed available and that she hoped that Grace and Harry would be able to adjust to it. Entertaining the Fosters, especially Harry, was initially easy. They were enthralled with our television set. There was nothing like it in South Africa at that time. Harry stayed glued to the TV when ever he was in the house. He fell in love with our new Studebaker sedan and took great pleasure in washing and polishing it. The only disappointment he had was that he could not drive it. He did not have a license and would have found it difficult to drive on the right side of the road.

A day or two after their arrival the Fosters were introduced to Anita's mother, father, and younger brother Richard as well as my mother. Harry blended very well and adjusted easily to the different circumstances he found in the United States. Grace on the other hand was often dismayed by what she saw and experienced. She was surprised to learn that Anita did her own house cleaning and laundry. Grace had servants to do such chores for her back in Durban. The first time Anita took the Fosters on the New York subway during a visit to Manhattan, Grace was shocked at the number of "Kaffirs" that rode in the subway cars with white people. She was used to the restrictions imposed by South Africa's apartheid policy. The skyscrapers and the throngs of people in the streets and the stores of Manhattan amazed both of them. They were also impressed with the tremendous variety of things that were available at such reasonable prices.

Anita's mother and my mother would often baby sit Randy so that Anita could take the Fosters to Manhattan and other places of interest. Richard, Anita's younger brother, often accompanied Anita when she took the Fosters into the city. This helped to reduce the strain on Anita of escorting the Fosters everywhere. They got to see a show at the Radio City Music Hall and a couple of live on stage TV shows which they enjoyed very much. Visits to museums and parks were not of as much interest to the Fosters. After about four weeks Harry made arrangements to take a passenger ship, I believe it was the Queen Mary, to England. He planned to visit family members he had not seen for many years. Apparently Grace was not keen on spending much time with Harry's relatives and she decided to take a bus tour across the United States to California. She wanted to see as much of America as she could and was very disappointed that

Anita could not go along with her. Grace planned to fly from California to England and meet Harry there for their return to South Africa. During the fifth week of their visit Harry departed New York on a ship bound for England. A couple of days later Grace departed New York on a tour bus headed for the West Coast.

All things considered, I believe the Fosters enjoyed their visit to the United States. Without a doubt their visit was a tremendous burden on Anita and she did a magnificent job of fulfilling an obligation that was rightfully mine. I think that most wives placed in that sort of situation would have been less than gracious. The Fosters had made my visits to Durban a very pleasant experience, and I was grateful that Anita was able and willing to make their visit to the United States an equally pleasant experience. In the months and years following the departure of the Fosters we did receive a card or a letter now and then. However the intervals between receiving these correspondence became longer with the passage of time. A few years later one of the Foster's letters informed us that they were selling their home in Durban and planned to emigrate to New Zealand. After that there was no further correspondence. I assume that they emigrated as planned, but I do not have a clue where they might have settled in New Zealand.

EASTWARD AROUND THE WORLD

The ship departed Staten Island during the afternoon for my first voyage around the world. The first port of call was Lisbon, Portugal a beautiful city with a population just under a million people. The ship spent two days there discharging and loading general cargo. The company's agent in Lisbon was a man forty or fifty years of age and fluent in English. Two or three hours were spent explaining the Waybill system to him and he had no difficulty understanding it. However, he did say that it was an unnecessary additional document he would have to bother with. I went ashore and sampled some of the restaurants. The food and wine were excellent and the prices were very reasonable. The city itself was bright and clean and for the most part the people were friendly. Because of our short stay there I was not able to see as much of the city and surrounding area as I would have liked to.

After departing Lisbon the ship steamed past Gibraltar and into the Mediterranean Sea and on to the port of Algiers, Algeria. Again I spent a couple of hours with the company's French agent explaining how the

Waybill procedure was to be implemented. He had no difficulty understanding the procedure but was somewhat less than enthusiastic about it. This of course was done in addition to my duties with discharging and loading cargo. As with my previous visit to Algiers, I found the Muslim peddlers and shop keepers to be somewhat unpleasant. Their system of haggling over every purchase was annoying. Fortunately the ship remained there for only a day and a half.

The next port of call was the beautiful city of Genoa, Italy. The ship arrived there after two days of steaming from Algiers. A short time after docking I was able to sit down with the company's agent and introduce him to the Waybill procedure. He accepted the added paper work with more grace than enthusiasm for which I was grateful. Genoa is a beautiful cosmopolitan city with many fine restaurants and upscale shops. Four of our passengers disembarked there. I went ashore as often I as I could and took in as many of the sights as circumstances would allow. There is one place in Genoa that most tourists make sure they visit. That place is the grave yard. It is large and has an amazing number of ornate mausoleums and fine statuary. In many ways it is truly a city of the dead. There was also a church that had a large unexploded bomb quite visible in the entrance way. The bomb had been defused and left where it had fallen as a clear sign of a miracle. After three days the ship sailed for Alexandria, Egypt.

ALEXANDRIA

The run across the Mediterranean to Alexandria was uneventful. Once the ship was cleared and secured to a dock, I asked the agent to give me some of his time so that I could explain the new Waybill procedure to him. This agent was a relatively young and energetic man and quite full of his own importance. He looked more European than Egyptian and quickly brushed me off saying that he was much too busy. Instead he assigned one of his subordinates to sit down with me. This subordinate was an elderly Egyptian and wore the customary Fez, a brim less hat that resembles a bright red up side down flower pot. Although his command of English was far better than my command of Egyptian or Arabic, I was sure that he did not understand everything I was telling him. During our discussions he informed me that he was a retired Admiral of the Egyptian Navy. I did not know that Egypt even had a navy. It seemed strange to me that a person with his background would be little more than a clerk under this young pompous agent. The Waybill procedure was explained to him in

detail and he assured me that he understood everything. With some misgivings I returned to my regular shipboard duties. When the cargo operations were finished I made a check of the condition of the cargo in each
hold. In number three tween deck space there was a Ford pickup truck
lashed down on the port side bound for Bombay. When the ship left New
York there had been a large wooden case secured in this truck's cargo bed.
The case was there when the ship arrived in Alexandria, but it was missing
as we were making ready to depart. The Egyptian longshoremen had pilfered the case and God only knows how much more of our cargo. I alerted
the Chief Mate that the ship would have a loss claim when it reached
Bombay, which indeed it did.

BEIRUT

It took about a day of steaming from Alexandria to Beirut, Lebanon.
Beirut was a cosmopolitan city much different than Alexandria. It was
said to be the Paris of the East and had a very obvious French atmosphere.
There were many wide boulevards with tall buildings, hotels, shops, restaurants, and night clubs. The population was between a quarter and a
half million people mostly Muslim with a minority of Christians. The
company's agent, an elderly man, invited me to come to his office in one
of the high rise buildings to introduce him to the Waybill procedure. He
was a Christian and during the three hours I spent in his office there was
some discussion of the Arab and Jewish problems in adjacent Israel. Much
to my surprise he felt that the Arabs were in the right and the Jews were
wrong. Since I was politically ignorant of the facts, I listened to his comments politely and said very little. When we were finished with the Waybill indoctrination he invited me to visit his home in one of the high rise
apartment buildings the following afternoon. Arriving there at the appointed time I was greeted by a very attractive young lady who led me
into the parlor. There the agent greeted me and introduced the young
lady as his daughter. A short time later she brought a tray with cups of
Turkish coffee and sweet cakes. After some small talk he handed me two
packages and said these are gifts, one was for me and the other for Walter
Isbrandtsen. I thanked him and assured him that I would get the other
package to Walter when the ship returned to New York. Upon opening
my package I found a very ornate box inlaid with an elaborate design in
mother of pearl. The box contained a variety of dried sweet fruits.

After two days the cargo operations were complete and the ship departed Beirut for a short run to Port Said and the Suez Canal. The ship had to wait for a day and a half as an east bound convoy of ships was assembled. The S S Flying Cloud was one of eight ships in the east bound convoy. Before starting the passage through the canal a crew of Arabs came aboard to get the ship ready. A row boat was rigged under a cargo boom on the fore deck and another on the aft deck ready to be placed in the water on short notice. Each boat had a crew of four Arabs. A large wooden box was hung over the bow of the ship from a special davit located there for that purpose. The box contained a powerful spot light and one or two men to work it. Night was falling as the convoy started through the canal. The crew in the spot light box illuminated the markers along the edges of the canal with the powerful beam from their light. This was done so the pilot on the bridge could see the sides of the canal and keep the ship in the center. The ships moved at rather slow speeds in order to avoid making any wakes. By daybreak the convoy was close to the mid point of the canal. All the ships came to a stop. The pilot ordered the two row boats put into the water. Then the Chief Mate on the bow with his crew and me on the stern with my crew lowered a mooring line down to each boat. The Arabs rowed their boats to the bank and hauled the mooring lines up the embankment to the top and placed the eye of each line over bollards located there. The lines were pulled taught and the ship was snugly moored to the bank of the canal. A short time later the west bound convoy came steaming by with a fair tidal current helping them. Once the west bound convoy was past, the mooring lines were taken aboard and the row boats were hoisted aboard and our ship along with the other ships resumed steaming east towards the port of Suez. As the ship passed through the Suez Canal Mount Sinai could be seen in the distance off the port side. The distance between Port Said and the port of Suez is more than a hundred miles. At the port of Suez the row boats, light box, and their Arab crews were quickly off loaded and the ship entered the Gulf of Suez.

JIDDA

The S S Flying Cloud steamed through the Gulf of Suez and down the Red Sea to the port of Jidda in Saudi Arabia. The heat during the passage was unbearable because a following breeze caused a stifling atmosphere on the ship. The ship anchored in Jidda harbor and port officials came aboard and cleared the ship. A cloud of black flies also came aboard. Since our stay there would be less than twenty four hours, sea watches were not broken. A tug boat brought a large steel barge alongside and a gang of Arab longshoremen came aboard. They were under the charge of a young man in flowing white robes who was one of the thousand or more princes in that country. No one was available to discuss the Waybill procedure, so this port was a pass. The prince who spoke English rather well was an arrogant twit who would not accept any advice from the ship's Mates. There were six Cadillac limousines to be discharged from number two hold. The hatch had eight large steel pontoon covers. The prince refused to remove any more than two of them to open the hatch. As each of the six vehicles were hoisted up with the ship's cargo gear they spun around so that they were caught on the pontoons still covering the hatch. This put large dents on the hoods and trunks of these vehicles. The Arabs receiving them ashore must have thought these vehicles were designed and built that way. We were glad to see this clown of a prince and his gang of long-shoremen leave the ship. We were equally glad to see the barge pull away without further damage to the vehicles. As soon as the hatch was covered and the cargo gear secured, the anchor was pulled up and the ship departed Jidda.

PORT SUDAN

The ship made a short run across the Red Sea to Port Sudan, Sudan. This place was a sea coast outpost on the edge of a desolate desert. A river of sorts flowed through this port to the sea but there was little vegetation worth mentioning. Once the ship was cleared and secured to the dock, the hatches were opened and cargo operations were begun. The long-shoremen were the most unusual I have ever seen. They were the original FuzzyWuzzys, actually the Beni-Amer people, made famous from the wars between the Sudanese and Anglo/Egyptian armies from 1875 to 1889. At a place called Tofrek, an army of Fuzzy-Wuzzys defeated a British army regiment and broke the famous British square. Rudyard Kipling wrote a poem about them worth quoting in part here:

We've fought with many men across the seas,
And some were brave and some were not:
The Paythan and the Zulu and the Burmese;
But the Fuzzy was the finest of the lot.

—

He's a daisy, he's a ducky, he's a lamb!

He's a ninja-rubber idiot on the spree,
He's the only thing that doesn't give a damm
For a Regiment of British Infantry!
So here's to you, Fuzzy-Wuzzy, at your home by the Sudan;
You're a poor benighted earthen but a first-class fighting man;
And here's to you, Fuzzy-Wuzzy, with your 'ayrick head of 'air
You big black bounding beggar — for you broke a British square!

Aboriginal might be the best way to describe them. They were very black, thin, and wiry with a huge mass of black kinky hair that covered their heads like a cloud. None were more than five feet tall. Otherwise naked to the waist they wore a skirt like garment that went to their knees. Each one carried a short sword with a blade about eighteen inches long secured by a leather belt. Some wore sandals, but most were barefoot. They were the fiercest looking people I have ever seen. Their facial features were European rather than Negroid. They had thin aquiline noses and thin lips. The eyes of most of them were somewhat blood shot, and they were always coughing up and spitting out yellow mucus. This may have indicated some significant health problems. Although they worked with surprising efficiency, they required the supervision of an Arab foremen. They completely ignored anything any of the ship's officers said to them. It was not just a language barrier. They had an arrogant disdain of white men. Like the other Mates, I avoided any confrontation with them. Again the local agent had no interest in the Waybill procedure and nothing was done with regard to it. Part of the cargo loaded there consisted of bales of hides, sacks of coffee beans, and bags of dom nuts, a hard nut used to make shirt buttons. Cargo operations were completed in less than two days, and the ship departed for Djibouti in Eritrea.

DJIBOUTI

The ship steamed along the coasts of Sudan and Eritrea, passed through the Bab El Mandeb into the Gulf of Aden, and entered the port of Djibouti. This was another small dusty city on the edge of a desert. There were the ever present flies in great numbers which seem to be a universal condition of Muslim seaports. The native longshoremen appeared to be more civilized than those of the last port. Arabic was the spoken language and few understood English. Our stay in Djibouti was short. Some general cargo was off loaded, and a quantity of bagged Ethiopian coffee was loaded.

This coffee was treated as special cargo and each individual bag was counted and stowed with care. As in the two previous ports, the agent had little interest in the Waybill procedure. His position was that any notations regarding a shipment of cargo would have to be done by the ship's personnel. No one on board expressed any regrets as we departed Djibouti and its dust, flies, and heat.

A PLAGUE OF LOCUSTS

The ship set a course for Karachi, Pakistan across the Arabian Sea which put us in sight of Oman on the Arabian coast part of the time. With the shoreline barely in sight on the western horizon we saw a huge black cloud over the land. This cloud was moving eastward and drifting across our course line. There was much speculation on the bridge as to what this cloud could be. Some thought it was just a line of rain squalls while others thought it might be a sand storm. Within an hour the black cloud extended from the shoreline all the way across the ship's course line like a thick black fog blocking out the sight of anything ahead. Not knowing what we were steaming into, all the doors and port holes were closed. On the radar screen the cloud appeared as if it were solid land. A lookout was sent to the bow, the Captain was called to the bridge, and the engine telegraph was put on standby, all standard procedures in restricted visibility. Without reducing speed, the ship steamed into the cloud. It was unbelievable. The cloud was composed of locusts, an insect resembling a grasshopper. They were about three or four inches long and a dark red or maroon color much like a boiled lobster. In about two minutes they covered all the exposed decks to a depth of twelve inches or more. The surface of the sea was red with locusts on both sides of the ship. They got into everything. I now knew what the Biblical stories about a plague of locusts really meant. There could be no edible vegetation left on the land where they were and now a stiff off shore breeze was blowing them out to sea. Once the ship passed through the cloud, the Chief Mate had the seamen wash down the decks with the fire hoses. When I finished my watch and returned to my cabin I found one of these locusts resting on my port hole curtain. Out of curiosity I kept it as a pet all the way to Japan feeding it bits and pieces from my evening dinner salad every day. The lonely locust prospered quite well on my tid bits, but jumped ship when we reached Nagasaki.

KARACHI

Other than the deluge of locusts, the run across the Arabian Sea to Karachi was uneventful. Once the ship was cleared for the port it went right to a berth at a dock. Four more of our passengers, a Protestant Minister, his wife, and two small daughters got off. They were going inland to some missionary outpost. Karachi had changed a good deal since I was last there in 1946. Instead of British, the port officials were all Pakistani. Although there were some Europeans to be seen in the city, they were a mere fraction of what were there on my first visit. I was able to introduce the company's agent to the Waybill procedure with some success which made me feel better about this added assignment. The ship's Purser informed me that he had a girl friend in Karachi and invited me to go ashore with him to visit her which I did. She was a nurse at the Seventh Day Adventists Hospital and a Syrian by nationality. She was also a Christian and had a friendly out going personality. Although a little on the plump side, she was never the less rather attractive. This relatively modern Christian hospital in this otherwise Muslim nation did seem odd to me. The Purser and I were given a tour of the hospital and later we were introduced to some of the staff over tea and cakes. One of the administrators, a man about thirty years of age, insisted on entertaining us and some staff members by playing music on a carpenter's saw. Following this recital he gave everyone present a lecture on the blessings of good behavior and the sin of fornication. I could not help but think that his lecture was directed at the only two rogue seamen present, the Purser and me.

It was very hot in Karachi and learning that our ship was not air conditioned, the Purser's girl friend nurse offered us the use of the hospital's air conditioned rooms for the night. We accepted her offer and returned to the hospital later that evening to spend the night. I did not get as much sleep as I had expected. She was on duty that night and made a point of looking in on the Purser and me every hour while she was making her rounds. Even so, I did enjoy a night of cool air in a comfortable bed. In the morning the Purser's girl friend invited us to attend a dinner party with her later that evening. It was being given by a wealthy businessman who had some interest in the hospital. Cargo operations were completed that afternoon and sea watches were to be set at midnight. Even so, the Purser and I went with his girl friend to the dinner party which was held in an outside garden of a large restaurant. Food and beverages were served to about thirty people seated at one long table. Our Pakistani host was very gracious and informed us that our ship had delivered some structural steel for his business. When the party was over he was kind enough to drive us back to our ship well before midnight. The ship departed Karachi shortly after sunrise the next morning bound for Bombay.

BOMBAY

The run south along the coast of India to Bombay took about two days. Upon arrival a pilot came aboard and guided the ship into Bombay harbor. With the help of a tug boat it proceeded through the locks to a berth at the Victoria docks. Once pratique was granted a horde of coolies came aboard and opened the hatches. The cargo gear was set in place and cargo operations started. Two more of our passengers, an elderly couple, got off. This left only two passengers, another elderly couple on a voyage around the world. I managed to take the company's agent aside for a while to explain the Waybill procedure to him. He was quick to inform me that the Waybill would be useless there. The Bombay Port Authority accepts all cargo discharged there but does not sign for it. They hold it in their warehouses until the consignees picks it up which could be weeks or months after the ship left. The Port Authority would not acknowledge or accept any responsibility for any damage or loss to the cargo. The continuity of custody was actually broken when the cargo was discharged in Bombay. All I could do was to prepare a report on the Bombay Port Authority situation for the home office.

Bombay was the largest city in India and rather cosmopolitan. The absence of British authority was noticeable. Everything was now run by the Indians. The police maintaining order in the street traffic were still predominately Sikhs with their impressive turbans. Several of the better hotels and shops were run by Europeans and Anglo Indians. Businesses seemed to be thriving so the move to independence did not bring on any significant change in the welfare of the people in Bombay. The caste system was still in place in spite of all the slogans about equality. There were still the very wealthy, the less wealthy, the middle class shop keepers, the poor, and the destitute. One day a priest from the Anglican Church, an Englishman, came to the ship and invited the Christians in our crew to attend services at his church. As far as I know none of them did so. A couple of times I left the ship in the early evening to do some souvenir shopping in the city. When returning to the ship after dark it was necessary to walk in the streets between the warehouses. The coolie longshore-men slept in mass in the open on all the sidewalks in the dock side area. What they did for shelter when it rained I have no idea. Cargo operations went on for about five days and through a weekend. The largest segment of cargo we loaded consisted of a thousand tons of baled cotton. When the last load of cargo was safely stowed in the holds, the hatches were covered and the ship made ready for a sea passage. It was late afternoon when the lines were taken in and the SS Flying Cloud departed the Victoria docks and Bombay. Once clear of the harbor a course was set for Colombo, Ceylon (now Siri Lanka).

COLOMBO

Two and a half days after departing Bombay, the ship arrived in Colombo. The ship went immediately to a dock and was cleared for the port with no delay. I managed to spend an hour with the company's agent and briefed him on the Waybill procedure. After my deck watch with the cargo operations, I went ashore do see what the local shops had to offer. Ceylon was famous as a place to buy semiprecious jewels. It had been raining on and off during the day so I took my new clear vinyl plastic rain coat with me. I went into a large jewelry store on the main street and was met at the door by its Arab proprietor. He invited me to sit at a table with him and ordered one of the clerks to bring some soft drinks. Then he asked me what he could show me. I asked him to show me a variety of stones including some star sapphires. Responding to his orders, one of the clerks brought three trays containing dozens of rings with different stones of various sizes to the table. I picked out three of them and asked how much he wanted for them. He responded with a price that was extremely high. As was expected, I made a very low offer for them. We kept haggling for a few minutes. He would lower the price a little, and I would raise my offer a little. All the while he kept looking at my rain coat. Finally he asked me to let him see it and try it on. The clear plastic rain coat impressed him a great deal and he asked if I would sell it to him. He had never seen anything like it before. I told him that it was very expensive and that he could buy several good quality cloth rain coats for what the plastic rain coat cost. Then I went back to haggling over the price of the rings I had picked out. He wanted that coat desperately. Finally I let him have it for the three rings and two more unmounted star sapphire stones. I believe that was the only time that I got the best of an Arab trader in a haggling exchange. He was delighted with the exchange and so was I. After buying a few more souvenirs I returned to the ship. The next day the ship departed Colombo for our next port of call, Singapore.

SINGAPORE

The S S Flying Cloud steamed across the southern part of the Bay of Bengal, into the Andaman Sea, and through the Strait of Malacca to Singapore. While steaming through the Strait of Malacca we passed an American built Liberty ship on a reciprocal course. Boldly displayed on its smoke stack was the yellow hammer and sickle on a red background of the Soviet Union. They were still using one of our lend lease ships which were never returned nor paid for. Singapore was a remarkable city. It was a very busy city with clean streets and many fine buildings. The population represented almost every race on the face of the earth. The administrators and officials were mostly English or European, the traffic cops were Sikhs, the shop keepers were either Arab, Chinese, Indian, or Malayan, and the Longshoremen were a mixture of all of them. The gangs working cargo on our ship appeared to be mostly Chinese. The company's English agent was very receptive to my explanation of how the Waybill procedure should be applied and he assured me that he would do his best to implement it. Our remaining two passengers got off in Singapore. They were going to have to wait there for about two or three weeks for the next Isbrandtsen ship to arrive. Then they could continue on their around the world cruise. There was some regulation that prevented them from going all the way on our ship.

After a day of cargo operations, When I finished my evening meal, I went ashore and took a taxi to the world famous Raffles Hotel. There were some shops either in or adjacent to the hotel offering a variety of goods, oriental ceramics, jewelry, clothing, fine furniture, and wood carvings. I purchased a pair of beautifully carved head busts made of a tropical red wood in one of the shops and then went into the hotel's dining room. Once seated at a table near the dance floor I ordered a gin and something drink and sat back to enjoy the floor show. A Filipino dance troupe and their musicians came onto the floor and performed the bamboo dance. It was a delightful performance, and after some searching the following day, I managed to buy a recording of the bamboo dance music named Tingaling. Although the ship's stay in Singapore was short, only two days, it was very pleasant in spite of the heat and humidity. Singapore is only about one degree north of the equator, approximately sixty miles.

MANILA

The S S Flying Cloud departed Singapore and steamed for four days across the South China Sea to Manila on the Philippine Island of Luzon. More than seven years had passed since I was last in Manila. The harbor had been cleared of the ships that had been sunk or stranded there during World War II. The city now had many new buildings and was bustling with economic activity. The ship went immediately to a new modern pier and started working cargo as soon as pratique was granted. The company's agent spent a few hours with me while I explained the Waybill procedure and we reminisced about the war years. He informed me that General Cinco and his band of brigands had just been recently been put out of business on one of the southern islands. It was General Cinco's band of guerillas that Ted Loos and I almost ran afoul of south of Tacloban on Leyte in 1945. The agent had been interred in a Japanese prison camp during the war but fared relatively well. He was an American and had lived in the Philippines most of his life. Our stay in manila was short, about two days. I managed to spend one afternoon wandering along the main street and sampling some of the local beer in one of the hotel bars. The street was crowded with a multitude of vehicles, the most interesting of which was a jeep modified into a small type of bus. They were constantly picking up and dropping off one or two passengers. I was surprised at how Manila had changed since 1945. The morning after cargo operations were finished, the ship departed Manila bound for Hong Kong.

HONG KONG

Steaming time between Manila and Hong Kong was a little less than three days. The approach to Hong Kong harbor had to be done with some care. There was a peninsula bordering the southern approach to the harbor that was part of Communist China. The Chinese army had set up some cannons on the end of the peninsula and would open fire on any ship that came within five miles. That was probably the maximum range of those cannons. One of the Isbrandtsen ships, the S S flying Arrow, had been hit by a couple of shells from Communist Chinese cannons a few months before. We gave them about seven miles clearance on our approach. Once into the harbor the ship anchored and several small craft and a couple of barges were soon along side. Since our stay in Hong Kong would be less than twenty four hours, sea watches were maintained. Once pratique was granted there were several vendors, tradesmen, and stevedores all over the ship. Cargo was discharged on to barges and loaded from barges on each side of the ship. Tailors and shoemakers were showing samples of their wares and taking measurements of many of the crewmen promising to have the made to order clothes and shoes back on board before the ship sailed.

The company's Hong Kong agent was a Chinese gentleman who spoke perfect English. He was very friendly and gave me ample time to acquaint him with the Waybill procedure. As soon as I was finished with my shipboard duties, I had one of the tailors measure me for a sports coat and slacks. He offered a variety of materials to choose from. Then I took a water taxi ashore to Hong Kong Island. The British colony of Hong Kong consists of Hong Kong Island and a portion of the mainland named Kawloon. There were hotels, restaurants, and shops offering every type of merchandise one could imagine. After a brief tour of Hong Kong Island I caught one of the ferry boats that ran over to Kawloon. There again there was a multitude of restaurants and shops. Every where I looked there were people selling things, making things, or carrying things. It was the busiest place I had ever seen. Many of the shops offered exquisitely hand crafted furniture, jewelry, and clothing. The population was a mixture of European and more numerous Chinese. There were no beggars on the streets and every one appeared to be relatively well off.

When I returned to the ship, my tailor was there with my sports jacket and slacks basted and ready for a final fit. He accomplished the fitting quickly and left the ship. Seven or eight hours later he was back on board with the finished jacket and slacks just about an hour before sailing time. They were a perfect fit and the cost was a fraction of what tailor made clothes would have cost me back home in New York. The speed with which things were accomplished there was amazing. In less than twenty four hours cargo operations were complete, stores brought aboard, and all the custom made cloths, shoes, and specialty items delivered to the ship. As the anchor was hauled up I was sorry that I could not spend more time in this fabulous place. With the help of a pilot, the ship made its way through the harbor and all the anchored vessels and numerous other water craft to the pilot station. The pilot got off and a course was set for Keelung, Formosa.

KEELUNG

At this time the Chinese civil war was still going on. The Communist Chinese held the main land and many of the off shore islands, and the

Nationalists Chinese held the island of Formosa (now Taiwan) and two small islands, Kemoy and Matsu, close to the main land. As the SS Flying Cloud passed by these two small islands we could see aircraft and hear the faint sounds of explosions off in the distance. When we were about half way across the Formosa strait the ship ran into a heavy rain storm. Suddenly a National Chinese destroyer came out of the rain and mist and ran close alongside with its guns trained on us. Once they established our identity and our destination they turned away and disappeared in the rain. These were dangerous waters and we were steaming through a war zone. Our destination, Keelung, was located on the northern tip of Formosa. When we arrived a pilot came aboard and guided the ship through the crowded harbor to a berth at a pier. As we passed through the harbor we could see about thirty of forty merchant ships of various sizes nested together at an anchorage. They were all ships that had been seized in the waters around China by the Nationalist Chinese Navy because they were carrying cargo to or from the Communist Chinese. Nothing was said about what had become of the crews of these merchant ships.

Keelung was not at all like Hong Kong. The company's agent was a rather brisk Chinese man who listened with some restrained patience as I explained the Waybill procedure to him. It is doubtful that he gave it any more attention than he had to. When I finished my deck watch, the Purser, the Radioman, an Engineer, and I went ashore to have dinner at a nearby restaurant. Once we were seated in the restaurant I noticed that the place was dingy and somewhat untidy. Two waitresses served our table but neither understood English. We managed to get our orders placed in spite of the language problem. However when the food was brought to the table we were disappointed with the quality of the food and annoyed by the slovenly manner of the waitresses. Surprisingly none of us suffered any ill effects from eating the food. I resolved to avoid trying any more restaurants in Keelung. Fortunately the ship finished cargo operations in a day and a half so our stay there was short. The ship departed Keelung in the afternoon and set a course for Nagasaki, Japan.

NAGASAKI

The sea passage between Keelung and Nagasaki took a little less than three days. The ship arrived in the morning and went directly to a berth at a pier. As soon as pratique was granted the hatches were uncovered and cargo operations were started. The company's local agent, a Japanese fellow, listened politely as I explained the Waybill procedure and when I was finished I was not sure how well he understood what I was saying. He was either too proud or too polite to ask any questions. Cargo operations during the day were hectic. The Japanese longshoremen were so fast it was difficult to keep up with them. All five hatches were working and cargo was being transferred on both sides of the ship, on to the pier and on to barges. After dinner when cargo operations were shut down for the night, the Chief Mate suggested that some of us should go ashore for some beer and relaxation. He and I and two of the Engineers left the ship and walked a few blocks to a bar. We went in, found a table, and ordered a round of beer. The bar was run by a woman and a couple of younger girls served the tables. After our beer was served, the woman came over to our table and politely asked us to drink our beer and leave. She said that she did not like to serve Americans nor to have Americans in her bar. Obviously she disliked Americans. Of course Nagasaki was one of the cities that suffered having the atom bomb dropped on it. The Chief Mate then suggested we go to a Japanese bath house and relax in a hot bath. We found a taxi and told the driver what we wanted. He drove us a good distance up the hill from the dock area through winding narrow streets to a hotel. We went inside and when our wishes were made known, the proprietor brought out several young women to take us to the baths and serve our needs. At this point I decided I did not want to spend the night there, so I told my companions that I would see them back at the ship later. When I walked out onto the street it was pitch black. There were no street lights, no taxis, no moon, nothing but darkness. I decided if I walked down hill I would eventually reach the waterfront. It was a long scary walk along dark empty streets until I finally saw the lights of the ship. The S S Flying Cloud was the only ship in the port and the only lights to be seen. Cargo operations resumed the next morning and were completed a day later. With all five hatches secured the ship departed Nagasaki and proceeded on to Kobe.

KOBE

The passage took us around the southern part of Kyushu Island, through the Osumi Strait, past the island of Shikoku, into the Kii Strait, and then into Osaka Bay to the port city of Kobe. Japan is a very hilly and mountainous country. On this passage there was one active volcano quite visible from the ship. There were also lumps of white matter floating on the surface of the water in one area and we were told that this was a form of volcanic pumice that had washed into the sea. When we arrived at the port of Kobe a pilot was taken aboard and the ship went directly to a berth at a pier. All five hatches were opened and gangs of longshoremen came aboard to work the cargo. The ship was expected to be in Kobe for five or more days because there was a lot of cargo to be discharged and a good deal to be loaded. Kobe was a large city with a population of over a million people. The company's agent was an American, a recently retired Navy Captain who was very receptive to the Waybill procedure when I explained it to him. He also told me that he could procure anything I might want from the local military exchange. I asked him to buy a set of good table dishes for me. A few days later he came aboard the ship and had a complete set of Norotaki dinner dishes in a wooden case for me. The cost was a fraction of what they would have cost back home and I thanked him for his kindness.

On the passage to Kobe the engineers reported that one of the ship's generators had burned up and would have to be repaired or replaced. During the first day in Kobe a group of Japanese technicians from the local electric company came aboard and removed the damaged generator. Three days later they returned with the repaired generator. The ship's Engineers were amazed at the quality of the repair. The wiring in the generator had been completely rewound and the repair technicians did not have any design drawings to refer to as they repaired the generator. The ship's Engineers said that the generator was better now than it was when it was originally installed. They were not only surprised at the quality of the repair but also with the speed with which it was accomplished.

I pulled the midnight to eight in the morning watch so I was able to go into town while the shops were open. The second day in Kobe I went ashore in the afternoon and wandered around the city. I found a store that sold optical goods and a pair of Ziess 7X50 binoculars were displayed in the window along with other binoculars. I went in and asked the clerk to let me examine the Ziess binoculars and try them out. They were, as I expected, excellent. The price was about $200. When I handed them back to the clerk, he handed me a pair of Japanese 7X50 binoculars and asked me to try them as well. Much to my surprise the Japanese binoculars were better than the Ziess binoculars, and they had a price of about $30. I bought the Japanese binoculars. Then I remembered that I had brought the damaged German binoculars I had acquired in La Spezia with me on this voyage. I asked the clerk if they could repair binoculars and he said that they had a repair shop in the rear of the store. The next day I returned to the store with the German binoculars and left them there to be repaired. They were repaired and ready for me two days later. The Japanese technician had returned the German Kreigs Marine binoculars to like new condition. Now I owned two pair of very good binoculars. The amount of money I was charged for the excellent repair work was less than $10.

On my walk back to the ship I saw a bar with a sign over the door showing a white horse and on the window were the words "White Horse Lounge." Since it was hot and I was thirsty, I went in to relax over a beer. There were three other patrons seated at a table and they greeted me with a friendly hello as I entered. They were officers off one of the British ships in the port. I took a seat near them and ordered a beer. We exchanged some small talk and they informed me that this was their favorite watering hole. The proprietor and owner, an older Japanese lady who spoke flawless English, came over and introduced herself as Noriko Kuzi. She was very gracious and spent some time exchanging information with me. She said that officers from British merchant ships often patronized her place, but that American officers rarely ever did. When I asked her how she learned to speak English so well, she told me that her father had been a professor at Tokyo University and that she had studied language and music there. In fact she said that she had studied piano under Walter Guiseking, a famous German pianist. As I was leaving the White Horse Bar I assured her that I would return.

The next evening after dinner on the ship, the Purser, the Second Engineer, and I went to the White Horse Bar and had a pleasant evening drinking beer and chatting with Noriko and the two girls who waited the tables. We asked Noriko if there was a restaurant she would recommend because we wanted to try some authentic Japanese cuisine. She said that she could arrange a formal banquet type dinner at a nearby hotel if that was what we wanted. All she would have to know is how many there would be for dinner and what time of the evening they would prefer to eat. She also said that we should allow about three hours for the dinner. We thought this would be great and told her that we would let her know the next day how many to expect for such a dinner the following evening. That would probably be our last night in Kobe and a fitting way to end the visit. The next evening the three of us returned to the White Horse Lounge and asked Noriko to arrange the dinner for six of us at about seven o'clock the next evening. She asked us to meet at her place and she would have a couple of taxis ready to take us to the hotel. A little after six o'clock the following evening the Purser, Radioman, two Engineers, the Chief Mate, and I went into the White Horse Lounge. While we were having a round of drinks, Noriko made a phone call. A short time later two taxis pulled up in front of the lounge and the six of us with Noriko got into them. The taxis drove us a short distance and deposited us in front of a rather dingy looking building. With Noriko leading us we entered the building and were surprised by what we saw. The interior of the place was beautiful. We took off our shoes and left them in the lobby and a servant girl provided us with slippers. Then we entered the banquet room. It was a large well lighted rectangular room with some statues in ancient Japanese armor in two of the corners. A long low table was arranged parallel to a glass wall which looked out on a formal garden. There was a pool close to the glass wall with large multi colored carp swimming about various types of water plants. As darkness fell strategically placed lights made the garden and the pool take on a beauty impossible to describe.

The proprietor invited us to seat ourselves on cushions placed on the floor along the length of the table. As soon as we were all seated, a kimono clad serving girl knelt beside and a little behind each of us. Servants brought out a variety of hors d'oeuvres on platters and jugs of warm sake wine which the serving girls transferred to our individual plates and cups according to our wishes. Three geisha girls in traditional dress and carrying stringed instruments seated themselves at one end of the room. Throughout the dinner they played and sang a variety of Japanese songs which were remarkably pleasing to the ear. Platters of thinly sliced raw beef were brought to the table for our approval and then taken to a nearby stove and cooked. The cooked beef was then brought back to the table and the serving girls quickly added portions to a bowl of whipped raw egg for each of us. They also placed a variety of vegetables and rice on our individual plates. There were additional courses of fish and fowl prepared to perfection. Following this there was some type of sweet cakes and nuts served to complete the dinner. Green tea was also served throughout the meal. We spent a full three hours eating and drinking with each of us being pampered by our own serving girl. All agreed that it was an outstanding evening. We gave Noriko money enough to cover the cost of the dinner and a substantial gratuity. Since it was late we took the taxis back to the ship and said farewell and many thanks to Noriko. The ship departed Kobe the following morning.

SHIMIZU

The next port was Shimizu where we arrived after about two days steaming. Shimizu was a small city of less than a quarter million people. Our stay there was short, about a day and a half. The same company agent was on hand to take care of the ship's business. Since there seemed to be little to do or see in Shimizu, I did not go ashore there. The spectacular cone shape of Mount Fuji was visible on the distant horizon. It was easy to see why the Japanese considered Mount Fuji a symbol of their nation. As soon as the cargo operations were completed, the hatches were covered and the ship departed for Yokohama.

YOKOHAMA

The run to Yokohama was short, only about a day. The ship went directly to a dock upon arrival, and again the company's agent was on hand. He could travel from port to port on the Japanese rail system much faster than the ship could by water. Yokohama had changed a great deal since I was last there in January 1946. All the wartime damage had been covered over by new modern buildings. Business was booming everywhere. Whenever I had any free time I went ashore and did a good deal of window shopping. There were large stores and small shops all selling a fantastic variety of goods at bargain prices. The rate of exchange between the Dollar and the Yen was about four hundred Yen to the Dollar. Arts and crafts objects, textiles, toys, instruments, jewelry, and a host of other things were in abundant supply. On every trip ashore I found something new and different which I could not resist buying. Fortunately cargo operations were completed in less than four days, and my bargain shopping was curtailed. Twelve passengers boarded the ship on its last day in Yokohama. They were a mixture of government civilians and business people returning to the States. The ship had a full load and was down to her marks when the hatches were covered and the cargo gear stowed for an ocean passage.

SAN FRANCISCO

The distance between Yokohama and San Francisco was somewhat more than forty five hundred miles. The passage took thirteen days and some hours, and generally the weather was good all the way across the Pacific Ocean. The ship picked up a pilot at the Farallon pilot station and proceeded into the port. San Francisco was a beautiful sight with the sun shining on the distant buildings as the ship approached the Golden Gate Bridge. It is hard to describe the feeling of pleasure that came over me as the City By the Bay came into view. Although I was still a long way from home, I was back in the United States. Port officials, Agriculture, Customs, and Immigration cleared the ship a short time after we docked. Our passengers disembarked and once they had their baggage they disappeared into the city. I went ashore and telephoned Anita and was brought up to date on everything at home. Cargo operations were started and a portion of our cargo was discharged in San Francisco. Night Mates and Night Engineers relieved the ship's officers from four o'clock in the afternoon till eight o'clock the next morning, so most of us took our evening meals in some of the fine restaurants in town. I was surprised to learn that the International Settlement where I spent so many pleasant evenings no longer existed. All the clubs and restaurants had moved to another part of the city referred to as the Tender Loin district. However, the Domino Club and Paoley's restaurant were still in business. We only had three nights in San Francisco, and then the ship departed and steamed down the California coast to Long Beach.

LONG BEACH

Long Beach is the port for the city of Los Angeles and covers a large area. The ship went directly to a berth at a pier and cargo operations were begun a short time after docking. Night Mates and Night Engineers again relieved the ship's officers at four o'clock in the afternoon and cargo operations also stopped until eight o'clock in the morning. This gave me the evenings free to explore Long Beach and Los Angeles. This area was entirely different from San Francisco. It was somewhat more informal and casual dress seemed to be the accepted attire for the evening. The land around Long Beach was relatively flat and there were numerous machines that resembled giant crickets located on lots scattered about. These were actually pumps extracting oil from the Los Angeles basin. There were some hilly areas around Los Angeles and during my wandering around I took a ride on an inclined street car named "Angels Flight" that climbed a rather steep hill I just rode this strange street car up and down for the novelty of it. On my second evening ashore I toured an amusement area known as the "Pike" that had a "Coney Island" atmosphere. It was crowded and much too honky-tonk for my tastes. Unlike San Francisco, much of the local population appeared to be of Mexican origin and there were many restaurants that featured Mexican fare. After three days of cargo operations, the hatches were covered and the ship departed Long Beach for Balboa and the Panama Canal.

THE PANAMA CANAL

The run south along the California and Mexican coasts to Panama was uneventful except for the passage across the Gulf of Tehuantepec. There we encountered strong easterly winds and relatively rough seas. Less than a day was lost in Balboa waiting to start the transit of the Panama Canal. This was my second passage through the canal, only this time I was going from the Pacific side to the Caribbean side. It was still a spectacular experience. The locks, the huge lake, the cut through a mountain, and the pristine manicured lawns and trees on each side were a pleasure to behold. Once through the canal a harbor pilot replaced the canal pilot. Then outside Cristobal harbor we dropped the harbor pilot and set a course for New York via Mona Pass. The weather was good and six days later the S S Flying Cloud steamed into the New York pilot station and then to pier 29 in Brooklyn. It was 8 May 1953 and the ship had traveled approximately 24,500 nautical miles and had visited 26 ports in a period of four months. I had circumnavigated the earth and at last I was home again.

HOME AGAIN

Anita was on the pier when the ship docked. As soon as sea watches were broken and Customs and Immigration cleared the ship I hastened ashore to take her in my arms. We only had about fifteen minutes. I had to leave her waiting on the pier and go back on board while the ship's hatches were opened and cargo discharge operations were begun. Company rules would not allow me to bring her aboard the ship so she had to wait for about three hours until I got off watch. The rough and tough longshoremen were very gentlemanly. One of them found a chair for Anita to sit on close to the Customs shack. The foreman working the gang close to where she was sitting ordered his men to refrain from using fowl language because there was a lady present. The longshoremen were very careful not to say anything offensive where she might hear it. From time to time the foreman would ask her if she wanted anything to eat or drink. If she did he would have had one of his men fetch it. Chivalry was not dead on the Brooklyn waterfront. It was late afternoon by the time I finished checking out the special cargo and finished my watch. I went to my cabin, changed my clothes, gathered the items purchased during the voyage, and headed for the gangway. With my arms loaded I joined Anita on the pier and we went to the car. An hour and a half later we were home in Islip. I was surprised and pleased to see how much the baby had grown. Since his name was Arthur Randolph Murray III, we decided to call him Randy to avoid any confusion.

The next day I was back aboard the S S Flying Cloud a little before 0800. There was a message there for me to meet with Walter Isbrandtsen at 26 Broadway as soon as possible. I was in his office by 0930. After initial greetings Walter got right down to business. He had read the reports I had sent in on the Waybill procedure, and with one exception, he was pleased with what I had accomplished. Walter said that the agent in Alexandria, Egypt claimed that he had not been given any information on the Waybill procedure. It was obvious to me that the retired Egyptian Admiral, the agent's clerk, either did not understand what I told him, or failed to pass on what he had been told to the agent. There was also the possibility that the agent was trying to avoid the extra paper work the Waybill procedure entailed by claiming that no one had given him any information on it. I gave Walter a full account of my efforts with the agent's clerk and suggested that it might require some added pressure to get the agent's cooperation. Considering that it cost the Isbrandtsen line practically nothing to get all of their port agents in the around the world service indoctrinated in the Waybill procedure, Walter had little reason to complain. After a little more small talk and a cup of coffee with Walter I returned to Pier 29 and resumed my shipboard duties.

I got another night and a Saturday and Sunday at home in Islip. The following Monday the S S Flying Cloud departed New York for a coastwise run down to Norfolk. Since there was no relief Mate available, I had to make the coastwise trip. The ship was scheduled to be in Norfolk for at least three days. Anita decided to fly down to Norfolk so we could spend a couple more nights together. She made arrangements for her mother and my mother to look after Randy while she was gone. The afternoon of the first day in Norfolk I met Anita at the Norfolk airport and was surprised to see that she was ashen when she got off the plane. She said that the plane was constantly buffeted by storms all the way from New York and that she and many of the other passengers were terrified until the plane touched down in Norfolk. She said that she would not take a plane back to New York. I had reserved a room at the Southern Hotel in Norfolk and we went there directly from the airport. After a couple of cocktails and dinner, Anita felt much better. We had two pleasant nights together and then on the morning of the day the ship was due to sail, I put Anita on a Greyhound bus to take her back to New York.

From Norfolk the ship went to Charleston, South Carolina and spent two days there loading cargo. Then the ship returned to New York and Pier 29. Three more days were spent loading cargo and I was able to get home every night. Time just seemed to rush by. Visits with my mother and Anita's family were pleasant but much too short. Anita informed me that she was not happy with my shipping out for such long periods and that she wanted me to find shorter voyages or some other type of employment. Now that we had a house, a mortgage, and a baby and all the obligations that go along with that, I could not afford to quit shipping out. However it was obvious that something would have to be done. After the cargo was topped off, and twelve passengers settled in, the S S Flying Cloud departed New York for another voyage around the world, and once again I was the Second Mate. However, for this trip Anita had prepared a "care Package," a carton containing a variety of canned goods to supplement my shipboard diet, which I was glad to take with me.

THE SECOND VOYAGE AROUND THE WORLD

My second voyage around the world on the S S Flying Cloud was much like the first. This time however there were three additional ports of call. Our first port after leaving New York was the Azores. The ship anchored off the largest of the islands and discharged cargo into barges brought alongside by tug boats. The stop over was less than twenty four hours so sea watches were maintained. From the Azores the ship went to Lisbon. There cargo was discharged as well as loaded and six of our passengers got off. The ship then went into the Mediterranean Sea to Algiers. From there the ship went to Genoa for a lay over of three days to work cargo, and four more of our passengers disembarked. The next port of call was Naples where I had an opportunity to visit Sorento and the ruins at Pompeii. Sorento had a cathedral with pillars studded with semi precious stones and spectacular art work. Walking around the ruins of Pompeii was like stepping back two thousand years in time. One evening while in Naples I tried to get a ticket to see a performance at the opera house. No tickets were available at any price. The Italians are devoted to their opera and the opera house was sold out for that evening's performance. The ship sailed before I could find time to visit the Isle of Capri. There was so much to see and so little time. The next ports of call were Alexandria, Beirut, Port Said, then through the Suez Canal and on to Jidda, Saudi Arabia.

The ship had taken on a large load of oranges in wood crates destined for Jidda. Again the ship anchored in Jidda harbor and barges were brought alongside. The same young obnoxious arrogant Arab stevedore boss came aboard with the Arab longshoremen. The hatches were opened and the crates of oranges were off loaded from the tween deck spaces to the barges. The longshoremen stacked the crates of oranges in vertical columns from the decks of the barges to the height of the ship's main deck. This was a height of about thirty or thirty five feet. I called the young Arab stevedore boss aside and told him that he should have the rectangular crates cross tied to prevent the outer tiers from falling off the barges. In a rather haughty voice he told me that he knew what he was doing and did not need any advice from me. When the tug boat pulled the first barge loaded with the oranges away from the side of the ship the barge began to rock just enough for the outboard tiers of crates to fall into the water. Most of these crates broke upon impact releasing the oranges. This scenario continued as each barge pulled away. It was a colossal, foolish, and unnecessary waste. As the ebb tide current flowed out of the harbor in the evening the surface of the water was covered with thousands of oranges.

From Jidda the ship went on to Port Sudan, Djibouti, Karachi, and Bombay. A large part of the cargo taken aboard in Bombay was bales of cotton for Japan. Our two remaining passengers, an elderly missionary couple, got off here. After a stay of four days the ship departed Bombay at night. I came on watch at midnight and a short time later the ship was scheduled to change its heading when it reached a predetermined position to follow a new course. The course change was about twenty degrees to port. The weather was good and there was a steady twenty knot wind broad on the starboard bow. There was also a pattern of wind driven waves running about ten feet in height. The ship was steady rolling gently about five degrees to port and starboard. As I turned the ship on its new heading it put the wind and waves on the starboard beam. Once the ship steadied up on the new heading I switched the steering to the "Iron Mike" (automatic steering) and walked out on to the starboard wing of the bridge. The ship took a sudden roll of about ten degrees to port and then a roll of fifteen degrees to starboard. The next roll to port was twenty degrees followed by a roll of twenty five degrees to starboard. Remembering one of my lessons in naval architecture class I realized what was happening and rushed into the wheel house and switched the "Iron Mike" off just as the ship took a roll of thirty degrees to port. As the ship took a thirty five degree roll to starboard, I spun the wheel to bring the ship around to the right and the severe rolling stopped. Once steady on a new heading, the ship resumed rolling about five degrees to port and starboard. A minute later the Captain came rushing into the wheel house and wanted to know what had caused the sudden heavy rolling. I explained that we had just experienced harmonic motion. When the ship is holding a steady course and the period and angle of the waves coincide with the natural period of roll of the ship, each successive wave will cause the ship to take a steeper roll. If the course were not changed, the ship would roll over. He seemed skeptical but there was no other explanation for the heavy rolling in such relatively moderate seas. This phenomena is probably the reason that some perfectly sound ships disappear in good weather on calm seas without a trace.

The next port of call after Bombay was Colombo followed by Singapore. Again I was able to spend a pleasant evening at Raffles Hotel. Six passengers for San Francisco came aboard including two young women from the U S Information Service. The ship departed Singapore and set a course for Iloilo on the island of Panay in the Philippines. The course took the ship through the Natuna Islands, across the South China Sea, then through the Balebac Strait and into the Sulu Sea. The British Admiralty chart of the Sulu Sea used for this passage had a survey date in the late 1800's. There was a caution note printed on the chart in the center of the Sulu Sea. It read, "Navigate with extreme caution. Most of the Sulu Sea has not been surveyed." It was the middle of the monsoon season and the ship encountered one very heavy rain squall after another. Visibility in the heavy rain was so poor the bow of the ship could not be seen from the bridge. At these times the Captain would be on the bridge, the engine telegraph would be on "Stand By," fog signals would be sounded on the ship's horn, and one of the Mates or I would be monitoring the Radar screen. During one of these squalls a solid line crossing our course several miles ahead appeared on the Radar screen. It appeared that the ship was heading for the shore of an island where according to the chart there should be no island. The engine was put on "Slow Ahead" and the Fathometer was monitored for depth of water. It indicated there was no bottom at a thousand fathoms. As the ship got very close to the solid line on the Radar screen, the engine was put on "Dead Slow Ahead." The Fathometer was still showing no bottom. When the Radar indicated that the ship was crossing the line we looked over the side through the deluge of rain. What we saw was our ship passing through a line of dirty bubbles and oil sludge. Apparently a tanker had crossed our course line while cleaning its tanks and left the residue in its wake. It was this oily residue that gave such a strong echo on our Radar screen, and caused the Captain and the Mates to experience some long moments of anxiety.

ILOILO

Iloilo is a port on the island of Panay. It had a single pier, a couple of large sheds, and little else. The town was some distance from the pier and there was little incentive for anyone to venture that far from the ship to visit the town. Filipino longshoremen loaded about five hundred tons of bagged raw sugar on the ship. There was obviously some political unrest in the area because the shipper's representatives who visited the ship carried pistols on their belts. It seemed that there were Communist rebels roaming around the area causing some mischief. The loading was accomplished in a couple of days without any incidents and the ship departed for Manila.

MANILA, HONG KONG, KEELUNG, & KOBÉ

Once the ship was secured at a dock most of the seamen off watch went ashore to enjoy the pleasures of the city. Manila was a much more inviting place for shore leave. There were many bars, movie houses, hotels, and plenty of available women. The Third Mate was a big muscular six foot plus Scandinavian fellow who felt he would be invincible going into some of the bars off the main street. Although the majority of the Filipino men hanging around those bars were small and thin, two of them jumped him when he came out of one of the bars. While one of them confronted him from the front, the other hit him with a club from behind and knocked him cold. When he was lying on the ground they relieved him of his wrist watch and money. Luckily his injuries were not too severe and he was able to return to the ship for first aid and comfort. Manila could be a fun town, but it was also a dangerous town. Seamen who were foolish enough to wander into the back streets were fair game for robbers and muggers.

After four days of cargo operations the hatches were secured and the cargo gear stowed away and the SS Flying Cloud departed Manila. A course was set across the South China Sea for Hong Kong. There was dense fog as the ship approached Hong Kong harbor and the Captain decided to anchor and wait for the fog to lift. The ship anchored well off the Chinese coast and a good distance from Hong Kong. According to the International Rules, the anchor bell was rung every minute. The Radar screen was set on the twelve mile range and showed several targets at various distances from the ship. After two or three hours had passed, there were several targets closing in on the ship. They soon formed a perfect ring around the ship, and that ring kept getting smaller and closer to the ship. Since we were just off the coast of Communist China, and what the targets represented was unknown, the Captain decided to weigh anchor and proceed on to Hong Kong in spite of the dense fog. Once the anchor was up and the ship started to sound the fog signal for a vessel underway on the ship's horn, the targets on the Radar screen began to scatter. Fortunately the fog began to lift as the ship approached the pilot station. Within an hour the ship was anchored safe and sound in busy Hong Kong harbor.

Sea watches were not broken because the scheduled stay in Hong Kong was less than twenty four hours. As soon as I got off watch I went ashore once again in this fascinating city. The variety, quality, and relatively low cost of everything was mind boggling. One merchant offered me a Chinese rug for about three hundred dollars that would normally sell for a couple of thousand dollars back in the United States. Unfortunately I could not bring it back with me because it was made in Communist China and there was a strict embargo on any products made in the Peoples Republic of China. However there was an abundance of products made in the Crown Colony to more than satisfy my desires. Included in my purchases were gold and jade jewelry, native costume dolls, toys, wood and ivory sculptures, silk brocade robes and a fine suitcase to carry these items. Time ashore in Hong Kong was much too short. A few hours after I returned to the ship the cargo operations were completed. The hatches were covered and secured for sea and the ship departed for Keelung, Formosa. This time the ship had good weather all the way from Hong Kong to Keelung. There was really nothing of interest to attract me to go ashore in Keelung. Our stay there was about a day and a half, and then we departed for Japan.

Kobe was the next port of call. Before arriving in Kobe the ship's officers asked me to arrange another banquet for them like the one we had on our last visit to Kobe. The two young women passengers overheard our conversations about the banquet and boldly asked to be included. The first evening I was free I went to the White Horse Lounge and was greeted warmly by the owner Noriko and her serving girls. I had brought a gift of a couple of records of classical piano music for Noriko and she was very pleased with them. I asked Noriko if she could arrange another banquet like last time, only this time I asked her to include the two young women. She said that she would be pleased to do so and would set it up for the following evening. The following evening five of the ship's officers, the two young women, and I went to the White Horse Lounge and from there with Noriko took taxi cabs to the hotel. The hotel proprietor and his staff provided an outstanding banquet just like the last time. However the young women complained frequently about the food, the way it was served, the music, and having to sit on the floor. The serving girls were not accustomed to serving women and seemed somewhat embarrassed and awkward in having to do so. The attitude and bad manners displayed by the young women embarrassed me and some of the other officers. It had been a mistake to include them, and as we were leaving the hotel I apologized to Noriko for having brought them along. She smiled and said that such banquets were generally the province of men, and only occasionally would include women of high standing. I managed to get in some souvenir shopping and one more evening at the White Horse Lounge before the ship sailed.

NAGOYA, SHIMIZU, YOKOHAMA

Our next port was Nagoya. The U. S. Navy had a large presence there both in ships and men. The lay over there was about forty eight hours and cargo operations went on around the clock. As a result I was not able to find time to go ashore. The next port was Shimizu. As it was on the last voyage the ship spent only two days there. During a break in cargo operations I took a brief walk ashore. Although there were no shops or markets of any interest near the waterfront, I felt that a stroll through any Japanese town was always interesting. The people were extremely industrious and polite. The streets were clean and the buildings were in good repair. There was one thing about Japan that I noticed on my previous trips there and again this time. There always seemed to be the faint aroma of burnt pine wood in the atmosphere. This may have been caused by the type of charcoal often used for cooking. The odor was not unpleasant, it was just something peculiar to Japan. From Shimizu the ship went on to Yokohama.

In Yokohama cargo operations took four days and I was able to get ashore to visit the shops and make a few more purchases. The rate of exchange was about four hundred Yen to the Dollar and everything seemed to be very inexpensive. Shopping for things in Japan was a pleasure. The Japanese merchants asked a fair price and there was no haggling. It was indeed a far cry from shopping for anything in the Muslim countries. On our last day in Yokohama six more passengers, two Oriental couples and one American couple, came aboard for the Passage to San Francisco. With a full load of cargo and twelve passengers, the S S Flying Cloud departed Yokohama for San Francisco.

BACK IN THE UNITED STATES

The passage to San Francisco was uneventful. My four to eight watch schedule limited occasional encounters and socializing with the passengers which was fine with me. The passengers and some of the cargo were discharged in San Francisco and three days later the ship sailed down the California coast to Long Beach. After another three days the ship departed Long Beach and continued south along the coasts of California and Mexico to Panama and Balboa. Again the only heavy seas encountered where as the ship was crossing the Gulf of Tehuantepec. It seems that the Gulf of Tehuantepec is always rough because the mountains in Mexico funnel and increase the force of the prevailing winds across that body of water. After transiting the Panama Canal the ship proceeded directly to New York. On 3 October 1953 I left the S S Flying Cloud and took a long overdue vacation. I had spent the last ten months as Second Mate on that ship.

When I got home my first born, Randy, was not quite at the toddler stage but he was able to crawl about quickly. All three grandparents were delighted with him and were always available to baby sit. This gave Anita and me a chance to get around and visit many of our friends. Walter Isbrandtsen requested that I visit him at 26 Broadway and I spent a full day reviewing the progress being made with the waybill system. Generally the system was successful in reducing the company's liability for damaged cargo in most ports of call. However there were a few ports like Bombay, India where the port authority took custody of the cargo but would not accept responsibility for any damage that might occur while the cargo was in their custody. Naturally this time spent in the home office was without compensation. It was expected of a loyal dedicated employee. The ten days between assignments went by much too quickly. On 15 October 1953 I signed on the S S Flying Trader as Second Mate.

THE S S FLYING TRADER

The S S Flying Trader was a Victory ship built during the War and was not configured to carry passengers. The accommodations for officers and crew were somewhat better than those of the wartime Liberty ships, and with a steam turbine engine the S S Flying Trader could cruise at fourteen knots. Captain Hardy, the ship's Master, was a man in his forties and an American with a pleasant personality. The Chief Mate was a short stocky fellow in his fifties and possessed a gruff unfriendly personality. He was a naturalized citizen, a German immigrant of the Jewish persuasion. I often thought that he would have some interesting stories to tell, but he was far too introverted. He had a strong guttural accent, a sour attitude, and a rather short temper. The Third Mate, Ted Tooker, was a fellow my own age with an easy going personality. We hit it right off on the trip down the coast loading cargo. The Chief Engineer was an older fellow and the three Assistant Engineers were all young men in their early thirties or late twenties. The coastwise voyage lasted ten days and on 27 October the S S Flying Trader departed New York for the Azores Islands. I was on my third voyage around the world.

THE THIRD VOYAGE AROUND THE WORLD

From the Azores the ship sailed on to Lisbon, Portugal then into the Mediterranean Sea to Genoa and Livorno in Italy. Then the ship went on to the North African ports of Tripoli, Libya, and Alexandria, Egypt. The next port was Beirut, Lebanon, the Paris of the East. With its mixed population of Christians and Muslims, fine hotels, restaurants, and night clubs Beirut was a pleasant place to visit. One evening Ted and I went into a large dimly lit French style night club to have a drink or two and see the floor show. There was an orchestra playing popular dance music and the floor show involved three or four exotic belly dancers who put on an excellent performance. When the floor show ended a very attractive raven haired young woman came to our table and asked if she could join us. She was a courtesan and came from Naples, Italy. Her English was very good and Ted asked her what she would like to drink. Without any hesitation she replied that she would like some Champaign. Ted ordered a bottle

S S Flying Trader
Victory Type Cargo Ship, Isbrandtsen Line

and after the three of us had consumed a glass I reminded Ted that I had to return to the ship because I had the midnight to eight watch. He decided to stay at the club so I covered my share of the tab and left. Ted returned to the ship about two in the morning. He told me that after two more bottles of Champaign he had barely enough money left for a taxi back to the ship. The young woman quickly lost any interest in Ted as soon as his money ran low and she went off to another table. Ted said that in spite of the high cost, he enjoyed the evening in the night club since it was the last civilized place we would see for some time.

After departing Beirut the S S Flying Trader proceeded to Port Said where we had a day long wait for the East bound convoy to form up. We were one of the last ships in an eight ship convoy. With the canal light box installed over the bow, a long boat rigged under a boom on the fore deck and another rigged on the aft deck with their Arab crews standing by the ship was ready for the transit. Our canal pilot came aboard just after sunrise and the convoy started through the Suez canal a short time later. By mid afternoon we were about half way through the canal. It was very hot with a strong wind blowing off the Sinai desert across the canal. The French canal pilot passed the word that the East bound convoy would have to tie up to the Sinai bank of the canal to allow the West bound convoy to pass. The sandy bank sloped up about two hundred feet from the water's edge to the top where the bollards spaced about two hundred feet apart were located. The Chief Mate on the fore deck with his crew and I on the aft deck with my crew got the two long boats launched with their Arab line men in them. Our crews then got the mooring hawsers ready to be lowered to long boats. Preparations for mooring to the canal bank went smoothly up to this point.

A VERY CLOSE CALL

Under my supervision my crew passed the eye end of one of our heavy hawsers through a stern chock and lowered it down to the waiting long boat. Then the crew kept feeding the hawser out as the Arabs in the long boat rowed to the edge of the bank. When the boat reached the bank two of the Arab line men took hold of the eye of the hawser and hauled it up the bank. When they reached the bollard at the top they spread the eye above it and let go. The eye slipped off the top of the bollard and slid back down the bank and into the water. Meanwhile the forward hawser was made fast to a bollard and the Chief Mate's crew were taking a strain on it to pull the bow over to the bank while the strong wind off the Sinai desert was pushing the stern of the ship away from the bank. I phoned the bridge that I had a line in the water so they would not use the propeller to move the stern toward the bank. There was only a very slow turning capstan on the stern for hauling on lines, so I ordered the crew to haul the hawser in by hand. The Arabs in the long boat rowed quickly under the stern to take the eye of the hawser again. By this time the ship was at a forty five degree angle to the canal bank and still swinging out. I could see the canal pilot on the port wing of the bridge waving his arms frantically and pointing up the canal at the approaching West bound convoy. They were less than a mile and a half distant with a huge tanker as lead ship. This convoy had the fair tidal current and could not stop.

At the rate at which the stern was swinging away from the bank, I could see that the whole length of the hawser would run out of the chock before the Arabs would have the eye back up to the bollard. I had my crew secure the end of the hawser to the eye of another hawser. This they did just in time and the second hawser secured to the first began running out through the chock. It took what seemed like an eternity of time for the Arabs to finally get the eye of the hawser up the bank and over the bollard. By this time half the length of the second hawser was out and the ship was completely across the canal blocking the channel. My crew put a few turns of the hawser on the capstan and started to pull the hawser in. The capstan had only one speed which at that moment seemed to be about one revolution per hour. Actually the capstan made about ten revolutions per minute and pulled in about six feet of the hawser with each revolution. There was about six hundred feet of hawser leading from the stern of the ship to the bollard on the canal bank. In complete frustration and exasperation, the pilot threw his cap on the port bridge wing deck and shouted some expletives in French at everyone on the aft deck.

As a strain was taken on the hawser the tanker leading the West bound convoy was only a couple of ship lengths away. I was awed by the speed of its approach. There were another eight or ten ships behind it. A collision seemed inevitable. The tanker was carrying a full load, possibly gasoline. All I could imagine was the two ships coming together with the screech of steel being rendered followed by a conflagration of fire and explosions as the gasoline poured from the ruptured tanks of the other vessel. What would the other West bound ships do? Would they crash into the sterns of the ships ahead of them, or would their pilots run them aground on the opposite bank to avoid collision? The Suez Canal could be rendered use-less for weeks and possibly months while the wreckage was cleared away. If I survived, what would I say at the inevitable court of inquiry? In all prob-ability I would be the scapegoat since I was the officer in charge at the stern and responsible for the actions of the crew. I had thoughts of the arm chair admirals and Monday morning quarterbacks telling the world of all the actions I had failed to take to prevent the catastrophe. Though trou-bling, these thoughts did not take my attention away from the task at hand, and that was to pull the stern of the ship toward the canal bank as quickly as possible.

The capstan was able to overcome the force of the wind, and the haw-ser became taught as the capstan slowly pulled it in. The stern began swing-ing back towards the bank as the tanker was little more than a ship's length away. Some men on the tanker's forecastle were racing down the ladders and running aft. The tanker's Mate and a couple of his crew held their positions while the pilot guided the tanker as close to the opposite bank as he dared. As the bow of the tanker was even with the stern quarter of my ship we were at an angle of about forty degrees to the canal bank. There was just enough space for the tanker to slip by with four or five feet of clearance. The tanker's Mate leaned over the forecastle bulwark and smil-ing at me said, "That was mighty close, mister."

I replied, "Do you really think so?" By the time the second ship in the West bound convoy was abreast, the S S Flying Trader was snug against the bank. A major catastrophe had been narrowly avoided, and I am sure the experience took a year or two off my life.

The S S Flying Trader resumed its passage through the canal to Suez where the pilot and the Arab canal men were disembarked with all of their equipment. From Suez the ship sailed down the Red Sea to Jidda in Saudi Arabia, then across the Red Sea to Port Sudan. From there the voyage continued on to Djibouti then across the Arabian Gulf to Karachi, Paki-stan and on to Bombay, India and Colombo, Ceylon. Without passengers life aboard ship was somewhat less formal. Ted, the Third Mate, and I had purchased a couple of cases of wine in Lisbon. We developed a habit of having a glass of wine in one or the other of our cabins before dinner. Quite often the Radio Operator and the Chief Steward would join us. Many sea stories and accounts of life's experiences were exchanged during these before dinner sessions.

The Radio Operator was a peculiar fellow. He came from a family of means and was a flabby, overweight, bachelor in his forties. Often times he was rather sad to the point of being morose. He felt that he was a failure in life, and compared his position as a radio operator to that of his brother who was a West Point graduate and a high ranking Army officer. One evening while he, Ted, the Chief Steward, and I were having the usual glass of wine, he sat on the settee in my cabin and had an extremely sad look on his face. After a few sips of wine, tears began seeping down his cheeks. I asked him what was troubling him. Heaving a great sigh he said that he felt he was a complete failure, that he was accomplishing nothing with his life. Looking down at his shoes he said, "I feel so miserable that one of these days I am going to jump over the side." Putting a hand on his shoulder, Ted quietly said, "If you do, please do not do it on my watch." I couldn't help myself. I burst out laughing. All four of us were soon laughing uncontrollably. The Chief Steward said, "That is the most you can expect for shipboard sympathy" as we continued laughing. We never knew for sure what ever it was that brought on his bouts of depression, but the Radio Operator always left our drinking sessions in a much better frame of mind. He did not jump overboard.

The next ports of call were Singapore, Iloilo, Manila, and Hong Kong. In Hong Kong, after the evening meal was over, Ted, the Radio Operator, the Second Engineer, and I took a water taxi ashore to take in the night life. We had rain coats with us because it was threatening to rain that evening. Along one of the main streets we came across Hennycies Club. This was a large night club located on the second floor of a large building. There was a very wide stairway leading up to a foyer where there was a cloak room with an attractive girl and a large formal desk with an older Chinese lady sitting behind it. We deposited our rain coats with the cloak room girl and then headed for the entrance to the dance hall. The older Chinese lady informed us that there was a cover charge and that she would take us to a table and then bring some hostesses to keep us company. The Engineer was rather unpleasant with her as he gave her the cover charge. As he walked away I apologized to her for his rudeness and told her that he had been at sea too long. She gave me a smile in appreciation and led the four of us to a table on the edge of a large dance floor. An orchestra was playing popular American music and the club was quite crowded.

The Chinese lady left us for a short time and returned to our table with three very attractive Chinese girls wearing expensive cocktail dresses. These girls were introduced to my three companions and they all spoke perfect English. The older Chinese lady then placed her face close to my ear and said, "I have a very special girl for you. She has just come to Hong Kong from the interior and does not speak English very well, but I am sure you will like her." A few minutes later she came to the table with the most stunningly beautiful Chinese woman I have ever seen. She introduced her to me as Sin Som Wu and then departed. Miss Wu was probably in her early twenties although it is difficult to tell the age of Chinese. She was wearing a beautiful cocktail dress that revealed a breath taking figure. A waiter came to the table to take our orders. The other girls had to act as interpreters for Miss Wu as we ordered drinks and snacks and made conversation. After a couple of delightful hours, the Second Engineer and I had to make our apologies and depart. Both of us had to go on watch at midnight, and it was probably a good thing too.

Ted returned to the ship around 0700 and told me he had the most wonderful time of his life. He said that after midnight the girl he had been with took him home to her apartment. She drove him there in her sports car and her apartment was in a very up scale part of Hong Kong Island. She told him that she had left main land China with her family's wealth before the Chinese communists sealed off the border. Her husband did not make it out and was probably dead. She was independently wealthy and only acted as a hostess at the club for fun and the opportunity to meet interesting men. Ted did not elaborate on how he spent the night, but he did say that he had an open invitation to visit her on his next trip to Hong Kong.

From Hong Kong the ship went on to Keelung, and finally Kobe. There I took my evening meals ashore and spent some time at the White Horse Lounge when I was not required to stand watch on board. On a Friday evening, Noriko asked me if I could get the following Sunday off all day. She had something very special that she wanted to show me. I swapped time with Ted and took his watch on Saturday and that way I got the time off. On Sunday morning I met Noriko and two of her waitresses in front of the White Horse Lounge. From there the four of us took a taxi to the Kobe railroad station and Noriko purchased tickets for us. A three hour ride took us to Takarazuka, the Hollywood of Japan. We had lunch at a very nice restaurant and then toured an unusually well laid out zoo. Then we went into a large theater similar to Radio City Music Hall. We saw a spectacular stage show that rivaled anything I had seen at the Radio City Music Hall in New York. After the show we had dinner at a restaurant in another part of Takaruzaka and then took the train back to Kobe.

I had seen a part of Japan that I never knew existed. The Japanese always amazed me. Their culture seemed to range from the very ancient to the very modern. One day a Japanese woman could be wearing a kimono the design of which has not changed for many centuries, and the next day she could be wearing a modern European style dress with high heeled shoes. The ancient and the modern seemed to blend naturally in Japan. I thanked Noriko and the girls for a very pleasant day, and got back to the ship just before midnight. The following day the ship sailed for Nagoya, and then on to Yokohama to top off our cargo.

The voyage across the North Pacific from Yokohama to San Francisco was uneventful. Three days were spent discharging part of our cargo. Then the ship went down the California coast to Long Beach harbor where three more days were spent discharging and loading cargo. The run south to Balboa was smooth except for the transit of the Gulf of Tehauntepec where the wind was howling and the seas were rough. After passing through the Panama Canal the S S Flying Trader steamed on to San Juan, Puerto Rico. The ship reduced speed to about four knots while cruising along the north coast of Puerto Rico. This was necessary in order to arrive at the pilot station at daybreak. The ship went directly to a dock from the pilot station and began working cargo as soon as pratique was granted. Since the ship would be in San Juan overnight, I phoned John Haussler, a classmate, who lived there. He invited me to have dinner with him and his wife. That evening I met them at a very nice restaurant and enjoyed an excellent dinner and a good deal of entertaining conversation. John had a management position with a company involved in the importation of industrial material and to some extent shipping. He had done quite well since our graduation. The ship sailed the following afternoon for New York so I was not able to have a follow up visit with John and his wife..

Just north of the Bahama chain of islands the ship ran into a storm. There was no warning. One morning the dawn broke over a gray sea with a thick overcast sky and a wind that increased in force as the day progressed. By mid afternoon the ship was rolling heavily in thirty foot seas. This storm may have just been forming as we steamed into it. The wind reached gale force by sundown and the occasional rain squalls made standing watch on the bridge a miserable experience. The heavy seas slowed our progress and added another day to our run to New York. When the ship got north of Cape Hatteras the storm abated and soon died away completely. We had only been in the storm for three days but it seemed much longer. The rest of the run to New York was smooth. Somehow the storm was a fitting climax to the end of my third voyage around the world. It made getting home again a much sweeter experience.

When the ship was berthed at pier 29 in Brooklyn and sea watches were broken cargo operations got underway immediately. Anita was waiting for me on the pier. After a quick hello I had to leave Anita waiting on the pier while I went back on board to check out the special cargo. It was early afternoon by the time I was free to leave the ship and join Anita. We drove home to Islip and spent the rest of the day catching up on all that had past during the past four and a half months. Early the next morning I returned to the ship and resumed my duties with cargo operations. On 11 March 1954 the voyage articles were broken and the crew was paid off. Most of them left the ship and new seamen came aboard to fill out the crew for the coastwise run. Ted informed me that he was getting off the ship and going back to his home town on Long Island. His former wife had written to him and indicated that she wanted to try out marriage again. I could never understand why she had divorced Ted. It seemed that her parents did not approve of him and had pressured her to divorce him. Now she realized that she had made a mistake. I understood this situation completely from my own experiences. I wished Ted good luck and told him that I would miss his fellowship on the next voyage.

Four days later the S S Flying Trader steamed down the coast to Philadelphia, Norfolk, and Charleston. Then it made a straight run back to New York to top off the cargo. Ted's replacement, the new Third Mate, was a fellow named Al. He was my own age but had a much different personalty than Ted. During the coastwise run I realized that I could get along with him, but we would never be friends. He was a wise guy who did a minimum of work and took in slack as often as he could. Although he was married and had children, he had the attitude of a playboy. After two more days in New York the cargo was topped off, and on 24 March 1954, foreign articles were signed. In addition to a new Third Mate we had a new Radio Operator. He was a rather tall older man in his sixties and very much a gentleman. There was also a new Chief Steward, and the same grouchy German Chief Mate signed on again for this voyage. The rest of the crew were the usual mixture that came out of the National Maritime Union hiring hall.

With sea watches set and a pilot on board, the ship cast off from the 29th street pier and headed into the harbor. It was early evening and a dense fog settled across the harbor. After setting out the charts in the chart room I went into the wheel house and looked at the radar screen. The screen showed that the ship was rather close to the Staten Island shore. Al was in the wheel house with the helmsman and the Captain and the Pilot were in the wing of the bridge. I told Al that the ship was very close to Staten Island and that he should let the pilot know. He replied that the pilot knew we were close and that they were getting ready to drop the anchor. I heard the order given to drop the anchor and I left the wheel house. I went to my cabin and to bed hoping to get in a few hours of sleep before taking the watch at midnight.

Al came into my cabin at 2330 and awakened me. I realized that there was something wrong. The ship was unusually quiet. The normal sound from the engine room when the ship was underway was missing. I asked Al if we were still at anchor. He replied,"No." "Well are we underway?" I asked. Again he replied, "No." Then with a grin he said, "We are hard aground on Staten Island." I got dressed quickly and went up to the bridge. There was no one there. Looking forward I could see that I was almost at eye level with the bluff at the Quarantine Station on Staten Island. Reviewing the entry in the log book I learned that the ship had dropped the anchor and its forward motion had run the bow right up on a clear section of the beach. Had it gone aground a couple of hundred yards either way, it would have destroyed a pier and some small craft. It had been high tide when the S S Flying Trader went aground. This was the worst possible time and it meant that we would have to wait until the next high tide to float the ship off the beach. I went down to the main deck and with a lead line I took soundings all around the ship. The bow was well up on the beach but the depth of water increased as I went aft. More than three quarters of the length of the ship was floating free of the bottom. The anchor chain led under the bow and under the hull.

Although my watch was over at 0400 and I was relieved by the Chief Mate I had no desire to go back to bed. As dawn broke I walked up to the bow, and looking down I could see much of the beach exposed. The tide was way out. It must have dropped seven or eight feet since the ship went aground. There was dry beach under the stem of the bow, and there was a small group of people on the bluff looking at the ship. A man was walking his dog along the beach coming toward the ship. When they reached the ship the dog raised his hind leg and urinated on the stem. Somehow this seemed to be the appropriate thing to do. There would no doubt be an army of reporters and photographers from the news media on hand as the morning wore on to give further embarrassment to the ship and the Isbrandtsen line.

The next high tide was due at about noon and there was a good deal of activity preparing to refloat the ship. The operations manager and the port captain came aboard to add their expert advice. Two tug boats were brought on scene to help pull the ship off of the beach. The engineers shifted as much fuel and water aft as they could to help raise the bow section off of the bottom. At 1000 all the experts felt that there was sufficient water depth due to the rising tide to get the ship off. With the ship's engine going astern and both tugs pulling from each stern quarter the ship did not slide off the beach. Instead it seemed to pivot from side to side but otherwise did not budge. Judging by the length of anchor chain that was out and the depth of the water, the experts reasoned that the ship was sitting on its anchor about a third of the length of the ship from the bow. The anchor was the pivot on which the ship swung from side to side. The experts were afraid that the anchor might have punctured through the hull. Soundings were taken of number one and number two holds, but there was no indication of any flooding. Finally after about two hours of trying various rudder angles, engine speeds, and direction of pull by the tug boats, the ship slid off the bank into deep water.

The S S Flying Trader returned to a berth at pier 29 and divers were deployed to examine the ship's bottom for damage. There was some doubt about the ship being able to start its voyage. If the divers found significant damage to the bottom, the Underwriters might declare the ship unseaworthy. The voyage would then be canceled, the cargo would be off loaded, and the crew would be discharged. Fortunately the divers found no significant damage, just a large dent where the ship had been sitting on the anchor. A little over twenty-four hours after running aground, the S S Flying Trader departed New York on its next voyage around the world. The grounding did cast a dark shadow on the ship. It was a very poor way to begin a voyage, and the usually pleasant Captain Hardy remained rather sour throughout the voyage.

THE FOURTH VOYAGE AROUND THE WORLD

The same ports were visited as on the previous voyage. There was nothing of significant difference as the ship called at the Azores, Lisbon, Genoa, Tripoli, Alexandria, Beirut, Port Said, Jidda, Port Sudan, Djibouti, Karachi, and Bombay. While in Beirut wooden cases of dried dates were loaded and filled the tween deck spaces in number one and number two holds. These cases of dates were to be discharged in Bombay. As usual the S S Flying Trader went to a berth at a dock in the Victoria basin. There were seven or eight other cargo ships working cargo at the Victoria docks. My normal routine when working cargo was to go from hatch to hatch to check the progress of loading and discharging the cargo and then up dating the cargo plan. Any discrepancies or damage to any of the cargo items were also noted and recorded. When I went down into number one hatch tween deck I found several of the wooden cases of dried dates smashed and the contents strewn across the deck. The coolies who were placing the cases in slings to off load them were careless and indifferent to the damage they were doing. The Indian cargo checker for that hatch who should have been recording the number of cases being discharged and their condition was nowhere to be found. The coolies ignored my admonition to handle the cargo with more care. About half the cases discharged were damaged. Since the Bombay Port Authority took no responsibility for the cargo the loss and damage to this cargo would be charged against the ship.

I went to the Chief Mate and alerted him to the problem in number one hatch. He and I returned to number one hatch and went down into the tween deck space. The Chief Mate spotted the Indian cargo checker lying prone on top of some of the cases, sound asleep. He grabbed the checker by his trouser belt and pulled him horizontally off the cases and let him fall on the steel deck. The Indian checker was shocked awake and obviously hurt by his sudden contact with the steel deck. He staggered to his feet and started shouting to the coolies in Hindu. The coolies climbed out of number one hatch and ran along the main deck calling down to the coolies working in the other hatches. All the coolies left the ship and gathered on the dock. Some ran along the dock to the other ships and all the coolies working cargo on those ships went on to the dock. Soon there was a huge crowd of coolies on the dock before our ship. They were shaking their fists and shouting curses at our ship. All cargo operations in the Victoria docks came to a complete stop. About an hour later officials from the Bombay Port Authority came aboard the ship and complained to the Captain that his Mates were abusing the coolies on his ship. Their union had called a general strike of the port in protest. When the Port Officials were told what really happened they said that the Chief Mate would have to formally apologize to the union officials in order to end the strike. Reluctantly and with some bitterness, the Chief Mate made an apology and the strike was called off. This may have been an example of honesty and justice in the worlds largest democracy, India. Two days later with cargo operations completed, and no further incidents, the ship departed Bombay.

Our next port of call was Colombo, Ceylon. When I got off duty I teamed up with the Radio Operator and the two of us walked to the main shopping street in Colombo and located the jewelry store I had visited on previous trips there. Inside the store we spent an hour drinking Coca Cola, looking at various precious stones, and haggling with the Arab proprietor over the price he was asking for them. The Radio Operator purchased a large emerald cut smoky topaz stone, and I purchased a black star sapphire about the size of a large green pea. I paid the proprietor about twenty five dollars for the sapphire. I told the Radio Operator that when the ship got to Kobe I planned to have the star sapphire mounted in a ring at a jewelry store I was familiar with. He thought that was an excellent idea and said that he would do likewise with the smoky topaz he had purchased. The ship spent two days in Colombo and then steamed on to Singapore, Manila, Hong Kong, Keelung, and Kobe.

The first thing I did when I got ashore in Kobe was to take the star sapphire to the jewelry store and asked the proprietor about mounting it in a yellow gold ring. He brought his technician from the back of his store and asked me to describe what I wanted. I told him that I wanted the sapphire mounted in a ring with a pink white pearl diagonally mounted on each side of it. He asked me to make a sketch of what I wanted on a piece of paper he handed me. When both the proprietor and his technician understood what I wanted, I asked them how much it would cost. They conferred for a short time and then the proprietor said that it would cost between ten and twelve thousand Yen. The rate of exchange at that time was still about four hundred Yen to the Dollar. I gave him twelve thousand Yen and told him that the S S Flying Trader would be departing from Yokohama in two and one half weeks. He said that he would do his best to have the ring delivered to me in Yokohama before the ship sailed. The following day I took the Radio Operator to the jewelry store and he made similar arrangements with the proprietor to have his topaz mounted in a ring.

Again I went to my favorite watering hole, the White Horse Lounge and took the Radio Operator with me. Noriko and the waitresses gave me a very warm welcome. Later Noriko, the Radio Operator, and I had dinner at a near by restaurant, Noriko asked us if we could get the evening off two days hence. She said that she wanted to take us to a very special place that evening after midnight when she closed the White Horse Lounge. On the appointed evening the Radio Operator and I arrived at the White Horse Lounge a little after eight o'clock. We spent a few pleasant hours drinking beer and talking with Noriko and the girls until closing time, midnight. A taxi appeared at the door as Noriko was closing the lounge. Noriko, two of her girls, the Radio Operator and I got in. Noriko gave the driver some instructions and we drove for about a half hour through the very dark night to a bluff in the hills above Kobe. We left the taxi and walked a short distance to an overlook surrounded with a stone railing. Ahead of us was a high stonework reservoir that must have been centuries old. A stream of water was cascading down the center of the reservoir wall to the glen far below. As we stood there a full moon came slowly from behind the hill on the far side of the reservoir. The grotesquely shaped Japanese pine trees growing on the hill and the sides of the reservoir were silhouetted sharply by the moon light. The cascading water looked like liquid silver as it spilled down into the glen. It was all a spectacularly beautiful sight. There was some sort of cabaret in the glen far below showing a few yellow lights. The faint sound of music drifted up from the cabaret. A band was playing the ancient "Coal Miners" song. We stood there in complete silence for about an hour enjoying the magic of the moment. Then we got into the taxi and returned to the White Horse Lounge, where Noriko served us a night cap in spite of the hour. That reservoir and the pine trees in the moon light are a sight I shall always remember.

A couple of days later the ship steamed on to Nagoya, then to Shimizu, and then on to Yokohama. When sailing day from Yokohama came, the Radio Operator and I were beginning to think that the rings would not arrive from Kobe before we sailed. Sea watches were set at 0800 and the ship was scheduled to cast off at 1600. At about 1400 I was in the chart room setting out the charts for the voyage to San Francisco. I walked out to the wing of the bridge to get a breath of air. As I looked down at the activity on the dock as the last of the cargo was being loaded aboard, I saw a boy in a gray bell hop type uniform pedaling a bicycle down the dock. He came to the gangway and gave the watchman two small packages. One package was for me and the other was for the Radio Operator. My package contained the ring, beautifully done, and a letter. The letter explained that the cost of the ring was less than the twelve thousand Yen I had given the Jeweler and indicated that I had one thousand Yen left in the account. The jeweler wanted to know how I wanted it returned to me, in Yen, Dollars, or merchandise. The Radio Operator was equally pleased with his package.

The passage from Yokohama to San Francisco took almost two weeks. Again a few days in San Francisco and a few more in Long Beach and the ship was on its way to Panama. The passage through the Panama Canal was always interesting and the manicured lawns and pristine buildings a pleasure to behold. From Cristobal the ship went to San Juan, Puerto Rico. When I was able to get ashore I places a phone call to John Haussler and learned that he and his wife were on travel. There would not be a friendly visit this trip. The playboy Third Mate spent his evenings in the fancy hotels in San Juan drinking, chasing divorcees, and gambling. Twice he came aboard intoxicated to relieve me and I refused to allow him to take the watch. If anything were to go wrong, I would be held equally responsible for letting an intoxicated mate relieve me. Naturally he took offense at my reluctance to let him relieve me. I was glad when we finally cast off our mooring lines and departed San Juan.

The run from San Juan to New York was uneventful. Again Anita was waiting on pier 29 when the ship docked. When I finally finished with my shipboard duties and we were driving home to Islip, Anita said that these round the world trips were too long. She asked me to get on a shorter run or quit the sea altogether. When we arrived home in Islip, son Randy, now a toddler, looked at me and said, "I know you, you are my daddy." I realized then that these long trips would have to come to an end. When I returned to the ship the next morning the voyage articles were broken. It was 29 July 1954. I informed the Port Captain and Captain Hardy that I would not sign on for the next voyage. The Port Captain said that he would try to get a berth for me on one of the company's ships on the European run. Those ships were usually on a two month turn around, less than half the time of the around the world voyages. I had just completed four trips around the world and that was enough.

BACK ON THE NORTH ATLANTIC RUN

A week later I was assigned to the S S Flying Spray to relieve the Third Mate who was taking the voyage off. The ship was topping off its cargo in New York and departed for Saint Nazaire, France on 7 August 1954. The voyage across the North Atlantic was pleasant, and there were twelve passengers aboard who provided some entertaining conversation at meal times. The food was somewhat better than that served on the around the world ships. For one thing, the food was much fresher, and of better quality. All of our passengers disembarked when we reached Saint Nazaire. Aside from the remains of the German submarine pens, Saint Nazaire was a small rather sterile city. Because of the watch schedule I got a day off in Saint Nazaire. The Radio Operator, a fellow about my own age, and I took a train from there to the city of Nantes on the Loire River. We walked around Nantes for a while, and then had dinner at a small restaurant on the main boulevard. There was not much of any interest for us to see or do in Nantes so we took the train back to Saint Nazaire and were back on board the ship before sun down.

From Saint Nazaire the S S Flying Spray sailed around the coast of Brittany and into the English Channel to Antwerp, Belgium. Antwerp had not changed since I was last there over two years ago. Skipper Straza was as busy as before and the Robot Bar and the Coney Island Bar were still in business. The Radio Operator and I had an excellent dinner in one of the better restaurants. With the help of the ship's agent I was able to get a ticket for the opera. The agent said that I would probably not enjoy this particular opera because it was a mandatory performance. I do not remember the name of the opera. It was performed because of some arrangement between the opera company and the Catholic Church. When I took my seat for the evening performance I was surprised to see that most of the seats were empty. I soon learned why. The music score was not pleasant. There were less than a half dozen performers. The theme of the opera involved some sort of religious miracle that I had difficulty understanding. In order not to offend anyone, I suffered through the entire performance. I resolved that in the future I would listen more carefully to the opinions of the local people where operatic performances were concerned.

The ship sailed on to Rotterdam, Holland from Antwerp. The neatness and cleanliness of Rotterdam was impressive. While working cargo one day one of the Dutch longshoremen climbed out of the cargo hold and handed me a wallet. He indicated that he had found it under one of the cartons of cargo he was helping to off load. Examining the wallet I discovered that it belonged to a fellow with an Italian name and an address in Queens, New York. He must have been one of the longshoremen who loaded the cargo on board in Brooklyn. There were about fifty U. S. Dollars in the wallet, which was a lot of money in those days. The honesty of the Dutch longshoreman impressed me. In most ports a longshoreman finding such a wallet would simply pocket the money and say nothing. I thanked the Dutch longshoreman and gave him the equivalent of five dollars in Dutch Guilders. The wallet was then given to the Captain who placed it in the ship's safe, to be given back to its owner when the ship returned to New York. This experience led me to believe that the Dutch are an inherently honest people.

From Rotterdam the S S Flying Spray steamed through the North Sea to the Elbe River and on to Hamburg. This cosmopolitan city is always a pleasure to visit. There are numerous fine restaurants and many shops and large stores offering a variety of products for sale. Only three days were spent discharging and loading cargo. On the last day there twelve passengers came aboard for the voyage to New York. As the ship steamed down the Elbe River to the North Sea I was amazed at the number of coastal freighters and self propelled barges running up and down the river. Germany seemed to be in full recovery barely a decade after the end of the war. The passage across the North Atlantic was rather rough most of the way. The passengers kept pretty much to themselves and I think many of them had a touch of mal de mar. The day after our arrival in New York the voyage articles were broken, and the Mate whom I had relieved for the voyage came aboard to resume his duties. The Port Captain informed me that I going to be assigned to another ship in a couple of days.

On 2 October 1954 I signed on the S S Flying Foam as Third Mate for another voyage to the northern European ports. Captain Hamby, the Master, was also new to the ship. He was from one of the Southern States

S S Flying Foam
C-1 Passenger/Cargo Ship, Isbrandtsen Line

and had a "no nonsense" demeanor. The Chief Mate was a Dane in his forties with an arrogant attitude and a nasty disposition. The Second Mate was a naturalized Mexican with a short fuse and a somewhat introverted personality. The Radio Operator, Len Gordon, was a fellow my own age with a friendly easy going personalty. The Chief Engineer was a light skinned Negro about forty years old and a very dapper dresser. He ran a very efficient department and had a forceful personalty. There was no doubt that he was destined for a higher position in the company. I got a brief glimpse of the Chief Engineer's wife as she dropped him off one morning at the head of the pier. She appeared to be a rather attractive white woman. The three assistant engineers were younger men and kept pretty much to themselves. The Chief Steward was a Negro fellow from the West Indies who was rather efficient and kept a tight reign on his department. The rest of the crew were typical of the type of people that came out of the National Maritime Union. With this mix of people I decided to keep a low silhouette during this voyage.

After a short coastwise cruise the S S Flying Foam returned to New York to top off the cargo and take on twelve passengers. The voyage across the North Atlantic to our first port of call, Le Havre, was uneventful. The way the ship was configured, the six passenger cabins entered into the dining salon with three cabins on each side. The ship's officers and the passengers took their meals in the dining salon, and that was the only place I was able to see any of them. For the most part the passengers kept to their cabins when the weather did not allow them to sit out on the boat deck. The passage must have been very boring for them. The passengers disembarked in Le Havre shortly after the ship docked. We did not have much cargo for Le Havre so our stay there was less than forty eight hours. From there the ship went on to Antwerp, Rotterdam, and Hamburg. In each of these ports of call I saw the Chief Engineer go ashore dressed like a Wall Street banker. He wore a Brooks Brothers suit and overcoat topped off with a Hamburg hat. I do not know where he went in these ports, but I am sure he impressed whomever he was meeting. He made quite an impression on the waterfront of each of the ports where the ship called. When time and circumstances allowed, Len Gordon, the Radio Operator, and I would go ashore and take a meal at a good restaurant. This gave us a break from the monotony and poor quality of shipboard food. Cargo operations went well in each port and finally we were preparing to depart from Hamburg.

Sea watches were set on departure day and departure was scheduled for the evening. It was past midnight when the Elbe River pilot was dropped off at the pilot station. I stopped by the salon to have a cup of hot cocoa before retiring. Len Gordon was there and he asked me if I had seen the passengers when they came aboard. I said that I had been too busy on deck to pay any attention to them. Len informed me that two of the passengers were very attractive young women. They were sharing one cabin. He said that one of the young women was a blond angel and the other was an older brunette who looked like she knew her way around. The rest of the passengers were old married German couples. The two of us spent a little time speculating on whether Captain Hamby would take the high circle home or choose the southern route where we could expect better weather. I went off to my cabin and gave little thought to the passengers.

In spite of the time of year, late Fall, Captain Hamby took the northern most great circle route, the shortest distance between northern Europe and New York. He gambled on having good weather on this run and lost his bet. Steaming that far north took the ship out of the Gulf Stream during most of the crossing. Standing night watches on the open bridge wing was a cold miserable experience. The ship ran into one North Atlantic gale after another. There were days when the ship only averaged four knots speed. Gale force winds and heavy seas not only slowed our progress but made for a very uncomfortable passage. We were shipping water over the main deck constantly. The seas were running twenty five to thirty five feet in height and the ship rolled heavily as a result. Captain Hamby set up a wicker lounge chair in the wheel house and slept there fitfully during those nights when the ship was rolling its worst. Trying to eat anything in the dining salon was a challenge, and the food prepared by the cooks was quite limited.

The weather remained relatively bad for this time of year in the North Atlantic. As the days passed I noticed that the older passengers were shunning the two young attractive women. This was done in very subtle ways. When the young ladies came out on the boat deck for some air, the older couples there would slowly one after the other go back inside the house. At meal times the older couples avoided sitting near the young women. I had been told that the young blond angel was a war bride on her way to America to meet her G I husband. The fast looking brunette was a bit of a mystery. Passenger affairs were none of my business so I decided to ignore the subtle animosity that seemed to exist among the passengers.

However one night after midnight when I got off watch I joined Len in the darkened salon for a cup of hot cocoa. While we were sitting and drinking our beverages we heard some giggling coming from the cabin occupied by the young women. A short time later the door to their cabin opened and the Chief Engineer emerged with his arm around the brunette and they went off in the direction of his cabin. Len and I had not been noticed in the darkened salon, and to say the least we were both shocked. Half an hour later the Chief Steward emerged from the cabin with the blond angel giving him a lingering good night kiss. She was wearing a skimpy nightie. Now I understood why the older German passengers were avoiding these young women. They probably considered them to be harlots.

Len Gordon covered his radio watches on the basis of Greenwich Mean Time. The Mates watches were set on ship's time which changed as the ship steamed west across each time zone. Because of these differences in the times we stood our watches I did not get to see Len for a couple of days. The next time Len and I met for a midnight beverage he filled me in on what he had observed regarding the young women. There was a hot and heavy affair going on between the young women and the Chief Engineer and the Chief Steward. The brunette would sneak out of her cabin and go to the Chief Engineers cabin in the wee hours of the morning. At the same time the Chief Steward would sneak into the women's cabin and spend a few hours there. The old German couples occupying the cabins on either side of the young women's cabin must have heard the amorous noises as the Chief Steward and the blond angel enjoyed sexual pleasure. Len and I decided to say nothing to anyone about what was going on. Apparently only we were aware of the trysts. The Chief Engineer and the Chief Steward were violating some very serious rules. Carnal knowledge between passengers and crew is strictly forbidden on American Flag ships.

As Third Mate I had the eight to twelve watch, 0800 to 1200 and 2000 to 2400. The S S Flying Foam did not have a Purser, so Captain Hamby would occasionally take my bridge watch and have me sit in his office and copy the entries from the bridge log to the smooth log. Deciphering some of the entries in the bridge log was a real challenge. I did not mind bringing the smooth log up to date, and the Captain appreciated my ability to write and print legibly because he could not. This side line work helped me to develop a good rapport with the Captain, and I could not help having a feeling of guilt or betrayal toward the Captain. I had knowledge of the trysts between the young women passengers and the Chief Engineer and the Chief Steward, and I had failed to inform the Captain. On one hand it was my duty to inform the Captain. On the other hand If I were an informer I would be looked upon by my ship-mates as a rat no one could trust. I reasoned that there would be no great harm done if the transgressions of the Chief Engineer and the Chief Steward were never made known. Therefore with some feelings of guilt I kept silent.

When the ship was about three quarters of the way across the North Atlantic the weather became unusually good and the seas relatively smooth. One morning about mid way through my watch when I was in the wheel house checking the gyro and magnetic compasses, I heard a knock on the door to the Captains office which was just off the wheel house. Looking toward the Captains office, I saw one of the black gang, an Oiler, standing there. When the Captain opened the door, the Oiler said that he had something very serious to discuss. While leaving the office door open, Captain Hamby invited the Oiler to enter his office and have a seat. A moment later I heard the Captain bellow, "THEY DID WHAT!" Then he stormed into the wheel house and ordered me to have my standby man call every Mate and Engineer not on watch to report to the bridge immediately. I gave my standby man the order and he went below to get the Mates and Engineers. Captain Hamby gave me a nasty look and then turned and stared out the forward ports without saying another word. I had an idea of what had angered the Captain, but I could not imagine how the Oiler, who was also the Union Delegate, had any knowledge of the trysts.

After a few minutes had passed there were the two Mates, two Assistant Engineers, as well as me standing in the wheel house. The Captain spun around and glaring at the group of us said, "You are the worst bunch of officers I have ever had on a ship. You are disloyal, unreliable, and dishonest. You have betrayed the trust I had in you. You have let my ship become a whore house." The Chief Mate interrupted the Captain asking, "What are you talking about?" The Captain then went on to say that the Oiler had informed him that the Chief Engineer and one of the women passengers were observed copulating in the engine room fiddley. They were doing this on the gratings two decks above the heads of the Fireman, Oiler and Wiper who were on watch below in the engine room. The Oiler had also told the Captain that, in addition, the Chief Steward was " screwing" the blond female passenger and that this had been going on for some time. Apparently the unlicensed crew men knew what had been going on with the young female passengers and had kept the knowledge to themselves. However when the Chief Engineer was wanton enough to have sex with the brunette in the engine room fidley where the men on watch below could see them, the Oiler, the Fireman, and the Wiper were offended. As the Union Delegate, the Oiler felt obligated to complain on behalf of the crew to the Captain. When the Captain finished admonishing us, we Mates and Engineers protested that we had no knowledge of what the Chief Engineer and the Chief Steward had been doing. We claimed that we were as surprised and shocked as he was. The Captain accepted what we said, and then ordered me to have my standby man summon the Chief Engineer and the Chief Steward to his office. The Mates and the Engineers left the wheel house quickly and the Captain returned to his office. A short time later the Chief Engineer and the Chief Steward went into the Captain's office and the door was closed.

I do not know what Captain Hamby said to the Chief Engineer and the Chief Steward, but their faces were grim when they came out of the Captain's office fifteen or twenty minutes later. The Chief Steward's career was probably safe because he was a member of the National Maritime Union and he would be protected by the Union. However he would never ship out on an Isbrandtsen ship again, and if the word got around to the other companies he would probably find it very difficult to get another berth as Chief Steward. As far as the Chief Engineer was concerned his seagoing career was over. Even if his license were not revoked, he would be "black balled" with the other shipping companies. I could not understand how so intelligent and capable a man could throw away all that he had achieved by acting so foolishly. Taking the brunette woman into the fidley in day time was beyond stupidity. From the engine room floor plates there is a clear view through the gratings at every deck level all the way up to the sky light at the top of the fidley hatch. He should have known that he and the woman would be seen by the engine room watch below. Had the Chief Engineer been able to control his passion and just continued to sneak around during the late night and early morning hours, the Captain would probably never have been told of his transgressions. Naturally all the hanky panky came to an abrupt end.

There was a somewhat different atmosphere on board the S S Flying Foam during the remaining few days of the voyage. The Chief Engineer spent most of the time in his cabin and avoided showing himself in the public areas. Likewise the Chief Steward stayed out of sight as much as he could. Captain Hamby had little more to say about the affair with the passengers and maintained a rather dour countenance most of the time. When the ship finally docked at pier 29 there were several cars in the parking area at the head of the pier. Small knots of people were gathered at the pier entrance obviously waiting for the passengers to clear Immigration and Customs and then disembarking. As soon as I could get ashore I went to the head of the pier where Anita was waiting for me. She was very pregnant and showing it. She and I were standing just inside the pier entrance talking when the passengers began walking from the gangway to the head of the pier with some longshoremen carrying their baggage. There was an elderly couple with a very young soldier in uniform standing near us. The young blond woman passenger ran to the soldier, embraced him, and kissed him profusely while saying, "Darling I missed you so much." I could not help thinking — I know how much you missed that poor soldier. The brunette woman passenger was met by two hard looking men in three piece suits who gave her a rather cool greeting and then led her to their car. The older German couples were met by family members or friends and driven off in a variety of cars and taxi cabs.

Cargo operations began a short time later and the Chief Mate asked me to go into number three hold tween deck and check out the special cargo, bags of mail. I told him that my wife was waiting on the pier, and he said that he would have me relieved in an hour or less. We had carried a couple of hundred bags of mail from Europe and each one had to be checked as it was off loaded. No one ever came to relieve me and four hours had passed by the time the last bag of mail was checked off. It was after four in the afternoon and my time on watch was over. I found the Chief Mate and told him I did not appreciate his sticking me with checking the mail and lying about having me relieved in an hour. He responded with a typical nasty remark. This just fortified my dislike of this arrogant square head. When I finally joined Anita on the pier I apologized for the long delay in getting off the ship. Before leaving the ship I learned that the Port Captain had notified Captain Hamby that the next voyage of the S S Flying Foam would be on the around the world run. After a pleasant evening at home in Islip, I returned to the ship at 0800 the next morning. The shipping commissioner was there and the voyage articles were terminated and the crew paid off. Shortly after the articles were broken the

Chief Steward came over to me on the pier to say farewell. As we were shaking hands he asked me what I thought of his affair with the blonde passenger. Why he wanted my opinion I do not know. However I answered him honestly and told him that I understood the temptation, but thought that he had acted unwisely in yielding to it. He walked away with a very sad expression on his face. I never saw nor did I hear anything about the Chief Engineer. However I am sure that his career in the maritime field was over. Confirming that the ship was scheduled for the around the world run next trip, I informed Captain Hamby and the Port captain that I would not sign on for the next trip. The Port Captain asked me to make the coastwise run, and said that he would try to find a berth for me on another ship on the European run. I made the coastwise run and enjoyed the satisfaction of knowing that I would not be sailing with that lousy Chief Mate again.

When the S S Flying Foam returned to New York from the coastwise trip I got off. Len Gordon the Radio Operator also got off. He had no desire to spend the next four or five months on a voyage around the world. The two of us agreed to keep in touch as we went our separate ways. I got a call from the Port Captain informing me that he had a new assignment for me. Two days after leaving the S S Flying Foam, I signed on foreign articles as Third Mate on the S S Flying Independent. The date was 27 November 1954. The S S Flying Independent had just completed a coastwise run and was ready to depart New York for France. Anita was very unhappy about the quick turn around and said that I should think about giving up my sea going career and try to find something that would keep me home. She said that she could not tolerate the long absences, and did not want to raise children without a father at home. There was no arguing the fact that she was carrying a heavy burden alone. It was also obvious that these relatively shorter European voyages were no solution to the problem. The money I made going to sea provided a good standard of living but made a normal home life impossible. I felt that I had a tiger by the tail. I did not want to hang on, but I was afraid to let go.

Signing on the S S Flying Independent involved blending in with a new ship's company. Captain John Lewis was the master, and I had sailed with him about two years ago on one of my coastwise relief runs. As a tall, lean, well educated man in his fifties, he was the epitome of the Virginia gentleman. I was pleased to find him as the master. The Chief Mate and the Second Mate were Puerto Ricans and were an aloof tight knit team.

There was also an additional Cargo Mate, a man also in his fifties, who did not stand bridge watches. The Chief Engineer was an older man who kept to himself, and the three Assistant Engineers were men ranging in age from thirty to forty years. The Radio Operator was a quiet introverted fellow who kept his own council. The Chief Steward was a man from the mid west in his late forties. The rest of the unlicensed personnel were typical of the seamen supplied by the National Maritime Union. The Third Assistant Engineer, a fellow my own age, shared the same watch schedule with me. He was a Kings Point graduate and became friendly when he learned that I was a graduate of Fort Schuyler. We bantered back and forth about the advantages of one institution over the other.

The morning of the day following the day when the foreign articles were signed, the S S Flying Independent departed New York with a full load of general cargo and eleven passengers. One passenger, a tall slender attractive woman in her late thirties or early forties, had one cabin to herself. The other five passenger cabins were double occupancy. The passenger cabins were arranged the same way as those on the S S Flying Foam. Three cabins on each side of the dining salon, with their entrance doors leading from the dining salon. The rest of the passengers were a mixture of older American and European couples. The ship's officers and the passengers took their meals in the dining salon. However there was not very much fraternization between the officers and the passengers. Most of the time the passengers were seated at separate tables from the officers. At other than meal times I noticed that the single attractive woman passenger did spend some time talking with the Third Engineer.

The first port of call on this voyage was Bordeaux, France. The weather on the crossing was typical for this time of year in the North Atlantic. The waves were fifteen to twenty feet most of the time and the ship rolled comfortably. There was frequent rain and the wind made going on deck a cold and uncomfortable experience. It soon became apparent why the two Puerto Rican Mates were so tight. They were less than competent and their navigation was sloppy to say the least. However they covered each other's mistakes well. The Cargo Mate called some of their blunders to my attention and said that he wanted to be on the bridge with me whenever the ship was maneuvering in port. He said that the Captain would need all the help he could get. It was obvious that he had a strong dislike for the Puerto Ricans, and he had sailed with them longer than I had. When the ship reached the Bay Of Biscay the weather deteriorated. Wind and seas increased and the ship began to roll and pitch uncomfortably. Anita gave birth to our second son on 8 December 1954, but I did not learn of it till several days later. In December radio traffic increases considerably, and the Radio Operator did not get the message sent to me as soon as he normally would. I received congratulations from the Captain and the ship's officers when the Radio Operator finally got the news.

The ship entered the Gironde River and after some confusion finally got the Pilot for Bordeaux on board. The Second Mate almost had the ship heading for La Pallice instead of Bordeaux. He claimed that he did not understand the directions the Captain left in the night order book. The ship proceeded up the Gironde River to Bassans, the port for Bordeaux. We tied up at a dock in the evening and cargo operations began the following morning. The passengers were cleared and disembarked with all of their baggage a short time later. Cargo operations went on only till four in the after noon each day which made our stay in Bordeaux six days. The first evening there the Third Engineer and I went ashore to walk around the city and take in the sights. While we were walking by a park a group of two couples were walking towards us. One of the couples included the attractive woman passenger from our ship. The Third Engineer started to give her a hearty hello, but she shot him a stone cold look and walked on by as if she had never known him. He was surprised and obviously hurt by her slight. When the group was well past us, he told me that he had an affair with her during the passage. She had initiated the affair and he had spent time with her in bed in her cabin on several nights. He could not understand why she shunned him now. I told him not to feel hurt, and that her change of attitude was quite typical. I went on to tell him that some women act strangely on a ship when the lines are cast off. They become predatory and seek out a male companion to provide them sexual satisfaction and a feeling of security during the voyage. Much like a "Jekyll and Hyde" personalty, they revert back to their former demeanor when they are again on shore and free of the anxiety of an ocean passage. I also warned him that he should not tell anyone else of the affair. Fortunately he was much more discrete than the Chief Engineer on the S S Flying Foam.

Captain Lewis was an unusual master. He never raised his voice nor lost his steady calm demeanor although the two Puerto Rican Mates gave him much cause to do so. The Cargo Mate and I covered much of the cargo work they should have been doing. Captain Lewis made a point of telling us that he appreciated our willingness to pitch in and do extra work when it was obviously needed. Whenever he pointed out any of their blunders to the Puerto Ricans, they would offer him excuses covering each other's incompetence. The Captain always kept his composure and tried to instruct them on how they could improve their performance. The Cargo Mate and I did not show any animosity or annoyance towards the Puerto Rican Mates. Instead we just took on the tasks that they ignored or were too indifferent to address. In spite of the short comings of the Puerto Ricans, we all got along without any rancor or vituperation. Open hostility on a ship can cause a most unpleasant voyage, and that was something that we did not want.

Bordeaux is a beautiful city with fine parks, wide boulevards, and impressive buildings. It has a grandeur that equals that of Paris or Genoa. With the help of the ship's agent, Captain Lewis arranged a banquet for the ship's officers. There was a resort type inn and restaurant on the river's side that had been closed for the Winter season. The agent got the owner to open the restaurant for one evening and to provide an elaborate dinner for the Captain's guests. On the appointed evening, all the ship's officers who were not on watch were taken by taxi to the river side restaurant. It was an elegant place with chandeliers, deep carpets, and fine furniture in the dining room. There were ten people including the Captain and the agent at this dinner. Four waiters were present to serve the dinner. It started with cocktails and hors d'oeuvres for a half hour or so before we were seated at one long table. The table was set with an array of fine China and elaborate silverware. The first course served was fish and vegetables covered with a sauce that gave them a delightful flavor. White wine was served with the fish. Following the fish there was a course of veal and different vegetables served with a red wine. Desert consisted of a delicious concoction of cake and ice-cream. An excellent coffee was served with the desert. After about two hours of eating rich food we all sat back in our chairs satisfied and over fed. The waiters served a fine brandy to top off the dinner. This dinner was an unusual and generous gesture by the Captain, and he paid for the whole affair out of his own pocket.

On another day, the Captain had the ship's agent arrange a tour of the Adrian Droz distillery for the ship's officers. Only four of us took advantage of this tour. The Captain, the Chief Engineer, the Third Engineer, and I took a taxi to the Droz Distillery on the outskirts of Bordeaux. The current proprietor, one of the original Droz family, welcomed us to the distillery and acted as our tour guide. After seeing the processing area where the various liquors were manufactured and formulated, we were led into a long ground level building containing a row of huge oak casks. These casks were large enough to hold a full size automobile. There were a dozen of these casks, and each one contained a different liquor. We were introduced to the head chemist, an older, short, stocky man wearing blue coveralls. He handed each of us a four ounce glass tumbler. As we examined the intricate carvings on the face of each cask, he would pour about an ounce of the liquor from the cask into our tumblers. By the time we reached the seventh cask I was beginning to feel a little intoxicated, and declined any more samples, as did the others. I bought five bottles of the liquors representing some of the liquors I had sampled to take home to the States. By the time we returned to the ship I felt much more intoxicated. A short time later a feeling of nausea overtook me and I spent a few minutes in the head vomiting. That was the price of sampling so many different liquors in such a short period of time. However the visit to the distillery was an enlightening and pleasant experience.

The S S Flying Independent departed Bordeaux and headed across the Bay Of Biscay to the English Channel and on to Antwerp. After a few days discharging and loading cargo the ship departed Antwerp and went on to Rotterdam. From Rotterdam, the ship went on to Hamburg. During the passages along the French, Belgian, and German coasts and the river estuaries, and eventually into the harbors, both the Cargo Mate and I were on the bridge with the Captain while either of the Puerto Rican Mates had the watch. There were many navigational hazards as well as heavy ship traffic in these areas. The Captain did not trust either of these Mates to navigate the ship safely through these waters without help. When we were not merely keeping a careful look out, the Cargo Mate and I were taking bearings of navigation aids both visually and with the RADAR or the radio direction finder, and running a continuous plot of the ship's position. This helped to relieve the Captain of a good deal of worry. Neither the Cargo Mate nor I expected any over time pay for this extra effort. We liked and respected Captain Lewis and we felt obligated to help him in any way we could.

The ship was only about three quarters full when we finished loading cargo in Hamburg. No passengers were taken aboard for the voyage back to the United States. We were informed that the ship was going to be diverted to Cuba to pick up a cargo of sugar. As a result instead of leaving

Hamburg for the North Sea and steaming around the north of Scotland, the ship headed south down the English Channel. Gale force winds were encountered in the Channel and that coupled with the very strong tidal currents made for slow progress. During one of my night watches I picked up Dover Light bearing four points just after I came on duty, and three hours later it was not yet abeam. The ship's speed during that watch averaged about four knots. Once the ship passed Bishop's Rock and got on the great circle track for the Windward Passage the weather improved. The run took us southwest across the Atlantic Ocean, through the Bahama Islands, and around Cabo Maisi on the eastern end of Cuba to the port of Caimanera on the west side of Guantanamo Bay. The United States Naval Base was on the east side of Guantanamo Bay.

The S S Flying Independent berthed at a shore side dock, and as soon as pratique was granted the hatches were opened for cargo. There was a single railroad track that ran the length of the dock and a train of flatbed cars loaded with bags of sugar was soon alongside. Gangs of Cuban longshoremen began loading the sugar aboard. The loading was done from 0800 in the morning until 1600 in the afternoon with long periods of idleness while empty rail cars were exchanged for full rail cars. The whole operation was rather slow so it took the best part of five days to complete loading the sugar. This gave me an opportunity to see some of the night life of Caimanera. Although the town of Caimanera was small it was only a short distance from the city of Guantanamo. The people were generally friendly and many spoke English. There were a large number of young attractive girls hanging around the bars and restaurants in Caimanera. The word was that most of them were involved with the American sailors in the Naval Base. However I did not see any American sailors wandering around the streets of the town. The Third Engineer and I found a nice restaurant on the road to Guantanamo City. On the second floor of the restaurant there was a large open air room where there was a game of bingo every night. On the nights when we were not on watch, we made a habit of having a few drinks in the bar below and then playing bingo with the locals for a couple of hours. A well dressed Cuban woman about forty years of age ran the bingo game and she often seemed annoyed with us when we made some minor mistakes. The locals seemed to be amused by our joining them in the bingo game.

During the day watches while overseeing the loading of the sugar, I had an opportunity to talk with some of the longshoremen and the stevedore bosses. There was obviously some political tensions among the local populace. There was a band of rebels roaming the hills and mountains above the cities of Santiago and Guantanamo. Their purpose was to overthrow the government of President Fulgencio Batista. Many of the longshoremen expressed a good deal of sympathy towards the rebels, and they also recited many Communist type slogans. The bosses claimed that the rebels were Communists and would establish a Communist regime if they were ever successful in overthrowing the government. Most of the New York newspapers and the radio commentators always seemed to refer to the Cuban rebels as freedom fighters trying to depose a corrupt dictator. Considering that the United States was engaged in a deadly dangerous cold war (World War III) with the Soviet Union, I could not help but wonder why the news media back home were so poorly informed or misguided. As far as I could determine, these rebels were Communists. The news media were misleading the American people, and I did not know whether it was sloppy journalism or down right chicanery.

With the cargo operations complete, and the ship "full and down," the hatches were covered, the lines were cast off and the S S Flying Independent departed Caimanera and Guantanamo Bay. The ship steamed around Cabo Maisi on the eastern end of Cuba, turned north, passed through the Bahaman Islands, and set a course for New York. There were a few days of foul weather, but otherwise the run to New York was uneventful. As soon as I could, I got off the ship and went home to Islip to see Anita and the new baby as well as Randy. Anita let me know that she was still not satisfied with my shipping out schedule. Although the time I was away on the European run was less than half the time I was gone on the around the world run, she was still unhappy. I was being confronted with a dilemma. Captain Lewis had informed me that he wanted me to be Chief Mate on the next voyage of the S S Flying Independent. He said that he would not allow the Puerto Ricans to sign on again. A couple of voyages to Europe as a Chief Mate would give me enough sea time to allow me to sit for my Master's license. Getting an unlimited Captain's license was always a prime goal in my maritime career.

When I returned to the ship at pier 29 in Brooklyn the next day I got some alarming news. Captain Lewis informed me that the S S Flying Independent's next voyage would be on the around the world service. He also said that my promotion to Chief Mate had been approved by the head of the operations department of the Isbrandtsen Line. This was good news and bad news. One voyage around the world as Chief Mate combined with my previous sea time as Second Mate would give me sufficient sea time to take the examination for Master. In addition to that, the Isbrandtsen Line gave the Master and the Chief Mate of their vessels a generous bonus at the end of a successful voyage. This would increase my income for a voyage considerably. When I got back home that evening, Anita and I had a serious conversation on what I should do. She was adamant that I should not sign on for the next voyage. The fact that I could not earn anywhere near as much money ashore as I could by going to sea made no difference to her. Essentially I had to choose between a maritime career and my marriage. Upon return to the ship the next morning, I informed Captain Lewis that I would not be signing on for the next voyage. He expressed extreme disappointment and urged me to reconsider. The Port Captain also urged me to reconsider, and informed me that he would not have a berth available for me on any of the ships on the European run for quite a long while. I signed off foreign articles on the S S Flying Independent on 19 January 1955, and I had just reached thirty years of age. With great misgivings I informed the Isbrandtsen line that I was not going to ship out any more. This was an important decision. I was giving up one promising career, and heading into an unknown environment ashore to seek another.

ASHORE FOR EVERMORE

My maritime career spanned the period from 1943 to 1955, more than a decade. The timing of my decision to quit the sea may have been a little off, but in retrospect I believe it was the right decision. One might think that all the shipping companies I worked for were doomed because now they are all gone from the seas. Those companies were the Boland and Cornelius Steam Ship Company, the American Gulf and West Indies Line, the Isthmian Line, the Grace Line, the Farrell Line, and the Isbrandtsen Line. The demise of those maritime companies and many others was due to the chicanery and dishonesty of our self serving politicians and the two corrupt major political parties that offer them to the voters for elected office. At the end of World War II there were more than four thousand ocean going vessels under the American flag. The United States was not just the maritime nation it had always been, it was then the greatest maritime nation in the world. Driven by greed the big money men, both foreign and domestic, with the help of their stooges in the Congress reduced the number of American flag vessels to a mere token. This was accomplished by eliminating subsidies, modifying the Jones Act, and passing laws and introducing rules and regulations that made it impossible to profitably operate ships under the American flag. The world's trade routes are now dominated by foreign flag vessels. A midget nation like Panama has one of the world's largest merchant fleets, while the United States has one of the smallest.

There is another factor that reduced the size of the American merchant fleet. That factor is the actual tonnage of individual merchant vessels. During the war years the average tonnage of a cargo vessel ranged between five thousand and twenty thousand tons displacement. Only the largest passenger liners exceeded twenty thousand tons. Since the end of the war in 1945 there was a steady increase in the size of new ships. Vessels exceeding one hundred thousand tons displacement were built in shipyards in Europe and Asia. Naval architects developed designs for ships exceeding even these huge tonnage figures, and a few are already in service. Advancements in technology increased the size of ships, while labor saving devices reduced the number of seamen required to operate them. While ships were becoming larger and larger the crews that manned them became smaller and smaller. After World war II the average ten thousand ton displacement ship carried a crew of thirty five. The ships now ranging from fifty thousand to five hundred thousand tons displacement carry crews as small as twenty two in number. Unfortunately most of these ships and their crews serve under foreign flags.

A deck officer in the Merchant Marine, a Third Mate, a Second Mate, or a Chief Mate carries a great deal of responsibility. While he has the watch, whether at sea or in port, he is responsible for the safe operation of the ship as well as the safety of everyone on board. This could involve a multi-million dollar vessel, crew and passengers that could exceed several hundred people, and possibly cargo worth many millions of dollars. The legal authority of a deck officer to direct and manage subordinates assigned to him is absolute. However exercising that authority is often tenuous at best. A naval officer can give an order to a subordinate and it must be carried out without any hesitation or argument. There are severe penalties for any subordinate naval person who refuses to carry out a legitimate order. That is not the case with a merchant officer. A subordinate officer or seaman may decline to obey an order or may choose to carry out an order in a less than satisfactory manner with far less significant consequences. This fact of life makes it necessary for a merchant officer to develop leadership and management skills to assure his orders will be obeyed without any hesitation. There was a old adage drummed into me when I was a Midshipman. That was, "Familiarity breeds contempt." Which simply means that if you become too familiar with your subordinates, they will be more likely to challenge your authority. I learned this lesson early on and developed a habit of never becoming intimate with subordinates. I avoided taking any libations in any of the watering holes frequented by any of my subordinates. Being decent and reasonably friendly with subordinates was standard procedure, but on the bridge and on the deck it was strictly business. This habit made most of my dealings with seamen productive and free of rancor.

The ships I served on included Liberty ships, Victory ships, Tankers, Colliers, and C1, C2, and C3 class ships. With a few exceptions, none of these types of ships have survived the wrecking yards. During my career at sea I visited ports in the following foreign places, Afars and Issas, Algeria, Azores, Belgium, Ceylon, China, Cuba, Denmark, Egypt, Formosa, France, Germany, Haiti, Holland, India, Italy, Japan, Lebanon, Libya, Morocco, Mozambique, Namibia, Norway, Pakistan, Panama, Philippines, Portugal, Puerto Rico, Saudi Arabia, Singapore, South Africa, Sudan, Sweden, Trinidad, Tunisia, and Venezuela. I sailed with men of outstanding ability and high moral character as well as a few scoundrels of the lowest order of human kind. Living and working closely with such a variety of personalities had a profound influence on my own personality. I learned to accept people as they are — not as I wished them to be. Developing the ability to get along with and work with people regardless of how I evaluated them became a valuable asset.

The ability to visit foreign lands and observe foreign cultures was an opportunity that few people are fortunate enough to ever have. Although my maritime career was over, there were experiences in that endeavor that I shall treasure and remember for as long as I shall live. My decision to give up my career as a professional seaman was a correct decision. The responsibilities of being a husband and a father required that I be ashore, not roving the world on some ship for months on end. The pleasures of being with my family full time far outweighed my romantic desire to follow the sea and visit exotic and some not so exotic places. My love of the sea was occluded by my love for my wife and my children.

EPILOG

Reading *The Smooth Log* one might get the impression that I am a racial bigot. Nothing could be further from the truth. Where I make any mention of African, Asiatic, Indian, Chinese, Filipino, Negro, or Scandinavian people, there is no intention to disparage or degrade any of them. My voyages put me in close association with all races and all creeds both afloat and ashore. I have tried to describe these people as I remember them with my mind's eye. Most of the crews I sailed with were "checkerboard," that is, they were a mixture of black and white with a few Asiatics thrown in. The Negro seamen I sailed with were as competent and as industrious as the white seamen. In my opinion, true racial integration in the work place began on American merchant vessels. Negro seamen were paid the same wages, ate the same food, and shared the same living quarters as the white seamen. In this period of time, 1943 to 1955, racial tension on the ships which I sailed did not exist. The same cannot be said for conditions ashore during those years.

Reviewing what I have written about my experiences as a professional seaman there are certain truths that must be realized. Normally the crew of a ship are people captured in a small tight community. They are associating with each other twenty four hours a day seven days a week. Because of the close confinement personalities and personal habits of crewmen become more obvious to each other. It is inevitable that under those conditions opinions regarding character, morality, and honesty evolve. I may have been unduly harsh in evaluating some of the people I sailed with. If this is so, I owe them an apology. Conversely, many of the people I sailed with may have formed a less than admirable opinion of me. Most of the time it is impossible for one to know how others see one's self. The great Scottish poet and philosopher, Robert Burns, put it very well in his poem:

TO A LOUSE

O wad some Power th giftie gie us
To see oursels as ithers see us!
It wad frae monie a blunder free us,
An' foolish notion,
What airs in dress an' gait wad lea'e us,
An' ev'n devotion

As a wise man once said, "Time cures all wounds both physical and psychological." Suffice to say, that as I reflect on the past and my maritime career, I carry no grudges and I have no regrets.

GLOSSARY OF NAUTICAL TERMS

ABAFT, aft of or behind

ABREST, alongside or close to the side of a vessel

Aft, toward the stern of a vessel

ANCHOR, an object attached to a vessel by rope, cable, or chain used to hold it in place

ASHORE, on the shore or beach

ATHWART, from one side to the other of a vessel

ATOL, a small circular island, usually of coral, enclosing a lagoon

BAROMETER, an instrument measuring the pressure of the atmosphere

BATTENS, planks along the inner sides of a ship to protect the cargo

BATTEN DOWN, to make cargo hatches secure and water tight

BEACON, a navigational marker

BEAM, the widest part of a ship, usually at the middle of a vessel between bow and stern

BILL OF LADING, a receipt from a vessel for cargo received

BITTS, a pair of vertical steel posts for securing mooring lines

BLINKER LIGHT, a signal light capable of flashing dots and dashes

BOLLARD, upright iron or steel post on a dock for securing hawsers

BOW, forward part of a vessel's sides

BREAKWATER, a sea wall used for breaking the force of waves

BRIDGE, the athwartships platform from which the ship is steered and navigated

BROACHING, to be thrown broadside to the seas

BULKHEAD, transverse or longitudinal partitions on a vessel

BULWARK, the light plating of the ship's side above the main deck forming a railing

BUNK, a built-in bed on board a ship

CABIN, a room used for quarters for ship's personnel

CAMEL, a wooden float placed between a vessel and a dock acting as a fender

CHECKERBOARD CREW, a crew composed of both White and Negro men

CLINOMETER, an instrument for measuring the angle of roll of a vessel in degrees

COAMING, the raised framework about deck openings

COMPASS, an instrument for determining a course or a bearing

DAVIT, a curved metal spar projecting over the side of a vessel

DIP, to lower a flag part way and hoist it again as a salute

DISPLACEMENT, the weight of water displaced by a vessel

DRAFT, the depth of water to a vessel's keel

DUNNAGE, wood boards used to support or wedge cargo, or a seaman's personal effects

EMBARK, to go on board a vessel

ENSIGN, a national flag, or a junior merchant or naval officer

FAIRWAY, an open channel

FANTAIL, the after section of the main deck of a vessel

FATHOM, a length of six feet

FIDDLEY, the open space from the engine room floor plates to the sky light hatch

FORE PEAK, part of vessel below deck at the stem or the bow

FORECASTLE, an upper forward deck or compartment, crew's quarters

FREEBOARD, distance from waterline to main deck

GALE, a wind force of 28 to 55 knots

GALLEY, the kitchen on a vessel

GANGWAY, an opening in a bulwark to give entrance to a vessel

GYPSY HEAD, a drum for heaving in lines

GUNWALE, the upper edge of a vessel's side

HATCH, an opening in a vessel's deck.

HAWSER, a large diameter rope used for mooring or towing

HEAD, a water closet, a toilet

HOLD, the space below decks for the stowage of cargo

KNOT, one nautical mile per hour

LOG BOOK, the official record of a vessel's activities

LOOKOUT, a man positioned to observe and report any objects seen

MAIN DECK, the highest deck extending from the stem to the stern of a vessel

MIDSHIPMAN, a cadet officer in training

MOORING, securing a vessel to a dock, buoy, or anchor

MONSOON, wind with rain blowing for months from one direction in the Indian Ocean

MUG, a Midshipman below first class at the New York State Maritime Academy

MUSTER, to assemble a crew

NAVIGATOR, officer charged with the safe navigation of a vessel

OLD MAN, the Captain of the ship

PORT SIDE, left side of a vessel looking forward

PRATIQUE, to be granted the liberty of the port

QUARANTINE, restricted or prohibited the liberty of the port

REEF, a ridge of coral, rock, or sand close to the surface of the water

ROUGH LOG, the ship's log written up in pencil by the Captain and Mates

SALVAGE, to save or recover a ship or cargo from danger of loss

SHOT, a length of chain of fifteen fathoms, or ninety feet

SHROUD, a side stay from the masthead to the rail

SKIPPER, the captain of the vessel

SLOP CHEST, a small shipboard store providing clothing, tobacco, etc. for the crew

SQUALL, a sudden rain and wind storm usually of short duration

STARBOARD, the right side of a vessel looking forward

STERN, the after part of a vessel

SUPERCARGO, a non-watch standing officer or person on a vessel

SWELL, heave of the sea

THWART, the side to side seat in a boat

TROUGH, the hollow between two waves

TYPHOON, a hurricane in the Indian and Pacific oceans

UNDERWAY, a vessel that is not at anchor, made fast to the shore, or aground

WAKE, a vessel's track, or water left behind

WINCH, a machine on deck fitted with horizontal drums or gypsies for heaving in lines

WINDLASS, a machine used for heaving in an anchor chain or line

Printed in the United States
58222LVS00001B/133